THE HUMAN ELEMENT OF
BIG DATA
ISSUES, ANALYTICS, AND PERFORMANCE

THE HUMAN ELEMENT OF BIG DATA

Issues, Analytics, and Performance

Edited by
Geetam S. Tomar
Narendra S. Chaudhari
Robin Singh Bhadoria
Ganesh Chandra Deka

CRC Press
Taylor & Francis Group
Boca Raton London New York

CRC Press is an imprint of the
Taylor & Francis Group, an **informa** business

A CHAPMAN & HALL BOOK

CRC Press
Taylor & Francis Group
6000 Broken Sound Parkway NW, Suite 300
Boca Raton, FL 33487-2742

© 2017 by Taylor & Francis Group, LLC
CRC Press is an imprint of Taylor & Francis Group, an Informa business

No claim to original U.S. Government works

Printed by CPI on sustainably sourced paper
Version Date: 20160824

International Standard Book Number-13: 978-1-4987-5415-6 (Hardback)

This book contains information obtained from authentic and highly regarded sources. Reasonable efforts have been made to publish reliable data and information, but the author and publisher cannot assume responsibility for the validity of all materials or the consequences of their use. The authors and publishers have attempted to trace the copyright holders of all material reproduced in this publication and apologize to copyright holders if permission to publish in this form has not been obtained. If any copyright material has not been acknowledged please write and let us know so we may rectify in any future reprint.

Except as permitted under U.S. Copyright Law, no part of this book may be reprinted, reproduced, transmitted, or utilized in any form by any electronic, mechanical, or other means, now known or hereafter invented, including photocopying, microfilming, and recording, or in any information storage or retrieval system, without written permission from the publishers.

For permission to photocopy or use material electronically from this work, please access www.copyright.com (http://www.copyright.com/) or contact the Copyright Clearance Center, Inc. (CCC), 222 Rosewood Drive, Danvers, MA 01923, 978-750-8400. CCC is a not-for-profit organization that provides licenses and registration for a variety of users. For organizations that have been granted a photocopy license by the CCC, a separate system of payment has been arranged.

Trademark Notice: Product or corporate names may be trademarks or registered trademarks, and are used only for identification and explanation without intent to infringe.

Visit the Taylor & Francis Web site at
http://www.taylorandfrancis.com

and the CRC Press Web site at
http://www.crcpress.com

Contents

Preface...vii
Editors...ix
Contributors...xi

Section I Introduction to the Human Element of Big Data: Definition, New Trends, and Methodologies

1 **Taming the Realm of Big Data Analytics: Acclamation or Disaffection?** 3
Audrey Depeige

2 **Fast Data Analytics Stack for Big Data Analytics**...17
Sourav Mazumder

3 **Analytical Approach for Big Data in the Internet of Things** 49
Anand Paul, Awais Ahmad, and M. Mazhar Rathore

4 **Analysis of Costing Issues in Big Data**...63
Kuldeep Singh Jadon and Radhakishan Yadav

Section II Algorithms and Applications of Advancement in Big Data

5 **An Analysis of Algorithmic Capability and Organizational Impact**......................81
George Papachristos and Scott W. Cunningham

6 **Big Data and Its Impact on Enterprise Architecture**.....................................107
Meena Jha, Sanjay Jha, and Liam O'Brien

7 **Supportive Architectural Analysis for Big Data**...125
Utkarsh Sharma and Robin Singh Bhadoria

8 **Clustering Algorithms for Big Data: A Survey** 143
Ankita Sinha and Prasanta K. Jana

v

Section III Future Research and Scope for the Human Element of Big Data

9 Smart Everything: Opportunities, Challenges, and Impact 165
Siddhartha Duggirala

10 Social Media and Big Data 179
Richard Millham and Surendra Thakur

11 Big Data Integration, Privacy, and Security 195
Rafael Souza and Chandrakant Patil

12 Paradigm Shifts from E-Governance to S-Governance 213
Akshi Kumar and Abhilasha Sharma

Section IV Case Studies for the Human Element of Big Data: Analytics and Performance

13 Interactive Visual Analysis of Traffic Big Data 237
Zhihan Lv, Xiaoming Li, Weixi Wang, Jinxing Hu, and Ling Yin

14 Prospect of Big Data Technologies in Healthcare 265
Raghavendra Kankanady and Marilyn Wells

15 Big Data Suite for Market Prediction and Reducing Complexity Using Bloom Filter 281
Mayank Bhushan, Apoorva Gupta, and Sumit Kumar Yadav

16 Big Data Architecture for Climate Change and Disease Dynamics 303
Daphne Lopez and Gunasekaran Manogaran

Index 335

Preface

This book contains 16 chapters of eminent quality research and practice in the field of Big Data analytics from academia, research, and industry experts. The book tries to provide quality discussion on the issues, challenges, and research trends in Big Data in regard to human behavior that could inherit the decision-making processes.

During the last decade, people began interacting with so many devices, creating a huge amount of data to handle. This led to the concept of Big Data necessitating development of more efficient algorithms, techniques, and tools for analyzing this huge amount of data.

As humans, we put out a lot of information on several social networking websites, including Facebook, Twitter, and LinkedIn, and this information, if tapped properly, could be of great value to perform analysis through Big Data algorithms and techniques. Data available on the Web can be in the form of video from surveillance systems or voice data from any call center about a particular client/human. Mostly, this information is in unstructured form, and a challenging task is to segregate this data.

This trend inspired us to write this book on the human element of Big Data to present a wide conceptual view about prospective challenges and its remedies for an architectural paradigm for Big Data. Chapters in this book present detailed surveys and case studies for different application areas like the Internet of Things (IoT), healthcare, social media, market prediction analysis, and climate change variability. Fast data analysis is a very crucial phase in Big Data analytics, which is briefed in this book. Another important aspect of Big Data in this book is costing issues. For smooth navigation, the book is divided into the following four sections:

Section I: Introduction to the Human Element of Big Data: Definition, New Trends, and Methodologies

Section II: Algorithms and Applications of Advancement in Big Data

Section III: Future Research and Scope for the Human Element of Big Data

Section IV: Case Studies for the Human Element of Big Data: Analytics and Performance

Editors

Geetam Singh Tomar earned an undergraduate degree at the Institute of Engineers Calcutta, a postgraduate degree at REC Allahabad, and a PhD at RGPV Bhopal in electronics engineering. He completed postdoctoral work in computer engineering at the University of Kent, Canterbury, UK. He is the director of Machine Intelligence Research Labs, Gwalior, India. He served prior to this in the Indian Air Force, MITS Gwalior, IIITM Gwalior, and other institutes. He also served at the University of Kent and the University of the West Indies, Trinidad. He received the International Plato Award for academic excellence in 2009 from IBC Cambridge UK. He was listed in the 100 top academicians of the world in 2009 and 2013, and he was listed in Who's Who in the World for 2008 and 2009. He has organized more than 20 IEEE international conferences in India and other countries. He is a member of the IEEE/ISO working groups to finalize protocols. He has delivered the keynote address at many conferences. He is the chief editor of five international journals, holds 1 patent, has published 75 research papers in international journals and 75 papers at IEEE conferences, and written 6 books and 5 book chapters for CRC Press and IGI Global. He has more than 100 citations per year. He is associated with many other universities as a visiting professor.

Narendra S. Chaudhari has more than 20 years of rich experience and more than 300 publications in top-quality international conferences and journals. Currently, he is the director for the Visvesvaraya National Institute of Technology (VNIT) Nagpur, Maharashtra, India. Prior to VNIT Nagpur, he was with the Indian Institute of Technology (IIT) Indore as a professor of computer science and engineering. He has also served as a professor in the School of Computer Engineering at Nanyang Technological University, Singapore. He earned BTech, MTech, and PhD degrees at the Indian Institute of Technology Bombay, Mumbai, Maharashtra, India. He has been the keynote speaker at many conferences in the areas of soft computing, game artificial intelligence, and data management. He has been a referee and reviewer for a number of premier conferences and journals, including *IEEE Transactions and Neurocomputing*.

Robin Singh Bhadoria is pursuing a PhD in computer science and engineering at the Indian Institute of Technology Indore. He has worked in numerous fields, including data mining, frequent pattern mining, cloud computing era and service-oriented architecture, and wireless sensor networks. He earned bachelor's and master's of engineering degrees in computer science and engineering at Rajiv Gandhi Technological University, Bhopal (MP), India. He has published more than 40 articles in international and national conferences, journals, and books published by IEEE and Springer. Presently, he is an associate editor for the *International Journal of Computing, Communications and Networking (IJCCN)* as well as an editorial board member for different journals. He is a member of several professional research bodies, including IEEE (USA), IAENG (Hong Kong), Internet Society (Virginia), and IACSIT (Singapore).

Ganesh Chandra Deka is the deputy director (training) under the Directorate General of Training, Ministry of Skill Development and Entrepreneurship, Government of India. His research interests include ICT (information and communications technology) in rural development, e-governance, cloud computing, data mining, NoSQL databases, and vocational education and training. He has published more than 57 research papers at various conferences and workshops and in reputed international journals published by IEEE and Elsevier. He is the editor-in-chief of the *International Journal of Computing, Communications, and Networking*. He has organized eight IEEE international conferences as the technical chair in India. He is a member of editorial boards and a reviewer for various journals and international conferences. He is the coauthor of four books on the fundamentals of computer science, and he has published four edited books on cloud computing. He earned a PhD in computer science. He is a member of IEEE, the Institution of Electronics and Telecommunication Engineers, India, and he is an associate member of the Institution of Engineers, India.

Contributors

Awais Ahmad
School of Computer Science and
Engineering
Kyungpook National University
Daegu, South Korea

Robin Singh Bhadoria
Discipline of Computer Science and
Engineering
Indian Institute of Technology
Indore, India

Mayank Bhushan
ABES Engineering College
Ghaziabad, India

Scott W. Cunningham
Faculty of Technology Policy and
Management
Delft Technical University
Delft, The Netherlands

Audrey Depeige
Telecom Ecole de Management—LITEM
Evry, France

Siddhartha Duggirala
Bharat Petroleum Corporation Limited
Mumbai, India

Apoorva Gupta
Institute of Innovation in Technology and
Management (IITM)
New Delhi, India

Jinxing Hu
Shenzhen Institutes of Advanced
Technology
Chinese Academy of Sciences
Shenzhen, China

Kuldeep Singh Jadon
Institute of Information Technology and
Management
Madhya Pradesh, India

Prasanta K. Jana
Department of Computer Science and
Engineering
Indian School of Mines
Dhanbad, India

Meena Jha
Central Queensland University
Sydney, Australia

Sanjay Jha
Central Queensland University
Sydney, Australia

Raghavendra Kankanady
School of Engineering and Technology
Central Queensland University
Melbourne, Australia

Akshi Kumar
Department of Computer Science and
Engineering
Delhi Technological University
New Delhi, India

Xiaoming Li
Shenzhen Institutes of Advanced
Technology
Chinese Academy of Sciences
Shenzhen, China

Daphne Lopez
School of Information Technology and
Engineering
VIT University
Vellore, India

Zhihan Lv
Shenzhen Institutes of Advanced
  Technology
Chinese Academy of Sciences
Shenzhen, China

Gunasekaran Manogaran
School of Information Technology and
  Engineering
VIT University
Vellore, India

Sourav Mazumder
IBM Analytics
San Francisco, California, USA

Richard Millham
Durban University of Technology
Durban, South Africa

Liam O'Brien
Geoscience Australia
Canberra, Australia

George Papachristos
Faculty of Technology Policy and
  Management
Delft Technical University
Delft, The Netherlands

Chandrakant Patil
Texec Pvt. Ltd.
Pune, India

Anand Paul
School of Computer Science and
  Engineering
Kyungpook National University
Daegu, South Korea

M. Mazhar Rathore
School of Computer Science and
  Engineering
Kyungpook National University
Daegu, South Korea

Abhilasha Sharma
Department of Computer Science and
  Engineering
Delhi Technological University
New Delhi, India

Utkarsh Sharma
Department of Computer Science and
  Engineering
G.L. Bajaj Group of Institutions
Mathura, Uttar Pradesh, India

Ankita Sinha
Department of Computer Science and
  Engineering
Indian School of Mines
Dhanbad, India

Rafael Souza
Cipher Ltd.
São Paulo, Brazil

Surendra Thakur
Durban University of Technology
Durban, South Africa

Weixi Wang
Shenzhen Institutes of Advanced
  Technology
Chinese Academy of Sciences
Shenzhen, China

Marilyn Wells
School of Engineering and Technology
Central Queensland University
Rockhampton, Australia

Radhakishan Yadav
Discipline of Computer Science and
  Engineering
Indian Institute of Technology
Indore, India

Sumit Kumar Yadav
Indira Gandhi Delhi Technological
  University for Women
New Delhi, India

Ling Yin
Shenzhen Institutes of Advanced
  Technology
Chinese Academy of Sciences
Shenzhen, China

Section I

Introduction to the Human Element of Big Data: Definition, New Trends, and Methodologies

1

Taming the Realm of Big Data Analytics: Acclamation or Disaffection?

Audrey Depeige

CONTENTS

1.1 Big Data for All: A Human Perspective on Knowledge Discovery 4
    1.1.1 The Knowledge Revolution: State of the Art and Challenges of Data Mining...4
    1.1.2 Big Data: Relational Dependencies and the Discovery of Knowledge 4
    1.1.3 Potentials and Pitfalls of Knowledge Discovery 5
1.2 The Data Mining Toolbox: Untangling Human-Generated Texts 6
    1.2.1 Interactive Generation and Refinement of Knowledge: The Analytic-Self 6
    1.2.2 Looking into the Mirror: Data Mining and Users' Profile Building 7
    1.2.3 Accurately Interpreting Knowledge Artifacts: The Shadows of Human
        Feedback..7
1.3 The Deep Dialogue: Lessons of Machine Learning for Data Analysis............................8
    1.3.1 Human–Machine Interaction and Data Analysis: The Rise of Machine
        Learning..8
    1.3.2 Using Machine Learning Techniques to Classify Human Expressions 9
    1.3.3 Learning Decision Rules: The Expertise of Human Forecasting......................10
1.4 Making Sense of Analytics: From Insights to Value...11
    1.4.1 Complementarity of Data and Visual Analytics: A View on Integrative
        Solutions..11
    1.4.2 From Analytics to Actionable Knowledge-as-a-Service....................................12
1.5 The Human Aid: The Era of Data-Driven Decision Making (Conclusion)..................12
    1.5.1 Big Data and Analytics for Decision-Making: Challenges and Opportunities....12
    1.5.2 Exploring the Power of Decision Induction in Data Mining............................13
    1.5.3 It's about Time: Is Prescriptive Knowledge Discovery Better?........................13
References...14
Author...15

ABSTRACT Undeniably, Big Data analytics have drawn increased interest among researchers and practitioners in the data sciences, digital information and communication, and policy shaping or decision making at multiple levels. Complex data models and knowledge-intensive problems require efficient analysis techniques, which otherwise performed manually would be time consuming or prone to numerous errors. The need for efficient solutions to manage growing amounts of data has resulted in the rise of data mining and knowledge discovery techniques, and in particular the development of computer intelligence via powerful algorithms. Yet, complex problem-solving and decision-making areas do not constitute a single source of truth and still require human intelligence. The human elements of Big Data are aspects of strategic importance: they are essential to combine the advantages provided by the speed and accuracy of scalable algorithms, together with the capabilities of the human mind to perceive, analyze and make decisions e.g., letting people interact with integrative data visualization solutions. This chapter thus seeks to reflect on the various methods available to combine data mining and visualization techniques toward an approach integrating both machine capabilities and human sense-making. Building on literature review in the fields of knowledge discovery, Big Data analytics, human–computer interactions, and decision making, the chapter highlights evolution in knowledge discovery theorizations, trends in Big Data applications, challenges of techniques such as machine learning, and how human capabilities can best optimize the use of mining and visualization techniques.

1.1 Big Data for All: A Human Perspective on Knowledge Discovery

1.1.1 The Knowledge Revolution: State of the Art and Challenges of Data Mining

The rise of Big Data over the last couple of years is easily noticeable. Referring to our ability to harness, store, and extract valuable meaning from vast amounts of data, the term *Big Data* holds the implicit promise of answering fundamental questions, which disciplines such as the sciences, technology, healthcare, and business have yet to answer. In fact, as the volume of data available to professionals and researchers steadily grows opportunities for new discoveries as well as potential to answer research challenges at stake are fast increasing (Manovich, 2011) it is expected that Big Data will transform various fields such as medicine, businesses, and scientific research overall (Chen and Zhang, 2014), and generate profound shifts in numerous disciplines (Kitchin, 2014). Yet, the adoption of advanced technologies in the field of Big Data remains a challenge for organizations, which still need to strategically engage in the change toward rapidly shifting environments (Bughin et al., 2010). What is more, organizations adopting Big Data at an early stage still face difficulties in understanding its guiding principles and the value it adds to the business (Wamba et al., 2015). Moreover, data sets are often of different types, which urges organizations to develop or apply "new forms of processing to enable enhanced decision making, insights discovery and process optimization" (Chen and Zhang, 2014, p. 315) as well as "a knowledge of analytics approaches" to different unstructured data types such as text, pictures, and video format, proving to be highly beneficial (Davenport et al., 2014) so that data scientists can quickly test and provide solutions to business challenges, emphasizing the application of Big Data analytics in their business context over a specific analytical approach. Indeed, a data scientist student can be taught "how to write a Python program in half an hour" but can't be taught "very easily what is the domain knowledge" (Dumbill et al., 2013). This argument highlights the dependencies that exist for an effective analysis and up-to-speed discovery process.

1.1.2 Big Data: Relational Dependencies and the Discovery of Knowledge

Specialized literature and research on the topic conceals that Big Data involves working on data sets that are so voluminous that their size goes beyond the capability of popular software to extract, manage, and process data in a short time (Manovich, 2011). The question of what type of insights and understanding can be gained through data analysis, in comparison to traditional science methods, is an important one in the context of digitalization of the social sphere. This context relates to the span of simultaneous and instantaneous

Taming the Realm of Big Data Analytics

creation, collection, analysis, curation, and broadcasting of knowledge (Amer-Yahia et al., 2010) having demonstrated the benefits of spontaneous collaboration and analysis of interactions of vast amounts of users to tackle scientific problems that remained unsolved by smaller amounts of people. Yet, challenges arise when organizations need to adopt new technologies to process vast amounts of data while they also need to overcome issues related to the capture, storage, curation, analysis and visualization of data in their quest for optimized decision making and gaining new insights on potential business opportunities. Issues that organizations face to implement Big Data applications are related to the technology and techniques used, the access to data itself, as well as organizational change and talent issues (Wamba et al., 2015). These results indicate that human elements such as skills and knowledge required to implement and generate value from Big Data analytics (technical skills, analytical skills, and governance skills), as well as change management factors such as the buy-in from the top management, remain much needed to unlock its full potential.

1.1.3 Potentials and Pitfalls of Knowledge Discovery

Big Data and data intensive applications have become a new paradigm for innovative discoveries and data-centric applications. As Chen and Zhang (2014) recall, the potential value and insights hidden in the sea of data sets surrounding us is massive, giving birth to new research paradigms such as data-intensive scientific discovery (DISD). Big Data represents opportunities to achieve tremendous progress in varied scientific fields, while business model landscapes are also transformed by explorations and experimentations with Big Data analytics. This argument is supported by high-level organizations and government bodies, which argue that the use of data-intensive decision making has had substantial impact on their present and future developments (Chen and Zhang, 2014). Such potentials cover the improvement of operational efficiencies, making informed decisions, providing better customer services, identifying and developing new products and services, as well as identifying new markers or accelerating go-to-market cycles. However, it appears that very little empirical research has assessed the real potential of Big Data in realizing business value (Wamba et al., 2015). The process of knowledge discovery, as illustrated in Figure 1.1, is a good example of such value creation, as intrinsically guiding attempts to identify relationships existing within a data set and extracting meaningful insights on the basis of their configuration. This process is highly dependent on guided assumptions and strategic decisions as regards the framework and analysis strategies, so that "theoretically informed decisions are made as to how best to tackle a data set, such that it will reveal information which will be of potential interest and is worthy of further research" (Kitchin, 2014).

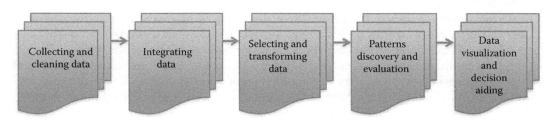

FIGURE 1.1
The knowledge discovery process and its potential for value creation.

Big Data is thus estimated to generate billions of dollars of potential value if exploited accurately, although this is notwithstanding the challenges correlative to data-intensive technologies and application. Such issues related to the collection, storage, analysis, and visualization stages involved in processing Big Data. In other words, organizations need to grow their capabilities to explore and exploit data, in a context where "information surpasses our capability to harness" (Chen and Zhang, 2014, p. 5), where pitfalls faced by organizations typically include inconsistencies, incompleteness, lack of scalability, irrelevant timeliness or security issues in handling, processing, and representing structured and unstructured data. In particular, it appears that organizations need to rely on high-performing storage technologies and adapted network bandwidth, as well as the capability to manage large-scale data sets in a structured way. The potential of Big Data emerges in the "proliferation, digitization and interlinking of diverse set of analogue and unstructured data" (Kitchin, 2014). Thus, the next steps are to cope with the volume of data to analyze and increment analytical data mining techniques, algorithms, and visualization methods that are possibly scalable, the aspect of timeliness constitutes a priority for real-time Big Data applications (Chen and Zhang, 2014). In this perspective, methods concentrating on the curation, management, and analysis of hundreds of thousands of data entries reflect the progression of new digital humanities techniques.

1.2 The Data Mining Toolbox: Untangling Human-Generated Texts

1.2.1 Interactive Generation and Refinement of Knowledge: The Analytic-Self

The evolution of humanist and social sciences toward the "mining" of human-generated data comes as an answer to the digitalization of businesses, which calls for the use of "techniques needed to search, analyze and understand these every day materials" (Manovich, 2011). The rise of social media communications early in the 21st century has provided researchers and data analysts with new opportunities to deepen their understanding of socially accepted theories such as opinion spreading, sentiment expression, ideas generation, amongst others. Research fields relying on such quantitative amounts of surfaced data include marketing, economics, and behavioral science (sociology, communications). In between the "surface data" and "deep data" has also emerged the pioneering discipline of digital ethnography, which offers a new approach for depicting and analyzing storytelling in social media, using interactive components such as user-generated data, and applying anthropological research methods in digital data analysis and planning. As an illustration, the increasing number of digital ethnography centers reveals the intersections made possible between anthropological and business perspectives on one hand, and between the individual or consumer behaviors, and the corporate world on the other hand. Such methods rely on the use of public data generated on online networks and social media, which constitute a pool of daily interactions. In this perspective, digital ethnography and other methods relying on the use of Big Data on digital platform places the user at the center, where self-representation and online identities emerge from the different interactions and strategies, which the user activates in various digital public spheres. In this perspective, the use of mixed research methods (both quantitative and qualitative) enables researchers to focus on the digital life of the users, combining techniques such as co-occurrences or network analysis (from a quantitative standpoint) with sentiment analysis (from a qualitative standpoint).

1.2.2 Looking into the Mirror: Data Mining and Users' Profile Building

Large data sets are being used in projects resonating with "digital humanities" application fields, as professionals start working with user-generated content (e.g., videos), user interactions (web searches, comments, clicks, etc.), user-created data (tags), and user communications (messages). Such data sets are extremely large and continuously growing, not to mention "infinitely larger than already digitized cultural heritage" (Manovich, 2011). These developments raise theoretical, practical, and ethical issues related to the collection, use, and analysis of large amounts of individually and socially generated data. The monitoring and collection of such user-generated interactions (voluntary communications such as blog posts, comments, tweets, check ins, and video sharing) has been on the rise and sought after by marketing and advertising agencies, reusing this data to analyze and extract value from "deep data" about individuals' trajectories in the online world (Manovich, 2011). The rise of social media combined with the emergence of new technologies has made it possible to adopt a new approach to understand individuals and society at large, erasing the long existing dichotomy between large sample size (quantitative studies) and in-depth analysis (qualitative studies). In other words, profiles or "persona" that were earlier built based on extended analysis of a small set of people is now rendered achievable at a large scale, relying on continuous data generated from daily user interactions.

The study of social interactions and human behaviors in the context of the consequently offers opportunities to analyze interaction patterns directly from the structured and unstructured data, opening the door to the development of new services that take into account how interactions emerge, evolve, and link with others or disaggregate across collective digital spheres. This view confirms the opportunities represented by consumers' data mining, since numerous companies see their customers spread around the world and generating vast amounts as well as fast moving transactional artifacts. However, previous work has reported that even though Big Data can provide astounding detailed pictures on the customers (Madsbjerg and Rasmussen, 2014), such profiles are actually far from complete and may also mislead people working with such insights. The challenge of getting the right insights to make relevant customer decisions is critical and is detailed in the next section.

1.2.3 Accurately Interpreting Knowledge Artifacts: The Shadows of Human Feedback

The Office of Digital Humanities, created in 2008, has opened the door for humanists to pursue their research work making use of large data sets (Manovich, 2011) that include transactional data such as web searches and message records. The use and analysis of such data sources does prelude exciting opportunities for research and practice, yet the analysis of millions and billions of online interactions represents a few "dark areas" that deserve attention from decision makers, those who will make final use of this new, large scale, user-generated data. In particular, there is a need to clarify the skills digital humanists will require in order to take full advantage of such data (Manovich, 2011), that is to say specific statistics and data analysis methods. This means that interpreting knowledge artifacts extracted from large-scale data sets and related visualization class for skills in statistics and data mining, skills that social researchers often do not gain, at least in the way they are initially trained. This view is supported by recent research work highlighting that Big Data shall be envisioned not only considering its analytical side, rather, acute human skills are critical: Big Data shall be approached "not only in terms of analytics, but more in terms developing high-level skills that allow the use of a new generation of IT tools and architectures to collect data from various sources, store, organize, extract, analyze, generate valuable insights" (Wamba et al., 2015, p. 6). There exists, indeed, a "large gap between what can be done with the right software tools, right data, and no knowledge of computer science and advanced statistics, and what can only be done if you have this knowledge" (Manovich, 2011), highlighting that researchers and professionals do need specialized skills and knowledge (statistics, computational linguistics, text mining, computer science, etc.) in order to be able to extract meaningful results of the collected data.

Organizations that capitalize on Big Data often tend to rely on data scientists rather than data analysts (Davenport et al., 2012), since the information that is collected and processed is often too voluminous, unstructured, and flowing as opposed to conventional database structures. The role of data scientist appeared early in the 21st century, together with the acceleration of social media presence and the development of roles dedicated to the storage, processing, and analysis of data, which Davenport (2014, p. 87) depicts as "hacker, scientist, qualitative analyst, trusted advisor and business expert," pointing out that "many of the skills are self taught anyway." Although such skills have become prevalent in today's context, the access to the data and its publication raises some questions related to the use, storage, and informational use of such user-generated data. Specifically, not all interactions on social media and in the digital world in general can be deemed as authentic (Manovich, 2011), rather such data reflects a well-thought curation and management of online presence and expressions. Reversely, the interpretation outcomes of data analysis can be rendered difficult in relation to the quality of the collected data, which may happen to be inconsistent, incomplete, or simply noisy (Chen and Zhang, 2014). This issue is proper to the "veracity" property of Big Data, inducing uncertainty about the level of completeness and consistency of the data as well as other ambiguous characteristics (Jin et al., 2015). Indeed, there always exists a risk of the data being "redundant, inaccurate and duplicate data which might undermine service delivery and decision making processes" (Wamba et al., 2015, p. 24).

Even though there exists techniques dedicated to virtually correct inconsistencies in data sets as well as removing noise, we have to keep in mind that this data is not a "transparent window into people's imaginations, intentions, motives, opinion and ideas" (Manovich, 2011), rather it may include fictional data that aimed to construct and project a certain online expression. Despite gaining access to a new set of digitally captured interactions and records of individual behaviors, the human elements of Big Data remains such that data scientists and analysts will gain different insights than those ethnographers on the field would get. In other words, one can say that in order to "understand what makes customer tick, you have to observe them in their natural habitats" (Madsbjerg and Rasmussen, 2014). This view is in line with the fact that subject matter experts in data science and therefore humans elements are much needed as they have "a very narrow and particular way of understanding" and are "needed to assess the results of the work, especially when dealing with sensitive data about human behavior" (Kitchin, 2014), making it difficult to interpret data independently from the context in which it has been generated considering it as anemic from its domain expertise.

1.3 The Deep Dialogue: Lessons of Machine Learning for Data Analysis

1.3.1 Human–Machine Interaction and Data Analysis: The Rise of Machine Learning

One of the questions raised by the use of Big Data analytics is as follows: Could the enterprise become a full-time laboratory? What if we could analyze every transaction, capture

FIGURE 1.2
Premises of Big Data's promises: from data collection to data analysis.

insights from every customer interaction, and didn't have to wait for months to get data from the field (Bughin et al., 2010)? It is estimated that data available publicly doubles every eighteen months, while the access to capture and analyze such data streams is becoming widely available at reduced cost. The first stages of the data analysis process are depicted in Figure 1.2, and used as a foundation by companies to analyze customer situations and support them in making real-time decisions, such as testing new products and customer experiences.

Companies may therefore make use of real-time information from any sensor in order to better understand the business context in which they evolve; develop new products, processes, and services; and anticipate and respond to changes in usage patterns (Davenport et al., 2012) as well as taking advantage of more granular analyses. Beyond these developments, the opportunities brought by machine learning research are noteworthy, and the methods that enable marshaling the data generated from customers' interactions and using it to predict outcomes or upcoming interactions, places data science as having the potential to radically transform the way people conduct research, develop innovations, and market their ideas (Bughin et al., 2010). Similarly, Kitchin (2014) states that applications of Big Data and analytics bring disruptive innovations into play and contribute to reinventing how research is conducted. This context calls for research aiming to understand the impact of Big Data on processes, systems, and business challenges overall (Wamba et al., 2015). Several large players in the technology industry have been using and developing such paradigms in order to refine their marketing methods, identify user groups, and develop tailored offers for certain profiles. Everyday information collected from transactions (payments, clicks, posts, etc.) are collected and analyzed in order to optimize existing opportunities or develop new services in very short times, even real time. Does it mean that Big Data applications make each of us a human sensor, connected to a global system, and thus has Big Data the potential to become the humanity's dashboard (Smolan and Erwitt, 2012)? Other researchers have reported worries of such possibility, because Big Data can typically expand the frontier of the "knowable future," questioning the "people's ability to analyze it wisely" (Anderson and Rainie, 2012). As the sea level of data sets is rising rapidly, the crunch of algorithms might draw right (or wrong) conclusions about who people are, how they behave now, how they may behave in the future, how they feel, and so forth in a context where "nowcasting" or real-time analytics are getting better.

1.3.2 Using Machine Learning Techniques to Classify Human Expressions

Other companies are going a step forward and seek to better understand the impact of dedicated actions/initiatives such as marketing campaigns on their customers: not only do machine learning technologies enable companies to gauge and classify consumers according to sentiment they express toward the brand, company, or site, rather the analysis also enables companies to trace, test, and learn (Figure 1.3) from user interactions how sentiment and referral about the brands are evolving over in place and time.

FIGURE 1.3
From data collection to prediction: a test-and-learn approach.

Where organizations may be interested to understand evolutions that exist within the collected data and how they can be meaningful—something that is traditionally casted as being specific to the human mind—data analytics software developed for such applications (data mining and visualization to answer customers) have claimed to have removed "the human element that goes into data mining, and as such the human bias that goes with it" (Kitchin, 2014). This tends to inaccurately suggest that data speaks for itself, not requiring any human framing neither efforts to depict meaning of patterns and relationships within Big Data. Kitchin (2014) coined this paradox: the attractive set of ideas that surrounds Big Data is based on the principle that the reasoning that underpins Big Data is inductive in nature, and runs counter to the deductive approach that dominates in modern science. Researchers shall be particularly cautious as regards Big Data, because it represents a sample that is shaped by several parameters such as the use of the tools, the data ontology shaping the analysis, sample bias, and a relative abstraction from the world that is generally accepted but provides oligoptic views of the world.

1.3.3 Learning Decision Rules: The Expertise of Human Forecasting

Previous research has argued that Big Data has the potential to transform ways decisions are made, providing senior executives with increased visibility over operations and performance (Wamba et al., 2015). Managers may for instance use the Big Data infrastructure to gain access to dashboards fed with real-time data, so that they can identify future needs and formulate strategies that incorporate predicted risks and opportunities. Professionals can also take advantage of Big Data by identifying specific needs and subsequently delivering tailored services that will meet each of those needs. Yet, while platforms enabling the analysis of real-time data may for some be considered as a single source of truth, decision-making capabilities do not solely rely on capabilities brought by machine learning technologies, rather it comes forward that experimentation, test-and-learn scenarios (Bughin et al., 2010), and human sense-making of the outcomes and patterns identified are essential to the organizational and cultural changes brought into picture. This attitude specifically highlights "the role of imagination (or lack thereof) in artificial, human and quantum cognition and decision-making processes" (Gustafson, 2015). In other words, "analysts should also try to interpret the results of machine learning analyses, looking into the black box to try and make sense out of why a particular model fits the best" (Davenport, 2014, p. 96). Another example of the role of the human thought process in Big Data is given by Wamba et al. (2015, p. 21), pointing out that "having real-time information on 'who' and 'where' is allowing not only the realignment and movement of critical assets …, but also informing strategic decision about where to invest in the future to develop new capabilities". Such perspective encompasses efforts from companies that have identified the right skills and methods they need in order to lead and conduct experiential scenarios as well as extracting value from Big Data analytics. These scenarios are represented in Figure 1.4, highlighting the role of data in decision making processes, while supporting the fact that the current digital transformation context has induced a "dramatic acceleration in demand

FIGURE 1.4
A structured path to decision making in Big Data projects.

for data scientists" (Davenport, 2014, p. 87). This is where the human elements of Big Data are commonly stronger: a rigorous analysis and decision making over the various scenarios identified via Big Data analytics require people to be aware that strong cultural changes are at stake. Executives must embrace "the value of experimentation" (Bughin et al., 2010) and act as a role model for all echelons of the company. In parallel to this, human interactions and especially communication and strong relationships are highly necessary, data scientists being "on the bridge advising the captain at close range" (Davenport, 2014).

1.4 Making Sense of Analytics: From Insights to Value

1.4.1 Complementarity of Data and Visual Analytics: A View on Integrative Solutions

Initiatives such as the Software Studies lab (Manovich, 2011) have focused on developing techniques to analyze visual data and exploring new visualization methods in order to detect patterns in large sets of visual artifacts such as user-generated videos, photographs, or films. The widespread preference for visual analytics (Davenport, 2014) is very noticeable in Big Data projects, for several reasons: they are easier to interpret and catch the audience's eye more easily, even though they may not be adapted for complex modelizations. Manovich's work highlights that human understanding and analysis is still needed to provide nuanced interpretations of data and understand deep meanings that remain uncovered. This is supported by the fact that even though sophisticated approaches have emerged in the field of data visualization, current available solutions are offering poor functionalities, scalability, and performances (Chen and Zhang, 2014). Very few tools have the capability to handle complex, large-scale data sets and transform them into intuitive representations, while being interactive. It is therefore certain that modeling complex data sets and graphically characterizing their properties needs to be rethought to support the visual analytics process. In other words, Big Data does not aim to substantiate human judgment or replace experts with technology, rather technology helps visualizing huge sets of data and detect patterns or outliers, where human judgment is needed for closer analysis and making sense out of the detected patterns. This may explain why visual analytics are extremely common in Big Data projects (Davenport, 2014), since they are much more appealing in order to communicate results and findings to nontechnical audiences. By processing structured and unstructured data, organizations are able to push some intelligence into their structure so as to support operations in the field, and implement innovative products and services (Wamba et al., 2015). Therefore, it comes forward that the combined ability of the technology to analyze huge sets of data with that of the human mind to interpret data undoubtedly gives most meaningful results, since human analytical thinking can't process such large data volumes, and computers' ability to understand and interpret patterns remains limited. In fact, data scientists or any other employees working with the analysis of data needs to be able to communicate well and easily explain the outcomes of analyses to nontechnical people (Davenport, 2014).

1.4.2 From Analytics to Actionable Knowledge-as-a-Service

We covered earlier how computational and human capabilities in the context of Big Data methods may compete in decision-making tasks (Gustafson, 2015). Now how do we get to know what people are willing to purchase and use and how do we deliver it to them? There does exist a few tools that capitalize on user-generated data in order to select and offer content of interest to the user, recommending actions on what to display, share, and interact with. Users can individually benefit from such insights by being proposed certain services that provide them with a detailed analysis of their own interactional data with the service or company they are using, such as exclusive content. In sum, the human contribution to the knowledge lifecycle, where users are both consuming and generating knowledge, is from both a direct and indirect data-centric point of view (Amer-Yahia et al., 2010): the participation from consumers is deemed as direct whenever it is from user-generated content, while indirect participations reflect online interactions in the digital world such as searching for information, consulting content, or browsing through websites. The confluence of possibilities epitomized by the growing adoption of crowdsourcing business models as well as cloud computing technologies requires "breakthrough in Machine Learning, Query Processing, Data Integration, Distributed Computing Infrastructure, Security, Privacy, and Social Computing" (Amer-Yahia et al., 2010). Yet, and despite the ubiquity of such techniques and solutions available on the market, the access to such technologies is often limited to an array of specialists who are able to make sense of the exciting potential of Big Data. This perspective highlights the necessity to "focus on the human side ... to make it psychologically savvy, economically sound, and easier to scale" (DeVine et al., 2012).

1.5 The Human Aid: The Era of Data-Driven Decision Making (Conclusion)

1.5.1 Big Data and Analytics for Decision-Making: Challenges and Opportunities

The rise of Big Data and the development of technologies enabling the close monitoring of usage patterns as well as of the ways individuals behave as consumers of products and services pave the way for the development of viable and sustainable innovations. Instant connectivity and the massive amounts of data generated by users have created a unique dynamic that "is moving data to the forefront of many human endeavors, changing the way that data-centric systems must be envisioned and architected" (Amer-Yahia et al., 2010). This argument is in line with research on Big Data applications, indicating that the majority of publications in the field address issues related to "replacing/supporting human decision making with automated algorithms" while a fair amount of such publications covers experimentation to "discover needs, expose variability and improve performance" as well as customizing actions for segmented populations (Wamba et al., 2015). This view contrasts with new forms of empiricisms claiming that paradigms are shifting from knowledge-driven science to data driven-science, where the emergence of digital humanities research engenders profound transformations in the ways we make sense of culture, history, and the economy (Kitchin, 2014).

Taming the Realm of Big Data Analytics

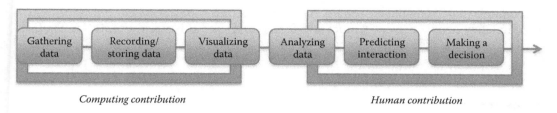

FIGURE 1.5
A balanced approach of Big Data: computational and human elements.

1.5.2 Exploring the Power of Decision Induction in Data Mining

This undoubtedly raises the question of how to best exploit and benefit from such rapidly evolving technologies, so as to capitalize on the digital transformation that is already underway (Bughin et al., 2010). A mere understanding of how data mining is powerful for developing new business models is merely sufficient for executives to meet the new reflective skills that are required in order to meet the demands brought by the introduction of such technologies. Davenport (2014) follows that direction, arguing that there should be no intermediaries between data scientists and decision makers, otherwise they may not understand issues involved in making the decision. This is illustrated in the end-to-end process in Figure 1.5.

The impact of data mining techniques and the experimentation that follows vary considerably in their degree of implementation and rate of adoption among businesses. Because its applications disrupt traditional models of working and identifying issues that were traditionally existing in companies, it is important that organizations first identify specific implications of such new technologies for their own businesses. Even though trends such as Big Data could extend the reach of organizations, improve management decisions, and speed the development of new products and services (Bughin et al., 2010), leaders need to allocate time to identify the implications of such technologies for their own businesses and activities.

1.5.3 It's about Time: Is Prescriptive Knowledge Discovery Better?

Big Data projects will only be successful as long as they serve real needs of businesses, developing strong communications between IT departments and the business. This leads us to the prescriptive aspects of Big Data (being able to make recommendations) that echo the human skills needed to make Big Data projects successful. Such skills relate to communication as well as trusted adviser skills (Davenport, 2014). Visualization of data is a good example of such communication skills, yet technologies able to generate visual displays remain more suitable when working on descriptive and predictive analytics, rather than for prescriptive analytics, whose inherent complexity is higher.

This chapter has underlined the importance of acquiring skills and knowledge to ensure a successful cross-functional adoption and implementation of Big Data techniques and methods. The present work has put forward critical insight into the key role of human elements in the design, execution, and measurement of Big Data strategies and operations. Overall, the exhaustive review of literature dealing with human aspects of Big Data (success factors or impact) has offered an opportunity to assess the role of the human mind in supporting Big Data initiatives. Indeed, the human aspect "has become top concern for companies' management since companies have realized that software is a product which is completely people driven" (Gupta and Suma, 2015) and this strictly applies to Big Data analytics and the discovery of knowledge.

References

Amer-Yahia, S., Doan, A., Kleinberg, J., Koudas, N., and Franklin, M. (2010, June). Crowds, clouds, and algorithms: Exploring the human side of big data applications. In *Proceedings of the 2010 ACM SIGMOD International Conference on Management of Data* (pp. 1259–1260).

Anderson, J. Q., and Rainie, L. (2012). Big Data: Experts say new forms of information analysis will help people be more nimble and adaptive, but worry over humans' capacity to understand and use these new tools well. Washington, DC: Pew Research Center's Internet and American Life Project.

Bughin, J., Chui, M., and Manyika, J. (2010). Clouds, big data, and smart assets: Ten tech-enabled business trends to watch. *McKinsey Quarterly, 56*(1), 75–86.

Chen, C. P., and Zhang, C. Y. (2014). Data-intensive applications, challenges, techniques and technologies: A survey on Big Data. *Information Sciences, 275,* 314–347.

Davenport, T. H. (2014). *Big Data at Work: Dispelling the Myths, Uncovering the Opportunities.* Boston: Harvard Business Review Press.

Davenport, T. H., Barth, P., and Bean, R. (2012). How 'big data' is different. *MIT Sloan Management Review, 54*(1), 22–24.

DeVine, J., Lal, S., and Zea, M. (2012). The human factor in service design. *McKinsey Quarterly, 1,* 118–123.

Dumbill, E., Liddy, E. D., Stanton, J., Mueller, K., and Farnham, S. (2013). Educating the next generation of data scientists. *Big Data, 1*(1), 21–27.

Gupta, S., and Suma, V. (2015, February). Data mining: A tool for knowledge discovery in human aspect of software engineering. In *2015 2nd International Conference on Electronics and Communication Systems (ICECS)*, pp. 1289–1293. IEEE.

Gustafson, K. (2015). The importance of imagination (or lack thereof) in artificial, human and quantum decision making. *Philosophical Transactions of the Royal Society A, 374*(2058), 20150097.

Jin, X., Wah, B. W., Cheng, X., and Wang, Y. (2015). Significance and challenges of big data research. *Big Data Research, 2*(2), 59–64.

Kitchin, R. (2014). Big Data, new epistemologies and paradigm shifts. *Big Data and Society, 1*(1), 1–12.

Madsbjerg, C., and Rasmussen, M. B. (2014). An anthropologist walks into a bar... *Harvard Business Review, 92,* 80–88.

Manovich, L. (2011). Trending: The promises and the challenges of big social data. In *Debates in the Digital Humanities*, Gold, M. K. ed. Minneapolis, MN: University of Minnesota Press.

Smolan, R., and Erwitt, J. (2012). What data says about us—What are we learning from the vast ocean of data? Truths about our measured world and our measured selves. Excerpted from The Human Face of Big Data. Fortune, p. 162.

Wamba, S. F., Akter, S., Edwards, A., Chopin, G., and Gnanzou, D. (2015). How 'big data' can make big impact: Findings from a systematic review and a longitudinal case study. *International Journal of Production Economics, 165,* 234–246.

Author

Audrey Depeige is the knowledge strategy manager in a leading software company developing Big Data analytics solutions and is simultaneously leading postgraduate research in the field of knowledge and innovation management. Her research and academic interests are evolving around co-opetition and innovation and relate more specifically to internal co-opetition, knowledge-based innovation, intraorganizational knowledge flows, and organizational behavior. Prior to starting academic research, she has been responsible for the development and support of innovation initiatives in the internal performance and innovation department of a leading optical manufacturing company.

2

Fast Data Analytics Stack for Big Data Analytics

Sourav Mazumder

CONTENTS

2.1 Introduction..18
2.2 Logical Architecture of Fast Data Analytics Stack 20
    2.2.1 Fast Data Analytics Core Capabilities (Fast Data Analytics Engine) Layer....21
        2.2.1.1 Flexible Data Ingestion..21
        2.2.1.2 Scalable Processing before Persistence 22
        2.2.1.3 Support for High-Level Domain Libraries......................22
        2.2.1.4 Support for Multiple Programming Paradigms 23
        2.2.1.5 Flexible Data Consumption...23
    2.2.2 Infrastructure Services Layer...23
        2.2.2.1 Distributed Caching 24
        2.2.2.2 Resource Management 24
        2.2.2.3 High Availability...24
        2.2.2.4 Monitoring 25
        2.2.2.5 Security..25
    2.2.3 Application Components Layer..25
        2.2.3.1 Data Conversion Components 25
        2.2.3.2 Machine Learning Components 26
        2.2.3.3 Data Exploration Components 26
        2.2.3.4 Integration Components 26
2.3 Technology Choices for Fast Data Analytics Stack...............................26
    2.3.1 Technology Choices for Fast Data Analytics Core Capabilities........26
        2.3.1.1 Apache Spark...27
        2.3.1.2 Apache Flink...30
    2.3.2 Technologies Used for Infrastructure Services 31
        2.3.2.1 Technologies for Caching 31
        2.3.2.2 Technologies for Resource Management............................33
        2.3.2.3 Technologies for High Availability 35
        2.3.2.4 Technologies for Monitoring 35
        2.3.2.5 Technologies for Security...36
    2.3.3 Technologies Available as Application Components for Fast Data
        Analytics Stack..36
        2.3.3.1 Technologies for Data Conversion Components 36
        2.3.3.2 Technologies for Machine Learning Components............38
        2.3.3.3 Technology Choices for Data Exploration Components.....40
        2.3.3.4 Technology for Integration Components...........................40
2.4 Applying Fast Data Analytics Stack to Big Data Analytics.................40
    2.4.1 Steps Involved in Big Data Analytics...41

2.4.2	Key Requirements of Steps Involved in Big Data Analytics	41
2.4.3	Mapping Key Requirements of Big Data Analytics to Fast Data Analytics Stack	42
	2.4.3.1 Mapping Time to Market to Fast Data Analytics Stack	42
	2.4.3.2 Mapping Integration with Existing Environment to Fast Data Analytics Stack	43
	2.4.3.3 Mapping Support for Iterative Development to Fast Data Analytics Stack	44
	2.4.3.4 Mapping Low Cost of Performance to Fast Data Analytics Stack	44
2.5	Deployment Options for Fast Data Analytics Stack	44
2.6	Conclusion	45
References		46
Author		47

ABSTRACT The rapidly evolving Big Data technology space has given rise to various tools and platforms in the last few years to deal with Big Data analytics. The new entrant to the Big Data technology space is the genre of technologies that are designed ground up with an analytics first approach instead of the storage first approach of existing Big Data technologies. In this chapter we call this genre of technologies Fast Data Analytics Technologies that originated from research work at Berkeley Amp Lab and Technische Universität Berlin. These technologies can be put together with other Big Data technologies to create the Fast Data Analytics Stack geared toward addressing the Big Data analytics needs of an enterprise from the creation of data products to operationalization of data products for day-to-day business use. In this chapter we'll delve into the details of features and technologies of the Fast Data Analytics Stack and discuss how the same can be used for achieving the various needs of Big Data analytics in an enterprise.

2.1 Introduction

From the very beginning, one of the biggest promises Big Data technologies brought to the table was the ability to generate actionable insights (*value*) right in time (*velocity*) from various (*variety*) types of high *volume* of data sets with reasonable accuracy (*veracity*). These insights are also called data products (Patil, 2012) in today's business world and the process of creating and operationalization of data products is commonly referred to as Big Data Analytics. These data products are sometimes geared towards solving existing business problem(s) and sometimes to changing the way existing business happens for better optimization and benefits. The needs around the data products vary from industry to industry and application to application; both from the perspective of immediate/tactical need as well as long-term potential of creating the future for the benefits of business and consumers.

Over the last 10 years or more, various Big Data technologies have become popular in the industry. They essentially tried addressing the challenges related to creation and operationalization of data products within stipulated time and cost. Data warehousing Appliances (Russom, 2011), the Hadoop Ecosystem (https://hadoop.apache.org), NoSQL Databases (Mazumder, 2010), Streaming Technologies (Wahner, 2014), and In-memory Databases (Evans, 2014) are a few examples of the Big Data technologies that fueled and helped the evolution of data products.

Fast Data Analytics Stack for Big Data Analytics

However, all of these Big Data technologies suffer from the *storage first* approach they are primarily built around. Hadoop, NoSQL Databases, and Data Warehousing Appliances require the data to be first stored within them and then analytics can be done on that data by accessing the data out of the store. In the case of Streaming Technologies, the extent of analytics that can be done on the streaming events without storing the data is considerably less because of lack of support for complex analytic needs and also they are not geared toward processing a high volume of batch data. The In-memory Databases work best for data storage and retrieval from memory and they too have very little support for complex analytics. The storage first approach eventually impacts the time for generating data products from the raw data and impedes right-in-time business decision making.

The latest addition to the Big Data technology innovation is a new genre of technologies that aim to address this issue associated with the storage first approach and instead they use Analytics First approach. These technologies are developed ground up to support data product creation and operationalization efforts in such a way that ingested raw data first go through all complex analytics steps needed to create the data product without requiring any intermediate storage. The final data product then gets stored (or pushed) to a persistent store for consumption of the data product. Sometimes even the data product may get accessed by the consuming applications online without the need of storing in a persistent store. This makes the Big Data analytics faster and more cost effective.

We call this genre of Big Data technologies Fast Data Analytics Technologies, as they support fast analytics and thereby help in generation of data products in a much faster and cost-effective way. Fast Data Analytics Technologies can be typically identified (and differentiated from other Big Data technologies) by the following key characteristics. First, using these technologies analytics can be done without the need of first storing the raw data in a persistent store. Second, they are agnostic of data storage technology. They can read from and write data to a variety of data storage systems including file servers, relational databases, NoSQL databases, HDFS (Hadoop Distributed File System), and message queues. Third, their engine supports end-to-end development of a data product (involving all steps like data ingestion from a data source, data cleansing, data transformation, aggregate creation, predictive model creation, prediction, data consumption/export to a data sink, etc.) within a single platform. And finally they can support both streaming data processing and batch data processing within a single platform. None of the other Big Data technologies provide all of these four capabilities within a single technology/framework.

Fast Data Analytics Technologies have evolved from research projects at various universities like the Amp Lab in Berkeley, California (https://amplab.cs.berkeley.edu/) and Technische Universität Berlin (http://www.tu-berlin.de/). However, they are capable of leveraging (and can be used along with) frameworks from other existing Big Data technologies like the Hadoop Ecosystem, NoSQL Databases, Data Warehousing Appliances, In-memory Databases, and Streaming Technologies. Fast Data Analytics Technologies are typically used together with other Big Data technologies for supporting end-to-end Big Data analytics requirements in an organization and they are collectively referred to as Fast Data Analytics Stack in this chapter.

In this chapter we aim to dive deep into the discussion of the Fast Data Analytics Stack. We'll start with discussing the logical architecture (technology agnostic) of the Fast Data Analytics Stack with the details around various ingredients across different layers of the stack. Next we'll map different technology options to the capabilities/services/components of those layers. We'll predominantly stick to the open source technologies. It is primarily because Big Data space is essentially fueled by open source initiatives and also because of the publicly available information about open source technologies. Finally we'll cover how the Fast Data Analytics Stack helps in implementing Big Data analytics and wrap up with the deployment options.

2.2 Logical Architecture of Fast Data Analytics Stack

The Fast Data Analytics Stack is essentially a platform for Big Data analytics that can support data product creation and operationalization from an end-to-end perspective. The central part of the Fast Data Analytics Stack is Fast Data Analytics Technologies. The Fast Data Analytics Technology is complemented with other Big Data technologies to form the overall Fast Data Analytics Stack. The key objective behind defining a platform like the Fast Data Analytics Stack is to ensure that the Fast Data Analytics Technology can be used effectively in an enterprise context.

As such there is no hard and fast rule of how the Fast Data Analytics Stack has to be assembled. An organization can use its own choice of Fast Data Analytics Technology and other Big Data technologies as deemed necessary in its particular context. This flexibility is the key value proposition Fast Data Analytics Technology brings to the Big Data technology landscape. Fast Data Analytics Technology can support a variety of Big Data and non-Big Data technologies (e.g., data sources, data sinks, analytics technique, programming paradigms, etc.) to easily fit itself into an existing technology landscape of any organization.

In this section we'll discuss logical architecture for the Fast Data Analytics Stack. This logical architecture is motivated based on BDAS (Berkeley Data Analytics Stack; https://amplab.cs.berkeley.edu/software/). It is, however, different from BDAS as we shall define it in a technology agnostic way around various defined layers with clear segregation of characteristics and responsibilities. This will help in using this logical architecture even with Big Data technologies not those are mentioned in BDAS and also the future ones that are in development (or yet to be conceived).

As shown in Figure 2.1, the logical architecture for the Fast Data Analytics Stack has three layers. The central layer represents the fast data analytics core capabilities, which are responsible for the efficient processing of data in a distributed way independent of storage infrastructure. These capabilities are the foundation of fast data analytics. In this chapter, in some places these capabilities are collectively referred to as the Fast Data

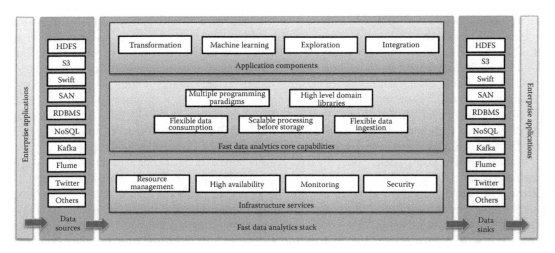

FIGURE 2.1
Logical architecture of Fast Data Analytics Stack.

Analytics Engine for the sake of brevity. The layer of fast data analytics core capabilities is complemented with two layers, namely, the infrastructure services layer and application components layer. The infrastructure services layer, below the fast data analytics core capabilities layer, groups a set of common infrastructure services that are used for effective cohabitation of the Fast Data Analytics Engine with other Big Data technologies in a cluster. The application components layer, on top of the fast data analytics core capabilities layer, groups a set of application components. These application components internally use the fast data analytics core capabilities to provide more advanced functionalities to the business applications. In the following sections, in a technology agnostic manner, we will discuss these three layers highlighting the various services/capabilities/components (also collectively referred to as *features* in some places in this chapter) encapsulated by each of them. We will also discuss the available (and brewing) technology choices that implement the features of these layers.

2.2.1 Fast Data Analytics Core Capabilities (Fast Data Analytics Engine) Layer

The heart of the Fast Data Analytics Stack is the fast data analytics core capabilities layer. The capabilities in this layer are the fundamental features of the Fast Data Analytics Stack. The features in the other layers of the Fast Data Analytics Stack essentially help in integrating the fast data analytics core capabilities to the enterprise ecosystem. These are the capabilities that essentially help to achieve data product creation and operationalization with lesser cost and higher performance. Next we'll discuss these capabilities in detail.

2.2.1.1 Flexible Data Ingestion

Big Data processing involves processing of various types of data. In today's business scenario, to create a data product one needs to consider various types of information available in an organization.

The process of creating a data product typically needs data from (a) various transactional applications (e.g., online customer transactions, status updates of inventory, user activities, social media updates, b2b data exchange, etc.) in real time; (b) data generated from conversational applications at various frequencies (e.g., customer support applications, social media instant messaging, social media blog, etc.), (c) data generated from observational applications (e.g., logs from various applications, sensor data, etc.), and finally (d) the relevant contents that get created inside as well as outside the organization in terms of documents, presentations, spreadsheets, blogs, and so on. These data might reside in different file servers, relational databases, NoSQL databases, and social media applications (like Twitter, message queues, online blogs, etc.). The capability of flexible data ingestion ensures that the data can be ingested from these various data sources easily.

The format of the data from these various data sources can be different too. For example, a relational database can provide data in row/column format in a text/csv file, the data extracted from NoSQL databases or social media can be in JSON format, the data from a Hive table may be available in Parquet format, and so on.

The actual data ingestion from these various data sources can happen in various mechanisms. The first mechanism can be getting the data in batches at a certain frequency (say, every 10 minutes or every 1 hour). The second mechanism can be getting the data in small or micro-batches (say, every 1 second, every 10 seconds, or every 1 minute). The third one can be intercepting a continuously flowing data stream within a stipulated time window (e.g., a time window of 1 minute, 30 minutes, or 1 hour). This essentially entails connecting to the source systems frequently or allowing the source system to push the data to the Fast Data Analytics Stack at regular time interval.

The flexible data ingestion capability is typically implemented with a set of inbuilt adapters available for the data source(s) to ingest the data from. If the adapter is not available for a new type of data source, typically the same can be developed with minimal effort.

2.2.1.2 Scalable Processing before Persistence

In business scenarios the importance of minimizing the time between the raw data got generated and preparation of the data product from the raw data on a regular basis is paramount. The acceptable time varies from business to business and application to application. But in every industry the need to minimize this acceptable time from its current value is increasing day by day. Sometimes this acceptable time has to be reduced to a very aggressive number for creating new business opportunities. Online real-time product recommendations to customers, real-time inventory status updates, and customized discounts in the retail industry; online real-time search and media recommendations in the media industry; next best action for customers and fraudulent transaction management in the financial industry; and real-time product quality assessment and supply chain optimization in the manufacturing industry are only a few examples of data products that have to be prepared very soon after the raw data gets generated on a regular basis. And the acceptable time for the same is reducing every quarter.

The capability of scalable processing before persistence helps immensely in minimizing the time between when the raw data gets generated and preparation of the data product. This capability is typically achieved by adopting three basic approaches. The first approach is to directly ingest and distribute the raw data from the source system to the memory of different machines in a cluster and store the data in a persistent store only after all of the analytics steps are completed. The second approach is executing the operations related to the processing steps in parallel with the various parts of the same data set (distributed in the memory of the different machines in a cluster). The third approach is to process the data in a lazy way (only when it is absolutely needed), which avoids unnecessary data reading, storing in temporary data structures, and data movement in each step.

This capability also ensures two important nonfunctional aspects of data processing. First, it ensures that during the end-to-end processing the raw data and the intermediate data is never lost in case any machine goes down. Second, it also ensures that the tasks/operations running on multiple machines in a cluster can be restarted and failed over in case of failure of some machines/processes.

2.2.1.3 Support for High-Level Domain Libraries

End-to-end processing of Big Data typically involves multiple steps. The data from various raw data sources are first cleansed to ensure that the noises in the data are removed. As a second step data from various data sources are aggregated so that they can be merged with each other. The third step is merging of the data from various data sources to create a single data set that has information about various aspects of the business problem to be solved. This step can also be associated with deep learning (Arel et al., 2010), natural language processing (Philips, 2006), and graph computing (Li et al., 2014). In the next step machine learning models (e.g., linear regression [Shalizi, 2015b], logistic regression [Shalizi, 2015a], clustering [Jain et al., 1999], and recommendation model [Agarwal et al., 2011], etc.) get

Fast Data Analytics Stack for Big Data Analytics

created with the use of that data set and then validation of the models happens. Finally, the aggregates and models are made available for consumption. Writing programs with low level APIs to achieve all these steps is a daunting task and takes a very long time before the target data product can be made available to the business.

The support for high-level domain libraries to achieve all of the aforementioned steps is of high importance to address the processing needs with the least effort and time. Typically Fast Data Analytics Technologies support this capability by providing many inbuilt libraries available to support machine learning models, graph computing, SQL-based tabular data processing, and so on. These libraries typically grow in number over a period of time with more support for newer and advanced functionalities.

2.2.1.4 Support for Multiple Programming Paradigms

Overall, data product creation typically needs efforts from various parts of an organization. This includes involvement coming from programmers (who will typically help in data ingestion, data consumption, etc.), domain specialists (who will help in validating the data, defining how to merge data without losing the context, etc.), and data scientists (who will apply predictive modeling technique on the data, validate the predictions, figure out a fix for missing data, etc.). Typically the people performing these roles come from various programming backgrounds the skills spreading across SQL, R, Java, Python, Scala, and so on. The capability to support multiple programming paradigms helps in supporting different programming skills available in an organization across these various roles.

2.2.1.5 Flexible Data Consumption

The consumption of a data product typically happens in various ways in an organization. Typically the data product has to be pushed to the data stores of other systems on a regular basis. However, the target system's data store can be of various natures. It can be a relational data store, NoSQL data store, local or cloud-based file system, and so forth. There may be a need for the target system to access the data product using SQL or language-specific APIs (Java, Scala, REST, etc.). Sometimes the data product may need to be pushed to a message queue. In all these cases the data format expected by the target system could be of different types including plain text, JSON, Parquet, Avro, etc. Also, the frequency at which the data product needs to be pushed to the target system on a regular basis or pulled by the target system can be different. The flexible data consumption capability addresses all these needs. Like in the case of flexible data ingestion, this capability is typically supported with a set of inbuilt adapters. If the adapter is not available for a new type of data sink, the same can be developed with minimal effort.

2.2.2 Infrastructure Services Layer

Like any other Big Data technology stack, the Fast Data Analytics Stack needs the ability to manage software and hardware resources for efficient execution of the Big Data analytics use cases. Most of the time, the Fast Data Analytics Stack is deployed on an infrastructure that is shared by other Big Data technologies and workloads. Hence, it is important that the Fast Data Analytics Stack be able to share the same infrastructure efficiently with other Big Data technologies used in the organization. Next we discuss the infrastructure services of the Fast Data Analytics Stack that help in achieving these goals.

2.2.2.1 Distributed Caching

The primary usage pattern supported by the Fast Data Analytics Stack is the situation where multiple user sessions run independent of one another for ingesting data, exploring data, aggregating data, creating machine learning models out of data, and making some predictions. However, many times there could be a need where multiple sessions need to share the aggregates/models created from the same set of raw data. The trivial approach to achieve this is to store the aggregates or models in a persistence store and then further reading them back from the persistence store. Though this approach works, it incurs additional time and cost associated with the disk I/O that must happen for storing the data and reading it back.

To address this concern, raw data, intermediate data aggregates, and machine learning models can be stored in a distributed cache so that they can be accessed across multiple sessions by the same or different users. Sometimes the same can be also used by other Big Data technologies.

2.2.2.2 Resource Management

The Fast Data Analytics Engine primarily uses CPU and memory of multiple machines in a cluster. Hence it is important to ensure that the computing resources of all nodes are reasonably utilized and shared appropriately across various sessions executing on the Fast Data Analytics Stack as well as with the sessions from other Big Data technologies running on the same infrastructure.

The key challenge of resource management for the Fast Data Analytics Engine is to manage the computation resources across long-running daemon processes and short-lived processes. Typically the worker processes (tasks) running on the data/slave nodes are short lived and they need to be managed along with other tasks running on the same nodes for optimal resource availability. On the other hand, the daemon/driver processes run on a master node and are long lived.

To ensure that these challenges can be addressed along with similar challenges of other Big Data technologies running on the same infrastructure, a centralized resource management service is needed. This centralized resource management service is responsible for managing these two types of processes specific to fast data analytics workloads along with other processes running on the cluster. The resource management service is typically implemented using a master–slave approach where the individual slave node runs a slave process. As and when computing resources become available in a slave node, the slave process reports to the master process (running in a master node) of the resource management service about the resource availability. The master process decides the requests that are going to get those available resources.

2.2.2.3 High Availability

In a Fast Data Analytics Stack there could be three types of high availability needs. The first situation is when an active master/daemon dies. In that case the requests have to be routed to a standby master process. The second case is where a task has to be rescheduled when a short-lived child process dies in a slave node or the slave node goes down. The third one is failover need if there are long-lived daemon processes running in multiple slave nodes; this is not a very typical situation.

The first situation is typically managed by the cluster level service. The second and third ones are the cases typically managed by the Fast Data Analytics Technology itself as it knows where to restart the process.

Fast Data Analytics Stack for Big Data Analytics 25

2.2.2.4 Monitoring

Like other Big Data technologies, the use cases (and technologies) running on the Fast Data Analytics Stack also need monitoring. The monitoring has to happen at multiple levels, namely, monitoring of services, monitoring of requests/loads, monitoring of software resources (thread pool, etc.), and monitoring of hardware resources. Typically the metrics gathered from all of the monitoring services are exposed using standard interfaces like JMX and SNMP. Then they are analyzed for troubleshooting, capacity planning, and outage prediction.

2.2.2.5 Security

The typical security features expected in case of a Fast Data Analytics Stack are the following:

- Authentication of various machines talking to each other while sharing the data to prove their identity to one another in a secure manner
- Sharing data with encryption (using SSL/TLS) across the network
- Access control for starting/stopping/modifying an analytics job
- Audit capabilities for the jobs
- Access control on log files
- Authentication and authorization using a centralized mechanism (like LDAP)

It is important to note that in case of a Fast Data Analytics Stack having security on who can access data is not important, as that is typically handled by the persistent layer used to get the data from or send the data to. Also, the security (encryption) of the data at rest is not within the scope of the Fast Data Analytics Stack for the same reason.

2.2.3 Application Components Layer

Application components are the ones that provide high-level functionalities to help implementation of data products by using fast data analytics core capabilities. Unlike infrastructure services these components are not used by the Fast Data Analytics Engine. Instead application components use fast data analytics core capabilities to provide high-level analytic components to be used in business applications. These components either run in a separate process space or provide libraries to be used while creating a data product. Typically these components provide implementations to address issues that are not catered by the Fast Data Analytics Engine or the ones that have broader usage. Some of the application components primarily support other Big Data technologies (or even non-Big Data technologies) but also have extended their functionalities to run on Fast Data Analytics Technologies as an additional feature.

2.2.3.1 Data Conversion Components

The data conversion components are the components that can provide implementation for data ingestion, cleansing, transforming, and aggregation for data in a way that can be easily used by the business level applications. Typically these components provide features that cannot be achieved using the fast data analytics core capabilities level. These components can also be the ones that can focus executing various steps (as mentioned earlier) together through declarative data flow definition.

2.2.3.2 Machine Learning Components

Machine learning components are the ones that are commonly used for analytics modeling involving regressions, clustering, recommendation, and natural language processing. As in the case of data conversion components, these components can serve broader use cases and features that are not addressed by Fast Data Analytics Technologies. They can also support creation and execution of the machine learning pipeline, which in turn abstracts various steps involved in creating a machine learning model and consumption of the same.

2.2.3.3 Data Exploration Components

The data exploration components support quick exploration of data and models in an ad hoc, interactive, and iterative way. The typical features provided by this capability are (a) support for a tabular view of results, graphs, and charts; (b) the ability to share data across various steps of the data product creation process; (c) the ability to store the steps and rerun the steps; and (d) sharing of the steps across multiple users. This ability is key to support the iterative nature of the data product creation/refinement process. Many times the exploration step in data product creation may involve exploration of data available in other technologies. Data exploration components help in achieving this too.

2.2.3.4 Integration Components

The integration components of a Fast Data Analytics Stack are meant to support integration of the overall data processing pipeline with the existing business process execution models. This is to ensure that the use cases of Big Data analytics can be run in unison with other use cases in the enterprise. Typically the integration components are common enterprise-level tools for scheduling and orchestrating business processes. They can call the data processing pipelines in part or whole using the capabilities provided by the Fast Data Analytics Engine.

2.3 Technology Choices for Fast Data Analytics Stack

In the last few years, multiple technologies have become popular that can support the various features of a Fast Data Analytics Stack. In this section we will discuss those technologies relevant to the different layers of the Fast Data Analytics Stack.

2.3.1 Technology Choices for Fast Data Analytics Core Capabilities

The Fast Data Analytics Technologies are the ones that correspond to the fast data analytics core capability layer of the Fast Data Analytics Stack. There are two Fast Data Analytics Technologies available that implement the features of fast data analytics core capabilities

Fast Data Analytics Stack for Big Data Analytics

to different extents. These two technologies are Apache Spark (https://spark.apache.org/) and Apache Flink (https://flink.apache.org/). These technologies are designed with the fast data analytics core capabilities in mind. In the following sections we'll discuss Apache Spark and Apache Flink and how each of them separately provides fast data analytics core capabilities within a single platform/framework.

2.3.1.1 Apache Spark

The most popular Fast Data Analytics Technology available now is Apache Spark. Apache Spark was originally developed at Amp Lab in Berkeley as a graduate project. The primary design objective was to achieve effective utilization of memory available in a cluster with a large number of machines to support machine learning algorithms and interactive queries on large-volume data sets. Spark provides most of the fast data analytics core capabilities described in the previous section to a considerable extent.

Spark supports ingestion of data from multiple data sources and in multiple formats. Data can be ingested in batch mode or in micro-batch (also called Spark Streaming). Spark does not support data ingestion in a real-time streaming mode. In batch mode, data can be ingested from a local file server, HDFS, any relational database, any arbitrary URI, and cloud data storage like S3 using core APIs of Spark. There are also components available that can help access data from NoSQL databases like Cassandra and HBase. Spark supports ingestion of data in text files, sequence files, and in Hadoop input format. In micro-batch mode, Spark supports data ingestion at a frequency as low as every one second. Out of the box, in micro-batch mode, Spark can read data from any TCP socket; messaging systems like Kafka and ZeroMQ; other streaming sources like Flume and Kinesis; storage systems like HDFS and S3; and social media like Twitter. On top of that, micro-batch mode also provides receiver interface that can be implemented for any other custom source. The support for various data sources is achieved through inbuilt adapters. There are also generic adapter interfaces available that can be implemented to develop a new one. The number of adapters for ingesting data from various data sources is continuously increasing to support more data sources.

Once the data is ingested, the data in Spark resides in memory in a distributed and resilient manner. Spark provides four abstractions for keeping the data in memory in a distributed and resilient manner, namely, Resilient Distributed Dataset (RDD), Dataframe, Dataset, and DStream. RDD (Zaharia et al., 2012) is the fundamental one among these various abstractions and essentially keeps the data in the memory of multiple machines in a distributed way. At the implementation level RDD is a collection of metadata information of data partitions across various machines and the lineage information for creation of the data. RDD gets created whenever data is ingested from a data source or as a result of processing an existing RDD using some transformation logic. But the RDDs don't have actual data materialized unless it is needed (lazy operation). Most of the time data get materialized when a processing pipeline is invoked either for consumption by any data access API or for storage in a target system through the call of an action method. However, if needed, data can be cached in memory explicitly to serve certain use cases. Data is not by default replicated in Spark. Instead, whenever a node goes down, Spark recomputes the data in RDD based on lineage information. Spark also can spill the data in local storage in case the memory is not sufficient. Work is ongoing in designing IndexedRDD, which can support efficient fine-grained updates for RDDs. RDD can handle any type of data, structured or unstructured.

Spark exposes another high-level abstraction for defining and processing data sets, which is called Dataframe. The Dataframe is a distributed collection of data organized into named columns. It essentially provides a tabular abstraction over RDDs depending on the tabular structure needed for an application. It is conceptually equivalent to a table in a relational database or a data frame in R/Python but with richer optimizations under the hood. Dataframes can be constructed from structured data files, tables in Hive, external databases, or existing RDDs.

Spark Streaming works on a high-level abstraction called discretized stream or DStream. DStream represents a continuous stream of data and is internally implemented as a sequence of RDDs. DStreams can be created either from input data streams from sources such as Kafka, Flume, and Kinesis, or by applying high-level operations on other DStreams. When a Spark Streaming program runs, it creates a DStream after each time (at a given frequency not less than 1 second) it pulls the data from the source and it generates a RDD.

Dataset API is the newest among the four abstractions. The key benefit Dataset API brings to the table is the structure awareness which in turn helps in better performance, optimum memory utilization, and also less coding. Data sets are strongly typed, immutable collections of objects that are also mapped to a relational schema. The encoder of Dataset API converts the data between JVM objects and relational representation. By using DataSet APIs one can get high-level functional transformation available for RDDs as well as access to a full set of relational constructs as in Dataframes. Over a period of time Dataset API can potentially become the single interface to be used in Spark for all sorts of structured data.

Spark provides the ability for parallel computation on distributed data (represented as RDD, Dataframe, Dataset, or DStream) in multiple slave nodes. Spark uses the abstraction of jobs and tasks for parallel computation on distributed data in multiple slave nodes. Jobs are the high-level requests submitted to Spark, which in turn instantiates a master/daemon/driver process. For each job, the Spark driver process creates multiple tasks running on various slave nodes. The driver also keeps track of those tasks in case any of them fail. The driver eventually also collates the results from various tasks. Spark uses Akka (http://akka.io/) for scheduling jobs between different slaves. It uses the actor model of Akka for passing messages between driver and slaves.

The Project Tungsten (Rosen, 2015) in Apache Spark has been under development for the last year or so. It is a high-level initiative that is geared toward further improvising the design of Spark's core engine. The key goals of Tungsten are (a) using application semantics to manage memory explicitly and eliminate the overhead of JVM object models and garbage collection, (b) cache-aware computation so that algorithms and data structures can exploit the memory hierarchy of the hardware, and (c) using code generation to exploit modern compilers and CPUs. The latest versions of Spark already have many features that are the outcome from Project Tungsten. Some examples are explicit memory management for aggregation operations in Spark's DataFrame API, customized serializers, binary memory management, cache-aware data structures, and optimized code generations for Spark SQL. There are also many long-term features getting developed under Tungsten. Examples are the ability to leverage SSE/SIMD architecture of modern CPUs and parallelism capabilities in GPUs.

One of the key goals of the Spark framework is to provide a platform that can be used by people with skills in various programming paradigms for data access and modeling. Given that, Spark supports multiple programming languages like Scala, Python, and Java for developers from various backgrounds. Spark also supports R language for data access and modeling, which is very popular with data scientists, that is known as SparkR.

Though the modeling support is limited right now, in the near future more machine learning algorithms will be available in SparkR. Spark SQL supports direct execution of jobs as SQL queries, which can be called from any standard JDBC/ODBC based SQL client. Spark provides support for REST-based interfaces for submitting and managing jobs.

Additionally, Spark also provides a rich set of high-level domain APIs for data aggregation, predictive modeling, graph computing, and relational queries. There are various components in Spark that are responsible for providing these high-level libraries, namely, Spark MLLib and ML Pipeline for machine learning; Spark GraphX for graph computing; and Spark SQL for relational queries. Spark does also provide a set of language-level APIs in Scala, Java, and Python (on the abstractions RDD, Dataframe, Dataset, and DStream) for common data processing constructs like Map, Reduce, Pipe, Join, Count, and various relational constructs as Spark transformations and actions. All these libraries can be used from a single code snippet where step-by-step processing can be done by using them to build a data pipeline from data ingestion to creation of a predictive model.

Finally, Spark supports multiple data storage systems that can be used to store the output from computation in a Spark cluster. The output from Spark can be stored in any relational database system, in HDFS, in a cloud storage system (like S3), in a local file system, and also to a message queue like Kafka. There are also some components available that can help to store data in NoSQL databases like Cassandra and HBase. The support for various data sinks are achieved through inbuilt adapters. There are also generic adapter interfaces available that can be implemented to develop a new one.

Figure 2.2 summarizes various features of Apache Spark in a layered architecture. The arrows represent the data flows from and to the various data sources and data sinks.

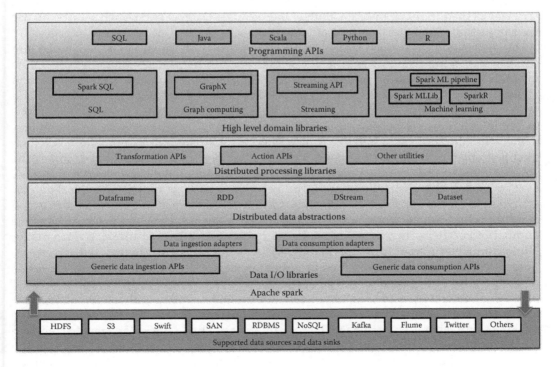

FIGURE 2.2
Components of Apache Spark.

2.3.1.2 Apache Flink

Apache Flink is other Fast Data Analytics Technology that is becoming popular. Apache Flink has its origin in a research project called Stratosphere. The idea of Flink was conceived initially in late 2008 by Professor Volker Markl from the Technische Universität Berlin in Germany (Ewen et al., 2012). Flink is also a platform for distributed general-purpose data processing with programming support in various languages. Flink uses stream computing as a fundamental to the fast data analytics approach. Every processing requirement is treated as stream computation, batch processing being a special case for a large streaming window. Though Flink came into news only in early 2014, because of its compelling features and maturity it became a top level Apache project within a year. Nevertheless, Flink still needs to properly support many of the fast data analytics core capabilities in terms of number and maturity.

As in Spark, Flink also supports various types of data sources to get the data in various formats. This includes local files, HDFS, cloud data storage (S3, Azure), relational databases, message queues (Kafka, Rabbit MQ), Flume TCP sockets, social media (Twitter), and NoSQL databases (Mongo Db, HBase, Redis). Flink supports data ingestion in low latency streaming mode as well as in batch mode. Flink also provides a generic interface for ingestion of data from any custom source. Like Spark, various inbuilt adapters are available for the supported data sources. The new ones can be developed by implementing a generic adapter interface if needed. In the Flink ecosystem the number of adapters for ingesting data from various data sources is continuously increasing to support more data sources.

To support data distribution in a resilient way, Flink provides DataSet for batch processing of static data. Flink also supports DataStream (for stream processing) APIs for unbounded real-time streaming data. DataSet APIs are similar to Spark's RDD, which supports the lazy way of materializing the data. Both of these APIs—DataSet and DataStream—can use the same set of high-level transformation functions.

The distributed data processing is achieved in Flink with the use of a distributed and scalable streaming dataflow engine. It executes everything as a stream (a hybrid engine for both stream processing and batch processing), supports mutable state of data, and allows cyclic dataflow. For distributed processing of data, Flink uses the similar job and tasks abstractions like Spark. However, unlike Spark, Flink executes tasks with iterations as cyclic data flow. To support this Flink provides two dedicated iteration operations, namely, Iterator and Delta Iterator. A data flow program (and all its operators) is scheduled just once. In the case of Iterator, for each iteration the step function consumes the entire input (the result of the previous iteration, or the initial data set) and computes the next version of the partial solution. Delta iterations run only on parts of the data that are changing. This approach significantly speeds up many machine learning and graph algorithms because the workload involved for a given iteration gradually decreases as the number of iterations increases. This native support of iteration within the engine makes Flink uniquely different from Spark. In Spark, an iteration is governed by the driver program and every iteration is executed as a separate task. Hence the driver program needs to decide where to start and end an iteration and accordingly to start new processes. In Flink, the iteration is inherent to a task and it knows how long to iterate. This eliminates the need for invoking separate processes multiple times and also optimizes the resources while iteration happens. The coordination of Flink's TaskManagers to complete a job is handled by Flink's JobManager after the driver program submits the job to the JobManager. The driver program can disconnect afterward. However, if the user-defined dataflow defines any intermediate results to be retrieved via collect() or print(), the results

Fast Data Analytics Stack for Big Data Analytics   31

are transmitted through the JobManager to the driver program. In that case the driver program has to stay connected.

Many performance-related improvements are planned for Apache Flink too. Two such improvements are the ability to dynamically increase and decrease the parallelism of a streaming job (for sustaining certain Service Level Agreements to be aligned with any change in environment) and changing key streaming operators (like user-defined state and windows) from Java Virtual Machine (JVM) objects to Flink managed memory for a better handle on memory management.

Flink also goes by the philosophy of supporting various programming paradigms for data processing and modeling so that people from various programming backgrounds can use them. Full support for Scala and Python are already there. However, Flink does not yet support execution of a job from a SQL query (using any standard SQL client). At present Flink does not have any support for R. Flink provides REST-based APIs for execution and management of jobs.

Flink does provide a rich set of high-level APIs for data aggregation, predictive modeling, graph computing, and relational queries. The domain libraries associated with Flink for this purpose are Gelly for graph processing, Flink ML Lib for machine learning, and Table API for relational query-like constructs that can be executed from Scala or Java (on both batch and streaming processes). Flink's high-level abstractions at DataSet and DataStream API level can be used for data transformation and data aggregation using Scala, Java, and Python. All these domain APIs can be executed from a single code snippet/driver program in Scala or Java to achieve end-to-end data pipeline from data ingestion to predictive model creation.

Finally, like Spark, Flink supports multiple data storage systems that can be used as sinks for the results generated as data products. The sinks can be relational database systems, in HDFS, in cloud storage systems (like S3), in local file systems, or NoSQL databases (MongoDB and HBase). Like Spark, various inbuilt adapters are available for the supported data sinks and new ones can be easily created by implementing a generic adapter interface.

Figure 2.3 shows various libraries, abstractions, and interfaces available in Flink in a layered architecture. The arrows represent the data movement from the data sources and to the data sinks.

2.3.2 Technologies Used for Infrastructure Services

Fast Data Analytics Technologies are typically geared with the ability to integrate with the standard solution for infrastructure services used in the Big Data technology landscape. This helps in easy integration of Fast Data Analytics Technologies in an enterprise ecosystem and also achieving optimal use of those solutions. In the following sub-sections we'll discuss in detail the technology choices available for each of the infrastructure services and the ways Fast Data Analytics Technologies leverage them.

2.3.2.1 Technologies for Caching

As discussed earlier, fast data analytics core capabilities can benefit from distributed caching service for sharing transformed/aggregated data and models with multiple users across multiple sessions. This need can also be extended where other Big Data technologies (non Fast Data Analytics Technologies) can use the aggregates/insights/models created by Fast Data Analytics Technologies without incurring additional disk operations. By using a distributed caching service the data is read from and persisted in a distributed

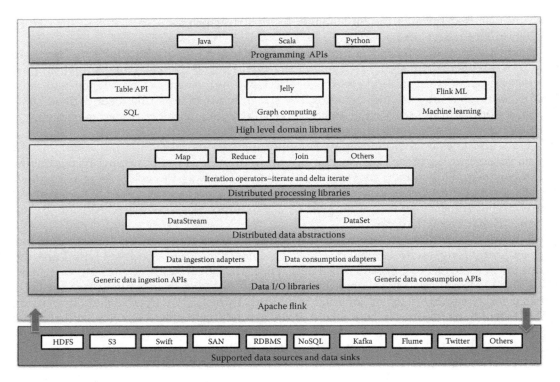

FIGURE 2.3
Components of Apache Flink.

caching layer. The caching layer in turn reads the data from and writes back to some persistent data store like HDFS, network file system (NFS), and cloud data storage. There are various choices available in the industry that provide such service.

2.3.2.1.1 Tachyon

Tachyon (http://tachyon-project.org/) is a memory-based distributed file system that can be used by various Fast Data Analytics Technologies (e.g., Spark and Flink) as well as other Big Data technologies (e.g., Hadoop MapReduce) for caching data in a distributed way. Using Tachyon, the Fast Data Analytics Technologies can store a working set of files in memory and avoid going to disk to load data sets that are used frequently. This enables different sessions of the same or different technologies (e.g., Spark, Flink, and Hadoop MapReduce) to access and share the same data available in the memory.

Tachyon also saves frameworks like Spark and Flink from recreation (or replication) of the data sets in memory to address the situation of node failure as the same is handled at Tachyon's level. Tachyon's unit for data distribution is a data block. Tachyon uses lineage information to reconstruct the data if a data block is lost because of node failure. This is in contrast to the other technologies that use replication to support failover.

Tachyon uses the Edge algorithm (Li et al., 2014) to achieve the lineage-based reconstruction of data. The Edge algorithm is based on three key design principles: check pointing of the edge of the lineage graph, favoring the high-priority files over low-priority ones for check pointing, and caching the data sets to avoid synchronous check pointing. Tachyon is data format agnostic and can support various data formats. Tachyon relies on other storage systems to persist the data and supports a variety of them (HDFS, S3, SAN, GlusterFS, etc.).

Fast Data Analytics Stack for Big Data Analytics

2.3.2.1.2 *Apache Ignite*

The other technology that can also serve as the distributed caching capability for Fast Data Analytics Technologies is Apache Ignite (https://ignite.apache.org/). There are two approaches available in Ignite. First, Ignite supports an in-memory distributed file system, which ensures availability of the data through replication (instead of recreating the data through lineage information). Like Tachyon, in this case the data can also be read from the underlying persistence file system and written back to it. In the second approach, Ignite supports the persisting of data in a distributed object cache. The data has to be mapped to objects so that the data can be stored and retrieved back from the underlying persistence storage system. Ignite provides inbuilt support for the second approach for Spark RDD, namely, IgniteRDD.

2.3.2.1.3 *Using Caching Layer of Distributed File Systems*

Many persistent distributed file systems provide facility of the caching layer where the data can be kept in memory once it is read from the disk. The Fast Data Analytics Technologies can potentially use this approach too. Open source solutions like HDFS, GlusterFS, and XtreemFS all provide such facilities. Licensed products like IBM's GPFS and EMC's Isilon also provide such facilities. The caching layers of these products can be turned on with appropriate configurations to achieve necessary performance by avoiding disk I/O.

2.3.2.2 **Technologies for Resource Management**

Fast Data Analytics Technologies come with their own ways of managing resources. While starting a job one can specify the computing resources to be used by daemon/driver processes and slave processes. However, this solution cannot be aware of the resource requirement of other components/technologies running on the same cluster. Hence it is better to use an external centralized resource management solution. There are two external resource management technologies available that are popularly used in Big Data clusters and also supported by the Fast Data Analytics Technologies. We shall discuss them next.

2.3.2.2.1 *Apache Mesos*

Apache Mesos (http://mesos.apache.org/) is the popular resource management framework used across different Big Data technologies like Hadoop, search, and streaming technologies. Mesos is part of BDAS. It abstracts CPU, memory, and storage, enabling fault-tolerant and elasticity for distributed systems. The Mesos kernel runs on every machine and provides applications with APIs for resource management and scheduling across entire on-premise data centers or cloud environments. Mesos consists of a master daemon that manages slave daemons running on each slave node. The applications (Spark, Flink, etc.) run tasks on these slaves. Figure 2.4 describes the resource distribution architecture of Mesos with the examples of Slave 1 and Slave 2 serving two applications or frameworks, Framework 1 and Framework 2 (say, Spark and Flink). The step numbers on the arrows in Figure 2.4 indicate the sequence of steps.

In a standalone cluster deployment, the slave nodes of Spark are managed by Spark Master. When using Mesos, the Spark Master's responsibility of managing the cluster is taken up by Mesos master. With Mesos when a driver creates a job and starts issuing tasks for scheduling, Mesos determines the slave machines that can handle the tasks. While deciding so Mesos takes into account other frameworks running on the same set of clusters (which are also controlled by Mesos). The integration of Apache Flink to run on Mesos is currently a work in progress.

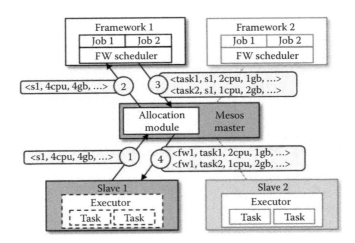

FIGURE 2.4
Resource distribution architecture of Mesos. (Courtesy of YARN Architecture, http://hadoop.apache.org/docs/current/hadoop-yarn/hadoop-yarn-site/YARN.html.)

2.3.2.2.2 Apache YARN

YARN (Saha, 2013), Yet Another Resource Negotiator, is a generic framework that can support resource management for different types of distributed programming models on HDFS. YARN is part of the Hadoop ecosystem. Hence to use YARN one has to download and deploy the Hadoop ecosystem (though it is not needed to run all services of the Hadoop ecosystem). Like Mesos, YARN is also a generic purpose operating system that can support various types of concurrent processes by allocating different computing resources to them. It is better to use YARN if a Fast Data Analytics Stack has to be deployed in the same cluster as Hadoop.

As shown in Figure 2.5, YARN has four key components: Global Resource Manager, Node Manager, Application Manager, and Pluggable Scheduler. These four components share the responsibilities of resource management and lifecycle management of a job. In a two-step process, resource allocation is done by YARN, and the application (e.g., Spark, Flink, and Hadoop MapReduce) handles the task execution.

Both Apache Spark and Apache Flink provide features so that they can be run on YARN easily. Apache Spark provides the option where the driver program on Spark can be run outside or inside of YARN. In the first option, namely, YARN client mode, YARN only manages the resources for Spark's slave processes (YARN client mode) and the driver program runs independent of YARN. In the second approach, YARN cluster mode, the driver process is managed by YARN, along with Spark's slave processes. Apache Flink provides an option close to the YARN client mode of Spark. In the case of Flink, the driver program typically runs outside of YARN and submits jobs to the Job Manager, which runs within YARN's resource management control. Apache Flink provides another way of running on YARN by use of Apache Tez (https://tez.apache.org/). Tez provides API for specifying a directed acyclic graph (DAG), placing the DAG vertices in YARN containers. It also provides API for data shuffling. Flink uses these facilities in a way that is equivalent to Flink's network stack. By replacing Flink's network stack with Tez, users can get scalability and elastic resource usage in shared clusters on YARN while retaining Flink's APIs, optimizer, and runtime. Flink programs can run almost unmodified using Tez as an execution environment.

Fast Data Analytics Stack for Big Data Analytics

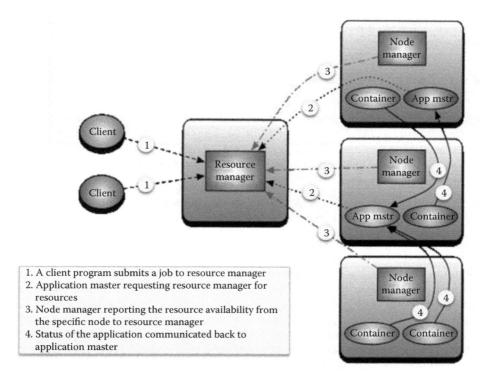

FIGURE 2.5
High-level architecture of YARN. (Courtesy of Mesos Architecture, http://mesos.apache.org/documentation/latest/mesos-architecture/.)

2.3.2.3 Technologies for High Availability

Apache ZooKeeper (https://cwiki.apache.org/confluence/display/ZOOKEEPER/Index) is the most popular general-purpose high-availability management solution used by most of the Big Data technologies. It provides a centralized service for maintaining configuration information, naming, distributed synchronization, and group services as aspects. Fast Data Analytics Technologies can use these services through a mix of specific components of ZooKeeper and application-specific conventions to avoid single point of failure. The situation of restarting a task in the same or another slave node in case of task failures is handled by the Fast Data Analytics Technology itself.

There are alternatives of ZooKeeper available, including Open Replica (http://openreplica.org/) and Consul (https://www.consul.io/). However, among all of these options ZooKeeper is the most widely and successfully used one for Big Data technologies.

2.3.2.4 Technologies for Monitoring

Typically Fast Data Analytics Technologies come with features for monitoring the jobs/tasks through their custom monitoring consoles. However, for more exhaustive monitoring requirements, external solutions need to be used. Use of Nagios and Ganglia are common standards in Big Data technologies for detailed monitoring, which can be also used for Fast Data Analytics Technologies. ELK (Elastic Search, Logstash, and Kibana) stack (Sissel, n.d.) is also popular these days for multiple levels of monitoring of a Big Data cluster. Both Apache Spark and Apache Flink can be integrated with these solutions with minimal effort because of their support for Java and REST-based APIs.

2.3.2.5 Technologies for Security

The security requirements are addressed by the respective Fast Data Analytics Technologies. They provide features to easily integrate with enterprise-level facilities (and requirements) like LDAP, SSL, Kerberos, Shared Secret, and the network firewall. Spark provides extensible support for these requirements. Flink's support for the security features is so far based on support available in the Hadoop platform.

2.3.3 Technologies Available as Application Components for Fast Data Analytics Stack

There are various technologies available in the Big Data technology landscape that can be used as application components in the Fast Data Analytics Stack. These application components are typically implemented by external initiatives/projects that are not part of the core Fast Data Analytics Technologies. That's the reason these capabilities can provide support for multiple Fast Data Analytics Technologies, other Big Data technologies, and sometime also for non-Big Data technologies. However, in many cases these application components actually start with a specific Fast Data Analytics Technology and then extends support for other technologies. In some cases even existing (non-fast data analytics based) application components extend their support to run on fast data analytics technology. At the enterprise level this helps in achieving optimal use of those application components as well as having a more centralized view and control across the various use cases. In the following sub-section we will discuss in detail the various types of application components.

Note that many of the application components are pretty new in the industry. Many of them are in the early stages. Some of them are still to be adopted in the mainstream industry.

2.3.3.1 Technologies for Data Conversion Components

Many application components are getting developed in the space that supports data transformation using Spark and Flink. These components are to provide support for data ingestion, data cleansing, data transformation, data aggregation, and end-to-end data flow pipeline covering all these tasks. The data conversion components typically use the high-level domain APIs available in Fast Data Analytics Technologies, including relational queries, graph computing, and transformation APIs. However, sometimes they can also directly use the capability of *scalable processing before persistence* of Fast Data Analytics Technologies. Next we'll discuss the key ones among these components that have potential for overall impact.

2.3.3.1.1 Apache MRQL

Apache MRQL (https://mrql.incubator.apache.org/) is a query processing and optimization system for large-scale, distributed data analysis. It is an SQL-like query language for large-scale data analysis on a cluster. The MRQL query processing system can evaluate MRQL queries in four modes: MapReduce mode using Apache Hadoop, BSP (Bulk Synchronous Parallel) mode using Apache Hama, Spark mode using Apache Spark, and

Flink mode using Apache Flink. The MRQL query language is powerful enough to express most common data analysis tasks over many formats like raw in situ data, XML, JSON, binary, and CSV. MRQL provides power constructs for executing SQL. However, it internally uses Spark or Flink's capability of scalable processing before persistence to execute them. In addition to SQL capabilities, MRQL can also enable users to express complex machine learning tasks, such as PageRank, K-Means Clustering, and Matrix Factorization, using SQL-like queries exclusively. The MRQL query processing system is able to compile these queries to efficient Java code and run on the backend run time engine like Spark, Flink, and Hadoop MapReduce.

2.3.3.1.2 BlinkDB

On top of Spark's SQL support, various SQL tools are in the process of development. BlinkDB (http://blinkdb.org/) is a new kind of SQL query engine that can allow trade-off between query performance and accuracy. It is a massively parallel approximate query engine for running interactive SQL queries on a large volume of data. BlinkDB presents the results in an annotated way with error related to accuracy. Users can pick and choose the result which is within the acceptable tolerance of accuracy for a given business context.

2.3.3.1.3 Sample Clean

Sample Clean (http://sampleclean.org/) is another new project useful for data transformation. Using Sample Clean, a pipeline can be run on BlinkDB to automate data cleaning using the pipeline concept. Sample Clean provides a set of physical and logical data cleaning operators that can be interchanged easily and can be composed out of each other. This project essentially aims to enable users to construct and adapt data cleaning pipelines easily and fast.

2.3.3.1.4 Hive on Spark

Support for Spark as an engine for executing Apache Hive queries is geared towards providing benefit to the users who are already using Spark for other data conversion and machine learning needs. In an enterprise, standardizing on one execution backend is convenient for operational management, makes it easier to develop expertise to develop various applications, debugs the issues, and makes further improvement in those applications. This feature of Hive is also aimed at helping organizations to have another option as the run time engine to run Hive queries (apart from Hadoop MapReduce and Tez). Hive on Spark (Zhang, 2015) supports all existing Hive features (Hive QL and all its extensions) and Hive's integration with authorization, monitoring, auditing, and other operational tools.

2.3.3.1.5 SQL Clients

Spark supports calling its jobs as SQL queries from any standard SQL client. This feature is compliant to Hive Query Language. Using this feature one can use ODBC/JDBC clients (like DB Explorer, Toad, Squirrel, Eclipse, etc.) to explore, transform, and aggregate the data using Spark. Also, using this feature one can access data directly from a Hive Table (in HDFS) and create/update a Hive Table. This feature supports use of various Hive UDFs too.

2.3.3.1.6 Cascading on Flink

Cascading (http://www.cascading.org/) is an application development platform for building applications that involve end-to-end data processing from data ingestion to data export. Cascading primarily supports technologies from the Hadoop ecosystem like MapReduce,

Pig, and Tez. From Cascading 3.0, it has also started supporting Apache Flink as one of the choices for executing data flows defined in Cascading.

2.3.3.1.7 *Apache Nifi and Spark*

Apache Nifi (https://nifi.apache.org/) supports powerful and scalable directed graphs of data routing, transformation, data aggregation, and system mediation logic. Users can specify a data flow to cover these various steps using a web-based user interface. Users can do design, execution, and monitoring of the data flow. Apache Nifi can be used to write a Spark streaming (micro-batch) application. This can cover data flow starting from ingesting data from a streaming data source; applying data transformation, aggregation logic on that data; and then finally moving the result to any data sink supported by Spark.

2.3.3.2 Technologies for Machine Learning Components

Various technologies are getting developed that run on Spark and Flink, and can support machine learning capabilities. In some cases these technologies use machine learning libraries available in Fast Data Analytics Technologies, and in some other cases they have separate implementation of the machine learning components that only depend on the capability of scalable processing before persistence of Fast Data Analytics Technolgies. Here we discuss a few of these technologies with high potential for adoption.

2.3.3.2.1 *Splash*

The framework Splash (Yuczhang, 2015) is a general framework for parallelizing stochastic learning algorithms on multinode clusters. Splash runs on Spark. The stochastic learning algorithms are the algorithms that can sequentially process random samples of the data from a large data set. The stochastic algorithms are very efficient in the analysis of large-scale data, as in the case of these algorithms the cost of preiteration does not depend on the overall size of the data. However, these algorithms are difficult to parallelize as they are typically defined as sequential procedures. Splash helps to develop a stochastic algorithm using the Splash programming interface without worrying about issues of distributed computing. The parallelization is automatic and efficient in the communication perspective.

2.3.3.2.2 *SystemML*

Apache SystemML (http://systemml.apache.org/), originally from IBM Research Lab, is a new open source project for machine learning that can run on Spark and is an alternative to Spark ML Lib. SystemML helps in flexible specification of machine learning algorithms in a declarative way. It also supports automatic generation of various types of runtime plans supporting different backend engines like process running on a single machine, Spark, and Hadoop MapReduce. In SystemML, machine learning algorithms are expressed in an R-like syntax that includes linear algebra primitives, statistical functions, and ML-specific constructs. This high-level language significantly increases the productivity of data scientists as it provides full flexibility in expressing custom analytics. It also helps in using data independent of the underlying formats and physical data representations. SystemML ensures efficiency and scalability through automatic optimization of a runtime execution plan. Compared to existing machine learning libraries, which mostly provide fixed algorithms and runtime plans, SystemML provides flexibility to define custom analytics and execution plans.

2.3.3.2.3 *KeystoneML*

KeystoneML (http://keystone-ml.org/) is a software framework, written in Scala, from the UC Berkeley AMPLab. It is designed to simplify the construction of large scale, end-to-end, machine learning pipelines with Apache Spark. KeystoneML shares some common concepts with Spark ML. However, there are a few important differences concerning the type safety and chaining that help in easier construction of pipelines. KeystoneML also presents a richer set of operators than those present in SparkML including featurizers for images, text, and speech. KeystoneML also provides several example pipelines that represent some of the state-of-the-art academic results on public data sets.

2.3.3.2.4 *Mahout on Spark*

The Apache Mahout (http://mahout.apache.org/) project provides an environment for quickly creating scalable and performant machine learning applications. Mahout provides implementation of various machine learning algorithms for regression, clustering, and recommendations. Mahout also supports some of its algorithms to run on Spark. At this point, this environment addresses mostly R-like linear algebra optimizations. The support for Flink as an engine for Mahout is a work in progress.

2.3.3.2.5 *H2O on Spark*

H2O (http://www.h2o.ai/#/) is an open source machine learning platform that has got widely popular recently. Sparkling Water (https://github.com/h2oai/sparkling-water) is a project from H2O that integrates H2O's machine learning engine with Spark. It provides utilities to help publish Spark data structures (RDDs, DataFrames) as H2O's frames and vice versa, using Spark data structures as input for H2O's algorithms, basic building blocks to create machine learning applications utilizing Spark and H2O APIs, and Python interface enabling use of Sparkling Water directly from PySpark.

2.3.3.2.6 *Apache SAMOA*

Apache SAMOA (https://samoa.incubator.apache.org/) is a framework for achieving machine learning on streaming data in a distributed way. SAMOA contains a programing abstraction for applying machine learning algorithms on streaming data (also known as distributed streaming ML algorithms). SAMOA enables development of new distributed streaming ML algorithms without directly dealing with the complexity of underlying distributed stream processing engines. SAMOA supports Apache Storm, Apache S4, Apache Samza, and Apache Flink as underlying stream processing engines. Using SAMOA users can develop distributed streaming ML algorithms once and execute them on multiple underlying distributed stream processing engines.

2.3.3.2.7 *Velox*

Velox (Crankshaw, 2014) is a project that also needs special mention here for its unique objective. So far enough work has happened (and still ongoing) in the industry to support creation of complex models using large data sets for addressing requirements like personalized recommendations, targeted advertising, fraud management, and sales prediction. However, not much work has happened for the deployment, management, and serving prediction requests using the models. Velox aims to address these issues using Spark as the backend engine. It is a framework for facilitating online model management, maintenance, and prediction serving, bridging the gap between offline model creation and online prediction by the model.

2.3.3.3 Technology Choices for Data Exploration Components

There are predominantly two types of technologies available for the data exploration components. The first one is interactive shell based and the second one is web-based interactive interface or notebooks. In the following sections we'll discuss both of them.

2.3.3.3.1 Interactive Shells for Data Exploration

Fast Data Analytics Technologies typically provide interactive shells based on the REPL (read–eval–print–loop) philosophy. These interactive shells can be started with required resources allocated to the daemon and slave processes. The interactive shells can be Scala based, Python based (so far only in Spark) or R based (so far only in Spark). Using the interactive scale one can do data ingestion, data transformation, data aggregation, and model building. However, the support for output would be limited to the tabular display of the data. Also, the steps cannot be saved for future use.

2.3.3.3.2 Interactive Web Interface (Notebooks) for Data Exploration

Notebooks are interactive web interfaces for data exploration in Big Data space. They are becoming the de facto standards for data exploration using various technologies. The two popular notebook technologies are Jupyter (http://jupyter.org/) and Zeppelin (https://zeppelin.incubator.apache.org/). Both of these technologies support various types of backends where backends are provided by the respective Fast Data Analytics Technologies as well as other Big Data (and non-Big Data) technologies. Spark has Spark Kernel (https://github.com/ibm-et/spark-kernel) for Jupyter. Flink does not have support for Jupyter so far. However, for Zeppelin both Spark and Flink have their own interpreters. Using notebooks one can execute steps for data analytics with rich visualization of data using various graphs/chart and advanced visualization tools. Also, the steps in an individual Notebook can be saved, rerun later, and shared.

2.3.3.4 Technology for Integration Components

The integration components are typically the enterprise-level tools (ETL tools, Message Queues, Enterprise Service Bus, etc.) for integration, scheduling, and orchestration of data pipelines. These tools can typically access the whole/part of the analytics pipeline executed in Fast Data Analytics Technologies using REST, SQL, and/or Scripting interfaces. Many times the integration can also be done by online synchronous calling of language-specific APIs of Java and SQL.

2.4 Applying Fast Data Analytics Stack to Big Data Analytics

In previous sections we discussed how the Fast Data Analytics Stack provides various features to help implement Big Data analytics in organizations. We have also investigated the various technology options available for implementation of those features using different Fast Data Analytics Technologies as well as other Big Data technologies in a Fast Data Analytics Stack. In this section we shall delve into the details of how those features/technologies can be mapped to the various steps of Big Data analytics.

2.4.1 Steps Involved in Big Data Analytics

As discussed earlier, the latest approach for Big Data analytics revolves around creation and operationalization of data products from a large volume of various types of data with reasonable accuracy and speed. The data product creation stage is a one-time development activity involving establishing steps for creation of insights and consumption of the data product. The data product operationalization stage involves periodically running a set of processes and subprocesses that create insights on a regular basis, helps consumption, and monitors the results or benefits of the data product.

Let us first discuss the steps involved in data product creation. The first step is to *define* a data product that can solve an existing business problem or create a new business opportunity. The process of defining a data product itself is time sensitive, as the very idea for a new data product (or enhancement of the existing one) has to be proven/tried out before business decision makers can invest on full-fledged operationalization of the data product. Otherwise alternative ideas have to be tried out. Once a data product is defined, in the next step one has to *infuse* the data product into the existing ecosystem of the organization. This essentially means adding a new business process (or refinement of existing ones) that will run in a periodic manner to create the data product on a regular basis. It also entails implementation of mechanisms by which other processes/applications can use the data product. The third step is to *refine* the data product based on the feedback from its regular use within the enterprise business processes. This step is similar to the define step but more focused on troubleshooting/debugging/tuning activities and sometimes exploring more to arrive at a better solution. Overall, the data product creation stage may be very time sensitive because of competitive market pressure for new capabilities, customer satisfaction, legal requirements, and various other business reasons.

The steps involved in the data product operationalization stage are essentially two. The first step is to *run* various processes and subprocesses for creating the insights and consuming the data product on a regular basis. The second step is to *track* the benefits and impact of the data product. The process of regularly tracking whether the data product is bringing in the anticipated benefits to the business is important. It proves the success of the initiative as well as provides feedback to tune the data product in the refine step. This stage is time sensitive too. The run step has to create the data product from the raw data on a regular basis in a periodic, real-time or near-real-time way so the insight is available for making business decisions and taking action in a timely manner. Similarly, the tracking step also needs to provide feedback in time before a wrong decision is made based on the anomaly/error in the insights.

2.4.2 Key Requirements of Steps Involved in Big Data Analytics

Following are the key requirements (or challenges involved) that can be abstracted from the characteristics of the various steps of Big Data analytics.

1. Time to market—There was a time when businesses were ready to wait for months or even a year to decide on new business strategies. However, in today's world, where everything is changing on a quarter-to-quarter basis, every business needs to change its strategy and direction in an agile manner. So the expected time from conceptualization of a new data product to regularly using the data product in a business process is typically very short in today's business context.

2. Ease of integration with existing environment—For the data products to work efficiently they need to be easily infused and running in existing environment. That essentially means ease of integration with existing source systems and consuming applications, reuse of existing software and hardware infrastructure, integration with existing processes, and reuse of existing skills.

3. Support for iterative development—Given the agility of the business environment, data products need to be changed/refined from time to time. Also, the initial phase of data product definition itself needs a number of iterations. That's the reason it is very important to have the support for iteration.

4. Low cost of performance—This requirement essentially means the ability to generate insights fast with less cost on a regular basis. Getting insights in real time (or near real time) using costly software and hardware clusters do not work in today's business scenario. The expectation is to arrive at the insights at lesser cost and sometimes on a pay-per-use basis.

2.4.3 Mapping Key Requirements of Big Data Analytics to Fast Data Analytics Stack

The Fast Data Analytics Stack provides support for addressing the requirements (and challenges) of Big Data analytics in a very effective way. It is primarily because Fast Data Analytics Technologies were developed from the ground up keeping these requirements in mind. In the following sections we discuss the mapping of these requirements with various layers and features of the Fast Data Analytics Stack.

2.4.3.1 Mapping Time to Market to Fast Data Analytics Stack

During the data product definition phase majority of the time goes to figure out how to get the data from a new type of data sources. If a data product needs data from a new type of data source, the challenge of ingesting data is a typical inhibiting factor given the new type of end point, data format, frequency of data ingestion, and so on. Similarly, there are challenges involved in adding a new data product in an existing environment. All these eventually impact the time to market of the data product creation process. The inbuilt adapters available for flexible data ingestion and flexible data consumption capabilities help immensely to cut down the time needed in addressing these challenges during the data product definition phase, infusion phase, and refinement phase. These capabilities also provide an easy way of creating a new set of adapters if needed.

The process of data product definition involves trying out different types of aggregates, various algorithms, and various feature sets to eventually arrive at the right data product. If one has to try out those various options without the support of high-level APIs it can become a very time-consuming task eventually delaying the time to market. Fast Data Analytics Technologies provide the support for high-level domain APIs for data aggregation, predictive modeling, graph computing, and SQL queries that help in achieving data product definition and refinement at a faster speed. They typically provide a large number of algorithms (which can be used through few API calls), SQL-based aggregation functions, machine learning pipeline creation based on configuration, and configuration-based cross-validation of parameters/feature sets. This capability also helps in the infusion phase in integrating the new aggregates/models in lesser time.

The process of integrating a new data product to run on the existing cluster is a typical inhibiting factor in an organization and delays time to market. The resource management capability and high availability capabilities in the Fast Data Analytics Stack, which can be easily integrated through configuration with the Fast Data Analytics Technologies, help in addressing integration during the infusion phase.

The overall definition time involved in data product creation can be reduced if the results (aggregates/models) from the intermediate steps can be shared with multiple people to parallelize the work as well as to get the feedback. The caching capability helps in achieving this too. This in turn helps in reducing overall time to market.

The integration components support most of the standard mechanisms of integration used today in an enterprise scenario. This helps to cut down time during the infusion phase for establishing day-to-day execution of the data pipeline. It also helps in quick integration with systems to track the benefits.

The data definition and refine steps need to be performed in small interactive substeps. This is needed for validating the results (aggregates/models) from each small substep. This in turn reduces the amount of rework, which eventually helps in reducing the overall time involved in data product creation. The data exploration components help as well. They can provide support to do execution and visualization in substeps, rerun those substeps, and share the results/visualization from those substeps with others, which in turn helps in reducing the overall time to market.

The data definition and refine steps can also benefit from the data conversion and machine learning components. Components like Blink DB, Sample Clean, KeyStoneML, Splash, and SystemML provide functionalities that can help in arriving at the right data product fast and with less effort.

2.4.3.2 Mapping Integration with Existing Environment to Fast Data Analytics Stack

Any organization has data sources ranging from relational databases, enterprise resource planning (ERP) systems (which typically support file based data exchange), NoSQL databases, message queues, etc. The format of the data in different data sources varies too. Also, there would be a need to pull the data from these sources at different periodic intervals. The flexible data ingestion capability of Fast Data Analytics Technologies helps immensely in supporting such various data sources available in the existing environment during the data product definition and refinement phases. Similarly, the flexible data consumption capability supports integrating with various types of downstream systems in an organization through export of data to those systems.

Every organization needs people in various roles to get involved in the data product creation process and they typically come from backgrounds of different programming skills. The support for multiple programming paradigms helps in reuse of the existing skills in an organization. Currently Fast Data Analytics Technologies support a majority of the popular programming languages in data science including SQL, Python, Scala, R, and Java.

The ability to reuse (and share with other applications) the existing resource management, high availability, monitoring, and security solutions helps in reuse of existing software and hardware infrastructure. As previously discussed, the Fast Data Analytics Stack is geared to achieving the necessary reuse while Fast Data Analytics Technologies provide an easy way of integration.

Many consuming applications in an organization may need to access the data product online. The integration components help in achieving this by a standard way of integration based on REST, SQL, and language-specific APIs. The same services also help in integrating the data product creation process with enterprise-level scheduling and orchestration tools.

Many of the existing components (in the Big Data technology landscape) for data conversion (Hive, Cascading) and machine learning (System ML, Mahout, SPSS) are extending their features for supporting Spark and Flink as their runtime engines. This will help in reusing the existing software investments in an enterprise.

2.4.3.3 Mapping Support for Iterative Development to Fast Data Analytics Stack

As previously discussed, step-by-step iterative development is important in the creation of data products. This not only involves trying out multiple data sources, algorithms, feature sets, and so on, but also requires participation from various types of people in the organization (i.e., developers, data scientists, and business owners).

The flexible data ingestion capability provides support for ingesting data from a variety of data sources to help data scientists to try out different types of data easily in an iterative way. Similarly, the flexible data consumption capability provides support for exporting data to various systems so that people in business roles can easily consume/validate the intermediate results. Support for multiple programming paradigms further aids this as data scientists and business users can have different programming skills and can use their own set of tools/programming paradigms to validate the intermediate results.

The caching service can help in sharing the aggregates and models easily with others, which in turn help in feedback-based iterative development. The visualization-based interactive exploration components help in feedback-based iterative development. They can provide support for this through the sharing feature, which can help sharing of the steps, results, and visualization from the substeps with others.

2.4.3.4 Mapping Low Cost of Performance to Fast Data Analytics Stack

The capability of scalable processing without storage helps in analyzing data in a distributed manner. This is the key proposition of the Fast Data Analytics Technologies for achieving high performance analytics on a large volume of various types of data at low cost.

However, in addition to that other features of the Fast Data Analytics Stack also helps in reducing the cost performance ratio. The caching service helps in attaining high performance in low cost by reducing the extra disk I/O and workload on other systems. The common resource management, high availability, security, and monitoring services help in executing the data product creation and consumption use cases in a common hardware and software infrastructure. This in turn further helps in reducing the total cost of ownership.

2.5 Deployment Options for Fast Data Analytics Stack

As discussed before, the Big Data analytics has two high level stages involved in its life cycle, namely, data product creation and data product operationalization. From the perspective of dealing with the various constraints and requirements of these two stages, appropriate deployment options have to be considered.

The data product creation stage is typically exploratory and open ended in nature. Data scientists/Data analysts need to try various data sets, different aggregation schemes, many predictive modeling algorithms, and different feature sets within a short time frame. Also, there may be a need for getting input/data from sources/people, which will have a wait time. Given this openness and exploratory nature this stage is a good candidate to be tried out in a cloud. Various cloud-based solutions are already available in the market from IBM, Databricks, Amazon, Qubole, etc. that can be used for data product creation. These cloud-based solutions can help an enterprises in executing of the data product creation stage in a more predictable manner. With the cloud-based solutions this stage can be executed in an elastic environment on pay-per-use basis without upfront investment in infrastructure and with the ability to shrink or expand infrastructure as and when needed. This in turn can help in addressing the openness and unknowns involved in this stage. For security of data transferred over wire SSL can be used for moving data in and out of cloud.

On the other hand, the data product operationalization stage typically is executed in a planned and controlled manner. Once an enterprise acquires necessary learning after the completion of the data product creation stage, this stage becomes more predictable with the least number of unknowns in terms of number and type of data sets, starting data volumes, resultant data volumes, and technology challenges. Even if there is a need to change this stage from the process perspective, the same typically happens in a controlled way. Hence this stage can be deployed using in-premise infrastructure. However, deploying this stage in a cloud makes sense too as Cloud can support growth of data volume in production in a cost effective manner.

2.6 Conclusion

The Big Data technology landscape is evolving from the storage first approach to analytics first approach. Fast Data Analytics Technologies are developed from the ground up to support data product creation and operationalization using the analytics first approach in a fast and cost worthy way. Apache Spark and Apache Flink are the two primary technologies in this category. Among these two technologies Apache Spark is more mature with its stability and availability of a large number of APIs for complex analytics need. It is ready for prime-time use by traditional enterprises. On the other hand, Apache Flink has a promising architecture given its approach of handling all types of data processing needs using the streaming approach and native iteration capabilities inherent to the runtime engine. However, it is relatively new and still needs more features and stability before it can be used for business applications in enterprises.

The Fast Data Analytics Stack can be typically built using Fast Data Analytics Technologies and other Big Data technologies to address enterprise-level requirements around reuse of infrastructure, processes, and skills. Many innovations are happening across various layers of the Fast Data Analytics Stack for supporting enterprise needs in a better way. Major work is going on for increasing the performance and efficiency at the fast data analytics core capability layer to ensure better cost to performance. In the infrastructure service, layer work is ongoing to support better caching, monitoring, and security needs in the future. In the application component layer many existing Big Data components are extending their support to run Fast Data Analytics Technologies as backend. Also many new components are getting developed focusing particularly to leverage the strength of efficient runtime of Fast Data Analytics Technologies.

Overall, Fast Data Analytics Stack is the future of Big Data analytics. Various big software companies as well as small-time software startups are investing in a big way in the Fast Data Analytics Stack for shaping the future of Big Data analytics in a way beneficial for both businesses and customers. However, proper due diligence to select appropriate technologies to be used in various layers of the Fast Data Analytics Stack (suitable for a given enterprise context) is key for successful implementation of business-critical data products using the Fast Data Analytics Stack.

References

Agarwal D., Chen B. (2011). Machine learning for large scale recommender systems. Retrieved January 12, 2016, from http://pages.cs.wisc.edu/~beechung/icml11-tutorial/.

Arel I., Rose Derek C., Karnowski Thomas P. (2010). Deep machine learning—A new frontier in artificial intelligence research. *IEEE Computational Intelligence Magazine*. Retrieved January 12, 2016, from http://web.eecs.utk.edu/~itamar/Papers/DML_Arel_2010.pdf.

Crankshaw D. (2014). Velox: Models in action. Retrieved January 12, 2016, from https://amplab.cs.berkeley.edu/projects/velox/.

Evans C. (2014). In-memory databases—What they do and the storage they need. *Computer Weekly*. Retrieved January 12, 2016, from http://www.computerweekly.com/feature/In-memory-databases-What-they-do-and-the-storage-they-need.

Ewen S., Tzoumas K., Kaufmann M., Markl V. (2012). Spinning fast iterative data flows. *Proceedings of the VLDB Endowment*, vol. 5, no. 11, pp. 1268–1279. doi:10.14778/2350229.2350245 (http://vldb.org/pvldb/vol5/p1268_stephanewen_vldb2012.pdf).

Jain A. K., Murty M. N., Flynn P. J. (1999). Data clustering: A review. *Journal of ACM Computing Surveys* (CSUR), vol. 31, no. 3, pp. 264–323. doi:10.1145/331499.331504 (http://dl.acm.org/citation.cfm?id=331504).

Li H., Ghodsi A., Zaharia M., Shenker S., Stoica I. (2014). Tachyon: Reliable, memory speed storage for cluster computing frameworks. *SOCC '14 Proceedings of the ACM Symposium on Cloud Computing*, pp. 1–15. doi:10.1145/2670979.2670985 (http://dl.acm.org/citation.cfm?id=2670979.2670985).

Lu Y., Cheng J., Yan D., Wu H. 2014. Large-scale distributed graph computing systems: An experimental evaluation. *Proceedings of the VLDB Endowment*, vol. 8, no. 3, pp. 281–292. doi:10.14778/2735508.2735517 (http://www.vldb.org/pvldb/vol8/p281-lu.pdf).

Mazumder S. (2010). NoSQL in the Enterprise. InfoQ. Retrieved January 12, 2016, from http://www.infoq.com/articles/nosql-in-the-enterprise.

Patil D. J. (2012). The art of turning data into product. Data Jujitsu. Retrieved January 12, 2016, from http://www.kdnuggets.com/2012/08/dj-patil-data-jujitsu.html.

Philips W. (2006). Introduction to natural language processing. Consortium of Cognitive Science Instruction. Retrieved January 12, 2016, from http://www.mind.ilstu.edu/curriculum/proto thinker/natural_language_processing.php.

Rosen J. (2015). Deep dive into Project Tungsten: Bring Spark closer to bare metal. *O'Reilly Community*. Retrieved January 12, 2016, from http://www.oreilly.com/pub/e/3474.

Russom P. (2011). The pros and cons of data warehouse appliances. TDWI. Retrieved January 12, 2016, from https://tdwi.org/~/media/TDWI/TDWI/Article%20Content/2005/08/Pros_and_Cons_of_DW_Apps%20pdf.ashx.

Saha B. (2013). Philosophy behind YARN Resource Management. Retrieved January 12, 2016, from http://hortonworks.com/blog/philosophy-behind-yarn-resource-management/.

Shalizi C. R. (2015a). Logistic regression. Retrieved January 12, 2016, from http://www.stat.cmu.edu/~cshalizi/uADA/15/lectures/12.pdf.

Shalizi C. R. (2015b). Regression: Predicting and relating quantitative features. Retrieved January 12, 2016, from http://www.stat.cmu.edu/~cshalizi/uADA/15/lectures/01.pdf.
Sissel J. (n.d.). An introduction to the ELK stack. Retrieved January 12, 2016, from https://www.elastic.co/webinars/introduction-elk-stack.
Wahner K. (2014). Real-time stream processing as game changer in a big data world with Hadoop and Data Warehouse. *InfoQ*. Retrieved January 12, 2016, from http://www.infoq.com/articles/stream-processing-hadoop.
Yuczhang. (2015). Splash: Efficient stochastic learning on clusters. Retrieved January 12, 2016, from https://amplab.cs.berkeley.edu/projects/splash/.
Zaharia M, Chowdhury M, Das T, Dave A, Ma J, McCauley M, Franklin M J, Shenker S, and Stoica I. (2012). Resilient distributed datasets: A fault-tolerant abstraction for in-memory fast data analytics. NSDI '12 *Proceedings of the 9th USENIX Conference on Networked Systems Design and Implementation*, p. 2–2. http://dl.acm.org/citation.cfm?id=2228301.
Zhang X, Ho S. (2015). Hive on Spark. Retrieved January 12, 2016, from https://cwiki.apache.org/confluence/display/Hive/Hive+on+Spark.

Author

Sourav Mazumder, a Big Data evangelist and architect, has around 20 years of information technology experience and 7 years in Big Data. Currently, he is part of the IBM Analytics Stampede and Spark Technology Center. Mazumder has experience in architecting high-throughput scalable data applications, real-time analytics, and petabyte scale database systems using the concepts of distributed computing, performance modeling, and Big Data technologies. Influencing key decision makers in Fortune 500 companies to embark into Big Data journey for over 5 years, Mazumder regularly publishes papers, books on Big Data Technologies and speaks in Big Data conferences. Mazumder is cochair of Big Data Applications for Enterprise, Industry and Business Track in IEEE Big Data Service 2016.

3

Analytical Approach for Big Data in the Internet of Things

Anand Paul, Awais Ahmad, and M. Mazhar Rathore

CONTENTS

3.1 Introduction: Background and Driving Forces 49
3.2 Sensor Deployment Scenario 52
3.3 Analytical Architecture 53
3.4 Intelligent Building 54
3.5 Proposed Algorithm 55
3.6 Implementation and Evaluation 56
3.7 Conclusions..58
References..59
Authors..60

ABSTRACT This chapter describes the analytical architecture system for the Internet of Things that demonstrates the collaborative contextual Big Data sharing among all the devices in a healthcare system. The analytical system involves a network architecture with the enhanced processing features for collected data received by millions of connected things. In the given system, various sensors (can be wearable devices) are attached to the human body to measure the data and transmit it to a primary mobile device (PMD). The amount of collected data is then forwarded to the intelligent building using the Internet to process and perform necessary actions. The intelligent building is composed of a Big Data collection unit (used for filtration and load balancing), Hadoop processing unit (HPU) (comprises HDFS and MapReduce), and an analysis and decision unit. The HPU and analysis and decision unit are equipped with the medical expert system, which reads the sensory data and performs actions.

3.1 Introduction: Background and Driving Forces

In healthcare system applications, the wireless body area network (WBAN) compromises an innovative model for wireless sensor networks (WSNs) in observing biomedical sensors, such as a biochip. These sensors can be attached to the human body or clothes (Xing and Zhu 2009; Alam and Hamida 2014; Cavallari et al. 2014) and can be used to measure the constraints related with the human body, usually observe physiological signals originating from different body organs, body motions, and the surrounding environment. The measured values can be collected and communicated to the main server using Internet

49

Protocol Version 6 (IPv6) over the Low-Power Wireless Personal Area Network (6LoWPAN) (Kushalnagar et al. 2007; Montenegro et al. 2007). It helps in connecting these nodes to the IPv6 network that plays a vital role in health diagnostics issues. With a view to investigating the amount of data collected, there is a need to transfer the data to some gateway node in order to produce results. For such application, a suitable example (e.g., ZigBee technology) can be employed that uses IEEE 802.15.4 PHY along with the MAC criterions in wireless transmission toward gateway nodes (Kiran et al. 2014). In this application, where data is remotely collected faces power grounds (Kiran et al. 2014). Since the sensor nodes are used for the collection of data, charging and replacing their batteries is a critical task.

Recently, the healthcare system's Internet of Things (IoT) was recognized as a revolution in information and communications technology (ICT). It has been in rapid development since the beginning of the 21st century. Mainly, IoT connects all the physical devices, such as sensors, actuators, entrenched sensors, and radio frequency identifications (RFID), to one medium, the Internet, and is considered to be an empowering technology to understand the visualization of a universal infrastructure of unified physical traits (Welbourne et al. 2009). Furthermore, IoT extends the usage of the Internet into our daily lives by connecting billions of smart devices (Kortuem et al. 2010; Ahmad, Paul, and Rathmore 2016), which bring significant change in the way we live and interact with other devices (Jara et al. 2012).

In IoT, smart technologies (e.g., sensors, actuators, RFID tags) are developing rapidly (Lee et al. 2010). Due to an increase in smart technologies, IoT applications are increasing day by day (Broll et al. 2009; Li et al. 2011). The aforementioned technologies are used for the development of smart homes and for monitoring of healthcare systems (European Commission Information Society 2008; National Information Council 2008; Alemdar and Ersoy 2010; Ahmad, Paul, Rathmore, and Chang 2016). The e-healthcare systems are integrated with wearable devices for the betterment of IoT (Castillejo et al. 2013). For chronic disease monitoring, a mobile base telemonitoring system was developed (Morak et al. 2012). The huge amount of sensor data collected from such applications should be available everywhere 24/7; the availability of sensor data depends on the Internet connectivity. The data generated from IoT applications is called Big Data because it is huge in volume. Such connectivity is the foundation of hyperconnectivity (Kiran et al. 2014). The number of devices connected to one another, 2 billion in 2015, will increase to 24 billion in 2020, according to GSMA (Malik 2011). In such situations, the bandwidth will be the critical problem for the healthcare system. The processing of sensory traffic will also be a big challenge. If we use traditional approaches for data collection and data gathering, then a huge amount of data will be lost due to these traditional approaches.

Based on the aforementioned technologies either an existing IoT architecture or new novel architecture should be designed for solving the problems of the healthcare system. New manufactured devices are rarely integrated into existing architecture, and this integration is an important element for enhancing the healthcare system in IoT. The development of smart systems require the following features: take care of human beings like patients at home, some people are outside, while some are inside thier cars, the desired system should constantly monitor the patients as well as provide the medications to the patients, and it should also diagnose and cure the diseases in real time. The problems of medical sensory data can be overcome by using fast aggregation and collection of data and by applying parallel efficient processing. This chapter presents a novel technique, the Hadoop-Based Intelligent Care System (HICS), a Big Data analytical approach that is based on the concept of multiple Hadoop HDFS and parallel processing.

In the recommended system, a human body uses wearable devices or other physical body sensors that measure the readings of blood pressure, pulse rate, diabetes, and car

Analytical Approach for Big Data in the Internet of Things

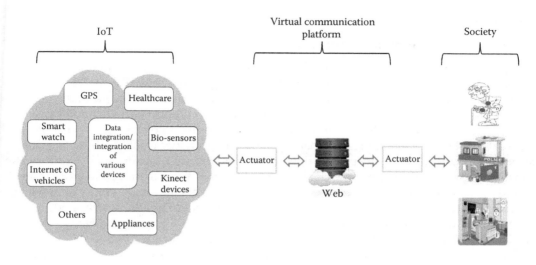

FIGURE 3.1
Factors influencing the human element in the Internet of Things.

accident information to the attached coordinator as shown in Figure 3.1. The measured data is then communicated to the primary medical device (PMD) using Bluetooth or ZigBee IEEE 802.15.4. The PMD is connected to the Internet through 3G/LTE/WiFi via gateways. Each gateway is responsible for collecting the measured data from various PMDs, which are then sent to the intelligent building (IB). IB provides the support to the recommended HICS network architecture that processes the immense volume of the incoming stream of data by capturing it using high-speed apprehending devices such as RF_RING and TNAPI (Fusco and Deri 2010) and comprehensive results in its collection unit. Afterward, the collected data is sent to the Hadoop processing unit (HPU) for further processing. The HPU performs the analysis algorithm including numerical calculations, assessments or other operations, and then generates results. Finally, the exploration and decision unit responds to the system (in case a patient requires a remote physician or ambulance, or there is a car accident) based on the results generated by the HPU.

The main contribution of this chapter is summarized as follows. The proposed network architecture is the first architecture designed for healthcare, in which the processing of real-time as well as offline data is done using Hadoop. Second, the network can also handle the enormous volume of data generated by the connected devices by breaking it down into components and performing analysis using Hadoop. Moreover, the intelligent building concept is introduced, which is mainly responsible for managing, processing, and analyzing incoming sensor data, and finally making decisions intelligently. The network not only handles the immense volume of data but also gives feedback to the users "anytime, anywhere, anyhow." The whole system is implemented in a real environment using Hadoop on UBUNTU 14.04. Sample medical and sensory data sets are tested to appraise the proposed system.

Next we discuss the proposed scheme including a sensor deployment scenario, which describes the functionalities of the medical and activity sensors, followed by the communication model for Hadoop-based HICS, and the network architecture including the intelligent building and its algorithm.

3.2 Sensor Deployment Scenario

The healthcare system comprises dynamic processes including pretreatment processing, in-treatment processing, and posttreatment processing, as shown in Figure 3.2.

In the figure, various sensors including activity sensors, medical sensors, and coordinator sensors are attached to human body parts. The human body parts include the wrist, ankle, heart, chest, and helmet (while cycling). These sensors collect heterogeneous data (such as diabetic and blood pressure data) and various activities (such as physical exercise, sitting, walking, climbing upstairs or downstairs, and cycling). During such activities, the sensors read the body temperature, heartbeat, blood pressure, sweating, and glucose level. In order to collect and aggregate data from various sensors and make the system energy efficient, we used a coordinator, which works as a sink node. The coordinator node acts as a relay node to collect the data and transmit it to the PMD. The communication between the PMD and coordinator is achieved through Bluetooth or ZigBee.

The coordinator receives health readings from various sensors attached to the body. Each sensor frame contains three main points of information: (1) globally unique device identifier (GDID), which uniquely identifies the sensor; (2) type, which identifies the type

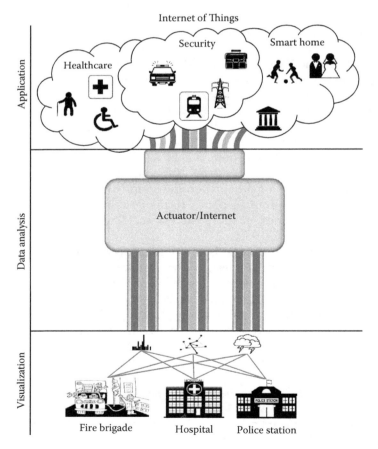

FIGURE 3.2
Deployment scenario for proposed system model.

of the sensor, such as glucose, blood pressure, or pulse rate; and (3) value, which contains the reading of the sensor. The coordinator aggregates and then encapsulates all sensor readings into a single packet in a proper format and sequence. It initially adds the packet header, which mainly contains the U_ID (user id) that uniquely identifies the sensor and the user. Later, it enlarges it by adding various sensor readings in the following sequence, depending upon the available readings: (1) glucose level reading, (2) blood pressure reading, (3) pulse rate, (4) temperature, (5) heart rate, and (6) breath rate. Moreover, all the readings from the various sensors are added for a particular time in a single packet. Since every sensor is not required to transmit data directly to the PMD, energy is saved. Moreover, the number of sensors on the patient's body depends on the patient requirement. Therefore, it is not compulsory that all of the sensors are attached to the user's body.

3.3 Analytical Architecture

Figure 3.3 illustrates the concept of the proposed healthcare IoT system. Various sensors are attached to the human body that are used to measure blood pressure, pulse rate, human

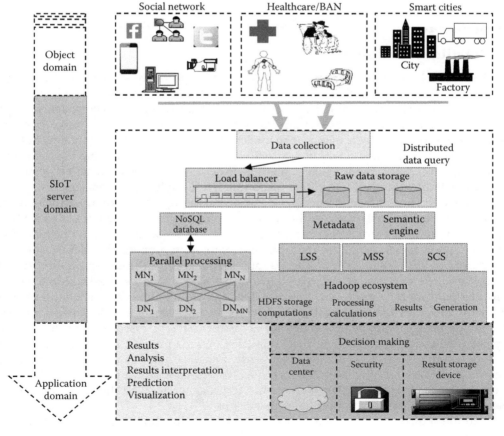

FIGURE 3.3
Application scenario for proposed healthcare IoT system.

motion, diabetics, car accidents, and so on. For a better understanding of the proposed system, we assume that all the users are equipped with smart devices. In our example scenario, we are considering a patient in a home, an elderly user, a user doing physical exercise, and a car carrying kids and adults. In these scenarios, if a patient's blood pressure or other disease crosses the defined threshold, or if an old man has a heart attack or a user doing physical exercise requires first aid, or has a car accident, the sensors transmit the measured data to the agent (e.g., raspberry-pi). Raspberry-pi is a device used to convert sensor data to mobile readable data. After the conversion, the mobile readable data is forwarded to the PMD using ZigBee or IEEE 8.2.15.4. Each mobile is equipped with the designed application, which shows the actual readings of the user. The PMD is connected to the intelligent building via the Internet (LTE/3G/WiFi). The intelligent building is a smart block used for storing, processing, and executing certain actions depending on the context of data. Therefore, for the example cases, the intelligent building executes individual actions for the patient (to record history of patient in hospital or change in the doctor prescriptions), for the elderly user (requiring remote physician or ambulance), for the physical exercise users (to provide first aid from a nearby hospital), and for the car carrying kids and adults (to inform the police station). A detailed explanation and working of the intelligent building, the core component of the system, is described in the next section.

3.4 Intelligent Building

The intelligent building is the central component of the proposed system. The building is a complete intelligent system that handles incoming high-speed Big Data from a large number of body area sensors using parallel processing by the Hadoop system. The system is responsible for collecting, processing, and analyzing health sensor data from a large number of people with sensors on their bodies. The intelligent building, we can say intelligent healthcare system, is mainly composed of a collection unit, a processing unit having the Hadoop system equipped with the intelligent medical expert system, sensor health measurement patient database, aggregation result unit, and finally the application layer services.

The collection unit is the entrance point for the incoming health data from the body area networks. It continuously collects the data from each registered person of the BAN network. It might have a single server performing all functionalities of the collection, filtration, and load balancing, or have multiple servers for each functionality depending on the complexity of the system. We considered multiple servers for the collection unit in which the collection server collects high-speed incoming WBAN sensors. It extracts the required information from each packet such as the GDID (globally unique device identifier), which uniquely identifies the sensors, U_ID (user id), and all sensor measurements squeezed in a single packet. Moreover, it filters all necessary data by discarding all unnecessary repeated information containing the same previous readings. It uses Hadoop libraries, such as Hadoop-pcap-lib, Hadoop-pcap-serde, and Hadoop Pcap Input, to process the incoming packet and generate sequence files from sensor readings encapsulated in the packet. For each distinct U_ID, one sequence file is generated. All the readings from that user are added to the corresponding sequence file.

When the sequence file has reached its size or time threshold, it is sent to the Hadoop processing units to process the sequence file by analyzing and calculating statistical parameters. The load balancer, which is sometimes the master node in the Hadoop setups, decides which data nodes will process the sequence file. Each processing server or data node has its GDID range for which it processes sequence files. The processing server is liable to process and analyze patient data that lies in its GDID range.

The Hadoop processing unit is composed of various master nodes and many data nodes. It uses the Hadoop Distributed File System (HDFS) on various parallel data nodes to store the data in blocks. Each data node is equipped with the same proposed algorithm using MapReduce implementation to process the sequence files either by calculating statistical parameters or by analyzing sensor measures in a sequence file to generate intermediate results for decision making. When the data node receives any sequence file from the collection unit, it applies the algorithm to the sequence file and generates intermediate results. Various mapper and reducer functions work in parallel to achieve the efficiency. The mapper function initially decides whether each sensor reading is normal and needs not be deeply analyzed or have some abnormal values that require analysis and emergency actions. It compares sensors and values with their corresponding normal threshold values, and if satisfied, then stores them in the database without further time-consuming analysis. When any sensor value from the WBAN sensor satisfies its corresponding serious threshold value, it generates an alert directly to the application layer service for a quick response. The application layer performs a quick action depending on the sensor, its value, and patient, such as calls the police in case of accidents, or calls the doctor or an ambulance in case of heart attack or a serious diabetes, blood pressure, or pulse reading. Apparently, when the sensor's reading is neither normal nor too serious, it requires analysis. The readings that lie in the aforementioned range are processed by calculating statistical parameters or performing other calculations depending on the algorithm to generate intermediate results for a final decision. Finally, the aggregation unit of the Hadoop processing system aggregates the results using the reducer from various parallel processing servers (data nodes) and sends them to the final decision server.

Decision servers are equipped with the intelligent medical expert system, machine learning (ML) classifiers, and other complicated medical problem detection algorithms for further analysis and decision making. It analyzes the current results, received from the processing unit, depending on the previous history of the patient using complex medical expert systems, ML classifiers, and so on. The concrete detail of the medical expert systems is out of the scope of the chapter. In our scenarios, we are using machine learning classifiers like REPTree, which is more efficient and accurate, as the decision server for various normal disease detection.

3.5 Proposed Algorithm

An algorithm is designed for the proposed HICS intelligent building system to process high-speed WBAN sensor data. The notations used for the proposed algorithm are SAVE_DB (), Analyze_Data (), Emergency () to represent some actions. SAVE_DB is responsible for storing sensor data into databases corresponding to the GDID and U_ID. The Analyze_Data function is the implementation of the expert system or ML classification algorithm, or other complex medical problem detection algorithms or statistical calculations of parameters. Emergency functions alert the application layer service to perform quick actions based on serious data received from sensors or based on the analysis results generated by processing servers.

Initially, at the collection unit, while receiving a packet from the co-coordinator node of BAN, all sensor measures, which are encapsulated in a packet, are extracted corresponding to the GDID, U_ID, and activity performed (if the activity reading is there). At the next step, these readings are added to a sequence file as one record corresponding to the GDID and U_ID in the particular sequence file. Therefore, for each packet there is one record added in a sequence file. When the sequence file reaches its particular time or size threshold, it is sent to the Hadoop processing system, i.e., Hadoop_Processing function. Hadoop_Processing considers the values from the sequence file containing readings from various sensors like the blood pressure sensor, diabetes sensor, and pulse sensor. The values initially checked whether they lie in a normal range such as blood pressure: not less than 70 and not greater than 140, diabetes: not less than 70 and not more than 200, and pulse rate: from 70 to 90. The data is just saved in the database if the sensor values lie within a normal range; they do not process further for analysis. On the other hand, if any one of the values from these sensors lies in a serious range by satisfying serious thresholds, such as blood pressure: below 40 and above 200, diabetes: below 40 and above 400, and pulse above 100 for adult and above 130 for a child, as well as a limit exceeding 0–240 bpm heart rate, 1–120 bpm breath rate, and 33°C–42°C temperature, then emergency action must be taken. Normal and serious threshold values for each type of sensor varies depending on the unit and intensity of the effect, and the activity performed while the readings are taken. Moreover, if the sensor readings are neither too serious nor too normal, then statistical calculations or other medical measures are performed on them to generate intermediate results for final analysis and decision making. These generated results are then sent to the decision server for making final decisions, disease classification based on the medical expert system, or classification algorithm installed on the decision server.

3.6 Implementation and Evaluation

The proposed algorithm is implemented using a Hadoop single node setup on a UBUNTU 14.04 LTS coreTMi5 machine with 3.2 GHz processor and 4 GB memory. MapReduce is used as a front-end programming with Hadoop-pcap-lib, Hadoop-pcap-serde, and Hadoop Pcap Input libraries for network packets processing and generating sequence files at the collection unit. The Map function of our implementation maps U_ID, Type, and corresponding sensor values. It compares the values with thresholds and generates action or alerts when required. Moreover, it generates intermediate results and sends it to the Reduce function as U_ID as a key and results in the value at the aggregation unit. The reducer aggregates the results, then sorts and organizes them. Finally, the decision is made based on the results. Hadoop MapReduce implementation of the whole system on various data nodes makes the algorithm be processed in a parallel environment efficiently. In addition, the algorithm is also implemented using simple Java programming to make a comparative analysis of Hadoop implementation.

Data sets are collected from the UCI repository and WISDM lab for evaluating the efficiency of the proposed system. The UCI diabetes data set (UCI Machine Learning Repository 1994a) contains the records of diabetes outpatients in various time slots such as pre-breakfast, post-breakfast, pre-lunch, post-lunch, pre-snack, pre-supper, and post-supper. Value parameter shows the patient-generated diabetes sensor's measure. It contains 13,437 records with different time stamps. The UCI ICU data set (UCI Machine

Learning Repository 1994b) holds the ICU sensed data of an 8.5-month-old, 5 kg weighted female kid patient having biliary atresia problem. She currently is in liver failure with coagulopathy. The data set includes various types of medical measurements from different devices including heart rate (bpm), respiration rate (breath/min), arterial pressure—mean (mm Hg), arterial pressure systolic (mm Hg), arterial pressure diastolic (mm Hg), arterial O2 saturation (%), tidal volume, and PIP (cm H20). It contains 7931 records in various continuous time stamps. The WISDM lab data set (WISDM Lab 2012) has two sensor-generated files: WISMDM_Transformed, which contains 5418 records from 15 sensors per record, and WISDM_raw, which covers more than 1,048,576 records from only 3 sensors. The WISMDM data set contains the measures corresponding to user activity, such as jogging, walking, and upstairs and downstairs movement. In addition, we also generated traffic accident data sets, which contains thousands of records of the location and time of accidents. Besides all these data sets, we also implemented other data sets containing different numbers of sensors to evaluate the system efficiency. Moreover, accidents and healthcare measures from data set files are replayed to the system as network traffic to check the real-time efficiency of the system.

Considering the diabetes patient, blood glucose measures are taken for analysis. A patient is monitored by considering his regular post-breakfast, post-lunch, post-supper, pre-breakfast, pre-lunch, pre-supper, and pre-snack measures. The system saves data into the database, analyzes data, or takes emergency action based on the values received from the user/patient. The graph of the first 30 blood glucose measures of the patient while post-breakfast, post-lunch, and post-supper is shown in Figure 3.4. The patient is an insulin-dependent diabetes patient. For this reason, the system just stores the value when it is less than 250 by considering it as an average threshold. However, when the received measure crosses the serious threshold, for example, 400 as at the 25th and 15th readings, the emergency action is taken of either admitting the patient in the hospital or requesting him to increase his insulin dose. In between diabetes values, the patient readings are analyzed and then some medicines are prescribed or insulin treatment is mentioned depending on the analysis results. While analyzing the post-meal patient measures, most of the post-supper readings crossed the average threshold but rarely after breakfast, as shown in Figure 3.4. For this reason, the patient is asked to change his food for dinner and also increase the insulin dosage.

Pre-meal diabetes measures are also considered for analysis purposes by the system, as shown in a scatter graph in Figure 3.5. In pre-meal analysis, pre-breakfast, pre-lunch, pre-supper, and pre-snack diabetes measures are taken as visible by the scatter graph. Nine times

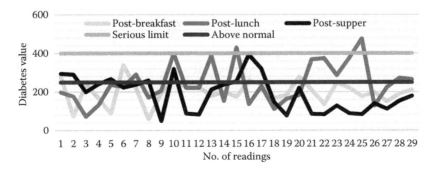

FIGURE 3.4
Post-meal diabetes measure of a patient.

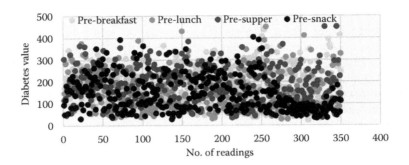

FIGURE 3.5
Pre-meal diabetes measure of a patient.

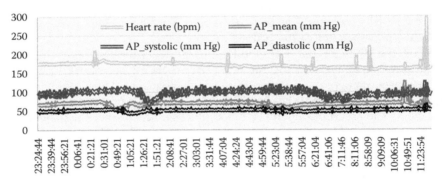

FIGURE 3.6
ICU patient measurements.

the glucose test crossed the serious threshold when quick action is taken in which the patient is suggested to increase the insulin dose. Most of the abnormal actions are at pre-lunch and pre-supper timings, which show the rise in glucose level at PM timings.

The system also analyzed the heart patient measurements related to heart rate (bpm), arterial pressure—mean (AP_mean, mm Hg), arterial pressure systolic (AP_systolic, mm Hg), and arterial pressure diastolic (AP_diastolic, mm Hg). The analysis report is presented in Figure 3.6. The considered patient is a small baby of age 8.5 months, for this reason; average heart rate threshold is 190 for her. Sometimes the heart rate crosses the average threshold such as at 0:24:41, 04:19:04, and 09:00:09. However, at that time other subordinary measures such as AP_mean, AP_systolic, and AP_diastolic are normal. For this reason, emergency action is not taken. Moreover, at the times of 11:26:54 and 11:27:54 the heart rate is enormously increased and AP_mean, AP_systolic, AP_diastolic also crosses the normal threshold. Therefore an alert is generated by the system, and the emergency call is made to save a life.

3.7 Conclusions

In this chapter, we discussed an intelligent healthcare IoT system using WBAN applications on Hadoop-based processing servers. The proposed system involves hospitals, emergency services, first aid, and police stations. The applications of the proposed network architecture include leveraging sensors, coordinators, PMDs, and the intelligent building. The system provides a promising solution for suppository nonacquiescence issues by automatically reminding users about their prescriptions, and helping and supporting them on various occasions (e.g., first aid, remote physician, police station, etc.). With a view to developing continuous follow-up and monitoring users' vital signs (anytime, anywhere, anyhow), a flexible system is developed, which is based on the intelligent machine. The intelligent machine receives data from various users, then processes and analyzes it using Hadoop, and then generates output for decision making. Based on the output, the machine executes individual actions (e.g., first aid, remote physician, reminding patient about the doctor prescriptions, car accident). The performance of the system is tested on Hadoop using a UBUNTU 14.04 LTS coreTMi5 machine with 3.2 GHz processor and 4 GB memory and compared with the performance of simple Java implementation. The final evaluations show that the performance of the proposed network architecture fulfills the required desires of the users connected to it, whether the input data is in real-time or offline while taking actions at the real time. In the future, we are planning to provide a security feature to the system such as confidentiality and user authentication. Moreover, more medical complex classifiers will be part of the system to make it more practical.

References

Ahmad, A., Paul, A., and Rathore, M. M. (2016). An efficient divide-and-conquer approach for big data analytics in machine-to-machine communication. *Neurocomputing*, 174, 439–453.

Ahmad, A., Paul, A., Rathore, M. M., and Chang, H. (2016). Smart cyber society: Integration of capillary devices with high usability based on cyber–physical system. *Future Generation Computer Systems*, 56, 493–503.

Alam, M. M., and Hamida, E. B. (2014). Surveying wearable human assistive technology for life and safety critical applications: Standards, challenges and opportunities. *Sensors*, 14(5), 9153–9209.

Alemdar, H., and Ersoy, C. (2010). Wireless sensor networks for healthcare: A survey. *Computer Networks*, 54(15), 2688–2710.

Broll, G., Rukzio, E., Paolucci, M., Wagner, M., Schmidt, A., and Hussmann, H. (2009). Perci: Pervasive service interaction with the internet of things. *IEEE Internet Computing*, 13(6), 74–81.

Castillejo, P., Martinez, J. F., Rodríguez-Molina, J., and Cuerva, A. (2013). Integration of wearable devices in a wireless sensor network for an E-health application. *IEEE Wireless Communications*, 20(4), 38–49.

Cavallari, R., Martelli, F., Rosini, R., Buratti, C., and Verdone, R. (2014). A survey on wireless body area networks: Technologies and design challenges. *IEEE Communications Surveys and Tutorials*, 16(3), 1635–1657.

European Commission Information Society. (2008). Internet of Things in 2020: A roadmap for the future. http://www.iot-visitthefuture.eu.

Fusco, F., and Deri, L. (2010, November). High speed network traffic analysis with commodity multi-core systems. ACM IMC 2010.

Jara, A. J., Zamora, M., and Skarmeta, A. F. (2012, June). Knowledge acquisition and management architecture for mobile and personal health environments based on the internet of things. In *IEEE 11th International Conference on Trust, Security and Privacy in Computing and Communications (TrustCom)*, 1811–1818.

Kiran, M. P. R., Rajalakshmi, P., Bharadwaj, K., and Acharyya, A. (2014, March). Adaptive rule engine based IoT enabled remote health care data acquisition and smart transmission system. In *2014 IEEE World Forum on Internet of Things* (WF-IoT), 253–258.

Kortuem, G., Kawsar, F., Fitton, D., and Sundramoorthy, V. (2010). Smart objects as building blocks for the internet of things. *IEEE Internet Computing*, 14(1), 44–51.

Kushalnagar, N., Montenegro, G., and Schumacher, C. (2007). IPv6 over low-power wireless personal area networks (6LoWPANs): Overview, assumptions, problem statement, and goals (No. RFC 4919).

Lee, S. Y., Wang, L. H., and Fang, Q. (2010). A low-power RFID integrated circuits for intelligent healthcare systems. *IEEE Transactions on Information Technology in Biomedicine*, 14(6), 1387–1396.

Li, X., Lu, R., Liang, X., Shen, X., Chen, J., and Lin, X. (2011). Smart community: An internet of things application. *IEEE Communications Magazine*, 49(11), 68–75.

Malik, O. (2011 October 13). Internet of things will have 24 billion devices by 2020. http://gigaom.com/2011/10/13/internet-of-things-will-have-24-billiondevices-by-2020/.

Montenegro, G., Kushalnagar, N., Hui, J., and Culler, D. (2007). Transmission of IPv6 packets over IEEE 802.15. 4 networks (No. RFC 4944).

Morak, J., Kumpusch, H., Hayn, D., Modre-Osprian, R., and Schreier, G. (2012). Design and evaluation of a telemonitoring concept based on NFC-enabled mobile phones and sensor devices. *IEEE Transactions on Information Technology in Biomedicine*, 16(1), 17–23.

National Information Council. (2008). Global Trends 2025: A transformed world. US Government Printing Office. http://www.acus.org/publication/global-trends-2025-transformed-world.

UCI Machine Learning Repository. (1994a). Diabetes Data Set. https://archive.ics.uci.edu/ml/datasets/Diabetes. Accessed January 31, 2015.

UCI Machine Learning Repository. (1994b). ICU Data Set. https://archive.ics.uci.edu/ml/datasets/ICU. Accessed January 31, 2015.

Welbourne, E., Battle, L., Cole, G., Gould, K., Rector, K., Raymer, S., Balazinska, M., and Borriello, G. (2009). Building the internet of things using RFID: the RFID ecosystem experience. *IEEE Internet Computing*, 13(3), 48–55.

WISDM Lab. (2012). Dataset. www.cis.fordham.edu/wisdm/dataset.php. Accessed January 31, 2015.

Xing, J., and Zhu, Y. (2009, September). A survey on body area network. In *5th International Conference on Wireless Communications, Networking and Mobile Computing (WiCom'09)*, 1–4.

Authors

Anand Paul earned a PhD in electrical engineering at National Cheng Kung University, Tainan, Taiwan, in 2010. He is an associate professor with the School of Computer Science and Engineering, Kyungpook National University, Daegu, Korea. He is a delegate representing Korea for the M2M focus group and for MPEG. His research interests include algorithm and architecture reconfigurable embedded computing. Dr. Paul has guest edited various international journals, and he is part of the editorial team for the *Journal of Platform Technology and Cyber Physical Systems*.

He serves as a reviewer for various IEEE/IET journals. He is the track chair for smart human computer interaction for ACMSAC 2015 and 2014. He was the recipient of the Outstanding International Student Scholarship Award in 2004–2010, the Best Paper Award in National Computer Symposium, Taipei, Taiwan, in 2009, and UWSS 2015, in Beijing, China. He is also an IEEE senior member.

Awais Ahmad earned a BS (CS) at the University of Peshawar and master's degrees in telecommunication and networking at Bahria University, Islamabad, Pakistan, in 2008 and 2010, respectively. During his master's research work he worked on energy efficient congestion control schemes in mobile wireless sensor networks. Currently, he is pursuing a PhD at Kyungpook National University, Daegu, South Korea. There he received research experience on Big Data analytics, IoT/SIoT, 4G/5G, machine-to-machine communication, and wireless sensor networks. He has received numerous prestigious awards: IEEE Best Research Paper Award: International Workshop on Ubiquitous Sensor Systems (UWSS 2015), in conjunction with the Smart World Congress (SWC 2015), Beijing, China; Research Award from the President of Bahria University Islamabad, Pakistan, in 2011; Best Paper Nomination Award in WCECS 2011 at the University of California, Los Angeles; and Best Paper Award in the 1st Symposium on CS&E, Moju Resort, Korea, in 2013.

M. Mazhar Rathore earned a master's degree in computer and communication security at the National University of Sciences and Technology, Pakistan, in 2012. Currently, he is pursuing a PhD, with Dr. Anand Paul, at Kyungpook National University, Daegu, South Korea. His research includes Big Data analytics, network traffic analysis and monitoring, intrusion detection, and computer and network security.

4

Analysis of Costing Issues in Big Data

Kuldeep Singh Jadon and Radhakishan Yadav

CONTENTS

4.1 Introduction 64
4.2 Need of Big Data 64
4.3 Major Sources of Big Data 65
4.4 Big Data Functional Issues 67
    4.4.1 Essential Classes of Information in Big Data 67
        4.4.1.1 Composite Multimedia and Mixed Information 67
        4.4.1.2 Objective and Contained Globe Information 67
        4.4.1.3 Portable Cloud Information Analytics 67
    4.4.2 Analysis Issues in Big Data Handling 68
        4.4.2.1 Organization of Storage for Big Data 68
        4.4.2.2 Study and Estimation for Big Data 68
4.5 Requirement of Big Data in Industries 68
    4.5.1 Existing Types of Data in Industries 68
    4.5.2 Different Data Storage Techniques Used in Industry 69
    4.5.3 Big Data Organization Structure 71
        4.5.3.1 Big Data Package Models 71
        4.5.3.2 Conveyed Record Framework 71
        4.5.3.3 Nonauxiliary and Semiorganized Information Stockpiling 72
        4.5.3.4 Information Virtualization Stage 73
4.6 Utilization of Hadoop in Big Data 73
    4.6.1 Procedure to Manage Big Data 74
    4.6.2 Performance Issues in Hadoop 75
4.7 Real Life Big Data Usage and Its Cost Factors 75
4.8 Conclusion 76
References 77
Authors 78

ABSTRACT In the present scenario, Big Data analytics is an important activity that is driven by the pervasive diffusion and adoption of, for example, RFID (radio-frequency identification), mobile devices, and social media tools. The Internet of things allows for the connection and interaction of smart devices as they move and exist within today's value chain. This allows for unprecedented process visibility that creates tremendous opportunities for operational and strategic benefits. However, the effective management of this visibility for improved decision making requires the combination and analysis of data from item-level identification using RFID, sensors, social media feeds, and cell phone GPS signals; in short, Big Data analytics. Millions of essential data are lost every day due to

63

traditional storage technologies, and this doesn't allow one to adapt the health service to the needs of patients or diseases, since nowadays there are no tools able to store and manage so much information, although the technology needed exists. The current architectures and systems used in the sector do not allow for managing greater volumes of data and even less in reasonable time. To allow for mass data storage in real-time technologies, Big Data are needed. Although Big Data analytics have tremendous potential for transforming various industries, many scholars and practitioners are struggling to capture the business value. This chapter focuses on the functional and analysis issues of Big Data in industries.

4.1 Introduction

Big Data is the greatest popular expression in business today (Krishnan, 2013). Each association, medium or large, is investigating the Big Data program for compatibility within its data resources. Big Data doesn't simply allude to having bigger volumes of information. We should consider the source(s) of the information. One reason for a major information usage is to join extra information sets into the present information and reduce the redundancy and complexity of data. In spite of the way that the probability of finishing objective appears to be sensible with the development of innovation.

In today's world where life without the Internet seems impossible, the measure of information that traverses the web is extensive as well as unpredictable. Organizations, foundations, human services frameworks, and every single entity in liveware uses heaps of information that are further utilized for making reports as a part requirements adherence. The procedure behind the outcomes that these entities demand asks for programming designers and organizations to test their information technology (IT). The test is done to ensure that the volume of information that is transmitted through the web safely reaches its destination.

Big Data is a popular expression in the IT and business world at this moment; however, there are different conclusions as to what these two straightforward words truly mean. Some say "Big Data" essentially alludes to a conventional information warehousing situation including information volumes in either the single or multiterabyte range. Such is not the situation. Today, Big Data isn't restricted to customary information distribution center circumstances; it incorporates constant or line-of-business information stores utilized as the essential information establishment for online applications that power key outside or inner business frameworks.

4.2 Need of Big Data

We desire to get informed—each website we visit, each online shopping basket we desert, each tweet we read; everything turns out to be a piece of this enormous accumulation of intertwined information that gets put away in an information distribution center and starts to characterize us. In the right hands, it can be used to make modified showcasing of stories that interface with customers in addition to driving results. In the wrong hands, it can be

Analysis of Costing Issues in Big Data 65

the opportunity to be, in the most ideal situation, only a hindrance but at its worst an attack of security. There are five stages for turning all your client information into a really effective promoting story. Companies can gather, join, picture, investigate, and enact the majority of the information and make genuine custom encounters from it (Stewart, n.d.).

Here are some important aspects that we must know regarding Big Data and its costs:

- The Big Data industry may increase to an extent of about $74.3 billion by 2017 as we compare with today's industries of about $18.2 billion.

- By better incorporating Big Data examination into social insurance, the industry could spare $320 billion a year, as per a late report—that is what might as well be called lessening the human services expenses of each man, lady, and youngster by $1200 a year.

- About 1.9 million IT occupations will be created in the United States by 2015 to do huge information ventures. Each of those will be upheld by 3 new employments made outside of IT—meaning an aggregate of 6 million new occupations on account of Big Data.

- 204 million messages were created by 1.8 million Facebook and 278,000 tweets. This involves the transfer of 200,000 photographs.

- United Parcel Service (UPS) is the greatest bundle shipping organization on the planet. It was established in 1907 and involves more than 16 million shipments of articles to more than 8.8 million of clients around the globe. Overall, 39.5 million of transactions were carried out from clients everyday. In the United States alone, UPS utilizes more than 55,000 drivers and has more than 100,000 vehicles. Worldwide UPS utilizes 399,000 individuals in 220 unique nations. Its revenue in 2012 was $54.1 billion. UPS assembles information at each conceivable minute and as of now stores more than 16 petabytes of information.

- Information is truly being delivered at the velocity of light, multiplying in size every 40 months. It is expected that by 2020 the measure of computerized data will have developed from 3.2 zettabytes today to 40 zettabytes.

- Today's server farms involve a territory of area equivalent in size to 6000 football fields. AT&T is thought to hold the world's biggest volume of information: its telephone records database is 312 terabytes in size and contains nearly 2 trillion columns. In the event that you copied the majority of the information made in only one day onto DVDs, you could stack them on top of one another and reach the moon—twice.

- By 2020, no less than 33% of all information will go through the cloud (a system of servers associated over the Internet).

- The White House has as of now put more than $200 million in Big Data ventures.

4.3 Major Sources of Big Data

Big Data is the accumulation of data assembled from various sources including

Internet data
Science data

Finance data
Mobile device data
Sensor data
RFID data
Streaming data
Shipment data
Sensors data
Stock market data
Healthcare data
Defense data

In Big Data we order the information in the accompanying classes (Figure 4.1):

Structured data or isolated data set (for example, relational data)
Semistructured data or data islands (for example, data content in XML files)
Unstructured data (for example, Word, jpg, mp3, mp4)

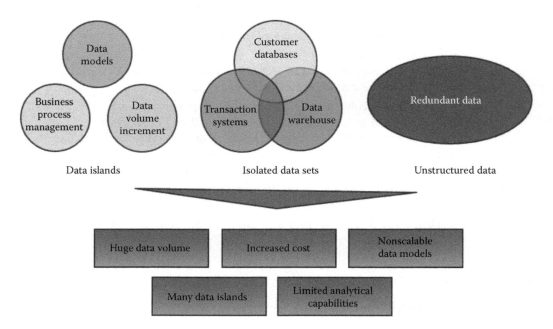

FIGURE 4.1
Traditional database management system.

Analysis of Costing Issues in Big Data 67

4.4 Big Data Functional Issues

Sending Big Data applications on a cloud environment is not a clear undertaking (Srinivasan and Nayar, 2012).

4.4.1 Essential Classes of Information in Big Data

There are a few essential classes of existing information preparing and applications that all appear to be more convincing with cloud environments and contribute further to its force. Some of them are as follows (Ji et al., 2012).

4.4.1.1 Composite Multimedia and Mixed Information

Nowadays clients store and prepare their interactive media applications' information in an appropriate way. The situation, in connection to cloud-based interactive media recovery system, 38 Multiprotocol Label Switching (MPLS), handled and analyzed data. These data are composite for cloud transport convention and cloud overlay system benefits.

4.4.1.2 Objective and Contained Globe Information

Individuals cooperating with one another in a web setting has led many organizations to success in the web space. There are likewise numerous challenges, for example, how to sort out huge information capacity, and whether to process the information in the real or virtual world. We should consider making a framework to show a new virtual cloud design for promoting the concept of a virtual world. The huge size of virtualized assets likewise should be prepared successfully and proficiently.

4.4.1.3 Portable Cloud Information Analytics

Advanced mobile phones or smartphones and tablets have sensors like GPS, cameras, and Bluetooth. Individuals and gadgets are all inexactly joined and trillions of such associated parts will produce a huge set of information. From now on, these broad data sets are more likely to be encouraged in considerable server farms and are permitted to go through the cloud. Moreover, dynamic indexing, analyzing, and addressing enormous volumes of high-dimensional spatial Big Data are big challenges.

As discussed earlier, sources of Big Data, like shipment data, sensors data, stock market data, healthcare data, and defense data, combined with late advances in machine learning and thinking, and also fast ascents in registering power and capacity, are changing our capacity to understand these undeniably huge, heterogeneous, loud, and deficient data sets gathered from an assortment of sources. In this way, scientists are not ready to come together around the fundamental components of Big Data. Some of them surmise that Big Data is the information that we are not ready to process utilizing preexisting innovations, strategies, and hypotheses. Regardless of how we consider the meaning of Big Data, the world is transforming into a "defenselessness" age while shifts of inestimable information is being created by science, business, and society. Big Data puts forward new difficulties for information administration and investigation for the entire IT industry.

4.4.2 Analysis Issues in Big Data Handling

We assume essential issues that we would experience while handling Big Data and we discuss our perspectives next.

4.4.2.1 Organization of Storage for Big Data

Current information management frameworks are not ready to fulfill the requirements of enormous information, and the expanding capacity limit cannot keep pace with the increasing amount of information. Therefore, an upheaval of current data systems is urgently needed. We need to outline various leveled stockpiling building designs. Furthermore, PC calculations are not ready to adequately store information that is specifically procured from the real world because of the heterogeneity of the Big Data. These systems could generate unexpected result for same nature of data. In this manner, how to recompose information is one major issue in huge information management system. Virtual server innovation can intensify the issue, raising the possibility for resources, particularly if correspondence is poor between the application, server, and capacity heads. We, likewise, need to take care of bottleneck issues of high simultaneous I/O operations and single-named hubs in the current master–slave framework model.

4.4.2.2 Study and Estimation for Big Data

While preparing an inquiry in Big Data, rate is a noteworthy demand. However, this might cost a great deal of time since it can't navigate all the related information in the entire database in a brief timeframe. For this situation, files will be an ideal solution. At present, files in huge information are just a simple sort of information, while Big Data is turning out to be more muddled. The organizational group for Big Data could support in better data preprocessing and handling. For approaching Big Data issues we can follow some ideal models like application parallelism and isolated application. The standard serial estimation is inefficient for Big Data. If there is adequate data parallelism in the application, customers can neglect the cloud's decreased cost model to use numerous PCs for a brief traverse of costs.

4.5 Requirement of Big Data in Industries

As discussed by Vasudeva (2012), the results are always required in concise form but data are mostly unstructured in nature, as shown in Figure 4.2.

4.5.1 Existing Types of Data in Industries

According to IMEX Research (2014), the web has produced a burst in information development as information sets, called Big Data, that are so expansive that they are hard to store, oversee, and break down utilizing customary relational database management system (RDBMS) which are tuned for online transaction processing (OLTP). In addition to the fact that this new information is unstructured, voluminous, streams quickly, and difficult to manage, it also lengthens the storage of data in RDBMS.

To benefit from the increase in Big Data, numerous organizations have developed solutions (for example, Hadoop) that are utilizing new parallelized preparing, product equipment, open

Analysis of Costing Issues in Big Data 69

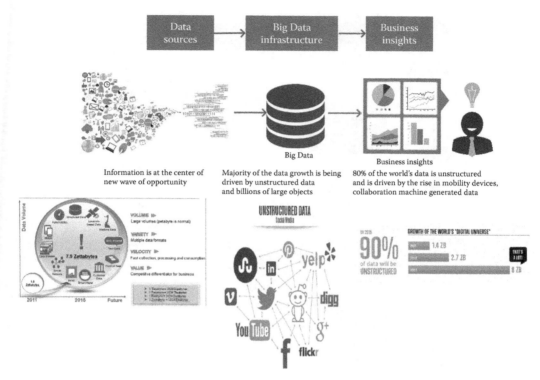

FIGURE 4.2
Existing Big Data format in corporate world.

source programming, and apparatuses to catch and dissect these new information sets and give a value/execution that is 10 times superior to any existing database/data warehousing/business intelligence systems. Although many people would only consider Google and Facebook as media organizations, they have been successful because of their capacity to furnish Big Data to further support their businesses (e.g., BigTable from Google).

4.5.2 Different Data Storage Techniques Used in Industry

The quick burst of computerized information catalyzed by the pervasiveness of the Internet and enormous development of the assortment of processing gadgets has led to another business sector for catching and dissecting noncustomary unstructured and machine-produced information (Ji et al., 2012). By far, most of information development is coming as information sets that are not appropriate for conventional social database merchants like Oracle. As shown in Figure 4.3, there has been a change in data storage and processing techniques used in different places. Not only is the information excessively unstructured and/or excessively voluminous for a conventional RDBMS, the product and equipment costs required to smash through these new information sets utilizing customary RDBMS innovation are restrictive. To exploit the Big Data increase, another type of Big Data organizations have risen that are utilizing ware equipment and open source programming innovations from information catch, operational mix, and progressed investigation to representation from these new information sets. IMEX Research trusts that some driving occupant merchants are unlikely to be players in the new Big Data period, more because

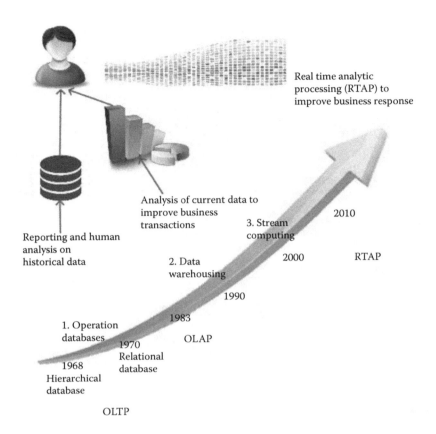

FIGURE 4.3
Change in the data storage and processing technique according to time and requirements of corporate world.

of their powerlessness to adapt to estimating issues and less as a result of an absence of specialized skill. Utilizing current Oracle evaluating models, we appraise Oracle valuing would be around 9 times more than normal for the Big Data sellers to tackle comparable issues. As corporate information sets develop, we are doubtful that Oracle could hold its evaluating power with a mixed database offering of conventional and Big Data arrangements if it somehow managed to go up against the Big Data players, regardless of positive transient support from moving to an incorporated SQL appliance like Exadata/Exalogic/Exalytics.

As we move toward Big Data, the following basic things are required:

1. Cloud infrastructure
2. Virtualization
3. Networking
4. Storage
    a. In-memory database (solid state memory)
    b. Tiered storage software (performance enhancement)
    c. Deduplication (cost reduction)
    d. Data Protection (back up, achieve, and recovery)

4.5.3 Big Data Organization Structure

Ji et al. (2012) discussed that 45% of overview respondents rank information development in their main three difficulties, trailed by framework execution and versatility at 38%, and system clog and availability structural engineering at 37%. Numerous scientists have recommended that business data base management frameworks (DBMSs) are not suitable for handling Big Data. Exemplary architecture's potential bottleneck is the database server while confronting crest workloads. One database server has confinement of versatility and cost, which are two important objectives of Big Data preparation. Keeping in mind the end goal to adjust different expansive information preparing models, four distinct architectures were exhibited in view of exemplary multilevel database application structural planning: apportioning, replication, disseminated control, and storing architecture. It is clear that option suppliers have diverse plans of action and target various types of utilizations. In these four architectures, we discuss the Big Data service model in some detail.

The majority of late cloud administration suppliers are using cross-breed structural engineering that is equipped for fulfilling their real administration prerequisites. In this area, we predominantly talk about Big Data building design from four key viewpoints: Big Data package models, conveyed record framework, nonauxiliary and semiorganized information stockpiling, and information virtualization stage.

4.5.3.1 Big Data Package Models

As we all know, cloud computing is a sort of innovation in the field of data storage, management, and correspondence that turned out to be a powerful asset to the IT and business world. Software as a Service (SaaS), Infrastructure as a Service (IaaS), and Platform as a Service (PaaS) are examples. There are a few IT suppliers that offer information administration services to the clients. Now, with the idea of Big Data coming up in the market, the cloud computing package model is steadily moving toward the Big Data package model, which is a combination of Database as a Service (DaaS), Analysis as a Service (AaaS), and Big Data as a Service (BDaaS). The description of these Big Data package models is as follows.

Database as a Service (DaaS) implies that database administrations are accessible applications conveyed in any execution environment, including on a PaaS. Be that as it may, in the Big Data setting, these would ideally be scale-out architectures, for example, NoSQL data is further spread into the memory database.

Analysis as a Service (AaaS) would be more acquainted with collaborating with an analytics stage on a higher deliberation level. They would commonly execute scripts and inquiries that information researchers or software engineers created for them.

Big Data as a Service (BDaaS) combined with Big Data stages are for clients that need to modify or make new Big Data lots. However, promptly accessible arrangements do not yet exist. Clients should first obtain the vital distributed computing infrastructure, and physically introduce the huge information preparing programming. For complex dispersed administrations, this can be an overwhelming test.

4.5.3.2 Conveyed Record Framework

Google File System (GFS) (Ghemawat et al., 2003) is a lump-based conveyed document framework that assists adaptation to noncritical failure by information parceling and replication. As a basic stockpiling layer of Google's distributed computing stage, it is utilized to peruse, include, and store yield of MapReduce (Dean and Ghemawat, 2008). Similarly, Hadoop has a disseminated record framework as its information storage layer called the Hadoop Distributed File System (HDFS) (Borthakur, 2007) and is an open-source partner of GFS. GFS and HDFS are client-level document frameworks that do not implement POSIX semantics and are upgraded for the instance of huge records (measured in gigabytes) (Rabkin and Katz, 2010). Amazon Simple Storage Service (S3) (Sakr et al., 2011) is an online open stockpiling web administration offered by Amazon Web Services. This document framework is focused at bunches facilitated on the Amazon Elastic Compute Cloud server-on-interest foundation. S3 plans to give adaptability, high accessibility, and low dormancy at merchandise costs. ES2 (Cao et al., 2011) is a versatile stockpiling arrangement of large information, which is intended to bolster both functionalities inside of the same stockpiling. The framework gives productive information stacking from distinctive sources, adaptable information dividing plot, record, and parallel consecutive filter. Likewise, there are a few general record frameworks that have to be noted, for example, Moose File System (MFS) and Kosmos Distributed File (KFS) framework.

4.5.3.3 Nonauxiliary and Semiorganized Information Stockpiling

With the accomplishment of Web 2.0, most IT organizations progressively need to store and examine the steadily developing information, for example, look logs, crept web content, and click streams gathered from a group of web organizations which are more often than not in the scope of petabytes. Be that as it may, web information sets are normally nonsocial or less organized, and handling such semiorganized information sets at scale bearing another test. In addition, straightforward circulated record frameworks, specified earlier, cannot fulfill the needs of administration suppliers like Google, Yahoo, Microsoft, and Amazon. All suppliers have their motivation to serve potential clients and their pertinent cutting edge of enormous information administration systems in the cloud environment. Bigtable (Chang et al., 2006) is a disseminated stockpiling arrangement of Google for overseeing organized information that is intended to scale to an extensive size (petabytes of information) crosswise over a huge number of merchandise servers. Bigtable does not bolster a full social information model. Then again, it gives customers a straightforward information display that underpins dynamic control over information design and arrange. PNUTS (Cooper et al., 2008) is a gigantic scale facilitated database framework intended to bolster Yahoo web applications. The principle focus of the framework is toward serving information for web applications, as opposed to complex inquiries. Upon PNUTS (Cooper et al., 2008), new applications can be effectively gathered and the overhead of making and keeping up these applications is not a great issue. Dynamo (DeCandia et al., 2007) is a very accessible and versatile disseminated key/esteem information-based store that is constructed for supporting Amazon's internal applications. It gives a basic essential key, just interfaced to meet the prerequisites of these applications. Be that as it may, it varies from key-quality stockpiling framework. Facebook proposed the configuration of another group-based information distribution center framework, Llama (Lin et al., 2011), a half-and-half information administration framework that consolidates the components of line astute and section shrewd database frameworks. They additionally portrayed another segment astute document group for Hadoop called CFile, which gives better execution than other record positions in information examination.

Analysis of Costing Issues in Big Data

4.5.3.4 Information Virtualization Stage

Information virtualization depicts the procedure of abstracting unique frameworks. It can be depicted as reasonable building of conceptual layers of assets. It is clear that by merging the enormous information and distributed computing we make IT framework and its application more dynamic and it is the only suggestion for consumption of large information. As of now, the innovation of the developing virtualization stage is just in the essential stage, which principally relies upon the cloud server farm incorporation innovation.

The fundamental thought behind data center is to influence the virtualization innovation to augment the use of processing assets. In this way, it gives the basic fixings, for example, stockpiling, CPUs, and system data transfer capacity as a service by particular administration suppliers at low unit cost. Coming to the objectives of Big Data administration, the majority of the examination foundations and undertakings bring virtualization into cloud architectures. Amazon Web Services (AWS), Eucalyptus, OpenNebula, Cloud Stack, and OpenStack are the most well-known cloud administration stages for framework as an administration (IaaS). AWS is not free but it has immense use in versatile stages. It is definitely not difficult to use and simply pay-as-you-go (means pay for service). Eucalyptus (Nurmi et al., 2009) works as an open source in IaaS. It utilizes virtual machine as a part of controlling and overseeing resources. Since Eucalyptus is the soonest cloud administration stage for IaaS, it consents to API perfect arrangement with AWS. It has a main position in the private cloud market for the AWS natural environment. OpenNebula (Sempolinski and Thain, 2010) has coordination with different situations. It can offer the wealthiest highlights, adaptable ways, and better interoperability to construct private, open, or half-and-half mists. OpenNebula is not a Service-Oriented Architecture (SOA) plan and has frail decoupling in processing capacity and system autonomous parts. CloudStack is an open source cloud working framework that conveys open distributed computing like Amazon EC2, utilizing clients' own equipment. CloudStack clients can exploit cloud registering to convey higher productivity, boundless scale, and speedier sending of new administrations and frameworks to the end client. At present, CloudStack is one of the Apache open source ventures. It now has adult capacities. On the other hand, it needs to assist reinforcement of the free coupling and part plan. OpenStack is an accumulation of open source programming ventures planning to construct an open-source group with researchers, designers, and ventures. Individuals in this group share the typical objective to make a cloud that is easy to convey, hugely adaptable, and loaded with rich components. The building design and segments of OpenStack are direct and stable, so it is a decent decision to give particular applications to undertakings. In current circumstances, OpenStack has a decent group and biological environment. On the other hand, despite everything positive, it has a few inadequacies like inadequate capacities and absence of business backings.

4.6 Utilization of Hadoop in Big Data

The Big Data environment has made Hadoop one and the same with (Chintamaneni, 2015)

- Devoted substantial servers ("simply get a group of thing servers, fill them up with Hadoop, and you can be similar to a Yahoo or a Facebook")

- Hadoop register and capacity on the same physical machine (the popular expression is "information territory"—you've got to have it else it's not Hadoop)
- Hadoop must be on direct joined stockpiling (DAS) ("nearby calculation and capacity" and "HDFS requires neighborhood plates" are customary Hadoop presumptions)

4.6.1 Procedure to Manage Big Data

Hadoop can keep running on sections or virtual machines. The new truth is that you can utilize virtual machines or sections as your Hadoop centers as opposed to physical servers. This spares your time from racking, stacking, and organizing those physical servers. You don't have to sit tight for another server to be requested and provisioned; or battle sending issues because of all the stuff that existed on a repurposed server preceding it being given over to you.

With programming characterized frameworks like virtual machines, you get a perfect and clean environment that empowers unsurprising arrangements—while conveying more noteworthy speed and cost reserve funds. Among the online courses, at Adobe, virtualized Hadoop could support in number of clusters. This could improve the execution of physical servers with low expenses.

Most server farms are completely virtualized. Is there any valid reason why you wouldn't virtualize Hadoop? Truly, the majority of the "Brisk Start" alternatives from Hadoop merchants keep running on a virtual machine or (all the more as of late) on holders (whether nearby or in the cloud). Organizations like Netflix have constructed a marvelous administration taking into account virtualized Hadoop groups that keep running in an open cloud. The prerequisite for on-premises Hadoop to keep running on a physical server is obsolete.

As described in Figure 4.4, the data is converted according to their usages and utility. The idea of information area is exaggerated. It's a great opportunity to at last expose this myth. Information area is a quiet executioner that hinders Hadoop appropriation in the undertaking. Replicating terabytes of existing endeavor information onto physical servers with nearby plates, and after that balancing/readjusting the information each time the server falls flat is operationally mind-boggling and costly. In reality, it just deteriorates as you scale your groups up. The web mammoths like Yahoo utilized this methodology around 2004 or 2005 in light of the fact that those were the times of 1 to 1.5 Gbps systems.

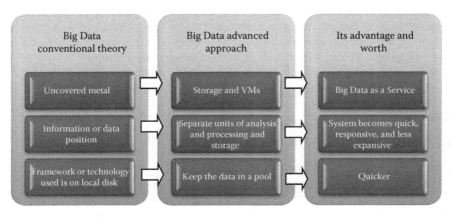

FIGURE 4.4
Conversion of data format accordingly.

Analysis of Costing Issues in Big Data

4.6.2 Performance Issues in Hadoop

Nowadays, systems are much quicker and 12 Gbps systems are ordinary. Research from the UC Berkeley AMPLab and more current Hadoop reference architectures have demonstrated that you can show signs of improved I/O execution with process/stockpiling division. Also, your association will profit by more straightforward operational models, where you can scale and deal with your process and capacity frameworks freely. Incidentally, even with a register/stockpiling co-area, you are not ensured about the information territory in numerous normal Hadoop situations. Ask the Big Data group at Facebook and they will let you know that just 35% of their Hadoop assignments keep running on servers.

A system containing HDFS does not require local storage. This is another of those conventional Hadoop inhabitants that is no more legitimate: neighborhood direct connected stockpiling (DAS) is not required for Hadoop. HDFS is as much a conveyed document framework convention as it is an execution. Running HDFS on neighborhood circles is one such execution approach, and DAS appeared well and good for web organizations like Yahoo and Facebook since their essential starting usage was gathering click stream/log information.

On the other hand, most undertakings today have terabytes of Big Data from various sources (sound, video, content, and so on) that as of now live in shared stockpiling frameworks, for example, EMC Isilon. The information insurance that undertaking grade shared capacity gives is a key thought to these ventures. Furthermore, the need to move and copy this information for Hadoop organizations (with the 3 times replication required for customary DAS-based HDFS) can be a huge hindrance.

At whatever time another foundation methodology is presented for applications (and a large portion of you have seen this before when virtualization was presented in the mid 2000s), the main inquiry is "Shouldn't something be said about execution?"

4.7 Real Life Big Data Usage and Its Cost Factors

Big Data isn't precisely new. Market pioneers have been putting away and dissecting multi-information sorts to increase their upper hand as well as to accomplish more profound experiences into client conduct designs that specifically affect their business (Bantleman, 2012).

The two most specific sectors are as follows:

- Telecommunications
- Retail

These two segments are put vigorously in information warehousing arrangements where vast amounts of client exchanges and cooperations are gathered and inspected after some time to decide key execution pointers, for example, income every year or per client or expense of client securing through online advancements or occasional crests. On the other hand, even market pioneers can't bear to store and oversee petabyte scale nitty-gritty information after some time in customary information distribution centers. Regularly they store, say, the last four quarters and after that delete the history of logged off tape, which isn't effectively open. The business challenge comes when Christmas falls on a Saturday, and they have to break down information from 7 years back to comprehend particular examples. Restoring more seasoned and voluminous information into the distribution center is exceptionally exorbitant.

Two important components become possibly the most important factor with respect to big business scale, Big Data administration, and investigation. To begin with, web pioneers, for example, Facebook, Google, and Yahoo, have added to a greatly adaptable capacity and register structural engineering to oversee Big Data. With the help of Hadoop, we can decrease the cost of Big Data by arranging the important information in various forms like parallel arrangement of similar kinds of set of information, etc.

Second, the innovation prerequisites to oversee Big Data have moved from the space of a couple of particular markets to a scope of divisions. Correspondence administrators that oversee petabyte scales today expect 15 to 110 times the information development because of the movement to 4G and LTE with expanding endpoint gadgets associated with the influence of a huge number of versatile applications. The utility savvy lattice is being dove into Big Data as urban areas over the globe joining the new "digitized network." Financial administrations organizations are seeing 100% compound developments in exchanging and alternatives information, which should be put away for a long time. Throughout the following 2 to 6 years, Big Data will be a key system for both private and open segment associations. Indeed, in the following 6 years, 65% of Big Data ventures are required to keep running on Hadoop.

Actually, customary database approaches don't scale or compose information sufficiently quick to stay aware of the velocity of creation. Also, composed information distribution centers are extraordinary at taking care of organized information, yet there's a high cost for the equipment to scale out as volumes develop.

A key empowering agent for Big Data is the minimal effort versatility of Hadoop. For instance, a petabyte Hadoop bunch will require somewhere around 130 and 260 hubs which costs ~$1.5 million. The expense of a bolstered Hadoop circulation will have comparable yearly expenses (~$5000 per hub), which is a small portion of an undertaking information distribution center ($20 million to $120 million). On introductory assessment, Big Data on Hadoop gives off an impression of being an awesome arrangement. Creative undertakings have Hadoop today—the inquiry is in what capacity they will influence it and at what pace will it get to be mission-basic and vital to an IT center.

The genuine cost, however, is in the operation and general administration or combination of Big Data inside of the current environment. As Big Data situations scale, for example, at Yahoo, overseeing 300 petabytes crosswise over 70,000 hubs require that more be added to convey extra stockpiling limit. Numerous Web 2.0 associations running Hadoop depend totally on the excess of information, yet in the event that you're a storage media or interchanges administrator, you should hold fast to standard-based security, catastrophe recuperation, and accessibility. As Hadoop exists today, it presents more mind-boggling administration and the requirement for gifted assets.

4.8 Conclusion

Big Data proposes immense business progress, lowering costs and versatile data quality. Despite the fact that Hadoop is moderately new, it's making extraordinary steps toward enhancing dependability and convenience. There is no deficiency of advancement originating from new companies and real donors to the Apache open source venture. The two zones that will have the most genuine effect in both simplicity of appropriation and expense are

- To influence existing SQL inquiry dialect and existing business intelligence devices against information inside Hadoop
- The capacity to pack information at the most granular level, which won't just decrease stockpiling prerequisites, yet will drive down the quantity of hubs and rearrange the foundation

Without these two capacities, expertise learning will require significant investment and cash, and won't keep pace with business requests. Information development rates will essentially outpace the expense of scale to oversee several terabytes to petabytes of Big Data that comes each day.

Chief information officers and chief technology officers must examine the genuine expense of Big Data. We know one thing is demonstrated: the advantages of utilizing Big Data will exceed IT speculation, thus for that, we thank our grassroots trailblazers. The charges will be imposed according to the amount of work.

References

Bantleman, J. (2012) The big cost of Big Data. http://www.forbes.com/sites/ciocentral/2012/04/16/the-big-cost-of-big-data/#183ffd6c6a21.

Borthakur, D. (2007) The Hadoop distributed file system: Architecture and design. Hadoop Project Website, 11.

Cao, Y., Chen, C., Guo, F., Jiang, D., Lin, Y., Ooi, B., Vo, H., Wu, S., and Xu, Q. (2011) Es2: A cloud data storage system for supporting both OLTP and OLAP. *Proceedings of 2011 IEEE 27th International Conference on Data Engineering (ICDE)*, pp. 291–302.

Chang, F., Dean, J., Ghemawat, S., Hsieh, W., Wallach, D., Burrows, M., Chandra, T., Fikes, A., and Gruber, R. (2006) Bigtable: A distributed structured data storage system. *7th OSDI*, pp. 305–314.

Chintamaneni, A. (2015) *Shared infrastructure for Big Data: Separating Hadoop compute and storage.* http://bigdatablog.emc.com/.

Cooper, B., Ramakrishnan, R., Srivastava, U., Silberstein, A., Bohannon, P., Jacobsen, H., Puz, N., Weaver, D., and Yerneni, R. (2008) PNUTS: Yahoo!'s hosted data serving platform. *Proceedings of the VLDB Endowment*, 1, 1277–1288.

Dean, J. and Ghemawat, S. (2008) MapReduce: Simplified data processing on large clusters. *Communications of the ACM*, 51: 107–113.

DeCandia, G., Hastorun, D., Jampani, M., Kakulapati, G., Lakshman, A., Pilchin, A., Sivasubramanian, S., Vosshall, P., and Vogels, W. (2007) Dynamo: Amazon's highly available key-value store. *ACM SIGOPS Operating Systems Review*, 41: 205–220.

Ghemawat, S., Gobioff, H., and Leung, S. (2003) The Google file system. *ACM SIGOPS Operating Systems Review*, 37: 29–43.

IMEX Research (2014) Big Data industry report. http://www.imexresearch.com/newsletters/newsLetterIndex_3_7_2014.html.

Ji, C., Li, Y., Qiu, W., Jin, Y., Xu, Y., Awada, U., Li, K., and Qu, W. (2012) Big data processing: Big challenges and opportunities. *Journal of Interconnection Networks*, 13(3–4): 1250009.

Krishnan, K. (2013) Ten mistakes to avoid in your Big Data implementation. TDWI Inc. https://tdwi.org/research/2013/02/ten-mistakes-to-avoid-in-your-big-data-implementation.

Lin, Y., Agrawal, D., Chen, C., Ooi, B., and Wu, S. (2011) Llama: Leveraging columnar storage for scalable join processing in the MapReduce framework. *Proceedings of the 2011 International Conference on Management of Data*, pp. 961–972.

Nurmi, D., Wolski, R., Grzegorczyk, C., Obertelli, G., Soman, S., Youseff, L., and Zagorodnov, D. (2009) The eucalyptus open-source cloud-computing system. *9th IEEE/ACM International Symposium on Cluster Computing and the Grid*, pp. 124–131.

Rabkin, A. and Katz, R. (2010) Chukwa: A system for reliable large-scale log collection. *Proceedings of USENIX Conference on Large Installation System Administration*, pp. 1–15.

Sakr, S., Liu, A., Batista, D., and Alomari, M. (2011) A survey of large scale data management approaches in cloud environments. *IEEE Communications Surveys and Tutorials*, 13: 311–336.

Sempolinski, P. and Thain, D. (2010) A comparison and critique of eucalyptus, open-nebula and nimbus. *2010 IEEE Second International Conference on Cloud Computing Technology and Science (CloudCom)*, pp. 417–426.

Srinivasan, N., and Nayar, R. (2012). Harnessing the power of Big Data—Big opportunity for retailers to win customers. https://www.infosys.com/industries/retail/white-papers/Documents/big-data-big-opportunity.pdf.

Stewart, A. (n.d.) The bigger the data the stronger the story: Five steps to breaking down Big Data into actionable insight. World Media Interactive Corporation. http://worldmedia.net/chief/files/WMI_Chief_whitepaper.pdf.

Vasudeva, A. (2012) NextGen infrastructure for Big Data. IMEX Research. http://www.imexresearch.com/newsletters/Newsletter2_22.html.

Authors

Kuldeep Singh Jadon is an assistant professor in the Computer Science Department of the Institute of Information Technology and Management, Gwalior, Madhya Pradesh, India. He earned a bachelor of engineering and a master of technology in computer science and engineering at Rajiv Gandhi Technological University, Bhopal, Madhya Pradesh, India. He is an active member of IEEE.

Radhakishan Yadav earned a BTech in computer science and engineering discipline at the Indian Institute of Technology (IIT) Indore, India. His areas of research include Big Data analytics, GPU data processing, security methodologies, and service computing architecture.

Section II

Algorithms and Applications of Advancement in Big Data

5

An Analysis of Algorithmic Capability and Organizational Impact

George Papachristos and Scott W. Cunningham

CONTENTS

5.1 Introduction 82
5.2 The Sectoral Adoption of Big Data Analytics 82
5.3 Key Constructs of Organizational Learning 86
5.4 Algorithms and Organizational Learning 88
    5.4.1 Organizational Learning 88
    5.4.2 Simplification 89
    5.4.3 Specialization 89
    5.4.4 Local versus Global 90
    5.4.5 Balancing Exploration and Exploitation in Learning 90
    5.4.6 Sensing Changes in the Environment 90
5.5 Organizational Impacts and Trade-Offs 91
5.6 Findings from Data Governance 94
5.7 Conclusions 97
    5.7.1 Individual Level: Persisting on Failing Courses of Action 97
    5.7.2 Organizational Level: Failure due to Inertia and Core Rigidities 98
    5.7.3 Organizational Level: Failure due to Architectural Innovation 99
    5.7.4 Problems from Architectural Innovation 100
Acknowledgment 101
References 101
Authors 104

ABSTRACT   Organizations face ever more complex environments and the need to adapt and increase their performance. A well-known trade-off lies between the convergence of performance-related factors to an organization's strategic orientation that produces inertia versus the need to sense opportunity and change in the environment and make the necessary internal changes. The advent of the algorithms has given rise to algorithmic governance and the notion that this trade-off can be addressed through the large-scale implementation of algorithms for data mining of Big Data. This chapter addresses the implementation aspects of data governance programs in terms of the two sides of this trade-off. It may enable improvements in organizational performance but at the same time it is necessary to managing unwanted effects inside and beyond the organization.

81

5.1 Introduction

There is increasing policy and corporate concern for the appropriate governance of algorithms (Lanier, 2014; Pasquale, 2015). Algorithms, at least in this definition, involve the deployment of machine learning algorithms trained on sources of Big Data. These algorithms result in decision rules, or routines, that are deployed in pursuit of organizational performance.

Governance, at least in this definition, involves making decisions about decision making in organizations (Denhardt and Catlaw, 2015). Fundamentally, the nature of governance then is about organizational exploration versus exploitation (March, 1991). Questions about governing this dilemma and the effect algorithms can have on organizational evolution reach beyond collection and use of data. Increasingly government and industry observers are concerned with the use of data in decision making, and the degree to which these decisions are contextually appropriate.

Organizations employ written rules, oral traditions, and systems of formal and informal apprenticeships to introduce-instruct new individuals in the ways the organization functions. Algorithms have an increasing role in this, making some parts of organizational memory more readily available than others. Availability is also related to the frequency of using a routine, the recency of its use, and its organizational proximity. Recently and frequently used routines are more easily evoked than those that have been used infrequently or in the distant past.

The interface between routines, as fixed procedures for machine analysis, and routines as sources of organizational memory and performance is further discussed and elaborated in this chapter. The chapter also revisits the tensions organizations face in their evolution and discusses the role of algorithms in exploration, exploitation, learning, and adaptation. Algorithms through their sheer data processing capability and output appear to have a range of unprecedented intra- and interorganizational effects. This chapter discusses the need and organizational capabilities for governing algorithms. It highlights the importance of getting data governance programs right (Thomas, 2014).

The organization of the chapter is as follows. In Section 5.2 we first describe the state of play with regard to a variety of new Big Data and machine learning algorithms. We broadly appraise the information needs of a number of different sectors. These strategic information needs therefore dictate the kinds of information systems that are required. Then, in Section 5.3, we adapt an organizational learning perspective. This material leads to Section 5.4 where we describe how these new systems are being utilized to enhance the capabilities of the organization. This leads to Section 5.5 where we discuss four trade-offs in organizational design that emerge as new systems are adopted. In Section 5.6 we compare and contrast expected organizational changes with the practical literature on data and information technology governance. The final section of the chapter discusses how, and if, the correct selection of algorithm actually delivers better organizational performance.

5.2 The Sectoral Adoption of Big Data Analytics

Organizations are collections of subunits that learn in an environment consisting largely of other organizations (Cangelosi and Dill, 1965). Organizational units use algorithms locally (e.g., optimization algorithms) but also to interface at a global level (e.g., enterprise resource planning). Algorithms simultaneously do two things: they have the potential to improve the absorptive capacity of the organization for absorbing and processing knowledge (Cohen and Levinthal, 1990), and they also introduce an additional intermediary layer for organizational learning (Levitt and March, 1988) between internal operations and the organization's environment. Their ubiquity and wide scope of use is fueled by ever-increasing quantities of data, and can have unprecedented consequences beyond what organizations can anticipate. Organizations interact strategically with other organizations and with their environment, and algorithms and Big Data are increasingly being sought out to provide strategic advantages.

A complementary function is to enhance organizational capabilities for verification monitoring and enforcement that underlie organizational interactions. Monitoring involves determining whether contractual, regulatory, or legal obligations have been met. It is enabled by embedded sensor networks. Stochastic monitoring is a more complex, and in some contexts a more efficient, monitoring mechanism. It requires a broader algorithmic foundation in an organization than merely passive approaches to monitoring.

Enforcement procedures involve ensuring that organizations that break their agreements receive appropriate censure. The coupling of electronic payment systems already ensures, in part, that new technologies can be leveraged in pursuit of contract enforcement. More complex and decentralized forms of enforcement require a stronger algorithmic foundation using block chains and other cryptographic foundations. These new algorithmic capabilities for monitoring and enforcement enable interactions in a wider variety of institutional forms with individuals and other organizations.

A major part of algorithm use in organizations involves strategic access to information. Information, in this economic sense, involves knowing who knew what when. It does not merely entail data, computing, or signal processing. Appropriately informed organizations can collect economic rents above and beyond their peers. We break information into three categorical qualities of information: uncertain, asymmetric, and incomplete (Rasmusen, 2006). A fourth quality of information, imperfection, signifies still greater informational challenges.

In an uncertain environment the organization is subject to stochastic shocks. Uncertainty may be epistemic in character, meaning that the organization lacks the necessary information to operate with full efficiency. (Some kinds of epistemic uncertainty are also considered under incompleteness below.) Alternatively, the uncertainty may result from human error. A final source of uncertainty may involve intrinsic variability in the systems being managed or exploited. This uncertainty may be variable in both space as well as time.

Industrial sectors facing uncertainty include extractive industries such as agriculture, energy mining, and environmental services. These sectors may not know the extent of their holdings, and they may face a variable market price once the resource is brought to market. The energy, logistics, and transport sectors face natural variability. Variable resources permit less extensive utilization and harvesting. Algorithms that permit organizations to better anticipate and counter environmental variability deliver new sources of competitive advantage. Algorithms that can be considered in this class include forecasting techniques and yield management algorithms. Supply chain management systems are also permitting organizations to pool information in response to variable market demands.

Uncertainty may be compounded by customer demands as well. This is where information asymmetry exists. Consumers know what they want, when they want it, and how much they are willing to pay to receive it. Through much of the consumer era consumers have received market surpluses because they, and they alone, know this information. As a result, many goods are provided at costs far below the utility value of the market.

Asymmetric information environments include the construction, finance, and government sectors, although they each constitute a somewhat special case. The construction industry routinely gains information rents from special understanding of the local social, political, and real-estate environments not readily available to the public. Many have argued that governments are also subjected to information asymmetry on the part of citizens who contract them to provide public goods and services. Criminals and terrorists also gain information asymmetry and hide among the public. The finance industry gains first mover advantages in markets and has inside knowledge of often opaque financial derivatives.

Reducing information asymmetry involves organizations targeting consumers. This can increase their profit margins by reducing the economic surplus of consumers. Many sectors gather customer data by segmenting customers into smaller targeted groups, and by implementing price description routines. Retail, commerce, and advertising industries all have implemented such responses. Telecommunications also face a similar challenge, although the sector's capability to discriminate by price is eroding by regulation and the proliferation of new technology. Manufacturing also faces a similar challenge, although the primary source of asymmetry is other firms that receive value-added surpluses through systems integration and services.

Many governments can also enhance the benefits of office holding if the quantity of public goods is also reduced. Consumer segmentation algorithms and pricing and promotion algorithms are particularly relevant for these cases. The political or governmental equivalent are citizen databases segmented by particular categories of interest. A variety of sophisticated algorithms capable of specific, and rapid, contingent action based on environmental conditions are being deployed in the finance industry.

An incomplete informational environment is one where the strategic actor may not actually understand the strategic game that they are playing. Actors may not understand the range of possible outcomes available to them, and they may not understand the means available to them in achieving their outcomes. Information incompleteness exists in the high-technology, pharmaceutical, and microelectronic industries and the government sector. They can be fundamentally transformed by reducing information incompleteness. New knowledge can cause the massive reconfiguration of existing products and production systems. New research and development can also create, or undermine, existing markets. Existing markets can be undermined by the development of new technologies and the entrants of new market participants.

Organizations best equipped to deal with information incompleteness can marshal their technical and creative resources. This may be coupled with the capability to rapidly deploy new products and prototypes. The organizations may also be able to better recognize and act upon environmental anomalies. These organizational capabilities can benefit the organization by preventing external disruption and by enabling the organization to more rapidly capitalize on new products.

There is a comparatively limited algorithmic capability for dealing with information incompleteness in a comprehensive manner. Algorithmic design environments are being developed that enable organizations to automatically explore and generate new products and technologies. Social and network analytic approaches are being used to analyze complex structuration. Topographic approaches are being developed to better understand and visualize diverse data sets. Data fusion techniques are being developed to reveal unforeseen connections across diverse data sets. Counterintrusion techniques are being deployed to recognize and highlight unusual activities as soon as they emerge.

In summary, an imperfect informational environment may suffer from multiple informational problems arising from information uncertainty, asymmetry, or incompleteness, or from entirely distinct informational issues. For instance, organizations may not understand where they are in a process. This may result from organizational forgetting, a lack of routines, or the complexity of the process. Algorithms for managing imperfection include knowledge bases, customer relationship management systems, or channel management systems. Many routine organizational systems for payment and personnel are aimed at reducing information imperfection. These systems are credited for increasing operational effectiveness, but the fundamental value of reducing information imperfection is still higher.

An example of information imperfection is healthcare. Healthcare organizations face a number of different sources of complexity, not least of which are the patients themselves. The insurance industry faces a mix of fundamental uncertainty and information asymmetry. Insurers must partial and apportion risk without themselves encouraging policyholders to take on more risk—the problem of moral hazard. The legal industry is also undergoing new changes created by automated search of relevant case law and the automated construction of contracts or other legal documents.

Table 5.1 summarizes the arguments of this section. It describes sources of information imperfection, and the sectors that are exposed to these sources. The table also summarizes the algorithmic remedies for imperfect information.

As described earlier, algorithms for supporting organizational information finding involve a range of systems, from simple accounting systems to more complete enterprise resource planning (ERP) systems. Unfortunately, it is not possible to simply deploy these algorithms without considering the organizational specific context (Hendricks et al., 2007).

TABLE 5.1

Information Quality, Sector Exposure, and Algorithmic Remedies

Information Quality	Sector	Remedies
Uncertainty	Logistics	Forecasting
	Transport	Yield management
	Agriculture	Supply chain management
	Mining and oil	Geographic information
	Environment	
	Energy	
Asymmetry	Retail	Customer segmentation
	Commerce	Psychographics
	Marketing and advertising	Pricing algorithms
	Manufacturing	Promotion algorithms
	Telecommunications	
	Construction and real estate	
	Finance	
	Government	
Incompleteness	High technology	Generative design
	Pharmaceuticals	Network analytics
	Microelectronics	Topographic analysis
		Data fusion
		Counterintrusion
Imperfection	Healthcare	Knowledge bases
	Insurance	Customer relationship management
	Law	Channel management

Algorithms are an intermediary layer between the organization and its environment. Machine learning algorithms, as discussed in this section, provide a seed around which organizational routines can form. Organizations have difficulty retrieving relatively old, unused knowledge or skills (Levitt and March, 1988). The effects of proximity stem from the ways that organizational history is linked to regularized responsibility. The routines that record lessons of experience are organized around organizational responsibilities and are retrieved more easily when actions are taken through regular channels than when they occur outside those channels (Olsen, 1983).

Generation of routines in this way is a core factor of performance consistency—learning reduces variability (Levinthal and March, 1993). Performance at the individual and organizational levels improve with repetition of activities. Unless the implications of organizational experience can be transferred from those who experienced it to those who did not, lessons learned are likely to be lost through turnover of personnel. In the next section we therefore review principles of organizational learning, with an eye toward a better understanding of the organizational impacts of Big Data.

5.3 Key Constructs of Organizational Learning

Organizations continuously try to improve their capacity and capability to process and analyze information, set objectives, and take action. Information technology makes the routinization of relatively complex organizational behavior economically feasible, for example, in the preparation of reports or presentations, the scheduling of production or logistical support, the design of structures or engineering systems, or the analysis of financial statements (Smith and Green, 1980). However, not everything is recorded and the process of encoding relevant data is costly. Costs are still subject to the costs of the information system itself. Nevertheless, it is hard to underestimate the scope of synergy and potential that information technology has to offer (Gunasekaran and Ngai, 2004; Melville et al., 2004). In this section we draw upon the literature of organizational learning to better understand how information technology impacts organizational learning, and therefore what governance challenges organizations will face when applying these technologies.

Increased performance consistency has its downsides for competitive advantage, as it requires little deviation from standard routines. Learning must increase organizational performance and reliability to produce a competitive advantage. Otherwise, the organization is at a disadvantage against more capable competitors (Levinthal and March, 1993). The necessary element of exploration in the face of exploitation driven learning is something that organizations need to address constantly through incentives, organizational structure, individual beliefs, or selection processes.

Organizations simplify their interactions with their environment by separating domains of activity and treating them as autonomous, in a sense they enact a particular environment around them (Weick, 1979). In this way they create buffers between them and their environment (Levinthal and March, 1993). The separation of problems, organizational units, and goals allows examination of proximal consequences and local experimentation. Problems and solutions of a global nature are reduced to the local level. This may enhance organizational control and coordination, but it also compartmentalizes individual and organizational experience. Algorithms are ideally suited to supporting and reinforcing this organizational attitude toward learning as in every case they assume a simplified version of reality.

Simplification can also be beneficial at an organizational level when it is difficult to trace the link between simultaneous learning activities and organization-wide performance, particularly in noisy business environments. In order to overcome these constraints, organizations have two options: generate more experience (this may not be available in new start-ups), or avoid taking simultaneous actions or decisions so that the effect of each one can be attributed to organizational performance. In this way learning for isolated subunits can often be quite effective (Cyert and March, 1992; Lave and March, 1993), while learning for interacting subunits in a noisy environment can be more difficult (Lounamaa and March, 1987).

Organizational unit specialization drives organizational focus and competences toward narrow niches in order to improve performance (Levinthal and March, 1988). Such a learning outcome is likely to capture the features of the environment the organization has experienced in the past, which have increased its competences. Specialization is advantageous provided that it leads the organization to improve the efficiency and to increase the use of the procedure with the highest potential.

However, a competency trap can occur when favorable performance with an inferior procedure leads an organization to accumulate more experience with it rather than with a superior procedure. This increases organizational inertia, i.e., the difficulty to implement anything other than incremental change to adapt to the contingencies it faces in the present (Tushmann and Romanelli, 1985). One example is the sequential exposure to new procedures in a developing technology (Barley, 1988). Improvements are processual, but learning organizations have problems in overcoming the competences they have developed with earlier ones (Whetten, 1987).

Making organizational learning effective as a tool for comprehending organizational history involves confronting three problems in the structure of organizational experience. First is the scarcity of organizational experience arising from the fact that eventually only one out of the many possible outcomes is realized. Second is the redundancy of experience problem. The repetition of organizational activities produces learning that tends to be less novel, that is, there are diminishing returns to such learning. Third is the complexity of experience. Deriving sound lessons from experience is hard.

These three organizational challenges carry direct implications for the trade-offs identified in earlier sections: (a) short-term organizational learning frequently takes precedence over long term, (b) local solution exploration tends to ignore the larger picture risks that pose a threat to the entire organization, and (c) organizational successes gather attention due to potential rewards compared to failures, which may be overlooked.

In order to cope with the short-term versus long-term trade-off, organizational action and responses sometimes take the character of preprogrammed exercises or capabilities (Starbuck, 1983) where responses to environmental triggers are drawn from an existing repertoire (Feldman, 1989; March and Simon, 1993). This is appropriate when the required response times are short and the organization does not have the time to respond effectively in a novel way. In short, the organization is faced with time compression diseconomies in developing organizational capabilities (Dierickx and Cool, 1989).

Organizational successes carry a premium of rewards compared to failures. Everybody wants to learn how to emulate successful organizational problem solving, and successful individuals are promoted and are more likely to reach top-level positions than individuals who have not. Their experience and confidence leads them to overestimate the chances of success from experimentation and risk taking (March and Shapira, 1987). As a result, failures tend to be overlooked.

Even when failures are not overlooked, ambiguity sustains the efforts of individuals in organizations to promote their favorite frameworks and provides the scope for conflicting interpretations. For example, leaders of organizations are inclined to accept paradigms that attribute organizational successes to their own actions and organizational failures to the actions of others or to external forces, but opposition groups in an organization are likely to have the converse principle for attributing causality (Miller and Ross, 1975). Similarly, advocates of a particular policy, but not their opponents, are less likely to interpret failures as a symptom that the policy is incorrect than as an indication that it has not been pursued vigorously enough (Ross and Staw, 1986).

These three challenges may compromise the effectiveness of organizational learning particularly because they complicate the task of maintaining an appropriate balance of exploitation and exploration. This suggests that great expectations should be met with caution (perhaps for Big Data too!). Conservative expectations may provide a basis for realistic evaluation and development of the role of learning in organizations (Levinthal and March, 1993). The four aspects of organizational learning that we want to use further in our analysis of information technology (IT) and organizations are discussed next.

5.4 Algorithms and Organizational Learning

Organizations co-evolve with their environment. They explore and learn from it; they utilize existing tools and solutions and come up with new ones. Through intraorganizational interactions the effects of these activities diffuse in the organization. Through interorganizational competition the effects of this process come full circle and form aspects of the organization's environment. This section provides an overview of the fundamental concepts related to organizational activity: exploration and exploitation, learning, and adaptation.

5.4.1 Organizational Learning

Our interpretation of organizational learning comes from three classical observations in the behavioral studies of organizations. First, organizational action is based on routines, collective recurrent activity patterns (Nelson and Winter, 1982; Cyert and March, 1992; Becker, 2004). Routines can include the forms, rules, procedures, conventions, beliefs, mental frameworks, strategies, and technologies of organizations and through which they operate (Nelson and Winter, 1982). Routines emerge and are matched to particular contexts and situations rather than being a calculated choice. Routines are based on interpretations of the past more than expectations of the future. Second, organizational actions are history-dependent (Lindblom, 1959; Steinbruner, 1974). They adapt incrementally to experience and evolve, in response to feedback about outcomes. Organizations and individuals learn by inferring lessons from their past activities and encoding them into routines that guide their behavior. Third, organizational behavior and performance is oriented toward particular objectives (Simon, 1955; Siegel, 1957).

Organizations collect information about available alternatives, their anticipated consequences, and then choose the set of actions best suited to reaching these objectives (Levinthal and March, 1993). Information demand and supply across and beyond the organization drives, at least in part, organizational operations, tasks, incentives, and individual responsibility. Information improves confidence in that the best future actions are chosen, and their implementation and effect are controlled (Levinthal and March, 1993).

Routines change through two mechanisms of organizational learning. The first is trial-and-error experimentation. The likelihood that a routine will be used increases when it is associated with success in meeting a target and decreases when it is associated with failure (Cyert and March, 1992). The second mechanism is organizational search from a variety of routines, and adopting better ones when they are discovered. Since the rate of discovery is a function both of variety and of the intensity and direction of search, it depends on the history of success and failure of the organization (Radner, 1975).

Organizations generate learning through simplification and specialization. The application of information technology can alleviate limitations related to either of them as it augments the inferential capabilities of individuals and organizations. Nevertheless, the question of inertia accumulation resurfaces. This is discussed next.

5.4.2 Simplification

Problem simplification and compartmentalization in order to control organizations has advantages and some weaknesses. Thus, a counterargument is made for tighter organizational coupling (Bower and Hout, 1988). Coupling makes issues that arise in a part of the organization visible to the rest of the organization, offering an organization-wide opportunity for learning (Levinthal and March, 1993). Available analytical and coordination information technology tools reduce the costs of dealing with organizational problems in a centralized way. Algorithms carry the promise of enhancing organizational coupling thus offering better problem detection, and an unprecedented level of diagnostics and localization of errors. They thus improve accountability within the organization and problem awareness, without the downsides of compartmentalization.

Algorithms play a part in reducing the command and control hierarchical layers in the system. Part of the appeal of more "flat" organizational forms is that they bring more organizational units in direct contact with the organization's environment (Ostroff and Smith, 1992). For example, this has manifested in lean and agile production systems (Christopher and Towill, 2000). The idea of increasing intra- and interorganizational coupling is tied also to the importance of linking to customers with customer resource management (CRM) systems and the idea of organizations being customer driven (Schonberger, 1990).

5.4.3 Specialization

Learning takes place simultaneously at different organizational units and organizational levels (Herriott et al., 1985). Two factors contribute to this. First, when equivalent performance outcomes can be achieved through learning of different units, then learning in one makes learning in another redundant to the extent that their adaptation alleviates the need for changes (Levinthal and March, 1993). This produces specialization of learning competence (Lave and March, 1993).

Second, adaptation pressure increases faster at the organizational units closer to the environment. This implies that organizational learning at the operational level may substitute frequently for learning at higher levels, which may end up having higher inertia. Such competency traps are particularly likely to lead to maladaptive specialization if newer routines are better than older ones. Whether in stable or turbulent environments, organizations end up having a number of specialized routines. However, in turbulent environments it is harder to set up response inventories and related knowledge (Levinthal and March, 1993). These kinds of environments require inventories of routines for future use without knowing in advance the precise nature of it.

5.4.4 Local versus Global

A trade-off arises between the survival of organizational units with specialized knowledge versus the survival of the whole organization (March, 1994). Learning in the proximity of current problems and action tends to ignore the larger picture risks that pose a threat to the entire organization (Levinthal and March, 1993). The effects of proximity stem from the ways path dependence is linked to regularized unit responsibility.

The routines that internalize lessons of experience are organized around organizational responsibilities and are retrieved more easily when actions are taken through regular channels than when they occur outside those channels (Olsen, 1983). In tightly coupled organizations, the returns of knowledge development to a particular unit depend on that developed in other units. When the environment changes, as it inevitably does, the match with well-adapted organization units is at risk. This may lead to a downward spiral where units in the organization find less and less value in their knowledge exploration activities that in turn results in a reduction of knowledge generation throughout the organization (Levinthal and March, 1993).

5.4.5 Balancing Exploration and Exploitation in Learning

The organizational learning challenges outlined earlier are part of the broader challenge of how organizations allocate their resources and activities between two broad kinds of activities: exploration and exploitation (March, 1991). Organizations that solely engage in exploration may have little returns on the knowledge they gain. Organizations that engage only in exploitation will risk their knowledge becoming obsolete. The challenge is to engage in sufficient levels of exploitation to ensure short-term survival, and sufficient exploration to ensure long-term survival (Cyert and March, 1992; Levinthal and March, 1993).

This is challenging because the needs of the organization change and because learning can change the balance as discussed. Developing a competitive advantage in one domain leads to performance increases in the short run. It becomes attractive for the organization to sustain its focus on the same activities due to their self-reinforcing nature (Levinthal and March, 1981), but in the long run it may lead to a potential decay of adaptive capabilities in other domains (Levinthal and March, 1993).

5.4.6 Sensing Changes in the Environment

Organizations need to develop the capacity to utilize exploration and exploitation and shift their balance. It refers to the capacity of an organization to sense its environment and make something out of it (Cohen and Levinthal, 1989, 1990, 1994; Lane et al., 2006; Lewin et al., 2011). An organization's absorptive capacity depends on the absorptive capacities of its individual members (Cohen and Levinthal, 1990). Organizational units formalize their procedures in order to respond promptly, effectively, and efficiently to recurrent issues (Daft and Lengel, 1986; Galunic and Rodan, 1998; Lin and Germain, 2003). This increases the likelihood that individual members will identify and act upon opportunities for the transformation of new external knowledge (Galunic and Rodan, 1998; Zollo and Winter, 2002). On the downside, employees that execute routine tasks only deal with a few exceptions and a narrow range of problems (Volberda, 1996). This reduces their absorptive capacity.

Absorptive capacity lies also on the individuals at the interface of the organization and the environment or the interface or organizational subunits (Cohen and Levinthal,

1990). Modern organizations invariably use information technologies in both interfaces. In this case organization members are assigned relatively centralized "gatekeeping" or "boundary-spanning" roles (Allen, 1977; Tushman, 1977; Tushman and Katz, 1980). A gate-keeper monitors the environment and translates information into a form understandable for internal staff to assimilate.

Nevertheless, a firm's absorptive capacity is more than just the sum of employee capacities. It also depends on knowledge transfer interfaces between organizational units, for example, between corporate and divisional research and development labs, design, manufacturing, and marketing functions. These communication interfaces deepen knowledge flows across functional boundaries and lines of authority (Katz and Allen, 1982). They promote nonroutine and reciprocal information processing and contribute to a unit's ability to overcome differences, interpret issues, and build understanding about new external knowledge. Thus, they enhance the knowledge acquisition and assimilation underlying a unit's potential absorptive capacity (Jansen et al., 2005).

5.5 Organizational Impacts and Trade-Offs

The capability to learn in the face of changing business environments is considered one of the most important sources of firm performance differences. They result in a long-term and sustainable competitive advantage (Argyris and Schon, 1978; Levitt and March, 1988; Burgelman, 1990; Senge, 1990). Successful organizations are those that have greater capacity and capability for learning and change (Prahalad and Hamel, 1990; Stalk et al., 1992). Organizational learning contributes in two ways to competitive advantage: it increases the average organizational performance, and it increases the consistency of organizational performance. In this section we discuss algorithmic capabilities and machine learning, and focus on particular impacts and performance dilemmas facing the organization.

Information technology has a major effect on organizational performance when time is particularly important. It can be used to scan an organization's environment for changes or opportunities. Under such conditions, appropriate use of information technology seems likely to improve an organization's competitive position. On the other hand, in many situations the main effect of information technology is to make outcomes more consistent. As work tasks are standardized and techniques are learned, variability in the time required to accomplish tasks and in the quality of tasks performed is reduced.

Learning processes do not necessarily lead equally to both increases in average performance and to reductions in variability. A loss of performance variability is not necessarily a positive for the organization, since variation enables organizations to unlock new capacities (March, 1991). Algorithms can help to increase the consistency of organizational performance and reduce organizational-memory-related costs. On the other hand, algorithms reduce the capability for exploratory deviations from routine that can unlock new sources of growth and potential.

Organizational learning formed by past successes and failures that accumulated over time can be an important basis of competitive advantage for a firm. Thus, organizations devote considerable energy to developing a collective understanding of their own competitive advantage. This depends on the frames within which the experience is being comprehended (Daft and Weick, 1984). Nonetheless, no experiences are reflected without bias in organizational history because of member conflict, turnover, and decentralization (March et al., 1991). Efforts to assign responsibility and to establish a favorable historical record are important facets of organizational life (Sagan, 1993).

These efforts gravitate toward a sustainable competitive advantage that becomes immediately evident in the marketplace. It tends to orient the development of knowledge and capabilities towards improving current organizational performance utilizing current organizational experiences. When short-term learning is effective it reduces the incentives to develop learning for the long term and can be a constraining factor. Therefore, learning can create its own traps (Levinthal and March, 1988).

Certain properties of this short-term orientation stem from cognitive limitations of individual inference and judgment (Kahneman et al., 1982; Sterman, 1989a,b, 1994; Cronin et al., 2009; Kahneman, 2011). Learning requires inferences from information and information retrieval from memory. Learning also involves the risky step of aggregating personal experience from a group of individuals (Levinthal and March, 1993). Research indicates that individuals are more likely to attribute their successes to ability and their failures to luck than they are to attribute their successes to luck and their failures to ability (Miller and Ross, 1975). This translates into biases in the estimation of risk. Thus organizational limitations compound the cognitive and inferential limitations that are already present in individuals.

Organizations address complex environments through a process of simplification, compartmentalization, and specialization as noted. Algorithms support simplification, because they are based on simplified representations of reality. The downside of simplification is that problems that fall outside of organizational boundaries are more likely to become ramified. Such problems may potentially grow more severe over time. Furthermore, organizational compartmentalization tends to restrict the flow of information between units with different expertise. This leads to less organization-wide knowledge of the significance of problems and of organization-wide opportunities for solving problems. If the organization responds to failure by increasing the rigidity of rule sets, then organizational structures can ossify. Particular maladaptive political structures can then become institutionalized (Boeker, 1989).

Nonetheless algorithms are a means ideally suited for supporting and reinforcing an organization-wide approach for learning and problem solving, even as they reinforce centralized hierarchies. Highly coupled hierarchical organizations, or so-called machine bureaucracies (Mintzberg, 1992), are places where an algorithmic approach to problem solving can thrive. However, these organizations may miss some of the opportunities for localized learning and discovery, which flat, decoupled organizations enjoy. The application of algorithms promises to bring higher levels of the organization closer to the environment. Standardized reporting, aggregated metrics, and real-time communication will equip executive decision-makers with the information they need to address organizational challenges. Such rapid turnaround of information can reduce inertia throughout the organization.

The effect of simplification and specialization is to improve organizational performance, *ceteris paribus*. Nevertheless, it is these same learning mechanisms that can ultimately lead to limits to growth. This is not attributable exclusively to individual and organizational inadequacies, as there are structural difficulties in learning from experience. The past is not a perfect predictor of the future, and the nature of everyday experience is far from ideal for effective causal inference (Brehmer, 1980).

The immediate consequence of organizational learning through simplification and specialization is that it renders the organization myopic with respect to the future. Short-term organizational learning frequently takes precedence over long-term learning. This can sometimes put organizational survival at risk. It is plausible that successful strategies for organizational survival in the short term may not be sustainable in the long term, or may ultimately lead to adverse results. Conversely, any consideration of long-term survival must inevitably consider short-term survival constraints (Levinthal and March, 1993).

The overemphasis on organizational success is a natural repercussion of the constant struggle for survival. The underlying assumption is that learning leads to greater organizational success. Nonetheless it is often at times of failure where there is the greatest opportunity for learning. When success and only success becomes associated with learning, a bias in prior experiences is introduced, which can lead to rigidities. Instead organizations lead the capabilities to overcome this and adapt.

Dynamic capabilities are key to maintaining an appropriate balance between exploration and exploitation. For exploitation, dynamic capabilities program behaviors in advance of their execution and provide a memory for handling routine situations (Van den Bosch et al., 1999). They typically require some formalization of rules, procedures, instructions, and communications to establish patterns of organizational action (Galunic and Rodan, 1998). They constrain exploration and direct attention toward specific aspects of the external environment thus reducing individual deviation from established or required behavior (Weick, 1979). This inhibits rich, reciprocal knowledge interaction and obstructs assimilation of new external knowledge by individuals.

For exploration, dynamic capabilities enable an organization to sense its environment, thereby creating new strategic resources through timely action (Teece et al., 1997). Under this perspective absorptive capacity is a dynamic capability. Learning should occur both from the external environment as well as from internal innovation processes (Kogut and Zander, 1992; Cohen and Levinthal, 1994; Iansiti and Clark, 1994; Teece et al., 1997; Eisenhardt and Martin, 2000; Zahra and George, 2002; Winter, 2003; Murovec and Prodan, 2009; Volberda et al., 2010).

Dynamic capabilities depend on individuals in the organization and the relationship of these individuals with algorithms. Algorithms may substitute for individual capacity or enhance and complement the absorptive capacity of individuals. The cumulative quality of absorptive capacity and its role in updating organizational knowledge are forces that tend to confine individuals, units, and organizations to operating in a particular technological domain. Organizations need to invest in inward- and outward-oriented absorptive capacity. If they don't invest in a particular expertise area early, they will not perceive knowledge coming from different units to be in their interest, even in the realization of the technological promise of the area. In other words, absorptive capacity leads to particular expectations and directly contributes to organizational inertia, a central feature in situations where organizations seek to maximize profit (Nelson and Winter, 1982).

Identifying and evaluating external knowledge is an important aspect of absorptive capacity. It needs to be maintained and is biased by prior experience. The embedded knowledge base, rigid capabilities, and path-dependent managerial cognition of organizations hinder their ability to identify and absorb valuable new sources of external knowledge (Leonard-Barton, 1992; Gavetti and Levinthal, 2000; Helfat, 2000; Langlois and Steinmueller, 2000; Tripsas and Gavetti, 2000). Power relationships can also have an influence on absorptive capacity (Todorova and Durisin, 2007). The balance of internal versus external capacities depends on the original sourcing, organizational embedding, and productive output of algorithms. Algorithms therefore alter or disrupt an organization's absorptive capacity.

The previous discussion identified four organizational impacts related to learning and adaptation:

1. Improving short-term versus long-term learning
2. Enhancing centralized learning versus the cost of local learning
3. Increasing algorithm efficacy versus cost of better implementation
4. Gaining better internal capabilities versus better external capabilities

These impacts involve trade-offs of short-term versus long-term learning, the trade-offs between centralized and local learning, trade-offs between decision efficacy and decision implementation, and the trade-offs between internal and external sources of organizational capacities. The following sections discuss qualifications of these impacts in light of the large-scale application of algorithms in organizations.

5.6 Findings from Data Governance

These previous organizational trade-offs, relating to algorithm use, must be qualified in light of a large and growing literature on algorithmic governance. This following section qualifies these findings in light of this literature. One of the most well-known models for data mining is Cross Industry Standard Process for Data Mining, or CRISP-DM for short (see Figure 5.1). It is a data mining process model that describes common steps that data mining experts use to tackle problems. There are six phases in the CRISP-DM model (Shearer, 2000). The CRISP data mining process can face domain-specific challenges and requirements for adaptation.

There are seven goals that data governance programs can accomplish: enable better decision making, reduce operational friction, protect the needs of data stakeholders, train management and staff to adopt common approaches to data issues, build standardized processes, enhance coordination, and enhance transparent and accountable processes (Thomas, 2014).

Data governance has become an all-encompassing term that can mean different things to different people. It is associated with terms such as data quality, metadata, data warehousing, data ownership, and data security. Data governance can also fail in more than one way to deliver on its promises because those involved in implementing it misinterpret its meaning, its value, and what it should look like in their organizations. One of the

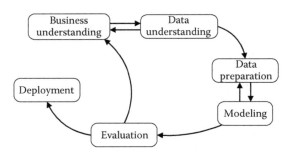

FIGURE 5.1
The data mining process. (Adapted from Shearer, C., *Journal of Data Warehousing* 5(4), 13–22, 2000.)

common definitional mistakes is to take data governance as equivalent with data management. Obviously, both require organizational commitment and investment.

However, data governance is business-driven, while data management is a diverse IT function that usually reports to the chief information officer. Data governance is the decision rights and policy making for corporate data, while data management concerns the operational level implementation of those policies. It follows that in an organizational setting it is important to define data governance and share that understanding across the organization. Data governance is the organizing framework for aligning strategy, defining objectives, and establishing policies for enterprise information (De Haes and Van Grembergen, 2015).

Any strategic level organizational initiative must be designed before being implemented. It should aim to tailor data governance to an organization's specific culture, structure, and decision-making processes. Implementation design requires outlining the scope and articulating the value proposition for decision making across functions or departments. For example, data governance will require a different implementation design at large, bureaucratic organizations, compared to high-tech companies with a flatter structure and informal culture.

Timing is critical in any strategic level initiative. While a governance "champion" might perceive the need for data governance and push forward, it is also important to get formal support and form a group of stakeholders. Necessary for this is answering the question of who needs to be involved and sponsor the initiative, before understanding what it involves and how it is to be carried out. It is important to engage a group of stakeholders in data governance design to produce the framework that will be used, including guiding principles, decision rights, and governing bodies. Otherwise, even if data governance is initiated it will stall and stop in its tracks because there will be no authorized group of stakeholders assigned to implement data governance and the clarity of what it involves.

When data governance initiatives manage to avoid errors in the areas mentioned, an organization probably has some sort of dedicated data governance cross-functional team assigned to it. The next hurdle is to avoid framing this as a one-off effort, another project that needs to be carried out. It is important that data governance initiatives are integrated in existing processes, where data are generated, used, and handled. Data governance should be seen as an ongoing part of organizational processes, directly related to the relation of an organization to its data and its function. Otherwise, there is a danger of data governance being seen as just another project with a finite date that people have to endure until it goes away or something that is not in their jurisdiction (i.e., none of their business).

The change toward permanent organizational data governance is a slow, long-term process involving few individuals at a time. They will need to be empowered to make decisions and be held accountable, so that decisions taken can be implemented and drive business improvements if errors are found in the process. The latter implies the need for organizational monitoring through committees that can review data governance-related rules. Involving decision-making bodies in the data governance process essentially institutionalizes data governance as a part of corporate policy making.

Bringing about organization-wide change cuts across deep-seated organizational paradigms and behaviors. This can be a challenge to a data governance effort. For example, corporations where the dominant culture stresses consensus over clear decision accountability may be less conducive to data governance programs. Organizational contexts where decision-making protocols are absent or obscure, where there is a mass mentality, or communication channels and planning are lacking can put a data governance initiative off track before it begins.

Data governance success requires explicitly establishing decision rights for individuals. This should be informed by organizational norms and structure. In the process intrinsic ideas about what decision making implies will be challenged. In order to overcome such challenges, the aims, value, and rewards of the data governance program must be clearly articulated and communicated in a stepwise fashion. The way this will manifest in each organization differs as each one must persevere and be patient in addressing its own challenges and biases.

The management of a data governance program expectations also requires attention. Securing senior level support and communicating the expected outcomes and their value is only part of the task. Implementing data governance and carrying out the necessary changes in data-related processes need to have the necessary resources to succeed. If during the implementation high-impact data issues are identified in the organization that should be improved, then procedures to validate, prioritize, or resolve a potentially increasing incoming stream of business problems should be in place.

Committing resources to identifying data governance issues without having a method and the authorization to resolve them will likely lead to frustration and mistrust. It may lead to a sense of expectations not being met and the danger of reverting back to the old way of doing things. In this situation convincing stakeholders and persevering with data governance will be an uphill battle. Gaining executive and management support for data governance through a well-motivated clear vision is an important success factor. Nevertheless, there is a limit to what senior support for a data governance program can be expected to achieve, as it may perceive that the value it can offer lies in its support, not participation. What needs to be put in place is a committee that will oversee the program.

The process of data governance has a think global–act local nature as the issues it seeks to address cut across intra- and even interorganizational boundaries and areas such as information privacy, security, and access policies. Attempting to address the range and variety of organizational issues in one go will likely come up against bottlenecks of prioritizing action, emergencies that need to be addressed, and resistance to change that is incumbent in every organization. There is no work-around for these kinds of bottlenecks except to take one step at a time.

Successful programs begin at small scale as narrow scope initiatives where value is clear for everyone to see and usually there are small delays involved in materializing outcomes. The process of resolving issues at this scale serves as a proving ground and raising awareness about data governance in an organic rather than a top-down way. This incremental approach requires more time but it allows demonstrating the value of data governance to stakeholders in a relevant context. A second-order effect is that because data governance is implemented several times in different parts of an organization, it illustrates that it is a core organizational process rather than a one-off project.

Data governance being an organizational process goes beyond implementation or application release. It requires performance measurement and monitoring as data streams are constant, new applications may be produced or acquired, and there is intra- or interorganizational user turnover. Data management is an ongoing activity overseeing data governance policies regarding data storage, access, maintenance, and resource allocation. Data governance and management approaches can potentially alleviate the potential downsides, trade-offs, and impacts of algorithmic implementation identified in the previous section. In contrast, a large-scale, one-off project will reveal its weaknesses in due time when novelty coming from data will impose new organizational demands. Every time this happens, compliance with existing standards needs to be monitored as well as the need to integrate new ones where necessary.

5.7 Conclusions

The previous sections discussed the learning challenges organizations face and the particular benefits the application of an algorithmic governance program may produce. Nevertheless, the answer to the question of whether organizations succeed because they have and apply the right algorithms is not a straightforward yes. Organizations are inherently human-centered constructs, so the advent of algorithms adds a further layer to them but does not overshadow their core nature. Their ability to rise and adapt to challenges, by managing their resources to match environmental change, that is, their dynamic capabilities, reside at the individual, firm, and/or network levels of analysis (Teece et al., 1997; Eisenhardt and Martin, 2000; Zollo and Winter, 2002). There are three corresponding reasons why organizations might not pay enough attention to past failures as much as successes and thus fail in the future.

1. Individual level—Managers commit to certain courses of action, the outcomes of which reflect on their personal careers. Thus, they have a motivation to stay at an organization until these courses of action bear fruit, even when evidence is mounting that they are not viable or sustainable anymore.

2. Organizational level—Organizations have core competences, the things they are good at. Past success reinforces them and adds to them. A change in their competitive environment arising from a new innovation will make them appear as core rigidities. In effect they will constitute existential threats rather than survival assets.

3. Organizational level—A change in the business environment arising out of a product/service innovation can have an adverse effect on an organization as well. This is because organizations with time come to mirror in their communication channels the functional arrangement of the products/services they provide.

5.7.1 Individual Level: Persisting on Failing Courses of Action

Research shows that past successes lead to persistence in the strategic orientation of the organization in the face of significant environmental change. Under such persistence organizational performance often declines. This kind of persistence is due to greater satisfaction with past performance, more confidence in the correctness of current strategies, higher goals and self-efficacy, and less seeking of information from critics (Audia et al., 2000).

Successful people tend to underestimate the risks of their actions and overestimate their gains (March and Shapira, 1987; Kahneman and Lovallo, 1993). Their effect can be considerable because this is the kind of people that the selection processes of organizations go for, and they are usually promoted to positions of power and authority (Levinthal and March, 1993). The end result for learning is that organizations systematically undersample failure. Organizational successes carry a premium of rewards compared to failures. Everybody wants to learn how to emulate successful organizational problem solving and successful individuals are promoted. At the same time, individuals who have been successful in the past are systematically more likely to reach top-level positions in organizations than are individuals who have not. Their experience gives them an exaggerated confidence in the chances of success from experimentation and risk taking (March and Shapira, 1987). As a result failures tend to be overlooked.

Trial-and-error learning and incremental search depend on the evaluation of outcomes as successes or failures. There is a structural bias toward postdecision disappointment in ordinary decision making (Harrison and March, 1984), but individual decision makers often seem to be able to reinterpret their objectives or the outcomes in such a way as to make themselves successful even when the shortfall seems quite large (Staw and Ross, 1978). Managers thus escalate their commitment to failing courses of action (Staw et al., 1981).

The complementary side to this is that understanding the business environment and how feedback loops operate is hard because it is hard to disentangle interactions and infer causality from situations that are dynamic (Sterman, 1989a,b, 1994). Research also shows that there is a tendency to attribute poor performance outcomes to external factors. This reduces the likelihood of strategic reorientation in a typical turbulent business environment and increases chances of failure. This is less so in stable environments where it is possible to infer the causes of substandard performance (Lant et al., 1992; Joseph and Gaba, 2015).

Algorithms provide the means to reduce the bias in the estimation of risk. Providing and updating data at the management level in a timely manner allows identification of the margin for persisting with a course of action that a manager has committed to. Identifying market trends and market response earlier may prove to save time and cost, and provide an opportunity for management-level auditing of strategic initiatives that particular managers may champion. On the other hand, because algorithms are also involved in carrying out organizational actions and are ubiquitous, it is sometimes hard to pinpoint the origin of true success.

5.7.2 Organizational Level: Failure due to Inertia and Core Rigidities

Core capabilities differentiate organizations strategically (Hayes et al., 1988; Prahalad and Hamel, 1990). They evolve and the survival of the organization depends on successfully managing this evolution. Core capabilities become institutionalized with time; they become part of the organization's frame of reference, arising out of the accumulation of decisions made in the history of the organization (Zucker, 1977; Pettigrew, 1979; Tucker, Singh, and Meinhard, 1990).

Core capabilities are an ensemble of knowledge sets, which are distributed and in constant flux from multiple internal and external sources. This implies that they cannot be managed as a single entity during the product/service development process. They are not easy to change either; because they are multifaceted they arise out of the combined interactions of values and norms of an organization, skills and knowledge base, technical systems, and managerial systems, which obviously includes algorithmic applications (Leonard-Barton, 1992).

New product, process, and service development initiatives are the locus of conflict between the need to evolve and the need to retain core capabilities (Leonard-Barton, 1992). Managers tend to avoid actions that challenge accepted modes of behavior (Weick, 1979). Thus institutionalized core capabilities may lead to novelty, but on the other hand they may lead to "incumbent inertia" in the face of environmental changes (Lieberman and Montgomery, 1988). It is also possible that external influences challenge their capabilities. Technological discontinuities can enhance or destroy the existing competencies of an organization (Tushman and Anderson, 1986). The effect of such occurrences ripples through the organization's internalized knowledge (Henderson and Clark, 1990).

Firms prefer to leverage the innovation mechanism in which they have built up some competence (Pennings and Harianto, 1992). Managers tend to avoid actions that challenge accepted modes of behavior (Weick, 1979). This implies that exploitation of existing expertise is prioritized over exploration of alternative innovation mechanisms (Levinthal and March, 1993). This can turn core capabilities to core rigidities and lead to competency traps (Levitt and March, 1988). This implies that organizations, particularly technology-based ones, have no choice but to challenge their competencies and innovate.

The means by which organizations can cope with these challenges are dynamic capabilities. They facilitate the ability of an organization to recognize a potential technological shift and the ability to adapt to change through innovation (Hill and Rothaermel, 2003). The particular difficulty involved in algorithmic applications is the expertise that needs to be in place for the firm to challenge its core capabilities. Even then, this might be met with resistance.

5.7.3 Organizational Level: Failure due to Architectural Innovation

Organizational form and structure facilitates knowledge and information processing. The communication channels of an organization, both formal and informal, develop along the personnel interactions that are critical to the tasks involved in designing and delivering products and services (Galbraith, 1973; Arrow, 1974). The architecture of organizational communication channels, with time, come to embody the architectural knowledge embedded in the design of its products and/or services (Henderson and Clark, 1990).

The development of formal and informal communication channels brings about the development of organizational information filters. These develop along communication channels to identify the information they need. As the tasks organizations face become standardized and less ambiguous, they develop filters to identify relevant pieces of information in their information stream (Arrow, 1974; Daft and Weick, 1984). The emergence of dominant designs in the industry in particular, and their gradual elaboration, have a formative effect on organizational filters. They become part of the knowledge around key relationships between the components of its products (Henderson and Clark, 1990).

Information filters and communication channels enable efficiency, particularly when facing recurring kinds of problems. Over time, organization employees acquire a store of knowledge about solutions to the specific kinds of problems that have arisen in previous projects. When confronted with such problems they don't reexamine all possible alternatives but focus on those that they find to be helpful in solving previous problems. In effect, an organization's problem-solving strategies summarize what it has learned about fruitful ways to solve problems in its immediate environment (Lyles and Mitroff, 1980; Nelson and Winter, 1982; March and Simon, 1993). Problem-solving strategies also reflect architectural knowledge, since they are likely to express part of an organization's knowledge about the component linkages that are crucial to the solution of routine problems. Employees may use strategies of this sort to solve problems in product components.

The strategies employees use, their channels for communication, and their information filters emerge in an organization to help it cope with complexity. They are efficient precisely because they do not have to be actively created each time a need for them arises. Furthermore, using them becomes natural as they become familiar and effective. Since product architecture is stable once a dominant design has been accepted, it can be internalized and thus becomes implicit knowledge. Organizations that are actively engaged in incremental innovation, which occurs within the context of stable architectural knowledge, are thus likely to manage much of their architectural knowledge implicitly by embedding it in their communication channels, information filters, and problem-solving strategies.

Component knowledge, in contrast, is more likely to be managed explicitly because it is a constant source of incremental innovation.

5.7.4 Problems from Architectural Innovation

For all their benefits, the particular filters and architecture of organizational communication pose some problems too. First, established organizations require significant time and resources to identify a particular innovation as architectural, since architectural innovation is often accommodated within old frameworks (Henderson and Clark, 1990). Radical innovation tends to make the need for new modes of learning and new skills quickly apparent. In contrast architectural innovation constitutes a new configuration of linkages between components making up a product or service.

Radical innovation changes the core design concepts of the product, making immediately obvious that knowledge about how the old components interact with each other is obsolete. The introduction of new linkages, however, is much harder to spot. Information that might warn the organization that a particular innovation is architectural may be screened out by the information filters and communication channels that embody old architectural knowledge. Since the core concepts of the design remain untouched, the organization may mistakenly believe that it understands the new technology. This effect is analogous to the tendency of individuals to continue to rely on beliefs about the world that a rational evaluation of new information should lead them to discard (Kahneman et al., 1982). Researchers have commented extensively on the ways in which organizations facing threats may continue to rely on their old frameworks or in our terms on their old architectural knowledge and hence misunderstand the nature of a threat.

Once an organization has recognized the nature of an architectural innovation, it faces a second major source of problems: the need to build and to apply new architectural knowledge effectively. Simply recognizing that a new technology is architectural in character does not give an established organization the architectural knowledge that it needs. It must first switch to a new mode of learning and then invest time and resources in learning about the new architecture. It is handicapped in its attempts to do this, both by the difficulty all organizations experience in switching from one mode of learning to another and by the fact that it must build new architectural knowledge in a context in which some of its old architectural knowledge may be irrelevant.

An established organization setting out to build new architectural knowledge must change its orientation from one of incremental search within a stable architecture to one of active search for new solutions within a constantly changing context. As long as the dominant design remains stable, an organization can segment and specialize its knowledge and rely on standard operating procedures to design and develop products. Architectural innovation, in contrast, places a premium on exploration in design and the assimilation of new knowledge. Many organizations encounter difficulties in their attempts to make this type of transition (Argyris and Schon, 1978; Weick, 1979). New entrants, with smaller commitments to older ways of learning about the environment and organizing their knowledge, often find it easier to build the organizational flexibility that abandoning old architectural knowledge and building new requires.

Established firms are faced with an awkward problem. Because their architectural knowledge is embedded in channels, filters, and strategies, the discovery process and the process of creating new information (and rooting out the old) usually takes time. The organization may be tempted to modify the channels, filters, and strategies that already exist rather than to incur the significant fixed costs and considerable organizational friction

An Analysis of Algorithmic Capability and Organizational Impact

required to build new sets from scratch (Arrow, 1974). However, it may be difficult to identify precisely which filters, channels, and problem-solving strategies need to be modified, and the attempt to build a new product with old (albeit modified) organizational tools can create significant problems.

In summary, for all the benefits that algorithms and their implementation through data governance programs brings, the extended use of all kinds of algorithms in modern organizations carries the potential of exacerbating particular problems and challenges. Organizations come to mirror in their communication channels the functional arrangement of the products/services they provide. The advent of the algorithms constitutes an additional layer overlaid along the communication channels. If the communication channels are hard to change due to inertia, this algorithmic layer may be just as hard to change as most employees see just the front end of an algorithmic application and don't have insight into its inner workings.

Acknowledgment

This work was partially funded by a European Commission FP7grant, grant number 619551.

References

Allen, T. J., 1977. *Managing the Flow of Technology*. MIT Press, Cambridge, MA.

Argyris, C., Schon, D., 1978. *Organizational Learning*. Addison-Wesley, Reading, MA.

Barley, S. R., 1988. Technology, power, and the social organization of work: Towards a pragmatic theory of skilling and deskilling. *Research in the Sociology of Organizations* 6, 33–80.

Becker, M., 2004. The concept of routines twenty years after Nelson and Winter (1982): A review of the literature. *Industrial and Corporate Change* 4, 643–677.

Boeker, W., 1989. The development and institutionalization of subunit power in organizations. *Administrative Science Quarterly* 34, 388–410.

Bower, J. L., Hout, T. M., 1988. Fast cycle capability for competitive power. *Harvard Business Review* 66, 110–118.

Brehmer, B., 1980. In one word: Not from experience. *Acta Psychological* 45, 223–241.

Burgelman, R. A., 1990. Strategy-making and organizational ecology: A conceptual framework. In J. V. Singh (ed.), *Organizational Evolution*, pp. 164–181. Sage, Newbury Park, CA.

Cangelosi, V. E., Dill, W. R., 1965. Organizational learning: Observations toward a theory. *Administrative Science Quarterly* 10, 175–203.

Christopher, M., Towill, D. R., 2000. Supply chain migration from lean and functional to agile and customised. *International Journal of Supply Chain Management* 5(4), 206–213.

Cohen, W. M., Levinthal, D. A., 1989. Innovation and learning: The two faces of R&D. *Economic Journal* 99(397), 569–596.

Cohen, W. M., Levinthal, D. A., 1990. Absorptive capacity: A new perspective on learning and innovation. *Administrative Science Quarterly* 35, 128–152.

Cohen, W. M., Levinthal, D. A., 1994. Fortune favors the prepared firm. *Management Science* 40, 227–251.

Cronin, M., Gonzalez, C., Sterman, J. D., 2009. Why don't well-educated adults understand accumulation? A challenge to researchers, educators, and citizens. *Organizational Behavior and Human Decision Processes* 108(1), 116–130.

Cyert, R. M., March, J. G., 1992. *A Behavioral Theory of the Firm*. Blackwell, Oxford.

Daft, R. L., Lengel, R. H., 1986. Organizational information requirements, media richness and structural design. *Management Science* 32, 554–571.

Daft, R. L., Weick, K. E., 1984. Toward a model of organizations as interpretation systems. *Academy Management Review* 9, 284–295.

Denhardt, R. B., Catlaw, T. J., 2015. Theories of public organization. 7th edition, Cengage Learning.

Dierickx, I., Cool, K., 1989. Asset stock accumulation and sustainability of competitive advantage. *Management Science* 35, 1504-1511.

Eisenhardt, K. M, Martin, J. A., 2000. Dynamic capabilities: What are they? *Strategic Management Journal* 21, 1105–1121.

Feldman, M. S., 1989. *Order without Design: Information Production and Policy Making*. Stanford University Press, Stanford, CA.

Galunic, D. C., Rodan, S., 1998. Resource recombinations in the firm: Knowledge structures and the potential for Schumpeterian innovation. *Strategic Management Journal* 19, 1193–1201.

Gavetti, G., Levinthal, D., 2000. Looking forward and looking backward: Cognitive and experiential search. *Administrative Science Quarterly* 45, 113–137.

Gunasekaran, A., Ngai, E. W. T., 2004. Information systems in supply chain integration and management. *European Journal of Operational Research* 159(2), 269–295.

Harrison, J. R., March, J. G., 1984. Decision making and post-decision surprises. *Administrative Science Quarterly* 29, 26–42.

Helfat, C. E., 2000. Guest editor's introduction to the special issue: The evolution of firm's capabilities. *Strategic Management Journal* 21, 955–961.

Hendricks, K. B., Singhal, V. R., Stratman, J. K., 2007. The Impact of Enterprise Systems on Corporate Performance: A Study of ERP, SCM and CRM System Implementations. *Journal of Operations Management* 25(1), 65–82.

Herriott, S. R., Levinthal, D. A., March, J. G., 1985. Learning from experience in organizations. *American Economic Review* 75, 298–302.

Iansiti, M., Clark, K., 1994. Integration and dynamic capability: Evidence from product development in automobiles and mainframe computers. *Industrial and Corporate Change* 3, 557–605.

Jansen, J. J. P., van den Bosch, F. A. J., Volberda, H. W., 2005. Managing potential and realized absorptive capacity: How do organizational antecedents matter? *Academy of Management Journal* 48(6), 999–1015.

Kahneman, D., 2011. *Thinking, Fast and Slow.* Allen Lane, UK.

Kahneman, D., Lovallo, D., 1993. Timid choices and bold forecasts: A cognitive perspective on risk taking. *Management Science* 39, 17–31.

Kahneman, D., Slovic, P., Tversky, A., eds. 1982. *Judgment under Uncertainty: Heuristics and Biases.* Cambridge University Press, Cambridge.

Katz, R., Allen, T. J., 1982. Investigating the Not Invented Here (NIH) syndrome: A look at the performance, tenure, and comunication patterns of 50 R&D project groups. *R&D Management* 12(1), 7–20.

Kogut, B., Zander, U., 1992. Knowledge of the firm, combinative capabilities, and the replication of technology. *Organization Science* 3, 383–398.

Lane, P. J., Koka, B. R., Pathak, S., 2006. The reification of absorptive capacity: A critical review and rejuvenation of the construct. *Academy of Management Review* 31(4), 833–863.

Langlois, R. N., Steinmueller, W. E., 2000. Strategy and circumstance: The response of American firms to Japanese competition in semiconductors, 1980–1995. *Strategic Management Journal* 21, 1163–1173.

Lanier, J., 2014. Who owns the future. Simon & Schuster.

Lave, C. A., March, J. G., 1993. *An Introduction to Models in the Social Sciences*. University Press of America, Lanham, MD.

Leonard-Barton, D., 1992. Core-capabilities and core rigidities: A paradox in managing new product development. *Strategic Management Journal* 13, 111–125.

Levinthal, D. A., March, J. G., 1981. A model of adaptive organizational search. *Journal of Economic Behavior and Organization* 2, 307–333.

Levinthal, D. A., March, J. G., 1993. The myopia of learning. *Strategic Management Journal* 14, 95–112.

Levitt, B., March, J. G., 1988. Organizational learning. *Annual Review of Sociology* 14, 319–340.

Lewin, A. Y., Massini, A., Peeters, C., 2011. Microfoundations of internal and external absorptive capacity routines. *Organization Science* 22(1), 81–98.

Lin, X., Germain, R., 2003. Organizational structure, context, customer orientation, and performance: Lessons from Chinese state-owned enterprises. *Strategic Management Journal* 24, 1131–1151.

Lindblom, C. E., 1959. The "science" of muddling through. *Public Administration Review* 19, 79–88.

Lounamaa, P., March, J. G., 1987. Adaptive coordination of a learning team. *Management Science* 33, 107–123.

March, J. G., 1991. Exploration and exploitation in organization learning. *Organization Science* 2, 71-87.

March, J. G., 1994. The evolution of evolution. In J. Baum, J. V. Singh (eds.), *The Evolutionary Dynamics of Organizations*, Oxford University Press, New York.

March, J. G., Shapira, Z., 1987. Managerial perspectives on risk and risk taking. *Management Science* 33, 1404–1018.

March, J. G., Simon, H. A., 1993. *Organizations*. Blackwell, Oxford.

March, J. G., Sproull, L. S., Tamuz, M., 1991. Learning from samples of one or fewer. *Organization Science* 2, 1–13.

Melville, N., Kraemer, K., Gurbaxani, V., 2004. Review: Information technology and Organizational performance: An integrative model of IT business value. *MIS Quarterly* 28(2), 283–322.

Miller, D. T., Ross, M., 1975. Self-serving biases in the attribution of causality. *Psychological Bulletin* 82, 213–225.

Mintzberg, H., 1992. *Structure in Fives: Designing Effective Organizations*. Prentice Hall, Englewood Cliffs, NJ.

Murovec, N., Prodan, I., 2009. Absorptive capacity, its determinants, and influence on innovation output: Cross-cultural validation of the structural model. *Technovation* 29, 859–872.

Nelson, R. R., Winter, S. G., 1982. *An Evolutionary Theory of Economic Change*. Harvard University Press, Cambridge, MA.

Olsen, J. P., 1983. *Organized Democracy*. Universitetsforlage, Bergen, Norway.

Ostroff, F., Smith, D., 1992. The horizontal organization. *McKinsey Quarterly* 1, 148–168.

Pasquale, F., 2015. The black box society: The secret algorithms that control money and information. Harvard University Press.

Prahalad, C. K., Hamel, G., 1990. The core competence of corporation. *Harvard Business Review* 68, 79–91.

Radner, R., 1975. A behavioral model of cost reduction. *Bell Journal of Economics* 6, 196–215.

Rasmusen, E., 2006. *Games and Information: An Introduction to Game Theory*, 4th ed., Wiley-Blackwell, Malden, MA.

Ross, J., Staw, B. M., 1986. Expo 86: An escalation prototype. *Administrative Science Quarterly* 31, 274–297.

Sagan, S. D., 1993. *The Limits of Safety: Organizations, Accidents, and Nuclear Weapons*. Princeton University Press, Princeton, NJ.

Schonberger, R. J., 1990. *Building a Chain of Customers*. Free Press, New York.

Senge, P. M., 1990. *The Fifth Discipline: The Art and Practice of the Learning Organization*. Doubleday, New York.

Shearer, C., 2000. The CRISP-DM model: The new blueprint for data mining. *Journal of Data Warehousing* 5(4), 13–22.

Siegel, S., 1957. Level of aspiration and decision making. *Psychological Review* 64, 253–262.

Simon, H. A., 1955. A behavioral model of rational choice. *Quarterly Journal of Economics* 69, 99–118.

Smith, H. T., Green, T. R. G., 1980. *Human Interaction with Computers*. Academic Press, New York.

Stalk, G., Evans, P., Shulman, L. E., 1992. Competing on capabilities: The new rules of corporate strategy. *Harvard Business Review* 70, 57–69.

Starbuck, W. H., 1983. Organizations as action generators. *American Sociological Review* 48, 91–102.

Staw, B. M., Ross, J., 1978. Commitment to a policy decision: A multi-theoretical perspective. *Administrative Science Quarterly* 23, 40–64.

Staw, B. M., Sandelands, L. E., Dutton, J. E., 1981. Threat rigidity effects in organizational behavior: A multilevel analysis. *Administrative Science Quarterly* 26, 501–524.

Steinbruner, J. D., 1974. *The Cybernetic Theory of Decision*. Princeton University Press, Princeton, NJ.

Sterman, J. D., 1989a. Misperceptions of feedback in dynamic decision making. *Organizational Behaviour and Human Decision Processes* 43(3), 301–335.

Sterman, J. D., 1989b. Modelling managerial behavior: Misperceptions of feedback in a dynamic decision making experiment. *Management Science* 35(3), 321–339.

Sterman, J. D., 1994. Learning in and about complex systems. *System Dynamics Review* 10, 291–330.

Teece, D., Pisano, G., Shuen, A., 1997. Dynamic capabilities and strategic management. *Strategic Management Journal* 18, 509–534.

Todorova, G., Durisin, B., 2007. Absorptive capacity: Valuing a reconceptualization. *Academy of Management Review* 32(3), 774–786.

Tripsas, M., Gavetti, G., 2000. Capabilities, cognition and inertia: Evidence from digital imaging. *Strategic Management Journal* 21, 1147–1162.

Tushman, M. L., 1977. Special boundary roles in the innovation process. *Administrative Science Quarterly* 22, 587–605.

Tushman, M. L., Katz, R., 1980. External communication and project performance: An investigation into the role of gatekeepers. *Management Science* 26(11), 1071–1085.

Tushman, M. L., Romanelli, E., 1985. Organizational evolution: A metamorphosis model of convergence and reorientation. In L. Cummings, B. Staw (eds.), *Research in Organizational Behavior*, JAI Press, Greenwich.

Van den Bosch, F. A. J., Volberda, H. W., de Boer, M., 1999. Coevolution of firm absorptive capacity and knowledge environment organizational forms and combinative capabilities. *Organization Science* 10(5), 551–568.

Volberda, H. W., 1996. Toward the flexible firm: How to remain vital in hypercompetitive environments. *Organization Science* 7, 359–374.

Volberda, H. W., Foss, N. J., Lyles, M. A., 2010. Absorbing the concept of absorptive capacity: How to realize its potential in the organization field. *Organization Science* 21, 931–951.

Weick, K., 1979. *The Social Psychology of Organizing*. Addison-Wesley, Reading, MA.

Whetten, D. A., 1987. Organizational growth and decline processes. *Annual Review of Sociology* 13, 335–358.

Winter, S. G., 2003. Understanding dynamic capabilities. *Strategic Management Journal* 24, 991–995.

Zahra, S. A., George, G., 2002. Absorptive capacity: A review, reconceptualization and extension. *Academy of Management Review* 27(2), 185–203.

Zollo, M. M., Winter, S. G., 2002. Deliberate learning and the evolution of dynamic capabilities. *Organization Science* 13, 339–351.

Authors

George Papachristos earned a PhD in supply chain operations strategy and transitions at the University of Patras, Greece. Since 2013 he has worked at the Delft University of Technology as a postdoc. His research interests include system innovation and sociotechnical transitions, innovation and technology management, system dynamics simulation, and operations strategy in closed loop supply chains.

 **Scott W. Cunningham** earned a PhD in science, technology, and innovation policy at the University of Sussex. After graduating from the University of Sussex he worked for a variety of companies, large and small, in the computer and software industry. He was a knowledge discovery analyst for AT&T and NCR, where he worked closely with Teradata. He also helped found a number of Internet start-up companies in Silicon Valley, one of which, DemandTec, eventually went public and was acquired by IBM. Since 2002 he has been an associate professor at the Delft University of Technology. His research interest focuses on Big Data for the social good, and he is an associate editor of *Technological Forecasting and Social Change*.

6

Big Data and Its Impact on Enterprise Architecture

Meena Jha, Sanjay Jha, and Liam O'Brien

CONTENTS

6.1 Introduction: Background and Driving Forces 107
6.2 Enterprise Architecture (EA) and Its Role in Big Data Solutions 109
6.3 Overview of the Entire Information Landscape 111
6.4 Big Data and Its Impact on Enterprise Architecture 115
     6.4.1 Big Data and Impacts on EA Application Architecture.................................. 115
     6.4.2 Big Data and Impacts on EA Technology Architecture 118
     6.4.3 Big Data and Impacts on EA Data Architecture 118
     6.4.4 Big Data and Impacts on EA Business Architecture 121
6.5 Summary 122
References 122
Authors 123

ABSTRACT   Business intelligence (BI) and data analytics (DA) have been used for years to evaluate bulk data, but these technologies reached their limits when the data involved became more ephemeral, unstructured, and high in volume. Big Data, which support BI and DA, are enabled by recent advances in technologies and architecture to handle unstructured and high volume data. However, Big Data problems are complex to analyze and solve. Challenges include classifying Big Data so as to be able to choose Big Data solution(s) to fit into the enterprise architecture (EA) of an organization. It is important to efficiently deliver real-time analytic processing on constantly changing streaming data and enable descriptive, predictive, and prescriptive analytics to support real-time decisions for BI. When a significant amount of data needs to be processed quickly in near real-time to gain insights, this is a form of streaming data. Streaming data changes constantly and can come in many forms (e.g., web data, audio/video data, and external data). Using streaming data for BI and DA is a new paradigm in analytics and will have impacts on technology infrastructure components and data architectures, since most data is directly generated in digital format today. The technology infrastructure components and the technology architectures as well as data architectures changes must be captured by an organization's existing EA to enable conducting BI and DA, using a holistic approach at all times, for the successful development and execution of an organization's strategy.

6.1 Introduction: Background and Driving Forces

According to Mayer-Schönberger and Cukier (2013), Big Data allows society to harness information in new and different ways to find useful insights or goods and services of significant value. According to Laney (2001), Big Data definitions include the three V's of data management: volume, velocity, and variety. However, Dumbill and Mohin (2013) suggests that Big Data has increased in popularity; however, it has yet to receive a concrete definition. The definition of Big Data according to Manyika et al. (2011) is "datasets whose size is beyond the ability of typical database software tools to capture, store, manage, and analyse." There have been different definitions of Big Data, but Big Data has broadly been reached on its potential to enhance decision making (Dumbill and Mohin, 2013).

We are awash in a flood of data today. In a broad range of application areas, data is being collected at unprecedented scale. Duffy Marsan (2010) suggested that by 2015, the world would generate the equivalent of almost 93 million Libraries of Congress. According to the Computing Community Consortium (2011), scientific research has been revolutionized by Big Data. Big Data is improving areas as diverse as healthcare, transportation, energy, and education. The development and distribution of Big Data technologies will allow people to live safer lives, conserve natural resources, receive personalized education, and much more.

Human elements such as social media are increasingly being used as an information source, including information related to risks and crises. The data on social media are unstructured, high volume, high velocity, and high variety. The technological advances in Big Data solution(s) have enabled handling of unstructured, high volume, high velocity, and high variety data.

Liebowitz (2013) suggests that the generation of data has contributed to the emergence of the Big Data phenomenon. As part of the Big Data phenomenon there has been massive growth taking place in data processing power, data visualization, data storage, network speeds, mobility, accessing real-time data, and higher semantic capabilities. Examples of technological changes include social networking, being always connected, and online blogging. These technological changes are being provided by companies such as Facebook, LinkedIn, Google, and Twitter. According to Lapkin and Young (2011), these changes were not predicted as mainstream activities a decade ago. However, these changes have actually defined the evolution of technologies, infrastructures, applications, users, communities, societies, and knowledge creation. They are an integral part of any enterprise, and enterprise architecture (EA) needs to address these technological changes for organizations to maintain their competitive advantage.

Big Data can be acquired, stored, processed, and analyzed in many different ways. Every Big Data source (live data, data from internal sources, and data from external sources) has different characteristics, including the frequency, volume, velocity, type, and veracity of the data. When Big Data is stored and processed, additional dimensions come into play, such as security, policies, structure, and governance. Data architecture of EA describes the structure of an organization's logical and physical data assets and the associated data management resources. All of this forms the information landscape of an organization, a key component of an EA. Choosing an architecture and building an appropriate Big Data solution is challenging, because so many factors have to be considered such as business, application, technology, and data changes.

As organizations grow and expand they are also likely to gain technologies that duplicate existing capabilities, with workflows in need of significant overhaul. One of the issues that organizations in such situations often encounter and must address is integrating Big Data, which can drive the alignment between the business's operating needs and the processes, applications, and infrastructure required to support ever-more dynamic requirements. As the demand for managing information increases, organizations need to focus their efforts on integrating their data, application, technology, and users across their entire information landscape (EIL).

According to the Federation of Enterprise Architecture Professional Organizations (2013), enterprise architecture provides pragmatic artifacts such as requirements,

Big Data and Its Impact on Enterprise Architecture

specifications, guiding principles, and conceptual models that describe the current state and an idea of how to get to the next major stage of evolution of an organization, often called the "future state." Enterprise architects need to document in the EA the current state, the future state, the gaps, and the roadmap to get to the future state, which can be used for the integration of Big Data. EA plays a major role in ensuring that organizations maximize the business opportunities posed by Big Data. Big Data disrupts traditional information architectures of an organization as requirements to handle unstructured, high volume, high velocity, and high variety data come into play. Traditional information architecture is not capable of handling Big Data solutions. Organizations may have the best technology and the best people, but if the internal architecture of the organization has silos and lacks data sharing, they are less likely to achieve success with Big Data.

Chen, Chiang, and Storey (2012) suggest that Big Data requires information technology (IT) leaders and technology specialists to acquire and apply tools, techniques, and architectures for analyzing, visualizing, linking, and managing big, complex data sets. Data integration requires capturing and integrating both structured and unstructured Big Data within the enterprise. Big Data as a part of the overall decision support system or business intelligence (BI) system can only be realized by data integration.

Key to success in any Big Data solution is to first identify the business needs and opportunities, and then select the proper fit-for-purpose solution. In fact, some identified use cases from the business might be best suited by existing technology such as a data warehouse while others require a combination of existing technologies and Big Data solutions (such as EMC Greenplum, IBM's InfoSphere, and Oracle Big Data Appliance), which are fueling business transformation. Jha et al. (2014) suggest that there could be legacy applications that need to be integrated to Big Data solutions. For this an EA is required to be developed. An enterprise architect needs to use the identified business needs and opportunities to generate a Big Data and EA roadmap by looking at the gap between current state without Big Data and future state with Big Data.

However, Big Data problems are complex to analyze and solve. Behind any information management practice lies the core doctrines of data quality, data governance, and metadata management along with considerations for privacy and legal concerns, which today have become the information landscape of an organization. Big Data is being generated at a high volume, with a rapid rate of change, and encompassing a broad range of sources and includes both structured and unstructured data. The ability to understand and manage the sources of the data, and then integrate the data from these sources into a larger business application, can provide significant value to the organization. Organizations that have had already developed its EA and now want to integrate a Big Data solution will face issues and concerns related to their information architecture, data architecture, business architecture, and technology architecture. Enterprise architecture plays a major role in ensuring that an organization maximizes the business opportunities posed by Big Data. In this chapter we discuss Big Data and its impact on enterprise architecture.

6.2 Enterprise Architecture (EA) and Its Role in Big Data Solutions

An EA is a conceptual blueprint that defines the structure and operation of an organization. The intent of an EA is to determine how an organization can most effectively achieve its current and future objectives. Lapkin et al. (2008) of Gartner define EA as follows:

"Enterprise Architecture is the process of translating business vision and strategy into effective enterprise change by creating, communicating and improving the key requirements, principles and models that describe the enterprise's future state and enable its evolution."

The scope of the EA includes the people, processes, information, and technology of the enterprise, and their relationships to one another and to the external environment. It is very important to capture architectural requirements for Big Data. The Rational Unified Process gives the following definition of a requirement: A requirement describes a condition or capability to which a system must conform; either derived directly from user needs, or stated in a contract, standard, specification, or other formally imposed document. An architectural requirement, in turn, is any requirement that is architecturally significant. Impact is the action of one object coming forcibly into contact with another. Big Data solutions have impacted architectural requirements such as capturing and storing unstructured data. According to Salim (2014), the four subsets of EA are greatly impacted by bringing Big Data solutions into an organization.

According to Gartner, enterprise architects compose holistic solutions that address the business challenges of the enterprise and support the governance needed to implement them. Integrating Big Data is a challenge for many organizations. EA can help develop the holistic solution to address this challenge. There are four types of architecture that are the subsets of overall EA:

- Business (or business process) architecture—This defines the business strategy, governance, organization, and key business processes. Business continuity and marketing architecture comes under this category.

- Data architecture—This describes the structure of an organization's logical and physical data assets and data management resources. Data governance architecture, master data management (MDM), reference data management (RDM), metadata management, and data security come under this.

- Application architecture—This kind of architecture provides a blueprint for the individual application systems to be deployed, their interactions, and their relationships to the core business processes of the organization. Reporting architecture, integration architecture, application portfolio management, and application security come under this.

- Technology architecture—This describes the logical software and hardware capabilities that are required to support the deployment of business, data, and application services. This includes IT infrastructure, middleware, networks, communications, processing, and standards.

If all four subset architectures of an EA can show the impact of Big Data, then the EA as a whole will render a holistic view of the information landscape and impacts of Big Data. Big Data solutions can be seen from many perspectives such as

- Storage—Requirement for lots of storage
- Distribution—Data stored in lots of places globally
- Database design—Lots of rows, lots of columns, lots of tables
- Algorithmic or mathematical—Lots of variables, lots of combinations, lots of permutations, summed up as one optimal answer among a large number of possibilities

Big Data and Its Impact on Enterprise Architecture

There are varieties of Big Data technologies. In distributed processing technology there could be parallel processing, or loosely or tightly coupled processing. In compression technology there could be data encoding and least-number-of-bit data function encoding. In proprietary hardware technology there could be performing algorithms at the data persistence layer, massive parallel platforms, networks, and quantum computer platforms. In reduced code set, it could be eliminating large amounts of DBMS (database management system) code and eliminating large amounts of online transaction processing (OLTP) code. The issue is if these technologies and requirements are not depicted in EA, the Big Data solution would be uncoordinated, inconsistent, and complex to handle. According to Porter (2008), an organization needs to understand its objectives and goals in using Big Data technologies and solutions as they do not come cheap. Handling all the technologies in an organization adds to the complexity of IT assets in the organization and can give rise to uncoordinated Big Data solutions, which will cost time and money to the organization. EA can address the issue of uncoordinated Big Data solution by

- Assisting the organization in opportunity recognition
- Architecting the holistic approach of information architecture
- Evaluating how applications will integrate knowledge via BI and service-oriented architecture (SOA)
- Updating the organization's infrastructure technology road map and watch list

6.3 Overview of the Entire Information Landscape

According to Oracle (2013), what has changed in the last few years is the emergence of Big Data, both as a means of managing the vast volumes of unstructured and semistructured data stored but not exploited in many organizations, as well as the potential to tap into new sources of insight such as social media websites to gain a market edge. The entire information landscape (EIL) deals with data landscape, technology, users, and applications within and outside the organization that are required for the operation of an organization.

The EIL is shown in Figure 6.1. There could be a number of applications in the organization such as supply chain management, human resources, and accounting that could be categorized as internal, external, applications on cloud, and so on. Big Data technologies include Hadoop, Greenplum, and Cloudera. The data landscape consists of Big Data, data in motion, and file system. Users can be external, internal, business, and so forth as shown in Figure 6.1.

When EA is being constructed it should provide a principles catalog, organization catalog, business service/function catalog, objective catalog, role catalog, and so forth under business architecture. The principles catalog captures principles of the business and architecture principles that describe what a "good" solution or architecture should look like. Principles are used to evaluate and agree on an outcome for architecture decision points. Principles are also used as a tool to assist in architectural governance of change initiatives. An organization catalog gives a definitive listing of all participants that interact with IT, including users and owners of IT systems. The business service/function catalog can be used to identify capabilities of an organization and to understand the level of governance that is applied to the functions of an organization. This functional decomposition can be

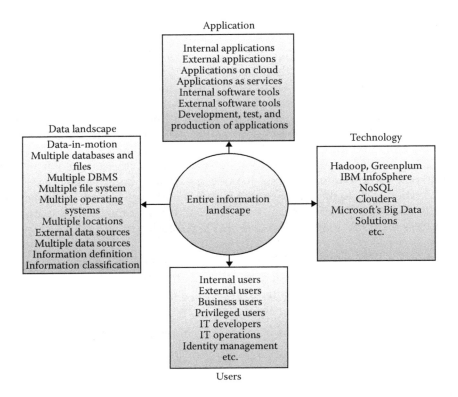

FIGURE 6.1
Overview of the entire information landscape.

used to identify new capabilities required to support business change or may be used to determine the scope of change initiatives, applications, or technology components. The business service/function catalog contains the following metamodel entities: organization unit, business function, business service, and information system service. The business service/function catalog provides a functional decomposition in a form that can be filtered, reported on, and queried, as a supplement to graphical functional decomposition diagrams. The purpose of the functional decomposition diagram is to show on a single page the capabilities of an organization that are relevant to the consideration of an architecture. By examining the capabilities of an organization from a functional perspective, it is possible to quickly develop models of what the organization does.

The objective catalog is a cross-organizational reference of how an organization meets its drivers in practical terms through goals, objectives, and (optionally) measures. The purpose of the role catalog is to provide a listing of all authorization levels or zones within an enterprise. Frequently, application security or behavior is defined against locally understood concepts of authorization that create complex and unexpected consequences when combined on the user desktop.

Under application architecture, EA provides an application portfolio catalog, interface catalog, and application/function matrix. The objectives of the application architecture is to develop the target application architecture that enables the business architecture and the architecture vision, while addressing the request for architecture work and stakeholder concerns and to identify candidate architecture roadmap components based upon gaps between the baseline and target application architectures. This requires internal and external applications, applications on cloud, application as services, internal software tools, external software tools, and any kind of development, test, and production of software. A request for architecture work is a document that is sent from the sponsoring organization to the architecture organization to trigger the start of an architecture development cycle. The architecture roadmap gives functional requirements, dependencies, relationship to opportunity, relationship to architecture definition document and architecture requirements specification, business value, and potential solutions to target architecture.

The application architecture shows different diagrams such as the application communication diagram, application and user location diagram, application use-case diagram, enterprise manageability diagram, process/application realization diagram, software engineering diagram, application migration diagram, and software distribution diagram.

For the purpose of the data architecture, EA provides a data component catalog, data entity, application/data matrix, conceptual data diagram, logical data diagram, data dissemination diagram, data security diagram, and data migration diagram. A data entity/business function matrix in data architecture depicts the relationship between data entities and business functions within the enterprise. Business functions are supported by business services with explicitly defined boundaries and will be supported and realized by business processes. The mapping of the data entity–business function relationship enables the following to take place: assign ownership of data entities to organizations; understand the data and information exchange requirements of business services; support the gap analysis and determine whether any data entities are missing and need to be created; define application of origin, application of record, and application of reference for data entities; and enable development of data governance programs across the enterprise (establish data steward, develop data standards pertinent to the business function, etc.).

Under technology architecture, EA provides a technology standards catalog, technology portfolio catalog, and application/technology matrix. The application/technology matrix documents the mapping of applications to technology platform. This matrix should be aligned with and complement one or more platform decomposition diagrams. The application/technology matrix shows: logical/physical application components, services, logical technology components, and physical technology components. The purpose of the application/data matrix in application architecture is to depict the relationship between applications (i.e., application components) and the data entities that are accessed and updated by them. Applications will create, read, update, and delete specific data entities that are associated with them. The data entities in a package/packaged services environment can be classified as master data, reference data, transactional data, content data, and historical data. Applications that operate on the data entities include transactional applications, information management applications, and business warehouse applications.

The technology standards catalog documents the agreed upon standards for technology across the enterprise covering technologies and versions, the technology lifecycles, and the refresh cycles for the technology. Depending upon the organization, this may also include location or business domain-specific standards information. This catalog provides a snapshot of the enterprise standard technologies that are or can be deployed, and also helps identify the discrepancies across the enterprise. If technology standards are currently in place, apply these to the technology portfolio catalog to gain a baseline view of compliance with technology standards. The technology portfolio catalog contains the following metamodel entities: platform service, logical technology component, and physical technology component.

There are a variety of Big Data technologies, which can be summed up as database technologies, hardware technologies, applications, and reporting tools. There are two open source foundations. The first is the Apache Software Foundation (ASF). The ASF provides support for the Apache community of open source software projects. The second is the Free Software Foundation (FSF). The FSF (2014) promotes the universal freedom to study, distribute, create, and modify computer software, with the organization's preference for software being distributed. The FSF was incorporated in Massachusetts, where it is also based.

Apache Hadoop is an open source distributed software platform for storing and processing data. Written in Java, it runs on a cluster of industry-standard servers configured with direct-attached storage. Using Hadoop, petabytes of data can be stored reliably on tens of thousands of servers while scaling performance cost-effectively by merely adding inexpensive nodes to the cluster. The Hadoop Distributed File System (HDFS) splits files into large blocks (usually 64 MB or 128 MB) and distributes these blocks among the nodes in the cluster. For processing the data, the Hadoop MapReduce ships code (specifically Jar files) to the nodes that have the required data, and the nodes then process the data in parallel. According to IBM (2014), this approach takes advantage of data locality in contrast to conventional HPC architecture, which usually relies on a parallel file system (computer and data separated, but connected with high-speed networking). Applications use an assortment of Big Data technologies such as open source, proprietary, traditional databases (OldSQL), nontraditional databases (NoSQL), and OLTP (New SQL) fully ACID. Database architectures for Big Data technologies are provided by EMC Greenplum, IBM's InfoSphere BigInsight, Microsoft's Big Data Solutions, and Oracle's Big Data Appliance.

EMC's Greenplum Unified Analytics Platform (UAP) is a unified platform enabling agile Big Data analytics by empowering data science teams to analyze structured and unstructured data in a unified platform. It comprises three components: the Greenplum MPP database, for structured data; a Hadoop distribution, Greenplum HD; and Chorus, a productivity and groupware layer for data science teams.

IBM's (2014) Big Data platform InfoSphere BigInsight includes software for processing streaming data and persistent data. BigInsight supports the latter, while InfoSphere Streams supports the former. The two can be deployed together to support real-time and batch analytics of various forms of raw data, or they can be deployed individually to meet specific application objectives.

Microsoft's Big Data Solutions brings Hadoop to the Windows Server platform and in elastic form to the cloud platform Windows Azure. The Hadoop Hive data warehouse is part of Big Data Solutions, including connectors from Hive to ODBC and Excel.

Oracle's Big Data Appliance caters to the high-end enterprise market, and particularly leans to the rapid deployment, high-performance end of the spectrum. It is the only vendor to include the popular R analytical language integrated with Hadoop and to ship a NoSQL database of its own design as opposed to Hadoop HBase.

Along with Greenplum, Aster Data, ParAccel, and Vertica are early pioneers of Big Data solutions before the mainstream emergence of Hadoop. All these solutions use the MPP (massively parallel processing) analytical database and have a Hadoop connector available.

NoSQL (Not Only SQL) is a new way of thinking about databases, founded on the belief that a relational database model may not be the best solution for all use cases and situations that require Big Data solutions. Some providers of NoSQL platforms are Redis, Riak, CouchDB, Membase, and Cassandra. NewSQL is a class of modern relational database management system that seeks to provide the same scalable performance of NoSQL systems for online transaction processing workloads while still maintaining the ACID guarantees of a traditional database system. The providers of NewSQL are VoltDB, Clustrix, xeround, and nuoDB memsql, to name but a few. ACID stands for atomicity (transaction cannot be subdivided), consistency (constraints don't change from before transaction to

Big Data and Its Impact on Enterprise Architecture

after transaction), isolated (database changes not revealed to users until after transaction has completed), and durable (database changes are permanent).

Case studies from market research and business literature suggest that a Big Data storage system based on the principle of cloud computing coincides with massive savings in IT infrastructure and operation. According to Gruman (2010), Walt Disney lowered its IT expense growth from 27% to 3%, while increasing its annual processing growth from 17% to 45% after setting up Hadoop Cluster on the cloud.

A Big Data ready cloud-computing platform provides the following key capabilities:

- Agile computing platform—Agility is enabled through highly flexible and recon-figurable data and analytic resources and architectures. Analytic resources can be quickly reconfigured and redeployed to meet the ever-changing demands of the business, enabling new levels of analytics flexibility and agility.

- Linear scalability—Access to massive amounts of computing power means that business problems can be attacked in a completely different manner. For example, the traditional extract, transform, and load (ETL) process can be transformed into a data enrichment process creating new composite metrics, such as frequency (how often?), recent in time (how recent?), and sequencing (what order?).

- On-demand, analysis-intense workloads—Previously organizations had to be content with performing "after the fact" analysis. The organizations lacked the computational power to dive deep into the analysis as events were occurring or to contemplate all the different variables that might be driving the business. With a cloud platform, these computationally intensive, short burst analytic needs can be exploited. Business users can analyze massive amounts of data in real time. This means uncovering the relevant and actionable facts across hundreds of dimensions and business metrics.

6.4 Big Data and Its Impact on Enterprise Architecture

Big Data influences EA design in many ways. Big Data solutions have impacts on business architecture, data architecture, application architecture, and technical architecture of EA.

6.4.1 Big Data and Impacts on EA Application Architecture

Application architecture describes the behavior of applications used in a business, and how they interact with each other and with users. It is focused on the data consumed and produced by applications rather than their internal structure. In application portfolio management, the applications are usually mapped to business functions and to application. The application architecture forms pillars of an enterprise architecture or solution architecture. According to The Open Group Architecture Framework (TOGAF 2014), the definition of application architecture is: structure of the structures and interaction of the applications as groups of capability that provide key business functions and manage the data assets. The application architecture also show the interfaces that the application provides for integration as well as the integrations to other applications and data sources the application requires to function.

IBM Systems Application Architecture provides document content architecture that specifies the format for documents to be exchanged among different word processors and other software, Systems Network Architecture Distribution Services for storing and forward document transmission, IBM Distributed Data Management Architecture for file sharing, and Distributed Relational Database Architecture for sharing relational databases (IBM, 2014). Application Architecture focuses on defining the applications within an enterprise. This includes identifying how applications interact with each other and the other elements within the business architecture. Application Architecture has a number of dependencies such as

- Services and processes—This dependency includes the services provided by the organization, the customers, core processes, value chain, process cuts (insourcing, outsourcing), work packages, and tasks involved in the organization. Implementation of Big Data solutions will have an impact on the services and processes of the organization. Services and processes need to be mapped to each other so that Big Data solutions can be integrated into EA. In services, a Big Data solution will impact client servicing such as customer relationship management (CRM), interactions and dependencies with other systems such as order entry/order management (OE/OM), factories such as cash/payment transaction factory and security transaction factory, cash accounts, custody accounts, wealth management, client reporting, and the way business administration works within the organization. It may also have an impact on other service providers that are collaborating with the organization implementing a Big Data solution. In process flows the organization needs to see how client data is being administered so that order cancellations do not occur due to incorrect client data.

- Component interaction—The software application interacts with a number of components such as order management, CRM, portfolio management, human resources and payroll, and reporting. There could be a case of data overlap. Portfolio management can also have the same data as CRM. A Big Data solution will impact many components in the organization such as order management and CRM. For example, Big Data is providing supplier networks with greater data accuracy, clarity, and insights, leading to more contextual intelligence shared across supply chains. Big Data technologies are getting beyond the constraints of legacy enterprise resource planning (ERP) and supply chain management (SCM) systems. For manufacturers whose business models are based on rapid product lifecycles and speed, legacy ERP systems are a bottleneck. Designed for delivering order, shipment, and transactional data, these systems aren't capable of scaling to meet the challenges supply chains face today. Some of the examples are Big Data and advanced analytics are being integrated into optimization tools, demand forecasting, integrated business planning and supplier collaboration, and risk analytics at a quickening pace for delivering orders and shipments.

- Functional cluster and architecture—This deals with data storage and process execution. Big Data solutions will impact the way applications and services are configured as resources on the cluster.

- Business components and applications—This includes the existing systems in the organization and what systems will be required in future. The business applications could be developed in-house or they could be packaged or bespoke

applications. These applications need to be integrated to Big Data solutions. The integration itself is a challenge.
- Value propositions, capabilities, and requirements—This focuses on client experience, organizations involved, and products and services supplied to provide consistent quality over time and automation of the processes. A Big Data solution will have an impact on business value propositions, solution/system capabilities, and system architecture requirements.
- Guiding principles—This dependency includes strategic principles such as package usage, business principles such as in-/outsourcing, technical principles such as platform technology, architecture principles such as service architecture, and data redundancy. A Big Data solution will impact strategic principles, business principles, technical principles, and architecture principles.

Application architecture within organizations need to integrate Big Data stores, which could be HBase, NFS, or HDFS. Figure 6.2 shows an overview of the impact of Big Data solutions on application architecture. An integration layer is required. An organization needs to clearly identify which applications can/should be integrated with Big Data solutions. There could be a possibility that not all applications can be integrated with Big Data solutions.

Big Data sources could be from, for example, e-commerce and market intelligence such as search and user logs, it could be from e-government and politics such as government information and services, or it could be from science and technology such as sensor and network content.

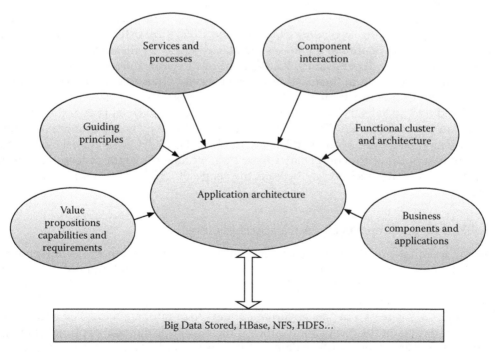

FIGURE 6.2
Big Data solutions on application architecture.

Existing application architecture have focused efforts on the data that is readily structured and thereby easily analyzed using standard tools. The very basic nature of Big Data is unstructured and hence it will have an impact on application architecture.

6.4.2 Big Data and Impacts on EA Technology Architecture

The technology architecture describes the hardware, software, and infrastructure environment that is required to support the development and host the deployment of the application components described in the application architecture. Big Data introduces new technologies in the organization that may not have been in the organization previously. There will be a need for a new type of storage that can support the Big Data processing needs. Applications with service-oriented EA in the cloud are emerging and will shape future trends in technology.

According to Zimmerman et al. (2013), technology domains are based on existing technology, hardware, and physical infrastructure categories. Big Data applications span a broad range of domains that require changes in technology domain of the organization. Expected technology domains are service-oriented enterprise architectures for services and cloud computing, and related service-oriented technologies and management. Ross, Weil, and Robertson (2006) suggest that the technological impact of Big Data from cloud vision has multiple aspects. Organizations are extending their technological capabilities to systematically managing their business operating model by developing and managing enterprise information architecture as the architectural part of IT governance.

Technology platforms include Mainframe, Linux, and Microsoft. Big Data solutions need to be hosted on a technology platform. Organizations need to assess the existing technology platform for Big Data solutions. Integration patterns include enterprise service bus and message queuing web services (SOAP and REST). Persistent data storage are the data artifacts such as relational databases, database tables, flat files, xml data stores, and message queues that hold persistent data. With the rise of personalized and social services, restructuring is occurring in the existing Internet service environment. From the Internet web service environment that focused on searching/portal sites, there is a demand for personalized and social services in the whole service area, such as telecommunications, gaming, and music shopping. This is why scale-out technology is becoming more important than scale-up storage. Moreover, DZone (2014) in its "NOSQL Technical Comparison Report" points out that for complicated functions, storage size, and processing requirements, data processing technology beyond the scope of OLTP is becoming increasingly important.

6.4.3 Big Data and Impacts on EA Data Architecture

According to Panahy et al. (2013), behind any information management lies the core doctrines of data quality, data governance, and metadata management along with considerations for privacy and legal concerns. Big Data needs to be integrated into the EIL and not seen as a standalone effort.

Thomas (2008) suggests that data governance helps an organization to take a holistic view and to manage data in the context of business process, and to support application integration needs. Different components of data architecture include data modeling, data design, and data delivery architecture. Data architecture requires information about master and reference data management, data warehousing business intelligence, transaction data management, structured technical data management, unstructured data management, metadata, analytical data, documents and contents, historical data, temporarily data, and Big Data analytics. All these data sources need to be organized in an information framework that can support data governance and data.

The key element of organizational structure is the business functions. Organizations need to know the kind of data required, captured, acquired, stored, and analyzed for business functions such as marketing, sales, supply chain, manufacturing, human resources, strategy making, finance, and information technology. Data is an asset to the organization. This asset must be managed to ensure competitive advantage and to reduce the complexity of the asset management in the organization. According to Russom (2012) and Hoffer, Prescott, and Topi (2012), information goals and principles are top priority for any organization, but they must be supported by data governance and information asset planning.

So while constructing the roadmap of information management framework we require data governance, information asset planning, data quality and management, data integration, information life cycle management, metadata management, data models and taxonomies, and information about master and reference data management, data warehousing business intelligence, transaction data management, structured technical data management, unstructured data management, metadata, analytical data, documents and contents, historical data, temporal data, and Big Data analytics. Figure 6.3 shows an EA data management framework.

In a high information technology-consuming context such as Big Data solution, data governance and data asset planning should be shown in the EA. Data governance and data asset planning remove risk of bad operational/transactional/in-motion data, which remove the risk of bad intelligence, reporting, and poor decision making.

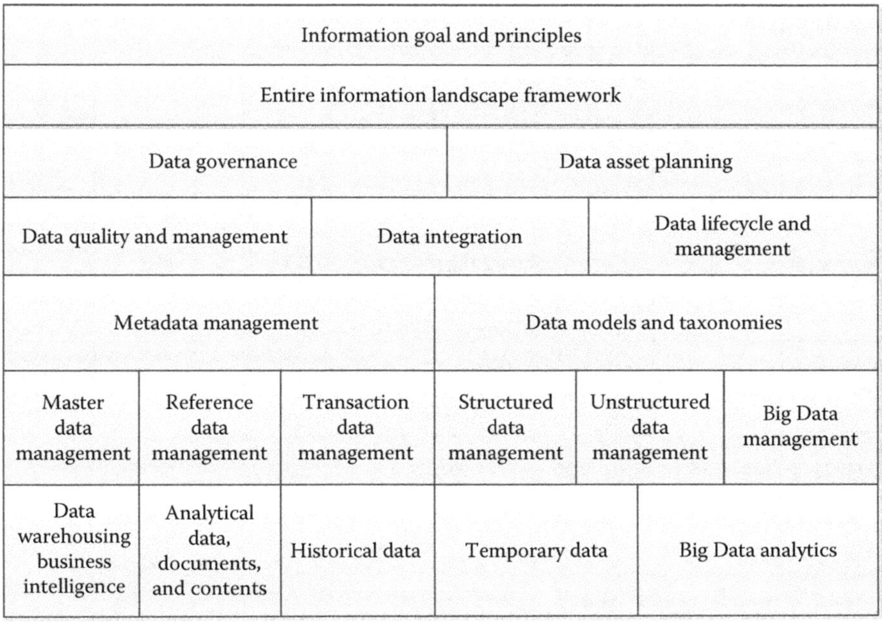

Information goal and principles					
Entire information landscape framework					
Data governance			Data asset planning		
Data quality and management		Data integration		Data lifecycle and management	
Metadata management			Data models and taxonomies		
Master data management	Reference data management	Transaction data management	Structured data management	Unstructured data management	Big Data management
Data warehousing business intelligence	Analytical data, documents, and contents	Historical data	Temporary data	Big Data analytics	

FIGURE 6.3
EA data management framework.

The following are the internal and external sources of Big Data that need to be integrated to the Big Data storage, processing, and analyzing platform as shown in Figure 6.4.

- Open data—A key source of data from governments and private institutions. Open relates to how accessible a data set is in terms of allowing others to use it without restriction.
- Internal enterprise data—Data that is collected by an organization about its own systems and processes. This data may not be digital, can consist of both quantitative and qualitative information, and can also be anonymized. A bank using anonymized customer transaction records to predict and proactively refill its ATMs is an example of this type of data.
- Little data—PwC (2014) suggests that small businesses can also make use of data analytics across data that they have about their own business, similar to Big Data, but on a smaller scale.
- My data—According to PwC (2014), internal data about a particular organization or individual is typically held securely with strict rules regarding access; for example, a hospital holding an individual's health records for its healthcare professionals, which would also allow them to diagnose the patient on the basis of other aggregate data on medical conditions.

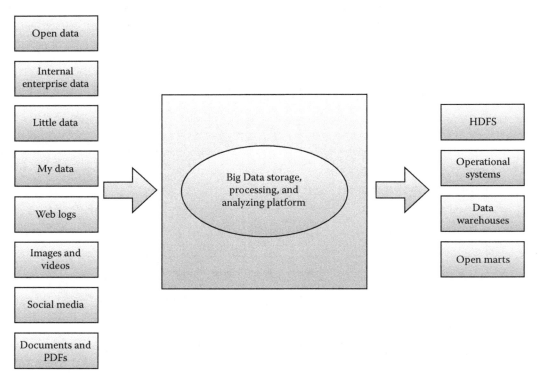

FIGURE 6.4
Integrating Big Data sources.

Big Data and Its Impact on Enterprise Architecture　　　　121

- Web logs—Web logs are personal web pages written in chronological order and maintained through specific software that helps their administration. A web log, sometimes written as web log or weblog, is a website that consists of a series of entries arranged in reverse chronological order, often updated frequently with new information about particular topics.
- Images and videos—Today, images and image sequences (videos) make up about 80% of all corporate and public unstructured Big Data. As growth of unstructured data increases, analytical systems must assimilate and interpret images and videos as well as they interpret structured data such as text and numbers.
- Social Media—Social media are websites and applications that enable users to create and share content or to participate in social networking.
- Documents and PDFs—Portable Document Format (PDF) is a file format that has captured all the elements of a printed document as an electronic image.

Once the Big Data, which is unstructured data, is stored, processed, and analyzed, it can be stored in HDFS, operational systems, data warehouses, and data marts from where data can be used for business intelligence, reporting, OLAP, ad-hoc reporting, and modeling.

6.4.4 Big Data and Impacts on EA Business Architecture

According to the OMG Business Architecture Special Interest Group (2010), business architecture is defined as "a blueprint of the enterprise that provides a common understanding of the organization and is used to align strategic objectives and tactical demands." Business problems can be categorized into types of Big Data problems. This categorization could be used to identify proper fit of Big Data Solutions. Table 6.1 lists common business problems and assigns a Big Data type to each.

Categorizing the Big Data type helps in understanding the characteristics of Big Data and the technologies associated with it. The Big Data type allows the organization to understand its data categories (transaction data, historical data, or master data, for example), the frequency at which data will be made available, how the data needs to be processed (ad hoc query on the data for example), and whether the processing must take place in real time, near real time, or in batch mode.

TABLE 6.1

Big Data Types and Business Problems

Application	Business Problem	Big Data Type
E-commerce and market intelligence	Sentiment analyses	Web and social data
E-government and politics, defense	Policy and regulation analyses	Web and social data, biometrics
Science and technology	Utilities: predict power consumption	Machine-generated data
Customer service	Call monitoring	Human generated
Retail	Personalized messaging based on facial recognition and social media	Web and social data, biometrics
Healthcare	Fraud detection, help plan your diet, using mobile technology to help us try and live healthier lifestyles	Machine generated, transaction data, human generated

6.5 Summary

Data continues a massive expansion in scale, diversity, and complexity. Data underpins activities in all sectors of society. To deal with these, Big Data solutions are available and are now fairly commonplace in large organizations. Organizations want to store, process, and analyze Big Data for intelligent decision making to get the competitive advantage. Implementing a Big Data solution typically begins as part of an information technology project that will extract, store, and analyze large amounts of data in order to get competitive advantage.

New ways of working with Big Data has an impact on technology infrastructure components and data architectures. Since most data is directly generated in digital format today these impacts and changes must be captured by an organization's EA for conducting enterprise analysis, design, planning, and implementation, using a holistic approach at all times, for the successful development and execution of organizational strategy.

It is well understood that at present Big Data solutions are evolving and all organizations are using Big Data as a buzzword without an understanding of the impact of using Big Data solutions. Organizations need to prepare themselves for Big Data integration. The EIL deals with the users, technology, data landscape, and applications. These are in turn based on business architecture, application architecture, technology architecture, and information architecture, all of which are subsets of their EA.

References

Chen, H., Chiang, R., and Storey, V. 2012. "Business Intelligence and Analytics: From Big Data to Big Impact." *MIS Quarterly* 36(4): 1165–1188.

Computing Community Consortium. 2011. Advancing Discovery in Science and Engineering.

Duffy Marsan, C. 2010. "Government Transparency: Single Pool of Storage Could Save Money and Allow Better Access." First Amendment Coalition, August.

Dumbill, E., and Mohin, S. 2013. "Opportunities at the Intersection of Health and Data." *Big Data* 1(3): 115–116.

DZone. 2014. "NoSQL Technical Comparison Report."

Federation of Enterprise Architecture Professional Organizations. 2013. "A Common Perspective on Enterprise Architecture."

Free Software Foundation. 2014. "Free Software Is a Matter of Liberty, Not Price."

Gruman, G. 2010. "Tapping into the Power of Big Data." *Technology Forecast: Making Sense of Big Data*, 3: 4–13. Accessed September 14, 2013. http://www.pwc.com/us/en/technology-forcast/2010/issue3/index.html.

Hoffer, J. A., Prescott, M. B., and Topi, H. 2012. *Modern Database Management*, 10th ed. Prentice Hall, Upper Saddle River, NJ.

IBM. 2014. "What is the Hadoop Distributed File System (HDFS)?" ibm.com.

Jha, S., Jha, M., O'Brien, L., and Wells, M. 2014. "Integrating Legacy System into Big Data Solutions: Time to Make the Change." Asia Pacific Working Conference on CSE 2014, Plantation Island, Nadi, Fiji, November 4–5.

Laney, D. 2001. "3D Data Management: Controlling Data Volume, Velocity, and Variety." Meta Group Inc. http://blogs.gartner.

Lapkin, A., Allega, P., Burke, B., Burton, B., Scott Bittler, R., Handler, R. A., James, G. A. et al. 2008. "Gartner Clarifies the Definition of the Term Enterprise Architecture." Gartner Research, August 12.

Lapkin, A., and Young, C. M. 2011. "The Management Nexus: Closing the Gap Between Strategy and Execution." Gartner.

Liebowitz, J. 2013. *Big Data and Business Analytics*. CRC Press, Boca Raton, FL.

Manyika, J., Chui, M., Brown, B., Bughin, J., Dobbs, R., Roxburgh, C., and Hung Byers, A. 2011. "Big Data: The Next Frontier for Innovation, Competition, and Productivity." McKinsey Global Institute.

Mayer-Schönberger, V., and Cukier, K. 2013. *Big Data: A Revolution That Will Transform How We Live, Work and Think*. John Murray, London.

OMG Business Architecture Special Interest Group. 2008. "What Is Business Architecture?" Accessed January 14, 2015. bawg.omg.org.

The Open Group Architecture Framework (TOGAF). 2014. "Enterprise Architecture Profile." Accessed November 14, 2014. http://www.togaf-modeling.org/models/application-architecture-menu.html.

Oracle. 2013. "Information Management and Big Data: A Reference Architecture." White paper.

Panahy, S., Sidi, F., Suriani, L., Jabar, M. A., Ibrahim, H., and Mustapha, A. 2013. "A Framework to Construct Data Quality Dimensions Relationships." *Indian Journal of Science and Technology* 6(5): 4422–4431.

Porter, M. E. 2008. "The Five Competitive Forces That Shape Strategy." *Harvard Business Review*, January, 79–93.

PwC. 2014. "Deciding with Data: How Data-Driven Innovation Is Fuelling Australia's Economic Growth." Accessed January 19, 2015. http://www.pwc.com.au/consulting/assets/publications/Data-drive-innovation-Sep14.pdf.

Ross, J. W., Weil, P., and Robertson, D. 2006. *Enterprise Architecture as Strategy: Creating a Foundation for Business Execution*. Harvard Business School Press, Boston.

Russom, P. 2012. "Seven Reasons Why Master Data Management Needs Data Governance." TDWI Checklist Report, August.

Salim, S. E. 2014. "Service Oriented Enterprise Architecture for Processing Big Data Applications in Cloud." *International Journal of Engineering Sciences and Research Technology* 3(6): 647–655.

Thomas, G. 2008. "Data Governance with a Focus on Information Quality." The MIT 2008 Information Quality Industry Symposium, July 16–17.

Zimmermann, A., Pretz, M., Zimmermann, G., Firesmith, D. G., and Petrov, I. 2013. "Towards Service-oriented Enterprise Architectures for Big Data Applications in the Cloud." 17th IEEE International Enterprise Distributed Object Computing Conference Workshops, Vancouver, Canada, September 9–13.

Authors

Meena Jha has over 20 years of experience in teaching and research in software engineering. She is a faculty member at Central Queensland University, Sydney, Australia. Her research interests include Big Data, enterprise architecture, legacy modernization, enterprise systems, and software architecture. She earned a BTech and MTech at Birla Institute of Technology, Mesra, Ranchi, India, and a PhD at the University of New South Wales, Sydney, Australia. She is a member of IEEE and the IEEE Computer Society Australia.

Sanjay Jha has over 25 years of experience in systems engineering, systems information in mining industries, computer networking and security, and computer-aided design and manufacturing to name few. He teaches at Central Queensland University, Sydney, Australia. His research interests include Big Data, enterprise architecture, data security, and enterprise systems. He earned a BTech and MBA at the Birla Institute of Technology, Mesra, Ranchi, India. He is a member of IEEE, the IEEE Computer Society, and the Australian Computer Society (ACS) Australia.

Liam O'Brien has over 25 years of experience in research and development in software engineering. He is a solution architect at the Australian Department of Immigration and Border Protection, and previously he was a solution architect at Geoscience Australia, chief software architect at CSIRO, and a principal researcher at NICTA's e-Government Initiative researching service-oriented architecture (SOA), service migration, service integration, scoping of SOA, and cost and effort estimation. He earned a BSc and PhD and is a member of the Service Science Society Australia.

7

Supportive Architectural Analysis for Big Data

Utkarsh Sharma and Robin Singh Bhadoria

CONTENTS

7.1 Introduction 126
    7.1.1 Data Model 127
        7.1.1.1 Variety 127
        7.1.1.2 Volume 128
        7.1.1.3 Velocity 128
7.2 Need for Big Data Infrastructure 129
    7.2.1 Ideal Change in Big Data 129
    7.2.2 Research Communities and Specific Scientific Data Infrastructure
        Requirements 130
    7.2.3 General Scientific Data Infrastructure Requirements 131
7.3 Architectural Epigrammatic for Analysis of Big Data 131
7.4 Scientific Data Infrastructure Architectural Model 136
7.5 Performance Parametric Considerations for Big Data Architecture 137
    7.5.1 Sizing of Clustering 137
    7.5.2 MapReduce Algorithm 138
    7.5.3 Input Data Set 138
    7.5.4 Data Node 138
    7.5.5 Data Locality 138
    7.5.6 Concurrent Activity 138
    7.5.7 Network Considerations 139
7.6 Capacity and Scalability Consideration for Big Data Architecture 139
    7.6.1 CPU 139
    7.6.2 Memory 139
    7.6.3 Disk 140
    7.6.4 Network 140
7.7 Conclusion 140
References 140
Authors 141

ABSTRACT The term Big Data was coined because of the huge data sets available with a large disparate complex structure for processing, analyzing, and recognizing for further results or processes. Big Data analytics deals with research into massive amounts of data to reveal hidden information and secret correlations. With the help of these useful and deeper insights into the data, companies and organizations can overpower their competitors. This is the reason why the research in this field is gaining interest day by day and therefore it needs to be carried out more carefully and accurately. This chapter deals with the architectural perspective for Big Data, content of Big Data samples, methods, scopes, advantages, and challenges.

125

7.1 Introduction

In today's world the use of enormous data, produced by several emerging applications, such as social networking, microblogging sites, and other data-centric sites, has created the concept of Big Data. Characterization of Big Data is done on the basis of continuously evolving volumes of different data types (i.e., unstructured, semistructured, and structured) from high-speed-generating sources capable of generating data at a very high rate (e.g., web logs of websites). This heavy amount of data produces new opportunities for data-related analysis such as product ranking, review analysis, and fraud detection.

Currently, the research and scientific community showed great interest in addressing the challenges in analyzing, accessing, and storing this Big Data. Several products are already available in the market to support this storage and processing. The main working of these tools is parallel database management system.

Manyika et al. (2011) stated that Big Data refers to data sets whose size is beyond the ability of typical database software tools to capture, store, manage, and analyze. Therefore the concept of Big Data is totally dependent on the current data processing and storage capabilities available at any time. Gordon Moore, cofounder of Intel, stated in the famous Moore's law, that processor speeds or overall processing power for computers will double every two years or in other words the number of transistors on an affordable CPU will double every 2 years. Several explanations are available that show that the amount of data considered as big is not actually that big nowadays. According to Jacobs (2009), in the 1980s 100 GB of data was considered big. In today's time a personal computer can have more than that capacity. The amount of data ranging from terrabytes (1024 GB) to petabytes (1024 TB) to exabytes (1024 PB) can be assumed as big nowadays. Generally Big Data is identified by three V's: volume, velocity, and variety, as stated by the Gartner Group (Gartner, Inc. 2011). Sometimes veracity and value are also considered characteristics by some researchers.

Several sectors and industries felt the need to acquire important information from the use of Big Data. There are several reports that show the massive impact of Big Data on the corporate world; for example, Sears Holding Corporation and Wal-Mart stores use Big Data databases for marketing help, according to King and Rosenbush (2013). New reserves of oil and gas were searched by Chevron Corporation using Big Data processing on seismic data. Big Data also proved valuable to the medical field; a new healthcare system was developed using the data on the care of hundreds of thousands of patients and used it to enhance the treatment of new patients.

Governments also seem to be interested in the benefits of analysis of Big Data and finding solutions to some of the complex nationwide problems and challenges spreading across the field of science and engineering. New career opportunities can also emerge from research in Big Data such as data scientists, data visualizers, data architects, data engineers and operators, and data architects. Companies can increase their benefits by incorporating important leading roles such as chief data officer and chief analytics officer. Current systems such as traditional database management systems are not suitable for completely handling the aspects of Big Data, for example, some can handle the volume but not the velocity, and some can handle the velocity but not the variety.

As time evolves, the demand for evaluating and comparing the performance and costing aspects of these tools will rise. But sadly there is no such architecture or model to do such a thing on Big Data. This situation was dealt with earlier with the database architecture in the 20th century and the result was an architecture where companies developed their

Supportive Architectural Analysis for Big Data

own set of benchmarks and biased standards for evaluating performance. The goal of such structure was just to fulfill the demands of the corporate organizations and giving no importance to the technical aspects that can be verified. The same phenomenon is now carried out by the organizations for Big Data architecture.

Organizations may come up with their own suitable architectures, called "architecture specials," that were particularly designed for performance improvement for any specific benchmark having very few applications to other real-world applications. As a result of this variance in the standards used by different organizations, benchmark consortia such as the Standard Performance Corporation (SPEC) and the Transaction Processing Performance Council (TPC) were founded. As time progressed these standards evolved and reformed into TPC-A, TPC-C, and TPC-D.

Big Data architecture that can be accepted by all industry standards must be a model to cover up all the major concerns of the Big Data environment including the three V's of Big Data: (1) volume (data from social media, information from sensors); (2) velocity (RIFD tags, sensors, and smart metering produce the need of handling torrents of data); and (3) variety (structured numeric data, unstructured text documents, video, audio).

7.1.1 Data Model

Volume, variety, and velocity are the three major concerns of any Big Data system. Big Data systems always need to handle a huge amount of data, sometimes in the range of hundreds of exabytes (Ghazal et al. 2013). In our discussion we consider the volume aspect about data scaling. By variety we mean the capabilities to manage heterogeneous types of data like unstructured, semistructured, and structured data. In our model we incorporate all types of data into a single entity, which will suffice our requirements of variety. The velocity part of Big Data is mainly concerned with how frequent the data modification and retrieval is performed, commonly referred as extraction, transformation, and load (ETL). A Big Data system is different from the common business operation database where data is updated very rarely or remain static most of the time. In the case of Big Data, the system must be capable of staying current all the time.

All the models of Big Data have been constructed around the 3 V's of Big Data. Scale factors are used to scale data up to petabytes of data in the data generators for addressing the volume issue. Different sources of data are used for maintaining variety. Updating and refreshing data is done periodically to maintain the velocity (Ghazal et al. 2013).

7.1.1.1 Variety

Figure 7.1 shows the general architecture for the data model and the benchmark components, namely, structured data, semistructured data, and unstructured data, along with the relationship between them. Recently TPC published the TPC-DS benchmark from which we adapted the structured components of Big Data architecture (Wang et al. 2014). Semistructured and unstructured data have more importance for analysis in the field of Big Data. In TPC-DS mostly all the tables leaving some exceptions are used by explained Big Data architecture; giving more emphasis on web sales and stores, which contains only structured data. The data in these tables covers all information regarding the purchases done in stores and over the web. Other tables contain related information regarding items offered by the retailer, customer info having all the necessary records about clients, all other data containing websites used by customers, web page and website describing data, and all associated tables. A new table called item market prices is also added to facilitate

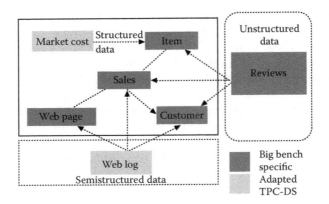

FIGURE 7.1
Big Data architecture for data model.

our functional design. This new table will keep the data for the comparison point of view of the user, so that the online comparison done by different users can also be provided.

The web log files containing the click streams are considered as a part of semistructured data. A link to the structured area containing items, web pages, online sales, customer, and associated dimensions has to be provided, because some of the clicks also result in sales. However, most of the clicks received are for the browsing activities not resulting in sales. The focus of these clicks is mainly on items and only concern registered users or guests. The Apache logs format is retained for the clicks. Run-time processing or late binding can be done for the web logs and then can be stored into a structured table/file.

7.1.1.2 Volume

The size of the tables involved will become the base for the size of the structured area, in accordance to a well-defined and standard quantity similar to the scale factor in TPC-DS. This scale factor will also affect the size of the semistructured and unstructured area. Therefore there will be complete uniformity for the size of the complete data set based on a single scale factor and can be determined and predicted for any volume. Consider the item market price table; the price from four different competitors is stored for each item. Thus, item market price has a size of

$$|\text{item}| \times 4$$

The buyers (making entries in web sales) and the visitors who do not end up buying make the clicks that affect the size of web logs. A single line item is represented by each row in web sales, thus the number of clicks to make a sale and the number of clicks per item will make the number of clicks per sale.

7.1.1.3 Velocity

In the life cycle of a Big Data system an integral part is the process of periodically refreshing the data. There are mainly three steps in the production data refresh process: (1) extraction of data, (2) transformation of data, and (3) data load. On multiple operational systems and ancillary data sources the data extraction step is executed consisting of numerous separate extraction operations. If we are running a Big Data application then it is not possibly necessary that the full list of these operational data sources resides on the same system, thus the metric that will be the result of measurement of data extraction performance may not be meaningful and appropriate to the scope of this benchmark. Therefore, generated files are in the form in which we represent data extract steps of the Big Data architecture.

The periodic refresh model for the tables in Big Data architecture have two aspects: (1) how much data the refresh process should include and (2) the interval of time for the periodic refreshing to occur. Both of these aspects are applicable to the structured, semi-structured, and the unstructured data.

7.2 Need for Big Data Infrastructure

7.2.1 Ideal Change in Big Data

Being a new technology driver, Big Data needs to remodel a number of infrastructure components, solutions, and processes to handle the following common challenges:

- Different research instruments and sensors are producing an enormous amount of data, which is growing exponentially.
- To ensure research continuity and cross-disciplinary collaboration we need to consolidate e-infrastructures as continuous research platforms, and also a governance model with delivering or offering persistent services has to be there.

The ideal change in modern e-sciences because of recent advancements in general information and communication technologies and Big Data technologies can be characterized by the following features:

- To make all e-science processes such as data storing, collection, classification, indexing and other components of the general data provenance and curation fully automated.
- Conversion into digital form of all processes, events, and products by means of multidimensional, multifaceted measurements, control, and monitoring; to digitize existing artifacts and other contents.
- To facilitate secondary research, mainly to reuse the initial and published research data with necessary data repurposing.
- For researchers to make available the global data and access over the network, including public access to scientific data.
- To allow fast infrastructure and service composition, and provisioning on demand for specific research projects and tasks there should exist necessary infrastructure components and management tools.
- To make sure secure operation of the complex research infrastructures and scientific instruments are highly advanced security and access control technologies that will allow creating a threat-proof, secure environment for cooperating groups and individual researchers.

The scientific data infrastructure (SDI) to be developed in the future should explore the benefit of the data storage/preservation, aggregation, and provenance, and support the whole data lifecycle in a large scale and during a long/unlimited period of time (Demchenko et al. 2012). Data security (confidentiality, integrity, availability, and accountability) and data ownership protection must be ensured by this infrastructure. There must be a trust on the SDI by the researchers to process their data on the SDI facilities and be ensured that their result of processing and stored research data are protected from nonauthorized access. Because of the distributed remote character of SDI, which is spanning over multiple countries having their own local policies, the issue of privacy is also raised. This is the task of another important component of SDI, the access control and accounting infrastructure (ACAI).

7.2.2 Research Communities and Specific Scientific Data Infrastructure Requirements

To analyze particular requirements for future SDIs to handle Big Data challenges, a short overview of some research infrastructures and communities, specially the ones defined for the European Research Area (ERA), is helpful. Requirements and practices of scientific communities analyzed by the existing studies of European e-infrastructures include those undertaken by the UK Future Internet Strategy Group Report, European Grid Infrastructure (EGI) Strategy Report, SIENA Project, and EIROforum Federated Identity Management Workshop (Demchenko et al. 2012).

It was also pointed out in the project the high-energy physics community that a huge amount of data, large number of researchers, and unique expensive instruments are generated and need to be processed continuously. The operational Worldwide LHC Computing Grid (WLCG) is also managed by this community, which supports the whole scientific data life cycle, and manages and accesses data, and protects its integrity (Demchenko et al. 2012).

In the evolution of European e-infrastructures, WLCG was an important step that is currently serving various scientific communities in Europe and internationally. The European and worldwide infrastructure for High Energy Physics (HEP) and other communities is managed by EGI cooperation. Analytical and low-energy physics and material science is characterized by short experiments, projects, and a highly dynamic user community. It requires advanced data management infrastructure and highly dynamic supporting infrastructure to allow distributed processing and wide data access.

Earth science and environmental community projects target on the data acquisition. As the data collected by these projects comprises data from land, sea, air, and space and in huge quantity, it requires an ever-increasing amount of storage and computing power. While tracking data use and keeping integrity, the SDI requires highly reliable suitable access control to huge data sets, policy-based data filtering, and enforcement of regional issues. Life sciences have general focus on drug development, new species identification, health, and new instrument development. All this work requires great computing power, storage capacity, data sharing, and collaboration.

Some of the data contains privacy issues such as biomedical data (healthcare) and must be handled according to the European policy on personal data processing. While some of the projects and communities are characterized by multilateral and collaborative work between researchers from all over the world, for this type of project a collaborative environment is needed to share data, research results, and collectively evaluate results.

Supportive Architectural Analysis for Big Data

7.2.3 General Scientific Data Infrastructure Requirements

On the basis of overview given above we can deduce the following necessary infrastructure requirements for the SDI for evolving Big Data science:

- It should be supportive for large data volumes produced at high speed in long-running experiments.
- Data accountability, confidentiality, integrity.
- Multitier interlinked data replication and distribution.
- Infrastructure provisioning on demand to facilitate data sets and scientific workflow.
- It should support dynamic user group creation and management, virtual scientific communities, and federated identity management.
- Secured trusted environment for data processing and storage.
- Binding of policies of data to ensure confidentiality, privacy, and intellectual property rights.

7.3 Architectural Epigrammatic for Analysis of Big Data

The present economy is basically driven by the globalization and the Internet, and their effect is multiplied by social networks and mobile computing; because of this Big Data is now an enterprise concern. If an organization has the capability to analyze, capture, and process Big Data, then it can increase the company's ability to respond to the dynamic market conditions and customer needs helping it to gain a better competitive advantage. The architecture for Big Data in presented in Figure 7.2.

The architecture of the client level consists of a distributed processing framework, distributed file system, and a NoSQL (Not Only SQL) database (Chan 2013). NoSQL databases work well with unrelated data because they are not SQL based, nonrelational, and store data in key-value pairs. A highly scalable, distributed data storage is provided by NoSQL for Big Data. The taxonomy of NoSQL includes ordered key-value store, key-value cache, key-value store, wide columnar store, eventually consistent key-value store, tuple store, and object database. Apache HBase is a popular example of a NoSQL database. Apache HBase provides random, real-time read/write access to Big Data. It is a distributed, column-oriented store, versioned, open source database. The distributed key-value design of the Oracle NoSQL database makes it capable of providing scalable, highly reliable, and available data storage across a configurable set of systems.

In the next layers there will be a distributed file system with scalability as a main feature, and a distributed processing framework that divides the computation and distributes it over large clusters so it can handle large volumes of data. File systems serviced by the Internet include Amazon Simple Storage Service, Google File System, and the open source Hadoop Distributed File System. The Apache Hadoop is a popular platform. For distributed processing of huge data sets across groups of computers, the Apache Hadoop framework is used and also is designed to multiply itself from a few servers to hundreds of machines, each providing local storage and computing. The two main components of Hadoop system

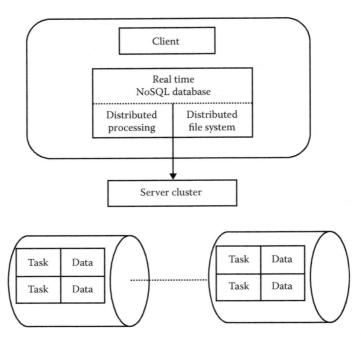

FIGURE 7.2
Big Data architecture.

are MapReduce and the Hadoop Distributed File System (HDFS). Functionalities of HDFS include distributing data files over big server clusters and providing large-throughput access to large data sets. Parallel processing of large data sets is done by the distributed processing framework MapReduce. It divides and distributes the computing tasks to every server in the cluster and collects the results.

Google's data storage system is the actual inspiration behind the creation of Hadoop which stores data in the form of BigTable (Bakshi 2012). Hadoop is an open source platform and Java-based framework. It does not work as a replacement to the warehouse, database, or ETL strategy. Hadoop includes data storage platforms, distributed file system, analytics, and a separate layer for parallel computation and workflow management. Real-time complex event processing cannot be performed on Hadoop. The task of HDFS is to connect the file systems of many input and output data nodes into a single big file system, as it runs through the nodes in a Hadoop cluster (Sagirogulu and Sinanc 2013). The services provided by Hadoop are (Ferguson 2012)

- Storing data on the clusters with the help of HDFS, a highly fault-tolerant distributed file system
- Distributed processing on clusters by MapReduce, a powerful parallel programming technique
- A distributed, scalable database HBase, for random read/write access
- For analyzing data sets that occur at a high-level language, a high-level data processing system called Hive
- A tool for transferring data between Hadoop and relational databases, Sqoop
- A system for serialization of data called Avro

Supportive Architectural Analysis for Big Data

- A workflow for Hadoop jobs that are dependent called Oozie
- For monitoring of distributed systems, a Hadoop subproject as data accumulation system called Chukwa
- A distributed and reliable streaming log collection called Flume
- For providing distributed synchronization and group services, a centralized service called ZooKeeper

High Performance Computing Cluster (HPCC) Systems is an open source, distributed data intensive computing platform for providing data workflow management services. The data model for HPCC is defined by the user unlike with Hadoop (Sagirogulu and Sinanc 2013). The complex problems can be easily stated with a high level ECL basis. It is ensured by HPCC that the nodes are processed in parallel and ECL is executed at the maximum elapsed time. The advantage of HPCC is that it does not require any third party tool like RDMS, GreenPlum, Cassandra, or Oozie. The components of HPCC are

- Thor, which is HPCC's data refinery, is a parallel ETL engine that provides batch-oriented data manipulation and enables data integration on a large scale.
- Roxie, which is HPCC's data delivery engine, is a highly parallel, ultra fast, high throughput, low latency, structured query response engine and allows efficient multiuser retrieval of data.
- Enterprise Control Language (ECL) has automatic synchronization of all algorithms, automatically distributes the workload between nodes, develops an extensible machine learning library, and is a simple to understand programming language modified for Big Data query transactions and operations.

In the server level of architecture of Big Data parallel computing, platforms are there that can handle the associated speed and volume. The three most important parallel computing options are high-performance computing (HPC), clusters or grids, and massively parallel processing. Clusters or grids are an example of parallel and distributed systems, a collection of interconnected stand-alone computers processing together as a single unit of computation resource composed in a cluster along with a grid that enables the selection, sharing, and dynamically aggregation at runtime of geographically distributed autonomous resources.

Client machines and clusters of loosely coupled servers of commodity complete the architecture for Hadoop, that will serve as MapReduce distributed data processing and the HDFS distributed data storage. In a Hadoop deployment, there are three main categories of machine roles consisting of master nodes, slave nodes, and client machine. Client machine has the following responsibilities: submit MapReduce job, retrieve the result of the job when it is finished, and load data into clusters. Master nodes are of two types: MapReduce nodes and HDFS nodes. In the HDFS nodes there are name nodes, whose task is to keep the directory of every file in the HDFS system. The jobs are further submitted to MapReduce nodes by the client application, containing job trackers that assign MapReduce tasks to the slave nodes.

After consulting the name nodes the job tracker determines the location of the data node in which the data resides, and then the task tracker is assigned a task that is in the same node, which can execute the task. HDFS, being a distributed file system, works good for the storage of large files, but it fails when fast individual record lookup is required. However HBase, built over the HDFS, provides fast record updates and lookups. Real-time, random read/write access to Big Data is provided by Apache HBase. The original design of HDFS was for high-throughput high-latency batch analytic systems like MapReduce, but HBase modified its design and improved it to work for real-time systems with low-latency performance. In this architecture a scalable fault-tolerant distributed data storage is provided by Hadoop HDFS for Big Data, distributed processing with fault-tolerance over large data sets across the Hadoop clusters is provided by Hadoop MapReduce, and real-time random access to Big Data is provided by HBase (Chan 2013). Figure 7.3 shows the Hadoop architecture.

The most popular form of large-scale parallel computers is clusters of commodity servers, yet they are not suitable for internode-dependent general-purpose application programming. A runtime system is proposed to address internode communication, which is called Distributed Software Multi-threaded Transactional memory (DSMTX). Massively parallel processing (MPP) is another option for a parallel computing platform. MPP is a combination of memory, storage, and computation to create a platform. In an MPP, the nodes are tightly interconnected by dedicated networking with high speed, which allows high-speed processor collaboration.

Big Data has not made the concept of data warehousing obsolete but still Big Data analytics of huge volumes of structured data use data warehousing as viable technology. Furthermore, there is some link between Hadoop-type Big Data architecture and data warehousing. Unstructured data such as data from social media and web applications, M2M devices, and sensors can be stored in Hadoop and be MapReduced later for meaningful insight. The data warehouse can then be integrated with the MapReduced data for further analytic processing.

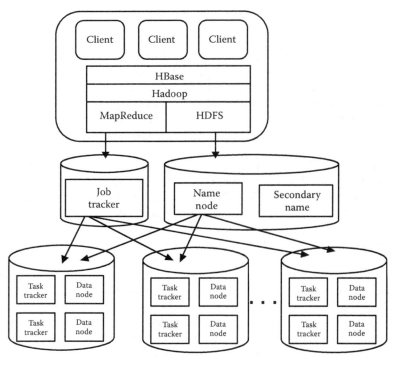

FIGURE 7.3
HBase clustering architecture in Big Data.

Conversely, for complex Hadoop jobs, the data warehouse can be a data source, simultaneously taking benefit of the heavy parallel capabilities of both the systems. The combination of historic data from the data warehouse and the real-time location data from smartphones and GPS can provide real-time leveraging for marketers to promote their targeted products to the individual customer based on customer profiling and real-time location data. Figure 7.4 represents an architecture designed for Big Data analytics.

There are various sources from which structured data can be captured including external systems, online transaction processing (OLTP) systems, and legacy systems. In its journey from source station to the targeted data warehouse it goes through the process of ETL. For creating business intelligence to improve decision processes and business operations, traditional business intelligence (BI) batched analytical processing tools, such as query and reporting, online analytical processing (OLAP), and data mining can be used.

The sources for semistructured and unstructured Big Data can be of a wide variety that includes data from geospatial devices, social media, clickstreams, sensors, mobile devices, call records, web logs, satellites, scientific research, and documents and reports. They all are loaded into HDFS clusters. Batched analytics can be performed across the Hadoop cluster where Hadoop MapReduce provides the fault-tolerant distributed processing framework. Analytical and operational applications can consume the insights resulting from business intelligence analytics and Hadoop MapReduce analytics.

Real-time events cannot be processed on Hadoop because of its high latency as it is a batch system. The quality of predictive analysis can be improved by geospatial intelligence using data about space and time. As an example, real-time location from smartphone

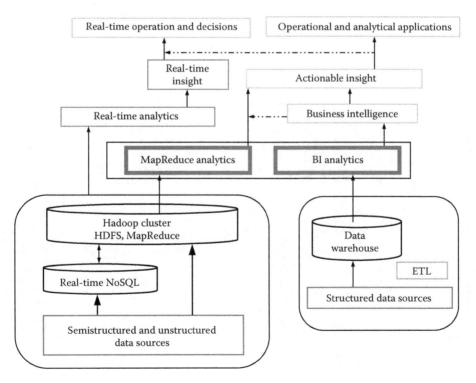

FIGURE 7.4
A supportive architecture for Big Data analytics.

usage can become a base for finding real-time recommendations of places of interest. The quality of predictions can be improved by combining this real-time information with the batched analytics. Some other examples of application of real-time analytics includes real-time web clickstream analysis, real-time trending of social media, real-time M2M analysis, and algorithm trading. Real-time read/write of Hadoop data can be provided by a combination of Hadoop and real-time NoSQL databases such as HBase. Some of the technologies that can be said to be emerging for Big Data real-time analytics are in-memory analytic systems, real-time analytics applications for processing of data stored in Hadoop, and collection and aggregation of real-time data for Hadoop.

7.4 Scientific Data Infrastructure Architectural Model

SDI architecture for e-science (eSDI) is illustrated in Figure 7.5 (Demchenko et al. 2012). Following are the layers of this model with "D" denoting the relationship to data infrastructure:

D1 Layer—This is the network infrastructure layer that is represented by the dedicated network infrastructure and general-purpose Internet infrastructure.

D2 Layer—Computing facilities/resources and data centers.

D3 Layer—This is the infrastructure virtualization layer represented by the middleware software, which support specialized scientific platform deployment and operation, and cloud/grid infrastructure.

D4 Layer—Shared layer for scientific instruments and platform-specific for different research areas.

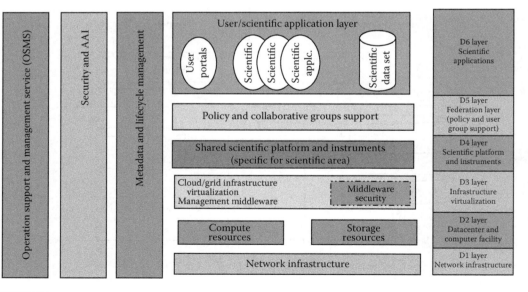

FIGURE 7.5
Architecture model for scientific data infrastructure.

Supportive Architectural Analysis for Big Data

D5 Layer—Layer for policy and federation including federation infrastructure components, includes collaborative user group support functionality.

D6 Layer—User portal/clients and scientific applications.

Three cross-layer planes are also defined: metadata and lifecycle management, security, and operational support and management system. The assurance of dynamic character of SDI and its distributed multifaceted community support is given by the D3 layer and D5 layer. Introduction of the federation and policy layer shows current practice in managing and building complex SDIs and allowing independent infrastructures to share resources and support interorganizational cooperation.

In e-SDI a separate lower layer is for network infrastructure. In Big Data the aspects of networking are becoming more important, for example, with clouds and computer grids. Although the problem of moving computing to the data location or conversely moving data to computing facilities in some particular cases can be solved, a specially designed internal MPP network infrastructure is required for processing highly distributed data on MPP.

A general view on the Big Data infrastructure can be visualized, which includes the common infrastructure for general data management, basically cloud based, and Big Data analytics requiring computing clusters with high performance, which in their own turn require a low-latency high-performance network. The components and services of general BDI include

Management tools for Big Data

Name-spaces, semantics, indexing/search, registries

Infrastructure for security (availability, access control, confidentiality, privacy, policy enforcement)

Collaborative environment

The Federated Access and Delivery Infrastructure (FADI) is defined as an important component of the general Big Data architecture and has the responsibility of connecting the different components of the cloud-/intercloud-based infrastructure combining federated access control and dedicated network connectivity provisioning.

7.5 Performance Parametric Considerations for Big Data Architecture

Several performance factors for a Hadoop cluster are described in this section.

7.5.1 Sizing of Clustering

As the data and processing requirements grow, the distributed architecture of Hadoop allows the expansion of the clusters. Due to the extra added nodes to the cluster, the corresponding name nodes and network infrastructure need to be sized. As the number of nodes increases in the cluster, the key metric of job completion time generally decreases.

7.5.2 MapReduce Algorithm

The data model of the algorithm, details of it, and the input size of the data sets have to be taken into account. One method of doing that is to place too much of the computation into reducers and not into the mappers and vice versa, making the algorithm more efficient. For example, more data for reducers is produced by the workload having very little processing in the mapping function, and therefore it will result in more network traffic between reducers and mappers. To achieve optimal results it is important to efficiently divide the algorithm, keeping in mind the functional differences of the reduce and map phases. A pipeline of smaller MapReduce jobs can be created for certain workloads in place of a single large MapReduce job, with the entire pipelining having the ability to finish faster than the single job.

7.5.3 Input Data Set

If the size of the input data set is large, then it will take a longer time to complete the processing and produce the result for the same algorithm.

7.5.4 Data Node

The proper sizing of the network, memory, CPU, and storage elements of data nodes is required. In the capacity planning section as discussed in Section 7.6, a more detailed review is given on this topic later. The job of MapReduce can vary in memory and CPU intensiveness. The time the map or reduce phase will take can be determined by the memory availability of such jobs and the capacity planning aspects. The time needed for job completion is decreased by fast processing and more memory. In accordance to the storage, the time required to read the HDFS blocks needed by the MapReduce algorithm and the typical disk data transfer rates combining can determine the total job time.

7.5.5 Data Locality

The availability of data locally on the data node can complete the task faster. The Hadoop JobTracker schedules the jobs optimally on such nodes where the data is available locally. Heavy load can be experienced in some instances by all the nodes that host a particular data block. The JobTracker is forced to schedule the jobs on any node available in such data miss instances. As the local availability of the data block needed is zero, the data block is requested by the task from a node that has data.

7.5.6 Concurrent Activity

MapReduce jobs run in parallel with the Hadoop clusters, apart from the background activities such as internal HDFS operations (e.g., rebalancing of data when nodes are removed or added and importing/exporting data from HDFS). The available resources for the newly submitted jobs are determined by all the running jobs in the cluster. The increase in priority of new jobs at the stake of existing jobs is one option. Speculative execution can be another strategy, where job completion by Hadoop infrastructure can be done by cleverly spreading several instances of the same task. Better performance for the scheduled jobs and less contention can be gained by less sharing of the cluster among the MapReduce jobs.

Supportive Architectural Analysis for Big Data

7.5.7 Network Considerations

During reading and writing data to HDFS, the interconnections of the cluster nodes are heavily used. Also, during the shuffle step and the MapReduce metadata communications among the nodes the network interconnects are highly utilized. There are other characteristics that need consideration. For the resiliency and availability of the network, it is very necessary to deploy a network that has the capability to scale up as the cluster grows and can provide the required redundancy. For the cluster nodes, the better technologies are those that allow network design with multiple redundant paths between the data nodes. Some other important characteristics are burst handling and queue depth. For the network traffic, read-write functions in HDFS and the shuffle step can be full of burst in nature. The network will drop packets if it can't handle burst effectively.

Therefore, for absorbing bursts, the network devices need an optimal buffer. Retransmission will be done for any dropped packet due to nonavailability of the buffer, which will in turn result in longer job completion time. Therefore a suitable architecture is with proper buffer and queues. The oversubscription ratio of the network is also an important consideration. Lower performance is seen due to dropped packets because of oversubscription. In converse, implementation cost of lower oversubscription is high.

7.6 Capacity and Scalability Consideration for Big Data Architecture

The following infrastructure capacity planning elements should be included to design an optimal Hadoop infrastructure with the aforementioned consideration. Storage area network (SAN) and blade computing systems are suggested by the traditional analytics. The Hadoop platform handles large data volume and reliability in the software tier rather than relying on the SAN and blade compute systems. Data is distributed across a cluster of balanced machines by Hadoop, and reliability and fault-tolerance is ensured by replication (Bakshi 2012). Discussed next are four elements of Hadoop infrastructure.

7.6.1 CPU

On each node there are 8 or 12 cores. The number of cores is comparatively larger or equal to the number of spindles. The mappers and reducers will be 2 less than the total number of hyperthreads (2 because of OS and daemon processing).

7.6.2 Memory

The application HBase is very memory-intensive. Assuming the catching parameters are enabled, a number of regions are kept in memory by each region server in HBase. By allocating up to 2 GB of memory, each region server can handle a few regions. The requirement for the memory is typically 4 GB per region server, but it depends on the access patterns and application load. About 1 to 2 GB of memory should be allocated per task for MapReduce, and additional memory for HBase for large clusters. Memory swapping of both MapReduce and HBase are not allowed as they can degrade the overall system performance.

7.6.3 Disk

At least two locations are recommended by the guidelines of the MapReduce disk planning to store HDFS and MapReduce intermediate files. For parallelism these partitions can be spread across the disk partition. By default 3 is set as the replication factor for HDFS and an additional 25% of the disk storage is required for intermediate shuffle files. Thus we can say that HDFS needs storage 4 times than the size of the raw data.

7.6.4 Network

A low-latency and high-throughput data network is required by each node in a HBase and MapReduce cluster. To avoid the master node from delisting the data nodes, the name nodes should be connected in a highly available fashion. On the top of the rack switches, racks with 1 to 2 gigabit network interfaces are connected by the nodes in a typical configuration. For a higher bandwidth workload, a wise choice will be a 10 gigabit network interface. Arrangement for large Hadoop clusters is generally done in racks. Network traffic across the racks is less desirable than the network traffic within the same rack. Replicas of blocks are placed on multiple racks for improved fault-tolerance by name nodes. Cluster administrators decide which rack a node belongs to. All the nodes belong to the same rack as assumed by default.

7.7 Conclusion

Governments and businesses are taking actions to exploit the values of and application of Big Data. This chapter presented an architecture for Big Data analytics and described the characteristics of Big Data. Big Data technologies are different from traditional SQL-based RDMS techniques because Big Data technologies deal with data of high volume, variety, and velocity (Chan 2013). The architecture discussed in this chapter used HDFS-distributed data storage, real-time NoSQL databases, and MapReduce-distributed data processing over a cluster of a commodity server. Running of real-time and batched analytics on the Hadoop platform were discussed. The relationship between the data mining analytic platform and traditional data warehouses are discussed. The main goal of this chapter was to provide insight into the architectural details of Big Data for those who want to take advantage of it.

References

Bakshi, K. 2012. Considerations for Big Data: Architecture and Approach. *2012 IEEE Aerospace Conference*, pp. 1–7.

Chan, J. O. 2013. An Architecture for Big Data Analytics. *Communications of the IIMA* 13(2): 1–14.

Demchenko, Y., de Laat, C., Membrey, P. 2014. Defining Architecture Components of the Big Data Ecosystem. *2014 International Conference on Collaboration Technologies and Systems (CTS)*, pp. 104–112.

Demchenko, Y., Zhao, Z., Grosso, P., Wibisono, A., de Laat, C. 2012. Addressing Big Data Challenges for Scientific Data Infrastructure. *IEEE 4th International Conference Cloud Computing Technology and Science (CloudCom)*, pp. 614–617.

Ferguson, M. 2012. Architecting: A Big Data Platform for Analytics. Intelligent Business Strategies, white paper.

Gartner, Inc. 2011. Gartner says solving 'Big Data' challenge involves more than just managing volumes of data [Press release]. Retrieved from http://www.gartner.com/newsroom/id/1731916.

Ghazal, A., Rabl, T., Hu, M., Raab, F., Poess, M., Crolotte, A., Jacobsen, H. A. 2013. BigBench: Towards an Industry Standard Benchmark for Big Data Analytics. *Proceedings of the 2013 ACM SIGMOD International Conference on Management of Data*, pp. 1197–1208.

Jacobs, A. 2009. The pathologies of Big Data. *Communications of the ACM* 52(8): 36–44.

King, R., Rosenbush, S. 2013. Big data broadens its range. *The Wall Street Journal, Business Technology Ed.* Retrieved from http://www.theretailingmanagement.com/?p=104.

Manyika, J., Chui, M., Brown, B., Bughin, J., Dobbs, R., Roxburgh, C., Byers, A. H. 2011. *Big Data: The Next Frontier for Innovation, Competition, and Productivity*. New York: McKinsey Global Institute.

Sagiroglu, S., Sinanc, D. 2013. Big Data: A Review. *International Conference on Collaboration Technologies and Systems (CTS)*, pp. 42–47.

Wang, L., Zhan, J., Luo, C., Zhu, Y., Yang, Q., He, Y., Gao, W. et al. 2014. BigDataBench: A Big Data Benchmark Suite from Internet Services. *2014 IEEE 20th International Symposium on High Performance Computer Architecture (HPCA)*, pp. 488–499.

Authors

Utkarsh Sharma is an assistant professor in the Computer Science and Engineering Department at G.L. Bajaj Group of Institutions, Mathura (India). He has worked in various areas including cloud computing and parallel algorithms, with specialization in evolutionary algorithms. He received his MTech in computer science and engineering from Jaypee University Noida (India). He has authored several research papers published in reputed conferences and journals including IEEE.

Robin Singh Bhadoria has worked in data mining, frequent pattern mining, cloud computing including service-oriented architecture and wireless sensor networks. He earned his bachelor of engineering and master of technology in computer science and engineering from Rajiv Gandhi Technological University, Bhopal, Madhya Pradesh, India. He is currently doing his PhD in computer science and engineering at the Indian Institute of Technology (IIT) Indore, Madhya Pradesh, India. He has published more than 45 articles in conferences, proceedings, journals, and book chapters of international and national repute including IEEE and Springer. Presently, he is serving as associate editor for the *International Journal of Computing, Communications and Networking*. He is also an editorial board member for various journals. He is an active professional member in IEEE (USA), IAENG (Hong Kong), Internet Society (Virginia), and IACSIT (Singapore).

8

Clustering Algorithms for Big Data: A Survey

Ankita Sinha and Prasanta K. Jana

CONTENTS

8.1   An Introduction to Big Data 144
8.2   Parallel Programming Models for Big Data 145
      8.2.1   Hadoop Ecosystem 145
           8.2.1.1   HDFS 146
           8.2.1.2   MapReduce Framework 146
           8.2.1.3   Apache Mahout 147
           8.2.1.4   Apache Spark 147
8.3   Big Data Clustering 147
      8.3.1   Clustering Techniques Based on a Single Machine 148
           8.3.1.1   Sample-Based Clustering 148
           8.3.1.2   Clustering Based on Randomization Techniques 153
      8.3.2   Clustering Based on Multiple Machines 154
           8.3.2.1   Parallel Clustering 155
           8.3.2.2   Clustering Based on MapReduce 156
      8.3.3   Other Big Data Clustering 159
8.4   Conclusion 159
Acknowledgments 160
References 160
Authors 161

ABSTRACT There is an explosion in the data generation from multiple sources such as social media, business enterprises, and sensors. We need to analyze such vast amounts of data, termed Big Data. However, Big Data cannot be processed using traditional methods. Data mining techniques are well-known and powerful knowledge discovery tools in which clustering plays an hidden patterns and gain some meaningful and accurate information. Clustering divides the data into groups called clusters, where intracluster similarity between objects is much higher than the intercluster similarity. Most of the traditional techniques are suitable for small data sets and generally executed on a single machine. However, with the increase in data size, it becomes impractical to handle large data on a single machine as it requires huge storage and computation capacity. The main objective of this chapter is to give the readers insight into clustering techniques available for Big Data. The pros and cons of each scheme will be discussed thoroughly with a brief discussion of some algorithms in each technique. The methods for Big Data computing will also be discussed to give researchers direction and motivation to deal with intricate data sets.

143

8.1 An Introduction to Big Data

With the advent of the era of information and technology, data in the digital universe has been increasing at an unprecedented rate. The amount of data generated amounts to 2.5 quintillion bytes every day and about 90% of the world's data has been generated in the last 2 years (IBM, 2015). This enormous data termed "Big Data" has the capability to reform many fields concerning humans directly such as healthcare, business, science, engineering, and bioinformatics (Chen and Zhang, 2014). In a 2001 research report, META Group (now Gartner) analyst Doug Laney defined Big Data as being three-dimensional, that is, increasing volume, velocity, and variety. Volume refers to the amount of data, variety refers to the number of types of data, and velocity refers to the speed of data processing. Sometimes other V's such as veracity, value, variability, and visualization also come into play. Veracity defines the correctness of source of data, and value means the data will create a lot of value for organizations, societies, and consumers. Variability refers to data whose meaning is constantly changing, and visualization specifies making all that vast amount of data comprehensible in a manner that is easy to understand and read.

Handling Big Data poses many problems in terms of storage and performing operations such as analytics and retrieval. Data clustering can be helpful in resolving such issues. Clustering is a powerful data mining technique that discovers natural groups of the underlying data sets and provides the same information kept by the original data sets. Moreover, handling smaller groups of original large data is much simpler and consumes less time. Clustering divides the data into groups called clusters, where intracluster similarity between objects is much higher than the intercluster similarity (Fahad et al., 2014; Shirkhorshidi et al., 2014). Clustering is used for high-dimensional, complex data to decrease its computational cost and increase its scalability and speed. Clustering of large data sets i.e., Big Data is a relatively new field. Hence, very few work has been done in this regard. In this chapter we perform a review of the existing clustering algorithms for Big Data along with their advantages and disadvantages.

The data is so huge and complex that it is incomprehensible with the existing techniques. The need is to make a gradual shift toward parallel and distributed storage and processing on cloud-based platforms, where resources can be made available on demand (Hashem et al., 2015). Apache Hadoop is the most popular software framework for writing parallel applications on a cluster of computers, consisting of commodity hardware (Apache Software Foundation, 2015b; Dean and Ghemawat, 2008; White, 2012). Various frameworks and tools available for parallel processing will be discussed later in Section 2 of the chapter.

The main challenges behind Big Data clustering are as follows:

- Computational cost—As the size of the data increases, the computation cost also increases, that is, the I/O and communication cost. The biggest challenge is to maintain the quality of clustering along with keeping computational cost in check.

- Scalability—The most important characteristics of Big Data is its volume and variety. The clustering algorithm should have the characteristic such that it should be able to handle a large flow of data and scale up dynamically, without degrading the quality of clustering.

- Speed—Velocity is another major factor of Big Data. We need to process the data as it arrives. The data may not be of any use afterward, so to maintain the speed of clustering is another important challenge.

Clustering Algorithms for Big Data
145

The main focus of this chapter is to give readers insight into various parallel clustering algorithms. We review some parallel programming models available to cluster huge data sets. The algorithms proposed for dealing with the problems for Big Data clustering is also discussed along with their advantages and disadvantages.

8.2 Parallel Programming Models for Big Data

An initial attempt was made toward achieving parallelism with the help of threads. POSIX threads provide a model-based string API in C/C++. Threads are also supported by other programming languages like Java and C#. Parallelism can also be achieved by creating processes by the use of the *fork()* system call provided by the operating system. However, these attempts toward parallelism were quite ineffective when applied to huge volumes of data, as these techniques were applied to a single machine where the storage and processing capability is limited. MPI was one of the earliest attempts made toward gaining multiple machine parallelism. MPI is a standard for developing a parallel programing system. MPI allows two processes to communicate with each other by the use of message passing. It supports a variety of message-passing functions that allow data transmission from one process to another. MPI is not a programming language; it is a library that incorporates programming languages like C or Fortran (Pacheco, 1997). Although MPI provides a solution to execute applications in parallel, it also has some weaknesses. It does not deal with node failure, and extra efforts are to be taken by the programmer for data distribution among the machines. Moreover, the machines have to be physically located in the same vicinity. We need a parallel programming paradigm on the cloud-based platform (Hashem et al., 2015). Various attempts have been made to make use of distributed storage and processing. Dryad was one such model, which can scale up from a very small cluster to large clusters. It is based on a directed acyclic graph (DAG), which defines the data flow of the application. The vertices of the graph define the operation to be performed on the data. Many features are provided by Dryad, like cloning, composition, merge, and encapsulation to build a graph. Dryad provides a number of functionalities like generating job graphs, scheduling of the processes, handling failures, collecting of performance metrics, and visualization of the job. Dryad keeps the inner details of concurrent programming abstract to the programmer (Chen and Zhang, 2014; Microsoft Research, 2015). However, Dryad's evolution has been discontinued by its developer Microsoft in late 2011 to put more emphasis on Hadoop. In the next section, we analyze some of the components of the Hadoop ecosystem, which are used for data processing and can be applied to clustering. There are many other components of Hadoop such as Hive, HBase, Sqoop, Oozie, Pig, and Zookeeper (Hashem et al., 2015; White, 2012) that are beyond the scope of this chapter.

8.2.1 Hadoop Ecosystem

Apache Hadoop is a software framework that allows distributed storage and processing over a cluster of commodity hardware and uses simple programming models. Like Dryad it can also scale from a few machines to thousands of machines. Each machine in the cluster has its own local storage and processing capability. Hadoop works on the principle of moving the process to data rather than moving the data to the process, which reduces the communication cost (White, 2012). Major components in the Hadoop ecosystem used for distributed storage and distributed processing are discussed next.

8.2.1.1 HDFS

Hadoop Distributed File System (HDFS), as the name implies, is a distributed file system to store data. It is a Java-based file system that stores data in a distributed fashion over a cluster of commodity hardware and provides scalability and reliability (Apache Software Foundation, 2015b; Dean and Ghemawat, 2008; White, 2012). It is highly fault tolerant as it replicates a file three times (this is the default; it can be changed according to requirement). So in case of node failure or crash there is no loss of data. It breaks the data into small chunks of 128 MB (default in higher versions of Hadoop earlier, it was 64 MB) and stores them in different nodes in the cluster, which are then fetched by the MapReduce program to be processed (Dean and Ghemawat, 2008). The final results are again written back into HDFS.

8.2.1.2 MapReduce Framework

MapReduce is a simplified programming model for processing large amounts of data sets in parallel. MapReduce efficiently utilizes the cloud resources and accelerates processing of Big Data on the cloud (Hashem et al., 2015). It assumes that every job is an entity and has no knowledge of jobs running in parallel (Dean and Ghemawat, 2008).

MapReduce communicates with HDFS to get the data for processing and also writes the final results back to HDFS. Initially the data are loaded into HDFS and divided into multiple blocks of predefined size. For each block, one meaningful record called input split is created. Each input split is processed by a user-defined map() method. The map() task processes the split and generates the intermediary output. The intermediate output is further processed by another user-defined reduce() method, which produces the final output. The number of reduce tasks can be decided by the programmer, depending upon the data size or requirement (Apache Software Foundation, 2015b). The working of MapReduce framework is depicted in Figure 8.1.

MapReduce works on the key-value concept, that is, the input and output are in the form of key-value pairs (Dean and Ghemawat, 2008). Map takes the input in the form of (k1, v1)

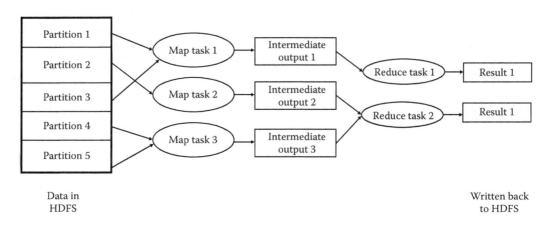

FIGURE 8.1
MapReduce framework.

Clustering Algorithms for Big Data

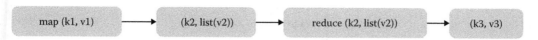

FIGURE 8.2
Input–output pair in MapReduce program.

and produces an intermediate output in the form of (k2, list(v2)) which is further taken as input to the reducer. The reducer produces the final output as depicted in Figure 8.2.

Although MapReduce is suitable for large volumes of data, it still has the following weaknesses:

- It uses multiple read and write back to the HDFS for an iterative program, which leads to an increase in time and cost.
- It is suitable for batch processing but not suitable for handling streams of data.
- There is no communication between the jobs, unlike MPI where jobs can communicate with each other.

8.2.1.3 Apache Mahout

Apache Mahout is a library of scalable machine learning algorithms. The core algorithms in Mahout are clustering, classification, pattern mining, evolutionary algorithms, regression, batch-based collaborative filtering, and dimension reduction (Chen and Zhang, 2014). It is implemented on top of Apache Hadoop and uses the MapReduce paradigm. Mahout also uses HDFS to store data (Apache Software Foundation, 2015c). It applies data science tools to find meaningful patterns in huge data sets. The main data science use cases supported by Mahout are collaborative filtering, clustering, classification, and frequent pattern mining. The implemented algorithms in Mahout are optimized for better performance (Chen and Zhang, 2014).

8.2.1.4 Apache Spark

Apache Spark was recently developed as an open source Big Data processing framework. It runs on the top of the Hadoop framework and can even run on Mesos, standalone, or in a cloud. It can access a variety of data sources like HDFS, HBase, Cassandra, and S3. Spark overcomes the weakness present in Hadoop MapReduce. It can run programs in the range of 100 times faster than MapReduce when running in memory and 10 times faster when it runs on disk. Spark does so by reducing the number of reads and writes to the disk. Spark is highly available, providing simple APIs in Python, Scala, Java, and SQL, and rich built-in libraries. Spark can also do real-time processing of large data streams, which is not present in MapReduce (Apache Software Foundation, 2015a).

8.3 Big Data Clustering

Several attempts have been made by industry and academia to cluster large data sets, both in terms of size as well as complexity. Earlier attempts were made on a single machine by using some sampling and randomization techniques. With the advent of parallel

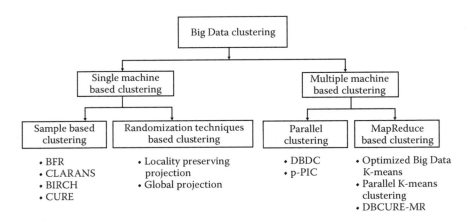

FIGURE 8.3
Big Data clustering techniques.

processing, there has been a gradual shift toward multiple machine-based techniques, which is the need of the moment (Shirkhorshidi et al., 2014). Figure 8.3 shows the various representative techniques to cluster Big Data.

8.3.1 Clustering Techniques Based on a Single Machine

In this section, we will review some of the existing single-machine-based techniques that were developed to curb the need of large-scale data clustering. In earlier attempts, samples of large data sets were taken and then instead of running the algorithm on the entire data set, the processing was done on these smaller samples and then the result extrapolated to the entire data set. This helped in decreasing the computational cost and memory required. As the data grew in size, the complexity also increased. Higher dimensional data sets also pose a problem in the existing approaches. Sampling can deal with large data volumes but was not efficient for high-dimensional data sets. The answer to this was dimension-reduction techniques, a process of intelligently reducing the number of random variables into consideration, without affecting the clustering result. A few important sample-based and dimension-reduction clustering algorithms are discussed in brief in the following sections.

8.3.1.1 Sample-Based Clustering

There are several sample-based clustering methods that have been developed for large data. We briefly describe a few popular clustering algorithms as follows.

8.3.1.1.1 BFR Algorithm

The BFR algorithm, developed by Bradley, Fayyad, and Reina in 1998, is a variant of the k-means algorithm. BFR clusters high-dimensional data in Euclidian space. The shape of the cluster is an important constraint in BFR. Data must be normally distributed about the centroid (Rajaraman and Ullman, 2012).

Clustering Algorithms for Big Data

The data set is divided into multiple small chunks that are stored in the main memory (the chunks should be small enough to be processed at once). Main memory also stores other information including

- *Discard set*—Points that are the representatives of the cluster. They are called discarded as they are not stored in memory; rather they are represented only through summary, the so-called discarded set.
- *Compress set*—Sets of points that are closer to one another, not to any cluster. The compress set is also discarded in the sense that it is not stored in the main memory, and is represented as a summary.
- *Retained set*—The sets of points that are neither close to any cluster nor to other points (i.e., the points in compress set). These points are stored in their original form in the main memory.

For d dimensional data, the compressed and the discarded sets are represented by $2d + 1$ values. The other data structures used are as follows:

- Number of represented points: N
- Sum of all components of all points in each dimension: SUM

$$SUM = \sum_{i=1}^{n} x^i$$

where $x^i \in R^n$ is a set of singleton points to be compressed
- SUM_i is the sum of components in the ith dimension
- The sum of squares of the components of all points in each dimension

$$(SUMSQ)_j = \sum_{i=1}^{N} \left(x_j^i\right)^2 \text{ for } j = 1, 2, \ldots, n \tag{8.1}$$

The points are not stored in their original form. Instead, they are stored using statistical tools: mean, variance, and standard deviation. The calculations can be easily done with the help of the aforementioned data structures.

$$mean_i = \frac{SUM_i}{N} \tag{8.2}$$

$$variance_i = \frac{SUMSQ_i}{N} - \left(\frac{SUM_i}{N}\right)^2 \tag{8.3}$$

$$Standard\ deviation_i = \sqrt{variance_i} \tag{8.4}$$

Steps of the BFR algorithm are as follows.

Step 1—Points close to a cluster are added to that cluster. To choose the level of closeness one of the following two approaches are used:

a. A point p is added to the centroid, which is closer to p and will remain close even after all the points have been processed. This decision is made based on the calculations mentioned in the original work by Bradley, Fayyad, and Reina (1998), discussion of which is beyond the scope of this chapter.

b. The probability of a point to belong to a cluster can be measured. This uses the fact that axes of the cluster consist of a normally distributed point about the axes of space. The calculation is made based on the Mahalanabis distance of the point. The *Mahalanabis distance* is the distance between a point and the centroid of the cluster, which is normalized by standard deviation of the cluster in each dimension (Bradley, Fayyad, and Reina, 1998). It is calculated by the formula

$$\text{Mahalanabis distance} = \sqrt{\sum_{i=1}^{d} \left(\frac{P_i - C_i}{\sigma_i} \right)^2} \tag{8.5}$$

where $P = [P_1, P_2, \ldots, P_d]$ is a point, $C = [C_1, C_2, \ldots, C_d]$ represents the centroid, and σ_i is the standard deviation. The Mahalanabis distance between all the points and its mean is calculated and based on the predetermined threshold value; the points are added to the closest cluster.

Step 2—Points that are not near to any cluster are clustered locally using any clustering algorithm. The newly formed clusters may be singleton or consist of two or more points. Clusters other than the singleton cluster are added to the compressed set. Singleton clusters become the updated retained set.

Step 3—Clusters formed in the previous state are the resultant of the points not belonging to any of the previous clusters. However, the newly formed nonsingleton clusters might be similar to one another and can be merged.

Step 4—Points that have been assigned to any nonsingleton cluster are written back to the secondary storage.

Step 5—The points remaining in the retained set can either be treated as outliers or can be merged with the cluster whose centroid is nearest.

The BFR algorithm has the following disadvantages. It provides a solution for large data sets that cannot fit into the main memory at once. However, it is very strict about the shape of the clusters. It always assumes that the clusters are normally distributed about the axes, which may not be possible in all cases. An algorithm proposed by Guha, Rastogi, and Shim in 1998, Clustering Using REpresentative (CURE), discussed later, overcomes the drawbacks of BFR.

8.3.1.1.2 CLARANS

Clustering Large Applications based on Randomized Sampling (CLARANS) is a spatial data mining algorithm that works efficiently on the spatial attributes of the data objects. CLARANS is a k-medoid clustering algorithm based on eminent algorithms, Partitioning

Around Medoids (PAM), and Clustering Large Applications (CLARA). PAM approaches to find k clusters of data objects where each cluster is having a representative data object called medoid, which is most likely located centrally within the cluster (Aggarwal and Reddy, 2013; Ng and Han, 2002; Rajaraman and Ullman, 2012; Shirkhorshidi et al., 2014). Initially, k-medoids are selected over x data objects, then other nonselected data objects are associated with one of the medoids according to the similarity or distance. So, k-centroids are formed around the medoid where each data object has the highest similarity or minimum distance with the medoid of that cluster. By the complexity analysis, it is found that the complexity of a single iteration is $O(k(x - k)^2)$, this makes PAM very costly to be applied to large data sets. It is suitable only for small-sized data sets, for example, 100 objects in 5 clusters. The complexity problem is addressed in CLARA, which is made suitable for large data sets. CLARA reduces the search space by sampling a small set of data from the large data set. PAM is applied on the small sampled data instead of the original large data set. If the sample selection is sufficiently random, then medoids of the sample would approximate the medoids of the entire data set. For better approximation, CLARA selects multiple samples from the large data and the best quality cluster is given as output.

The process of finding k medoids from x objects can be presented as a graph-searching problem. Each node in the graph $G_{x,k}$ is a set of k-medoids $(M_{m1}, M_{m2}, ..., M_{mk})$. Two connected nodes—$S_1 = (M_{m1}, M_{m2}, ..., M_{mk})$ and $S_2 = (M_{w1}, M_{w2}, ..., M_{wk})$—are called neighbors if the intersection set $(S_1 \cap S_2)$ is a k-1 item set. So each node is connected by $k(x - k)$ neighbors. As each node represents a medoid so it corresponds to a cluster. The PAM selects one of the nodes randomly and searches one of the accurate neighbors by traversing through the graph. All the $k(x - k)$ neighbors of a node are examined, which is a time-consuming task. This problem is resolved in CLARA by reducing the search area by applying PAM on sampled objects that correspond to a subgraph.

CLARANS refines PAM and CLARA to work on large data sets efficiently. CLARANS has some similarity and dissimilarity with both algorithms. Like PAM, CLARANS also traverses through the graph to search for the optimal solution. But unlike PAM, CLARANS does not traverse through all the neighbors of a node; it only traverses through a sample of neighbors. CLARANS also applies the sampling techniques to reduce the search space like CLARA. However, CLARANS does not restrict the search up to a particular subset (Ng and Han, 2002). Moreover, CLARANS samples the subsets dynamically in each iteration rather than taking a single subset in the beginning of the algorithm. This strategy in CLARANS assumes that all the subsets for an object are nonconflicting, so gives accurate results. Therefore, CLARANS is more efficient than CLARA and produces more accurate clusters by taking diverse subsets throughout the complete process.

8.3.1.1.3 BIRCH

BIRCH (Balanced Iterative Reducing and Clustering using Hierarchies) is an incremental clustering scheme. It is a one-pass clustering algorithm in the sense that it initially scans the input data once to give output as a set of clusters (Aggarwal and Reddy, 2013). However, in order to increase the quality of clustering, a number of optional scans can be added (Zhang, Ramakrishnan, and Livny, 1996). In each increment, BIRCH makes clustering decisions without scanning all the points or existing clusters. It uses measurements such that the natural closeness of the points is maintained (Aggarwal and Reddy, 2013; Rajaraman and Ullman, 2012; Shirkhorshidi et al., 2014; Zhang, Ramakrishnan, and Livny, 1996). The running time of BIRCH is linearly scalable; it makes an assumption that not all data points are equally important. It makes full utilization of the available memory and generates optimal subclusters. Another important feature of BIRCH is that it does not require the entire data set before the start of the algorithm; rather it scans the data incrementally.

Two data structures called clustering features (CF) and CF trees are used to accomplish the above purpose. CF is a triplet <N, LS, SS>; N represents the number of data points, LS is the linear sum of data points in a cluster, and SS is the square sum of data points in a cluster. CF is additive in nature (Zhang, Ramakrishnan, and Livny, 1996). Hence the merging of the existing clusters is very simple. The CF tree is represented in Figure 8.4.

The CF tree is a height-balanced tree with each nonleaf node having a maximum of B entries and a leaf node having a maximum of L entries. All the entries of the leaf node represent a cluster, satisfied by a threshold value. The size of the tree is also a function of threshold T and is related to the same inversely. As the threshold increases, the size of the tree decreases and vice versa. The parameters B and L are determined on the basis of the page size. Insertion in a CF tree is the same as an insertion in a B+ tree. The CF tree represents data in a very compressed form, as each entry in leaf node represents only a subcluster rather than the specific data points.

The BIRCH algorithm works with the following steps:

Step 1—Data is loaded into memory by means of a CF tree.

Step 2—A CF tree can be compressed into a desirable range (optional).

Step 3—Global clustering is performed.

Step 4—To increase the quality of clusters, refinement can be done (optional) by scanning the data set a few more times.

Zhang, Ramakrishnan, and Livny (1996) have experimentally proven that BIRCH has many advantages over CLARANS (Ng and Han, 1994) in terms of time as well as space complexity. BIRCH can also deal with outliers that are not present in CLARANS. However, CLARANS was later improved by its authors Ng and Han in 2002. Moreover, BIRCH cannot discover clusters of nonspherical shapes, which can be solved by the CURE algorithm, discussed next.

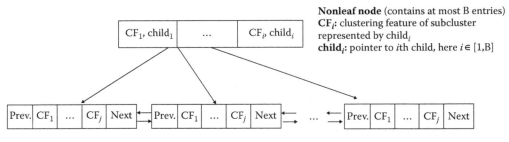

FIGURE 8.4
CF tree.

Clustering Algorithms for Big Data

8.3.1.1.4 CURE

CURE is a large-scale clustering algorithm in the point assignment class. It adopts a middle ground between a centroid-based and all-point approach. CURE can handle clusters of all shapes, as it does not assume clusters are normally distributed about the axes (Aggarwal and Reddy, 2013; Guha, Rastogi, and Shim, 1998; Rajaraman and Ullman, 2012; Shirkhorshidi et al., 2014). It is represented by a set of representative points, unlike BFR that takes centroids into consideration.

Initially, CURE draws well separated samples of data. It uses a combination of random sampling and partitioning to improve scalability. This sample needs to be clustered; any algorithm present in literature can be applied for this purpose. However, CURE handles odd-shaped clusters like S-bend and rings by using hierarchical methods (most suitable). As in hierarchical clustering, clusters having close enough pairs of points are merged into one. Each representative point is moved for a fixed fraction of distance (usually 20%) between its location and centroid of the cluster. In the next phase two representative points that are close enough are merged. In the final stage of the CURE algorithm, an assignment process takes place. Each data point in the secondary memory is compared with the representative points. Assignment is done on the basis of Euclidian distance, that is, point p is assigned to its nearest representative point. Two data structures are used by CURE to accomplish these tasks. One is heap data structure, which keeps the track of each cluster and its nearest cluster. The other data structure used is the k-d tree, which stores all the representative points for each cluster. The sequence of steps in the CURE algorithm are as follows:

Step 1—Random samples are drawn from the original data set.

Step 2—The samples from step 1 are partitioned.

Step 3—The partitions created in step 2 are clustered individually (local clustering).

Step 4—Outliers in the partial clusters are detected and removed.

Step 5—The partial clusters created in step 3 are clustered (global clustering).

Step 6—Finally the data in the disk is labeled.

CURE can discover clusters of many shapes and it is not very sensitive to outliers. However, algorithms like BIRCH and BFR can only discover clusters only of specific shapes.

8.3.1.2 Clustering Based on Randomization Techniques

Variety is an important feature in Big Data. The sampling techniques provide a solution to handle the size of the data set, but fails to handle high dimensional data sets. The complexity of the data set is directly proportional to the number of dimensions. Therefore, to deal with huge data sets on a single machine some dimension reduction techniques are implied, which are discussed in the following sections.

8.3.1.2.1 Locality Preserving Projection

As the name specifies, locality preserving projection, also called random projection, occurs when higher dimensional data is reduced to lower dimensional data, the distance between any two pair of points to be preserved in a probabilistic way. In many algorithms that work in the Euclidian space like k-means, pairwise distance determines the clustering structure. Johnson and Lindenstrauss (1984) proved that any n point set in d dimension can be projected into a lower dimension t (here $t \ll d$) by having an error of $1 \pm \varepsilon$ using a random orthogonal matrix (Aggarwal and Reddy, 2013, 259–276; Shirkhorshidi, Aghabozorgi, and Herawan, 2014). Let A be the original data matrix. A rotation matrix R of order $d \times t$ is created such that A' = A × R, here A' is the projection A in lower dimension, that is, the dimension of A' is t. For different types of random projections, the creation of the rotation matrix varies. Work done by Dasgupta (2000), Fern and Brodley (2003), and Boutsidis, Zouzias, and Drineas (2010) used the dimension reduction techniques to deal with huge amounts of data.

8.3.1.2.2 Global Projection

In global projection the aim is to keep the projected matrix A' as close as possible to the original data matrix A. To accomplish this purpose ||A' – A|| is minimized. Here A' has t dimensions and A has d dimension and $t \ll d$. A' can be represented as products of three matrices A' = PQR, where P, Q, and R have dimension d. The properties of the matrices P, Q, and R are determined by the type of approximation being followed. Several types of approximations present in literature are singular value decomposition (SVD) (Golub and Van Loan, 2012), CX/CUR (Drineas, Kannan, and Mahoney, 2006), Colibri (Tong et al., 2008), and CMD (Sun et al., 2007). SVD gives the best result among the various approximations (Aggarwal and Reddy, 2013).

8.3.2 Clustering Based on Multiple Machines

Algorithms based on a single machine provided a solution for clustering Big Data. A single machine has limited storage and processing capability. So, it is impractical to handle such data deluge by relying on the storage and processing capabilities of a single machine. Therefore, the algorithms based on single machines need to be modified and implemented on multiple machines. The data are divided and stored in distributed fashion across the different nodes to be processed in a distributed manner. The intermediate output is then merged and the process of the refinement of results continues until the optimal solution is generated. The various steps in multiple-machine-based parallel processing is depicted in Figure 8.5.

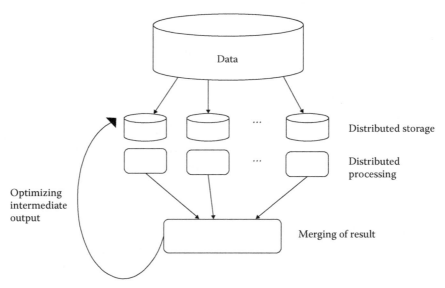

FIGURE 8.5
General steps in parallel processing.

8.3.2.1 Parallel Clustering

Many algorithms have been developed using multiple machines to cluster huge amounts of data. The algorithms discussed do not use the cloud computing paradigm for handling Big Data. A few such algorithms are discussed as follows.

8.3.2.1.1 DBDC

The Distributed Density Based Clustering (DBDC) algorithm discovers clusters of arbitrary shapes and sizes (Januzaj, Kriegel, and Pfeifle, 2004). DBDC doesn't use any parallel programming paradigm method mentioned earlier. It achieves parallelism by communicating the aggregated results between a central site and the clients.

A pictorial representation of the steps in DBDC is shown in Figure 8.6. DBDC clusters huge amounts of data at their site of generation and transfers the local models to the central site. An enhanced version of DBSCAN is used at the local nodes, where the information regarding the representatives in each local model is calculated during the execution. The details of the enhancements can be found in the original work of the authors (Januzaj, Kriegel, and Pfeifle, 2004). All the information that needs to be transferred to the central site, that is, the representatives and their corresponding ε ranges, are generated during the clustering process. DBSCAN is also used for global clustering (Aggarwal and Reddy, 2013; Shirkhorshidi et al., 2014). The motive here is to create such clusters, as if the clustering was being done on the entire data set rather than on their representatives. After the global clustering has been done, a global model is created, which is then sent to the client sites. The client site then updates their clusters, as a result of which some individual clusters may get merged (Januzaj, Kriegel, and Pfeifle, 2004).

The communication overhead between the nodes is less because the entire data set is not being transferred between the nodes, rather only some aggregated models are being transferred. Moreover, the communication is not iterative; the client sends the local models to a central site once and receives the global model. Therefore, the communication cost incurred is minimal. The quality of clustering achieved by DBDC is in the range of 30 times faster than its serial version.

8.3.2.1.2 p-PIC: Parallel Power Iteration Clustering for Big Data

p-PIC is the parallel version of the spectral clustering algorithm power iteration clustering (PIC). It is computationally much simpler in comparison to other spectral clustering

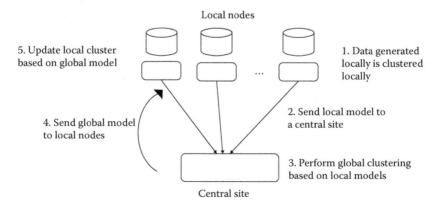

FIGURE 8.6
DBDC algorithm.

algorithms. PIC embeds the original data set in one dimension and does a series of matrix operations such as matrix vector multiplication and calculation of similarity matrix (Yan et al., 2013). PIC has three main components. First is similarity matrix calculation and normalization. Second is iterative matrix vector multiplication and third is clustering. However, with the increase in data size problems arise related to storage and calculation on Big Data matrices. p-PIC overcomes these problems in PIC by extending it to the parallel programming paradigm, MPI.

The p-PIC works on the master–slave architecture. There is one master and $p - 1$ slaves, where p is the total number of processors. The n points that are to be processed are represented by $\{x_1, x_2, ..., x_n\}$. p-PIC consists of the following steps:

Step 1—The master assigns the starting and the ending indices of the data to be processed by the slaves.

Step 2—The slave processors, after receiving the indices, first reads the entire data set of size n/p. Each slave calculates the similarity submatrix by performing the similarity calculation and normalizing the result by row sum in parallel.

Step 3—The slaves send their row sum to the master.

Step 4—The master on receiving the row sums from all the slaves, concatenates the row sum to obtain the row sum vector. After calculating the row sum vector, the master sets the initial vector to normalize the row sum and sends the same to all the slaves.

Step 5—The slaves on receiving the initial vector calculates the updated subvector by performing matrix–vector multiplication and sends the updated subvector to the master.

Step 6—The master after receiving the updated subvectors from all slaves, concatenates the subvector into the updated vector and checks for the termination condition. If the termination condition is met, then the algorithm stops, else go to step 4.

p-PIC induces a communication cost of $O(knp)$, which was not present in PIC. However, the overall computational complexity of PIC is p times higher than p-PIC. The computational complexity in p-PIC is $O(kn(n + 1)/p)$, whereas the same in PIC is $O(kn(n + 1))$. p-PIC also uses POSIX threads in each processor to calculate the matrix multiplication to further increase parallelism. The number of threads spawned was limited to the number of processors, that is, p. The use of POSIX threads in individual processors increased the speed by 5% (Yan et al., 2013).

The major drawback of p-PIC is there is a no fault-tolerance mechanism; if the master node fails, the entire algorithm fails. This can be easily handled by any MapReduce-based clustering technique where node failure is inherently handled by Hadoop.

8.3.2.2 Clustering Based on MapReduce

These algorithms use a cloud-based platform, MapReduce (discussed in Section 8.2.1.2), to cluster Big Data. Some of the representative algorithms in this category are discussed as follows.

8.3.2.2.1 PKMeans

PKMeans (Parallel *K*-Means clustering based on MapReduce) algorithm uses global variable *centers* that are chosen prior to the start of the algorithm and then recursively adds

Clustering Algorithms for Big Data

points to them by the mapper, and the reducer does the work of refining the centers. To optimize the algorithm a combiner is added intermediary to decrease the communication cost. The combiner in MapReduce does the work of combining the intermediate output from the mapper before sending the output to the reducer (Aggarwal and Reddy, 2013; Zhao, Ma, and He, 2009).

The three phases in PKMeans are explained as follows:

Phase 1 (Mapper)—The data is distributed across the different nodes in the cluster. A global variable center is provided as an input to the mapper along with the data chunk. The mapper assigns each point to its nearest center and produces the intermediate result as a set of clusters, that is, the index of the closest center, and the information about the sample.

Phase 2 (Combiner)—It combines the output of the same mapper. The partial sum of the values assigned to the same cluster is calculated in the combiner. The samples of the same cluster are recorded in the same mapper to calculate the mean value of the objects assigned to the same cluster.

Phase 3 (Reducer)—The reducer receives the data from the combiner, which contains the partial sum along with the sample number. The reducer sums them all and finds the number of samples assigned to the one cluster, and thus updates the global variable centers.

In the next iteration the updated value of centers is fed to the mapper. This process continues until the algorithm converges. The major drawback of this algorithm is that it is iterative in nature, and MapReduce jobs are sensitive to iteration, as with each iteration the number of reads and write increases. Rather, if the number of iterations is n, then the number of read and writes to the file system will also be equal to n. The next algorithm overcomes this problem in PKMeans.

8.3.2.2.2 Optimized Big Data K-Means Using MapReduce

Optimized Big Data K-means using MapReduce was proposed by Cui et al. in 2014. They showed their algorithm to be an efficient, robust, and scalable clustering algorithm. The K-means algorithm by nature is iterative. The major advantage of this algorithm over other MapReduce-based K-means is that it is iteration independent, which reduces the computation cost (I/O and network cost) of the algorithm and also increases the speed of clustering in the process. The various steps in this algorithm are represented pictorially in Figure 8.7.

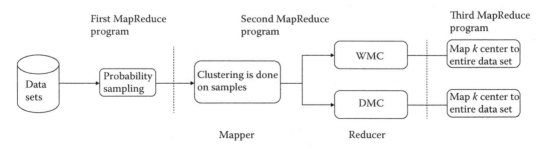

FIGURE 8.7
Optimized Big Data K-Means algorithm.

The algorithm uses three MapReduce programs in three steps as follows:

Step 1—Generate samples from the original data set. Probability sampling is used to generate samples from the original data set. Data is sampled using k and probability $p_x = \dfrac{1}{\varepsilon^2 N}$, where $\varepsilon \in (0,1)$ and N is the number of data points. The samples generated will be processed by one single machine.

Step 2—Clustering of samples and merging of results. Clustering of the samples generated in the first phase is done in the map() phase of the second MapReduce program, whereas the merging is done in the reduce() phase. If n is the number of objects, then $n \approx 2k^2$. The first MapReduce program generates $2k$ small-sized samples. Each sample is then clustered using k, and $2k^2$ centers are generated. The points need to be processed on a single machine, the value of k is chosen such that it complies with that. The centers generated are then fed to the reducer and merged to the generated k final centers. The merging process by the reducer can be done in one of the following two ways:

a. Weight-based merge clustering (WMC)—To merge two or more clusters, weight is assigned to keep the merging process even. The weights will be assigned on the basis of the number of points assigned to each of the merging centers.

b. Distribution-based merge clustering (DMC)—In this merging technique, $2k^2$ centers are separated into k groups, and each group has $2k$ centers. Each of these $2k$ centers are from the sample cluster. Each sample contributes one center. An intermediary clustering result is randomly selected. The k centers of the intermediate cluster are the first member from k different groups. The remaining members of the intermediate cluster are selected based on distances between the centers.

Step 3—Map the centers to the entire data set. The k points generated in step 2 are used to generate a Voronoi diagram in the third MapReduce program. The original data set is then mapped to the k centers using the Voronoi diagram.

The major drawback of this technique is that the final output is very much dependent on the sample initially selected. The basic feature of Big Data is variety (explained in introduction), so sampling may lead to problems of accuracy. Single-machine-based sampling techniques were present, so the obligation for MapReduce-based clustering techniques that use sampling is not provided. The input and output pairs have also not been clearly specified in terms of key-value pairs for the MapReduce program for any of the three MapReduce programs, which makes the algorithm difficult to understand.

8.3.2.2.3 DBCURE-MR

DBCURE-MR is a parallel density-based clustering algorithm that is a parallel version of DBCURE. Kim et al. (2014) proposed a density-based clustering algorithm DBCURE, which is a modified and improved version of DBSCAN. DBCURE starts by choosing an arbitrary point, which is an unvisited point in data set D, as a seed and inset the same in seed set S. A point p is selected from the seed set and all the points that are density reachable from p are retrieved. The τ-neighborhood of p is inserted into S. This process is repeated for all $p \in S$ until S becomes empty. The details of the algorithm can be found in the original of Kim et al. (2014); discussing all aspects of DBCURE is beyond the scope of this chapter.

Clustering Algorithms for Big Data

DBCURE finds each cluster one by one repeatedly. DBCURE-MR, the MapReduce version of DBCURE, finds all the clusters at once by expanding all core points in parallel. It uses a series MapReduce program discussed as follows:

- CONVAT-MR to estimate the neighborhood covariance matrix. The neighborhood covariance matrix for each point is calculated in parallel.
- NEIGHBOR-MR to compute the ellipsoidal τ-neighborhood. This discovers all pairs of points each within their ellipsoidal τ-neighborhood by performing similar joins.
- FINDCORE-MR discovers the core clusters. The result of this is the list of every core point with its τ-neighborhood; the resultant is called the core cluster table.
- MERGE-CLS-MR the core clusters discovered by the FINDCORE-MR are merged repeatedly in this phase. The merging is done on the basis of shared common core points. The resultant is the set of final clusters.

DBCURE-MR finds the clusters correctly as per the definition of density-based clustering and scales well with the MapReduce framework.

8.3.3 Other Big Data Clustering

Bahmani et al. proposed Scalable K-Means++ in 2012, which is an amalgamation of random initialization and K-means++. Random initialization selects the k centers in one go by using uniform distribution. K-Means++ does not use uniform distribution but the number of iterations taken by it to select k center is k. Scalable K-Means++ tries to find the k centers in a non-uniform manner by taking fewer k iterations. Cai, Nie, and Huang in 2013 also implemented k-Means in MapReduce to deal with large-scale heterogeneous data sets. He et al. proposed an algorithm in 2011 that is a parallel version of DBSCAN, where all the critical processes have been parallelized. They experimentally proved that the load is balanced among the nodes in the cluster. Main focus was on the spatial data points, which can be extended to complicated special objects and high dimensional data. Work has also been done to use GPU clusters instead of CPU clusters to further increase the speed. The algorithm presented by Andrade et al. in 2013, called G-DBSCAN, is a parallel version of the DBSCAN on GPU. They showed experimentally the performance gains is in range of 100× in GPU over the CPU implementation. Cui, Charles, and Potok (2013) conducted research and implemented a flocking-based clustering algorithm on a GPU. The performance was in the range of 30 to 60 times over the CPU implementation. GPU's disadvantage lies in its limited, nonorthogonal instruction set and programming model, which needs to be explored more.

8.4 Conclusion

Clustering is indispensable in the era of data deluge. With the remarkable increase in the digital universe, traditional clustering techniques need to be optimized and improved to deal with large-scale data sets. The clustering algorithm for Big Data should be scalable and fast, and the computational cost should be minimum. These requirements can be fulfilled by parallel and distributed computing based on the cloud. Furthermore, to increase

160 *The Human Element of Big Data*

the processing, GPU clusters are used instead of CPU clusters. The chapter provided an extensive review of the developments that occurred in Big Data clustering, starting from single-machine algorithms to multiple machine with shared memory and the gradual shift toward algorithms based on the cloud.

Acknowledgments

The research work of author Ankita Sinha is supported by the Council of Scientific and Industrial Research (CSIR), New Delhi, India (No. 09/085(0111)/2014-EMR-1). The author is grateful to CSIR, India for financial support.

References

Aggarwal, C. C. and Reddy, C. K. (eds.). (2013). *Data Clustering: Algorithms and Applications*. CRC Press.

Andrade, G., Ramos, G., Madeira, D., Sachetto, R., Ferreira, R., and Rocha, L. (2013). G-dbscan: A GPU accelerated algorithm for density-based clustering. *Procedia Computer Science*, 18, 369–378.

Apache Software Foundation. (2015a). Spark. http://spark.apache.org.

Apache Software Foundation. (2015b). Welcome to Apache Hadoop! http://hadoop.apache.org.

Apache Software Foundation. (2015c). What is Apache Mahout? http://mahout.apache.org.

Bahmani, B., Moseley, B., Vattani, A., Kumar, R., and Vassilvitskii, S. (2012). Scalable k-means++. *Proceedings of the VLDB Endowment*, 5(7), 622–633.

Boutsidis, C., Zouzias, A., and Drineas, P. (2010). Random projections for k-means clustering. In *Advances in Neural Information Processing Systems* (pp. 298–306).

Bradley, P. S., Fayyad, U. M., and Reina, C. (1998, August). Scaling clustering algorithms to large databases. *KDD*, 9–15.

Cai, X., Nie, F., and Huang, H. (2013, August). Multi-view k-means clustering on big data. In *Proceedings of the Twenty-Third International Joint Conference on Artificial Intelligence* (pp. 2598–2604). AAAI Press.

Chen, C. P. and Zhang, C. Y. (2014). Data-intensive applications, challenges, techniques and technologies: A survey on Big Data. *Information Sciences*, 275, 314–347.

Cui, X., Charles, J. S., and Potok, T. (2013). GPU enhanced parallel computing for large scale data clustering. *Future Generation Computer Systems*, 29(7), 1736–1741.

Cui, X., Zhu, P., Yang, X., Li, K., and Ji, C. (2014). Optimized Big Data K-means clustering using MapReduce. *The Journal of Supercomputing*, 70(3), 1249–1259.

Dasgupta, S. (2000, June). Experiments with random projection. In *Proceedings of the Sixteenth Conference on Uncertainty in Artificial Intelligence* (pp. 143–151). Morgan Kaufmann.

Dean, J. and Ghemawat, S. (2008). MapReduce: Simplified data processing on large clusters. *Communications of the ACM*, 51(1), 107–113.

Drineas, P., Kannan, R., and Mahoney, M. W. (2006). Fast Monte Carlo algorithms for matrices III: Computing a compressed approximate matrix decomposition. *SIAM Journal on Computing*, 36(1), 184–206.

Fahad, A., Alshatri, N., Tari, Z., Alamri, A., Khalil, I., Zomaya, A. Y., and Bouras, A. (2014). A survey of clustering algorithms for big data: Taxonomy and empirical analysis. *IEEE Transactions on Emerging Topics in Computing*, 2(3), 267–279.

Fern, X. Z. and Brodley, C. E. (2003, August). Random projection for high dimensional data clustering: A cluster ensemble approach. *ICML*, 3, 186–193.

Golub, G. H. and Van Loan, C. F. (2012). *Matrix Computations* (vol. 3). JHU Press.

Guha, S., Rastogi, R., and Shim, K. (1998, June). CURE: An efficient clustering algorithm for large databases. *ACM SIGMOD Record*, 27(2), 73–84.

Hashem, I. A. T., Yaqoob, I., Anuar, N. B., Mokhtar, S., Gani, A., and Khan, S. U. (2015). The rise of "big data" on cloud computing: Review and open research issues. *Information Systems*, 47, 98–115.

He, Y., Tan, H., Luo, W., Mao, H., Ma, D., Feng, S., and Fan, J. (2011, December). MR-DBSCAN: An efficient parallel density-based clustering algorithm using MapReduce. In *IEEE 17th International Conference on Parallel and Distributed Systems* (ICPADS) (pp. 473–480). IEEE.

IBM. (2015). What is Big Data? http://www-01.ibm.com/software/data/bigdata/what-is-big-data.html.

Januzaj, E., Kriegel, H. P., and Pfeifle, M. (2004). DBDC: Density based distributed clustering. In *Advances in Database Technology-EDBT 2004* (pp. 88–105). Springer.

Johnson, W. B., and Lindenstrauss, J. (1984). Extensions of Lipschitz mappings into a Hilbert space. *Contemporary Mathematics*, 26, 189–206.

Kim, Y., Shim, K., Kim, M. S., and Lee, J. S. (2014). DBCURE-MR: An efficient density-based clustering algorithm for large data using MapReduce. *Information Systems*, 42, 15–35.

Laney, D. (2001). 3D data management: Controlling data volume, velocity and variety. *META Group Research Note*, 6, 70.

Microsoft Research. (2015). Dryad. http://research.microsoft.com/en-us/projects/dryad.

Ng, R. T. and Han, J. (2002). Clarans: A method for clustering objects for spatial data mining. *IEEE Transactions on Knowledge and Data Engineering*, 14(5), 1003–1016.

Pacheco, P. S. (1997). *Parallel Programming with MPI*. Morgan Kaufmann.

Rajaraman, A. and Ullman, J. D. (2012). *Mining of Massive Datasets* (vol. 77). Cambridge: Cambridge University Press.

Shirkhorshidi, A. S., Aghabozorgi, S., Wah, T. Y., and Herawan, T. (2014). Big data clustering: A review. In *Computational Science and Its Applications–ICCSA 2014* (pp. 707–720). Springer International Publishing.

Sun, J., Xie, Y., Zhang, H., and Faloutsos, C. (2007). Less is more: Compact matrix decomposition for large sparse graphs. In *Proceedings of the Seventh SIAM International Conference on Data Mining*, 127, 366. Society for Industrial and Applied Mathematics (SIAM).

Tong, H., Papadimitriou, S., Sun, J., Yu, P. S., and Faloutsos, C. (2008, August). Colibri: Fast mining of large static and dynamic graphs. In *Proceedings of the 14th ACM SIGKDD International Conference on Knowledge Discovery and Data Mining* (pp. 686–694). ACM.

White, T. (2012). *Hadoop: The Definitive Guide*. O'Reilly Media, Inc.

Yan, W., Brahmakshatriya, U., Xue, Y., Gilder, M., and Wise, B. (2013). p-PIC: Parallel power iteration clustering for big data. *Journal of Parallel and Distributed Computing*, 73(3), 352–359.

Zhang, T., Ramakrishnan, R., and Livny, M. (1996, June). BIRCH: An efficient data clustering method for very large databases. *ACM SIGMOD Record*, 25(2), 103–114.

Zhao, W., Ma, H., and He, Q. (2009). Parallel k-means clustering based on MapReduce. In *Cloud Computing* (pp. 674–679). Springer.

Authors

Ankita Sinha earned an MTech in computer applications at the Indian School of Mines (ISM), Dhanbad, in 2013 and is working as a junior research fellow in the Department of Computer Science and Engineering at ISM. Her research focuses on the design of efficient algorithms for handling Big Data over cloud.

 **Prasanta K. Jana** earned an MTech in computer science at the University of Calcutta in 1988 and a PhD at Jadavpur University in 2000. He is a professor in the Department of Computer Science and Engineering, Indian School of Mines, Dhanbad, India. He has authored 133 research articles and coauthored five books. He has also produced seven PhDs. In recognition of his outstanding research contributions, he was awarded Senior Member of IEEE in 2010. He is on the editorial board of two international journals and acted as a referee on many reputed international journals. Dr. Jana has served as the general chair of the international conference RAIT-2012, cochair of the national conference RAIT-2009, and the workshop WPDC-2008. He has also acted as an advisory committee member with several international conferences. His current research interests include wireless sensor networks, parallel and distributed computing, Big Data, cloud computing, and data clustering. He visited University of Aizu, Japan; Las Vegas, USA; Imperial College of London, UK; and University of Macau, Macau, and Hong Kong for academic purposes.

Section III

Future Research and Scope for the Human Element of Big Data

9

Smart Everything: Opportunities, Challenges, and Impact

Siddhartha Duggirala

CONTENTS

9.1 Introduction.. 165
9.2 Applications.. 167
    9.2.1 Customer-Oriented.. 168
        9.2.1.1 Home Automation (Smart Homes).. 168
        9.2.1.2 Healthcare 169
        9.2.1.3 Workplace.. 170
        9.2.1.4 Retail 171
    9.2.2 Smart Manufacturing.. 171
    9.2.3 Transportation.. 172
9.3 Challenges.. 174
    9.3.1 Technology... 174
    9.3.2 Connectivity 175
    9.3.3 Security... 175
    9.3.4 Privacy, Confidentiality, and Intellectual Rights................................... 175
    9.3.5 Interoperability 175
    9.3.6 Organizational Talent.. 176
    9.3.7 Public Policy 176
9.4 Summary... 176
References.. 177
Author.. 178

ABSTRACT Hyperconnected technology is the prima facie of our hyperaccelerated world. We have 3 billion-plus devices connected to the Internet, including everyday machines. The Internet of things in its current form is sweeping the Internet into a network of interconnected objects that senses the environment, interacts with the physical world, and at the same time uses existing Internet standards for providing services for information transfer, applications, and analytics.

9.1 Introduction

We are living in a world of hyperaccelerated innovation. And this crazy speed is drastically altering people's demands and needs. Each one of our lives and work have undergone metamorphosis and they are still changing. It's hard to be surprised when a normal person says that they find it difficult to do everyday chores or even mundane jobs due to time constraint. Such a velocity is the new norm. And the technology is the prima facie reason for this transformation.

Technology has come a long way since the Industrial Revolution. Early on technological emphasis was more on manufacturing things. Slowly the emphasis moved to sharing of information. With the web and international networks, huge global multinational companies have sprouted up. The ones with the data, or rather information, are kings. A few interrelated technologies that marked this phase are interconnectivity and commodity hardware. In the earlier networks, bandwidth was seriously constrained and highly expensive. The applications were sparse, and only the basic exchange of e-mails or data between research organizations and maybe a few networked was possible. As the bandwidth increased, advanced uses emerged and slowly more devices were connected to the Internet, and the commoditization of networks and computers have led to even more systems online. And the World Wide Web emerged as it is today. Meanwhile media consumption through the Internet increased, and the forerunners like YouTube and Netflix flourished, and together with torrents consumed more than 65% of whole Internet bandwidth. And as we evolve toward the next-generation of interconnectivity, we are looking at possibly the biggest change of our perception: building a cyber-physical world from the information world (Ashton, 2009).

And this is the phase of evolution we are in right now. We have approximately 7.4 billion devices connected to the Internet, but it is estimated that the number of Internet connected devices can go up to 11.6 billion devices by 2020 (Cisco, 2016). These are not just the desktop computers or laptops or even smartphones for that matter; these are everyday things we use: a coffee machine, thermostats, AC, refrigerators, televisions, industrial machines, cars, etc. (Manyika, 2014).

This new era of computing is built upon sensors and actuators, and radio frequency identification (RFID), which are embedded in the environment all around us, resulting in humongous amounts of data that has to be captured, stored, and processed. Various Big Data technologies like Hadoop and NoSQL databases for efficiently storing the data and processing frameworks like Spark, and R and Python sciKits can be used to extract patterns and make decisions.

The value in the new era of computing lies in finding patterns and making effective decisions based on those patterns. This will result in service-based business models and pay-as-you-go, similar to traditional commodities. Cloud computing can provide the virtual infrastructure for utility computing, thereby integrating the devices, processing platforms, and visualization tools like Tableau, DataViz (Ren, 2010), and D3.js to form end-to-end solutions for users.

A major chunk of the value that is derived from this evolution lies in control and efficiency. Efficient infrastructure directly relates to higher comfort of living for people; for commercial establishments the main advantage comes from the cost savings in preventive maintenance and process optimizations by controlling and monitoring each and every process efficiently. This has led to the movement that has been termed the Internet of Things (IoT) (Lee, 2015). In simple terms, IoT implies connecting every electronic device to the Internet, monitoring their usage, and making relevant decisions. The term was first coined by Kevin Ashton in 1999, albeit in the context of supply chain management. However, in the last few years the definition has been expanded to include vast application areas like transportation, healthcare, manufacturing, and utilities. The definition of things has been modified heavily from what had been originally envisioned.

Smart Everything 167

IoT in its current form is sweeping the Internet into a network of interconnected objects that senses the environment, interacts with the physical world, and at the same uses existing Internet standards for providing services for information transfer, applications, and analytics.

Imagine every electronic device you own or interact with is connected to the Internet. The next major step after connecting every device online is to be able to control the devices intelligently. This is Smart Everything. The "intelligent control" here implies that all the devices that interact with you directly or indirectly should be able to work in a collaborative fashion provide to your needs, based on your context and your interests. This interest can be your pleasure, manufacturing efficiency in plants, increasing the service of the service companies (Kopetz, 2011).

The European Technology Platform on Smart Systems Integration, ETP EPoSS Project defines Internet of Things as, "the worldwide network of interconnected objects uniquely addressable based on standard communication protocols."

According to Forrester Research, "a smart environment uses information and communication technologies to make the critical infrastructure components and services of education, healthcare, real estate, transport, city's administration and utilities more conscious, interactive and efficient."

A more relevant definition could be: "IoT is network of interconnected, interoperable sensing and actuating devices providing ability to share information across platforms, enabling us to perceive common operating picture and thereby develop innovative and efficient applications. This is achieved by utilizing ubiquitous sensing, analytics" (Gubbi, 2015). This evolution is fueled by commonness of devices enabled by open wireless technologies such as Bluetooth, radio frequency identification, Wi-Fi, and 4G-LTE/3G. The technological evolution in embedded sensor and actuator nodes is the harbinger of the transformation of the current static Internet into a fully dynamic, integrated future Internet (Buckley, 2006; Tan, 2010).

Most home automation devices and the current generation of smart applications are heavily based on ubiquitous Wi-Fi and mobile data services. However, to fully reach IoT's true vision, technology needs to disappear from the consciousness of the user with shared understanding of context, pervasive communication networks, and analytical tools (Gubbi, 2015).

9.2 Applications

The value of IoT is derived differently in different application domains. In consumer products and in retail industry, the value is derived from emphasis on customers. While in industries value is derived from process efficiency. As the IoT ecosystem evolves, new application areas might arise; nevertheless let's focus on a few major classes of applications in which we will see more market implementations in the near future (Lopez, 2012).

1. Consumer-oriented applications
   a. Home automation
   b. Healthcare
   c. Workplace
   d. Retail

2. Smart manufacturing

3. Transportation

4. Smart cities and communities

5. Smart grids and supplies

In the following sections we will review a few use cases and how value can be created for some applications.

9.2.1 Customer-Oriented

Customer-oriented applications directly deal with the end consumer in one way or the other. They might deal with changing the environment as per the consumer's tastes or enhance the environment to let us build our best work. This class can further be divided based on the context of application (Microsoft, 2015).

9.2.1.1 Home Automation (Smart Homes)

Our homes are the most intimate part of our lives. We craft the place according to our wishes, likings, and requirements. We strive to make it a better place, even though in most cases the home is just a couple of rooms.

One of the most seen examples of home automation is Jarvis from the *Iron Man* films. Some of the features of Jarvis are access control, temperature and weather control, and it controls and manages everything from the houses to the Iron fleet autonomously and automatically under the instructions of Jarvis. In 5 to 10 years this is going to be a reality of our world. With cost-effective, intelligent machines to cater to our needs we are going to see the next big disruption in our social order. I'm not talking about robots or Skynet (which is hell-bent on destroying humanity, from the *Terminator* movie series). I'm referring to the intelligent software that controls most parts of our lives.

A few applications can be intelligent sensing and temperature control. One of the biggest names in this space is the Nest Learning Thermostat. The thermostat uses advanced machine learning techniques to learn the temperature preferences of users and sets the temperature accordingly.

Home security is one of the biggest concerns of modern-day life. It makes good sense to track what is happening at our homes even when we are away. To help with this, we install sophisticated security HVAC systems. And sometimes we use a service provider to monitor the security 24/7. What we are referring to in this smart context is not just another remote controlling/monitoring solution. We are intelligently connecting motion, smoke, and carbon monoxide (CO) sensors to security. These integrations make it easier for home-owners to take appropriate action before it is too late to notify the respective authorities. Canary is one of the best examples of home security. It automatically video records everything, has night vision capabilities, and becomes more effective as one uses it longer. Using devices like Dropcam Pro or Nest Camera we can monitor the security footage of our homes in real time and we can integrate these with door locks and other security features.

Most home automation systems have a central hub that plays an intermediary role in communication among the connected smart devices. The smart devices generally provide and consume the necessary sensory data available in the publisher–subscriber model. One commercial example of a smart home hub is Wink Hub, which supports various communication technologies like Bluetooth, Z-Wave, ZigBee, Wi-Fi, Lutron, and Clear Connect.

Smart Everything

For example, if you are using Jawbone to monitor your sleeping cycle, as soon as the Jawbone goes into sleep mode you can set up a protocol that closes the window curtains, closes doors, switches off the lights, and maybe plays some calm music and adjusts the temperature. You could also use Amazon Echo to control the devices using your voice directly (Microsoft, 2015).

HomeSeer, Samsung SmartThings Hub, and Insteon are a few commercially available smart home hubs. A few other smart home devices include Philips Hue lighting, WeMo, and Samsung SmartThings Outlet. This smart home automation doesn't stop at the new devices, there is a way to control already present appliances albeit in a few predefined ways using smart power outlets to switch on and off, appliance modules for controlling the motion, etc.

When studying home automation software, do not overlook Apple HomeKit, which was unveiled with much fanfare. With HomeKit, Apple strives to create a common language between smart devices and leverages Siri the voice assistant. Using Apple HomeKit the devices are connected through Bluetooth LE instead of Wi-Fi as in the case of Nest and Samsung SmartThings.

Other open source alternatives are OpenHAB, which is a vendor and technology agnostic home automation software written in Java and based on OSGi and can be controlled on any system that can use JVM. An advantage of using this software is that it can work offline, meaning the devices need not be connected to the Internet. Other open source alternatives are Home Assistant, which is based on Python 3, and Wosh based on ANSI C++.

9.2.1.2 Healthcare

Healthcare is one of the prominent fields for IoT. With smartphones, health bands, and fitness trackers, end consumers are given the power to maintain their health and fitness with personalized expert advice. By making healthcare equipment smart, hospitals can now efficiently function in monitoring and curing the diseases of patients. Business models are transformed to meet the demands of data-influenced customers (Bui, 2011).

It is being touted that by the end of this decade, this data-enabled personalized analysis of our health and fitness will be the norm. Customized cure plans and social technologies will enable us to monitor our health more effectively. As we embrace this model of taking care of our health, companies need to rethink their business models. A healthcare provider will become any provider with sufficient technology to analyze and provide personalized health monitoring to these individuals.

Of all the healthcare related IoT deployments, the most popular is smart bands and fitness trackers. With the help of the product like Jawbone Up and Fitbit HR we can now track how much physical work we have done in a day, such as our sleep patterns and number of kilometers walked. This data is accessible via an easy API through which we can integrate with other applications that track our diet and medical history. This can help us in supervising our daily fitness goals, and can accurately show how our physical work and diet correspond to our long-term goals. An example of using API is to integrate your Fitbit activity tracker account with the MyFitnessPal mobile app to track your daily fitness and provide personalized exercise recommendations. Or you can integrate this with the TrendWeight app to understand how your weight is changing day by day. Users generally wear a smart band or smart watch that continually tracks the heart rate, step count, and distance walked, and when connected to the mobile phone hub, it syncs this data to the mobile app, which in turn synchronizes the data with the cloud. Any of the aforementioned integrations directly access the data from the Fitbit cloud or Jawbone cloud (Lee, 2015).

Athletes use smart wearables to track injuries, heart rate intensity while training, and effectiveness of the training. Through the Internet, the connected athlete's body becomes a network of sensors. With Big Data processing the athlete's performance and blood oxygen and CO_2 levels, heart, and respiratory rates can be tracked and used to assess the current physical condition. Using this concept of the connected athlete, teams can now reduce injuries and thereby use analytics to gain a competitive edge. Athos is one such connected apparel currently on the market.

With the help of smart wearables and simple diagnosis devices, like blood pressure measurement from iHealth, doctors and patients can track their individual health. Doctors can easily track the health and current physical conditions of their patients, thereby reducing the chances of illness. After surgery, wireless sensors can be attached to a remote patient health monitoring system (Rohokale, 2011) making it feasible for the patients to be discharged as soon as possible. Healthcare devices can be implanted subcutaneously to monitor vital signals and these vitals are communicated to apps in the cloud. Hospitals can implement cloud-based operative compliance tools to track whether hospital workers are following hygiene guidelines by tracking the usage of the hand-sanitizer dispenser. Hospitals can also track whether medicine has been administered or instructions given to the patient. Many medicines are scheduled drugs and the dosage use of those medicines should be in stipulated ranges. Hospitals can track the usage of medicinal doses by using RFID tags on medicines. The doctors can track whether patients are taking medicines in required doses through the wearable devices and medicine dispensing machines.

Remote monitoring of patients also becomes less expensive for the patients through the use of IoT. Wearables like smart slippers can alert the proper authorities if an elder has stepped out of a geofence (this type of tracking can be used for toddlers as well) (Dohr, 2010). Health devices connected to smartphones can be used to quickly diagnose health conditions just by taking pictures. These diagnostics are low cost and can be shared with healthcare professionals around the world. An interesting example for this is in Africa where eyesight checkups are being done through smartphones.

Recently, Apple released ResearchKit. This is an open source framework that allows developers and researchers to create applications for healthcare research. Developers can use this framework to let users crowdsource data for study on a variety of conditions like diabetes, breast cancer, asthma, and Parkinson's disease. Clinical trails are now being examined based on the data received from IoT devices, accelerating a drug's time to market, thereby potentially saving lives.

9.2.1.3 Workplace

The Internet of Things has a huge potential to transform today's workplaces into more productive and efficient places. For example, by accessing, monitoring, and analyzing the usage patterns of the workplace machinery, rooms, and equipment, better office layouts can be designed. Monitoring employee engagement in various office events and meetings, better plans can be made to increase the engagement. This data can be cross-referenced with employee health data to recommend certain workshops or check-ups. Based on this engagement level data, company can sponsor relevant training, doubling the productivity of employees.

Unauthorized usage of office facilities and unauthorized access to confidential information can hurt a business financially or strategically. Using ambient motion sensors

Smart Everything 171

with smart ID card, security can easily track whether the employee has the authorization required to access specific areas of the office (Pore, 2014).

Many devices are left on overnight or longer. The energy and utility bills due to wastage can be a huge drain on the business. Using motion sensors and thermosensors, one can estimate the number of people in the office building and the places they are in right now. With this information the lights and other electric equipment can be switched off reducing wastage. Also, by tracking the usage statistics of various rooms, businesses can remodel the offices to suit the usage in a better way. For example, if there are 10 big conference rooms with 100 seating capacity but most of the time teams of 5 are using the conference rooms, then the business can remodel the conference rooms to fit 5 to 10 people, thereby increasing the number of rooms available for teams.

Another big productivity cog at the workplace is malfunctioning printers or nonfunctioning laptops. By understanding the usage statistics and health of the asset, the downtime for the machine can be reduced and proactively provide preventative maintenance.

9.2.1.4 Retail

Retail potential for IoT is an interesting extension to social media marketing, brand positioning, and inventory management. The primary purpose of any retail outlet is to engage the customer to buy something of higher value to maximize profit (Chaffey, 2009).

Imagine if a retail salesperson knows that a customer likes a particular style of clothes or the customer is going to a dress-coded event, the salesman can now direct the customer toward the rack having the dresses of her liking. Sometimes a customer could be browsing but lurks at a specific stall with T-shirts. Seeing this, a salesperson comes forward to help the customer, but to his distress the customer leaves without buying anything. However, if the store has information about the customer's previous visits and knows the stalls where he lurks every time, then the store can give a personalized deal to the customer thereby converting the browser to a paying customer. Customer tracking can be done via smartphone or by placing i-beacons at every stall. These beacons can be used to engage with the customer at a more personal level and change the positioning of the brands, bringing forward popular brands depending on the season.

Also, by tracking every item using smart sensors, real-time inventory can be tracked, and if a particular item is found to be low in quantity then an order can automatically be placed. The supply chain can also be made efficient by prioritizing the items that are completely sold out.

Smart windows can be installed in retail outlets, which lets users choose their desired fabric, color, and model, and if they like, place a direct order automatically deducting the cost from the customer's account. Once a custom order is placed, the material is sourced directly from the supplier and the apparel is sent directly to the customer. The apparel is tagged with a sensor that the customer and sales representative track it. This model of convergence of brick-and-mortar stores with digital stores is going to redefine the user experience for shopping in the coming years.

9.2.2 Smart Manufacturing

The primary goal of manufacturing is to build a product efficiently and with optimal use of resources. The industrial revolution helped in removing the inefficiencies in manufacturing by replacing high-skill workers with machines. The output of the machine is always consistent with the design inputs that are fed into it. As time progressed, the production of a machine was broken down into component and assembly lines to increase the efficiency of production. Automatic machines took place of manual labor in certain parts of production. And many advanced manufacturing plants have some sort of internal network connecting the automated devices. But these devices are based on propriety communication protocols and are only accessible in the internal network. Connecting these automated devices to the Internet will facilitate remote monitoring of key performance metrics. And all the stakeholders can know the current state of the plant wherever they are (Microsoft, 2015).

This radically improves the efficiency and streamlines the communication of information. Decisions can be made in real time with the current state information being readily available. If anything is out of acceptable range, then the relevant authorities can be quickly notified and the correction can be quickly done. Closing a manufacturing plant due to a fault in one machine not only hurts production, but it causes severe financial losses to the company. IoT reduces the burden through preventive maintenance alerts given to the authorities by analyzing the data captured and predicting the fault. This notion reduces the plant downtime but also immensely increases the safety of the plant. There are a lot of quality control tests done after the product is assembled on the assembly line. At this step if any product fails the quality control tests, then relevant people can be immediately informed and the wastage can be reduced. And depending on the type of failure, the communication can also be escalated.

In the world of cutthroat competition, companies that continually strive to produce the best quality items with the lowest price win the customer race. And by eliminating wastage, and increasing the safety, efficiency, and reliability of the manufacturing plant and reducing the downtimes of the plant, industrial IoT will pave a huge opportunity for manufacturing companies to move past the competition. Industrial equipment manufacturer GE has recently introduced the industrial IoT cloud for the industrial IoT application. In the future, we will see more action happening in converting the hardware equipment sales model to service-based models (Atzori, 2010).

9.2.3 Transportation

Transportation is the core constituent of any economy. In other words, with no efficient cost-effective transportation network, people and goods cannot be moved from one place to another, bringing a standstill to the economy. The financial development of a region would be unimaginable. This point is illustrated through the evolution of cities and towns. With heavy urbanization, the traffic lanes have become congested with private vehicles and fleets transporting goods and services. Fleet owners and vehicle drivers can no longer rely on the age-old model of intuition; they need hard-proof data and actionable insights on transport routes, and vehicle and driver conditions (Marr, 2015).

In the lines of evolution, digital information is the lifeblood of the transportation industry. Networks of sensors and computers are integrated in every aspect of transportation including fleet management, surveillance, passenger information, public transport, and private vehicle safety and maintenance. IoT is forcing the hand of the fleet managers and transport owners to share and analyze the data to derive monetary benefits. For example, in cases of public transport, real-time passenger information like count data allows transport owners to optimize the schedules of vehicles. Combined with the passenger information, route congestion, local events, and weather data, analytical software can suggest adaptive routes improving customer service, thereby increasing the monetary benefits. Vehicle owners can implement vehicular telematics through IoT, which in turn helps in notifying other vehicles when there is the possibility of collision or even notify the driver

Smart Everything 173

about the probable collision and notify the relevant authorities directly after an accident. This helps not only in preventing collisions through machine-to-machine communication and machine-to-human communication, but also expedites the process after an accident happens. Vehicle health analytics can be monitored by vehicle technicians, who in turn can perform preventive maintenance (Lee, 2015).

As smart transport evolves, vehicles need to adapt to the driving style and experience of drivers. Monitoring the state of the driver also becomes easier, for example, a simple photo-based drowsiness detection system can be deployed in the vehicle that communicates with the brakes system of the vehicle. If the driver is drowsy, the vehicle is automatically stopped at the nearest possible safe stop, thereby reducing the probability of accidents. With the widespread deployment of GPS, vehicle sharing has become a norm. Uber, Lyft, and other rider-sharing companies have permanent places on our smartphones. But there is always a concern about personal safety of passengers. Using driver-state monitoring, passenger information and GPS information of vehicles can be kept under surveillance reducing the chances of unwanted security attacks.

A few initiatives across the world exemplify IoT in transportation. The Dallas Area Rapid Transit (DART), which is one of the larger public transit providers in the United States with over 100 million annual passengers, uses Cisco IoT to improve fleet management and preventive maintenance. Indian Railways, one of the largest railways in the world, is planning to use IoT for wagon maintenance, security, energy saving, and improved customer experience (Marr, 2015). At the community level everything from the streetlights, to traffic signals, and the water management system can be interconnected to better control and manage the whole community intelligently (Belissent, 2010).

IoT and Smart Everything are unprecedented opportunities to build a better world for everyone. That being said, there are a lot of research and practical challenges while moving forward. Skeptics fear that allowing enormous digital monitoring and conscious artificial intelligence systems might give rise to Skynet. This concern might sound too far-fetched, but given the state of development if correct measures are not taken, then the future might not be much different from what has been depicted in the Terminator movie series.

The definition of IoT as per our understanding has been evolving for the last two decades. For example, retailers and consumer good manufacturers have used RFID tags to track and manage inventories. Right now, we stand at a very exciting stage of digital evolution. A variety of technological advancements have fueled the rise of Smart Everything. The dropping prices of the smart hardware make the sensors, network bandwidth, cloud storage, and processing power affordable to consumers and industry at large. There have been huge efforts toward ubiquitous low-cost wireless coverage, which stands as a pillar to widespread IoE adoption. IoT applications also benefit from the improvements in distributed processing and Big Data analytics (Microsoft, 2015).

As we enter into the IoE market economy, the supplier industry is poised to evolve in a discrete manner (Figure 9.1). In the first phase, IoT hardware suppliers will create efficient hardware solutions to solve individual problems. Sensors and connectivity will be the major focus in this phase. Device makers like Fitbit, Nest, Apple, or network suppliers like Cisco and AT&T will be the prominent players in their respective markets. We have already witnessed this phase from the start of 2013 and it's still going on as of now.

In the second phase of IoE supplier evolution, we will see startups and established companies alike focusing more on the storage, analytics, and security of the data produced. The generic cloud platforms Microsoft Azure IoT and Amazon AWS IoT (Barr, 2015) or the open source cloud platform Bluemix IoT from IBM (IBM, 2015) will strive to build platforms with all the security and analytics features required to build IoT applications.

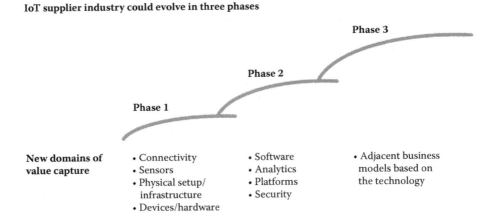

FIGURE 9.1
IoT supplier Industry evolution.

Vertical Cloud platforms like GE's Industrial IoT cloud (General Electric, n.d.) or Salesforce IoT cloud focusing on niche IoT application areas will start to hit the markets.

As we move on to the next phase of IoE implementation, interoperability between different vertical areas will be achieved and new business models and applications will be devised based on cross-classes of applications. Leveraging multiple sources of data, a fully contextual self-model of the world is built from amorphous structures we have right now.

9.3 Challenges

To deliver maximum benefits through IoT several hindrances need to be overcome (Want, 2015). A few of these challenges are technical, and others are social and regulatory. For example, businesses need to take proactive steps to include data-driven decision making enabled by IoT. Regulatory framework needs to support the innovation (Lee, 2015; Microsoft, 2015). For example, data sharing between consumers, companies, and even between countries needs to be streamlined. Another example can be whether to allow self-driving vehicles like the Google self-driving car onto public roads. If allowed, how will they be regulated? The classical problems with artificial intelligence also creep in when we mention smart homes or cities (Atzori, 2010; Lee, 2015; Microsoft, 2015).

9.3.1 Technology

For banal adoption of IoT, the cost of hardware needs to come down to a point that it becomes affordable for everyone. With the evolution of sensor technology and nanoelectronics, we can expect to get low-cost, low-power microelectronics with prices being dropped about 50% in the coming years. As we have already witnessed with smartphones, the average price has been slashed 30% to 70% in the last few years. Another technological inherence is that the sensors are mostly deployed in remote areas and they are expected to work several days with a single charge. And the batteries used need to be lightweight and economically viable. This implies that the sensor or actuator device needs to consume

Smart Everything 175

low power and cover larger ranges than the devices of the previous generation. And the energy consumption by these devices is also one concern for energy deficit economies of the future.

9.3.2 Connectivity

One of the major hurdles in bringing up IoT is that the Internet is not available in most parts of the world. For example, in India Internet penetration is only at 20% of the population. There are several efforts by governments all over the world to provide low-cost Internet services to the public. In India, hopefully with the push for Digital India and a nationwide fiber cable network plan, coverage will expand in the near future.

Most of the deployments for the IoT, as we have noted earlier, is mobile. This creates a huge challenge for data transmission, as the mobile networks can be rather spotty. In some cases the bandwidth required to transmit the data can be greater than the bandwidth available.

9.3.3 Security

IoT service providers and organizations need to have the means to secure the data from unwarranted and unauthorized access. In addition to that, they need to be able to deal with the new risks IoT deployment creates. With every device that is connected, new categories of security breaches can be introduced. Not only that, when these IoT systems control physical systems like energy grids or manufacturing plants, a security breach can have far more grave consequences than unauthorized access of data. Another risk that commercial IoT deployments face is that in the event of a security breach, commercial operations might fail causing enormous financial loss of the businesses.

9.3.4 Privacy, Confidentiality, and Intellectual Rights

Most of the data gathered through various sensors deployed throughout workplaces and personal devices is highly personal. The easy accessibility of this data might concern individuals about the privacy, confidentiality, and integrity of their data. Future IoT providers need to show compelling value and provide transparency on the data collection and utilization.

To fully unlock the potential of IoT, a common understanding on the data proprietorship and data access licenses for the data produced via connected devices is required across all stakeholders. The issue of data ownership between organizations can severely complicate IoT deployment. For example, consider a healthcare device manufactured by device company M is implanted into patient P by health service provider H. The health service provider monitors the data gathered by the device about patient P. The classic question arises as to who is the owner of the data gathered by the device: the healthcare provider, the patient, or the device manufacturer? This understanding is required beforehand to avoid violating the privacy and confidentially of the consumer.

9.3.5 Interoperability

As we have noted earlier in the chapter, the value of IoT is realized when we aggregate data from multiple sources and then a viable decision can be made based on the full current context. To realize this, multiple systems need to be able to cross-communicate and transfer data in an interpretable manner. This is not a simple task, as the integration needs to be done across systems, vendors, industries, and communication protocols.

There are about 400 standards related to IoT and several communication protocols like ZigBee, XMPP, and MQTT. And the one way to achieve the interoperability is to embrace the open standards. IoT consortiums like Open Interconnect Consortium, Industrial Internet Consortium, and Internet of Things Consortium are striving to bring about the much-needed standards and interoperability between multiple devices. Without standards, various companies will be building data silos that can be leveraged to extract any value.

9.3.6 Organizational Talent

Before IoT, in several organizations the IT department was abstracted away from the operational departments. For example, in a retail store the function of the IT comes in at the time of billing and static inventory management. But with the arrival of IoT, the IT departments were no longer alienated. IT departments are as equally responsible for successful operations as any other department. Every physical asset is embedded with a piece of IT that directly affects the operations. Companies need to nurture the talent to fit in this new realm where real-time data driven decisions can be made. The data generated often requires sophisticated programming and expertise to become actionable. And the analyzed data needs to be displayed in a format in which the decision makers can make an informed decision. And the employees are capable enough to tackle the challenges of security and data analysis of the data captured in a rightly manner. This challenges traditional business models and business relationships.

9.3.7 Public Policy

As noted earlier, certain IoT deployments call for regulatory monitoring and approval. This is due to the fact that IoT directly affects the physical things. So rules about liability must be firmly established. Policy makers need to create appropriate incentives for vendors, and at the same time create rules for data accessing, sharing, and usage.

Finally, IoT implementations are already showing potential for tremendous improvements in people's lives. From motivating people to stay fit to giving new tools to monitor and manage their health, decreasing pollution levels in cities, increasing the efficiencies in manufacturing, to providing customized deals to save energy and fuel, whatever might be the use case the profits are passed down to the people. The people are the major beneficiaries. By decreasing commuting time, saving time from the mundane tasks, and saving money on fuel, energy and providing safer communities and cities, peoples' lives will no doubt be enriched beyond measures.

But the data is after all just a tool that can be wielded to make the world a better place or make it a hell like no other. So, capturing the data is not the final deal for all IoT stakeholders; providing better service by following ethical and moral codes should be the final goal for the suppliers.

9.4 Summary

Smart Everything means the ability to connect every physical object, sensor, or any other source to the Internet and process the data to provide usage analytics and improve

Smart Everything

efficiencies. Depending on the context of the applications, they can be categories of several vertical classes of applications. Consumer IoT includes healthcare, wearables, and the workplace. Commercial IoT includes transportation, smart manufacturing, smart grids, and supplies. Social IoT includes smart communities and cities and environmental management. Whatever the application class, the major beneficiaries will be people. To realize the full potential of IoT several hindrances need to be resolved. The main ones among those are technology, connectivity, organizational talent, public policies, interoperability, security, and privacy. The evolution of IoE is marked by the product and services provided by suppliers.

References

Ashton, K. (2009). That "Internet of Things" thing. *RFID Journal*, 97–114.

Atzori, L. I. (2010). The Internet of Things: A survey. *Computer Networks*, 54(15), 2787–2805.

Barr, J. (2015). AWS IoT—Cloud services for connected devices. AWS Blog. Retrieved December 30, 2015. http://goo.gl/5Q9DUr.

Belissent, J. (2010). Getting clever about smart cities: New opportunities require new business models. Forrester Research.

Buckley, J. (2006). *The Internet of Things: From RFID to Next-Generation Pervasive Networked Systems*. Auerbach Publications.

Bui, N. Z. (2011). Health care applications: A solution based on the Internet of Things. International Symposium on Applied Sciences in Biomedical and Communication Technologies (p. 131). ACM.

Chaffey, D. E.-C. (2009). *Internet Marketing: Strategy, Implementation and Practice*. Pearson Education.

Cisco. (2016, February 3). Cisco Visual Networking Index: Global Mobile Data Traffic Forecast Update, 2015–2020. Available at http://www.cisco.com/c/en/us/solutions/collateral/service-provider/visual-networking-index-vni/mobile-white-paper-c11-520862.pdf.

Dohr, A. M.-O. (2010). The Internet of Things for ambient assisted living. *Seventh International Conference on Information Technology: New Generations* (pp. 804–809). IEEE.

General Electric. (n.d.). Predix: Industrial Internet of Things Cloud Platform. Retrieved December 30, 2015. https://www.ge.com/digital/predix.

Gubbi, J. B. (2015). Internet of Things (IoT): A vision, architectural elements, and future directions. *Future Generation Computer Systems*, 29(7), 1645–1660.

IBM. (2015). Internet of Things (IoT) Bluemix solutions. Retrieved December 30, 2015. www.ibm.com/cloud-computing/bluemix/solutions/iot/.

Kopetz, H. (2011). *Internet of Things in Real-Time Systems*. Springer.

Lee, I. L. (2015, July). The Internet of Things (IoT): Applications, investments and challenges for enterprises. *Business Horizons*, 58(4), 431–440.

Lopez, T. S. (2012). Adding sense to the Internet of Things—An architecture framework for smart objective systems. *Pervasive Ubiquitous Computing*, 291–308.

Manyika, J. D. (2014). The Internet of Things: Mapping value beyond hype. McKinsey Global Institute Report.

Marr, B. (2015, May 27). How Big Data and Internet of Things improve public transport in London. *Forbes*. Retrieved December 30, 2015. https://www.forbes.com/sites/bernardmarr/2015/05/27/how-big-data-and-theinternt-of-things-improve-public-transport-in-london/.

Microsoft. (2015). Capture value from Internet of Things. Retrieved December 30, 2015. http://goo.gl/pVHyts.

Pore, A. (2014, February 13). Designing a happier workplace. *Discover*. Retrieved December 30, 2015. http://discovermagazine.com/2014/march/11-designing-a-happy-workplace.

Ren, L. T. (2010). DaisyViz: A model-based user interface toolkit for interactive information visualization system. *Journal of Visual Languages and Computing*, 21(4), 209–229.

Rohokale, M. V. (2011). A cooperative Internet of Things for rural healthcare monitoring and control. *International Conference on Wireless communication, Vehicular Technology, Information Theory and Aerospace and Electronic Systems Technology* (pp. 1–6). IEEE.

Tan, L. W. (2010). Future Internet: The Internet of Things. *3rd International Conference on Advanced Computer Theory and Engineering* (pp. V5-376–V5-380). IEEE.

Want, R. S. (2015). Enabling the Internet of Things. *Computer*, 48(1), 28–35.

Author

Siddhartha Duggirala is a software engineer developing enterprise software products. He is fascinated by data and its impact on the world. He is a published author in the areas of data, analytics, and artificial intelligence. He is a graduate of the Indian Institute of Technology, Indore.

10

Social Media and Big Data

Richard Millham and Surendra Thakur

CONTENTS

10.1 Introduction 179
10.2 Introduction to Social Media 180
    10.2.1 Social Media Role in Events 180
    10.2.2 Political Power 181
10.3 Business 182
10.4 Introduction to Big Data 184
    10.4.1 Definition 184
    10.4.2 Traditional Structuring Techniques 184
    10.4.3 Social Media Analysis and Structuring Techniques 185
    10.4.4 Big Data Architectures 186
    10.4.5 Ontology 187
10.5 Case Studies 187
    10.5.1 Airbnb 187
    10.5.2 #FeesMustFall 189
10.6 Conclusion 189
References 190
Authors 193

ABSTRACT Big Data, whether originating from traditional or social media sources, is able to provide hidden insights into our lives to others through data analysis. However, before any meaningful data analysis can occur, the meanings within Big Data must be derived and Big Data must be structured accordingly. In this chapter, we briefly examine the role of social media in terms of cause–effect–solution with its effect on political power and business. An overview of data structuring techniques is given with a proposed feasible database architecture and ontology. Social media case studies are given to show how data generated from them could be structured for easier analysis.

10.1 Introduction

In this chapter, we investigate the role of social media as providing a "virtual" sense of community among users. This sense of community enables participants to adopt a cause–effect–solution approach where one or more members of a community identifies a cause; members of the community come together to produce an effect; and a solution from this effect ensues. Examples of this cause–effect–solution are outlined in social media's role in organizing political protests and its effect on business. In additional, several examples are given where social media played a unique role in events, both positive and negative. An introduction to Big Data structuring techniques, both for traditional and social media data, is given with a suitable database model and ontology. Case studies, one centered on political protests and one centered on business, will be given to demonstrate how data could be structured for easier analysis.

One of the forerunners of social media, e-mail, has always had the advantage of simplicity and ease of use. E-mail was conceived to be a simple duplex communication where one person sent a text message to another person who was connected to their network. Through the use of mail forwarding and multiple recipients, e-mail's original duplex communication changed to a multiplex communication. Through the addition of more features and the introduction of interactivity, e-mail, in part, spawned the further growth of different types of social media (Idugboe, 2015).

The role of social media has had a huge impact in a number of ways. Social media has dramatically changed the way that we communicate and interact with each other. Social media, through the facility of remote networking, enabled the development of communities and subcultures that without social media would not otherwise have been possible. Social media has brought people together and enabled the sharing of knowledge between people of different communities, cultures, countries, and continents. Social media has given many, especially those belonging to marginalized and minority groups, the ability to voice their opinions and concerns. In many different ways, social media has empowered the first creation of a global village, where everyone is a "virtual" neighbor of another (Strømmen-Bakhtiar, 2012).

10.2 Introduction to Social Media

Although there is much contention over the terms "social media" and "social networks," Ellison defines "social networks" to be web-based services that allow users to first set up their own public profile and delineate individuals with whom they wish to share a connection and then, within the system boundaries, navigate and view these links (Ellison, 2007). Besides developing links with other individuals, social media allows users to develop their own content and then work together with others to both improve the content and to have a shared understanding of this content (Westerman, Spence, and Van Der Heide, 2012).

As the Internet grew from the 1990s, the world's networked population has increased from the low millions to the low billions. During this same period of time, the prevalence of social media has become a reality for all levels of society including activists, regular citizens, governments, and nongovernment organizations (NGOs) (Shirky, 2011).

10.2.1 Social Media Role in Events

In this section, several examples are provided as to how social media is strongly intermeshed with people's lives and can help provide a solution to problems (carjacking, disruptions caused by earthquake, etc.). Social media can also provide a public backlash against an insensitive comment posted by a user.

Social media has been used to crowdsource help among unconnected users for a number of causes. One event occurred on April 7, 2012, when a man was carjacked in Johannesburg,

Social Media and Big Data 181

South Africa. The man, locked in the trunk of his car, messaged, via Twitter (a tweet) on his mobile, to his girlfriend about his situation. His girlfriend tweeted a description of his car and asked others to retweet (circulate the message) (Peters, 2012). Although only 7 people retweeted this message, one friend retweeted this message to user @Pigspotter, who posts warnings of speed traps and has 110,000 followers, who sent the message on to his followers. A Twitter frenzy erupted with police and private citizens on the lookout for the car. Within two hours, the car was found, with the boyfriend safe, in a town two hours away from Johannesburg (Smith, 2012).

Social media also plays the role of the positive interventionist in people's lives as demonstrated in the 2011 Japanese earthquake. During the disaster, Twitter published a mobile web page, in both English and Japanese, on how to use Twitter during an emergency and different hashtags for different relevant topics. As Japan has 115 million Internet-able mobiles for a population of 126 million, virtually every inhabitant could use Twitter to receive updates or send messages of distress. Although less popular in Japan, Facebook was leveraged by organizations and volunteers to crowdfund earthquake relief efforts. A Facebook page, Disaster Relief, as of October 2011, served as a central page for disaster information with over 680,000 "likes" by users. Facebook relayed information on blackouts and train service during the disaster and allowed every user, inside and outside the country, to get in touch with loved ones (Peary, Shaw, and Takeuchi, 2012).

Social media may also serve as an outlet for the public to backlash on a user and as a form of social control. Justine Sacco, a successful marketing executive, was heading to South Africa for Christmas 2013. At Heathrow Airport near London, she tweeted "Going to Africa. Hope I don't get AIDS. Just kidding. I'm White" before boarding her flight to South Africa. The tweet was meant to mock Westerners' consideration of HIV/AIDS as an "African thing" to which they are immune, despite the fact that there is an AIDS epidemic in the United States (Ronson, 2015a). Although Sacco only had 170 followers, which would have doomed the tweet to anonymity, a racism advocate Ronson (2015b), who searches Twitter for racist tweets, found it and widely posted it on social media. A media storm erupted as the tweet became the top worldwide trend. Before Sacco landed, she lost her job and gained infamy (Waterflow, 2015). To justify why he reposted the tweet and to explain social media's new influence, Ronson (2015b) stated: "A great renaissance of public shaming is sweeping our land. Justice has been democratized. The silent majority are getting a voice and are mercilessly finding people's faults. … The internet mob is using shame as formative social control." The propensity of social media as working as a social control, without restrictions or controls, may be queried through the act of one user asking Ronson during his reposting: "Were you a bully in school?"

10.2.2 Political Power

Social media, through the nature of the flat governance hierarchies and dispersed power of its networks, enables political activism by permitting grassroots members to participate in the political process without the guidance of institutions or organizations (Rheingold, 2002). Furthermore, social media's attributes of easy use and transparency make it very useful for social activists (Corera, 2015). Social media allows protestors to organize their thoughts and to synchronize their actions (Shirky, 2011). Social media can be termed to be an alternative online media that challenges the "news" as presented by mass media; coordinates protest interactions on the local, national, or international level; and provides a means of cooperation in terms of unifying protest messages and in engaging geographically dispersed people who may not know each other to participate in protests (Fuchs, 2006).

One of the earliest uses of social media as a political empowerment tool was during the impeachment trial of Philippine President Estrada in 2001. After the legislature voted to suppress crucial evidence against him that probably would have led to his acquittal, irate Filipinos used 7 million text messages to coordinate meeting places of protests. After days of massive protests, the evidence was allowed to be introduced and Estrada was forced to resign (Shirky, 2011). Social media's collaborative projects, where dispersed people work together to develop content, played a role in the Egyptian uprising of 2011 where such a project, Google Docs, allowed the development and dissemination of protests, tactics and demands (Joseph, 2012).

Social media allows formerly isolated people to join together in protest and to present alternate views in opposition to mainstream media. An example of social media exposing government malfeasance was the video posting of the killing of Neda Agha-Soltan by government forces during the Iranian protests of 2009, which created extensive denunciation of the Iranian government's tactics (Joseph, 2012). Alternative web-based news content was provided by Mohammad Nabbous who streamed live video of events in his city of Benghazi, the rebel stronghold in Libya, in early 2011 to his viewers. Blogs are often used by dissidents to present alternate views in comparison with mainstream media that are often controlled by authoritarian governments (Joseph, 2012). An example of social media, in this case Facebook, uniting dispersed and voiceless people is the Facebook group A Million Voices Against FARC, which was initiated by 6 people and grew to 3000 supporters within the first 24 hours and now has 230,000 members. FARC is Columbia's oldest and most powerful rebel group, who claim to represent the poor and oppressed, but was corrupted by the country's prolific drug trade and was transformed into kidnappers and murderers of innocent citizens (Neumayer and Raffl, 2008).

Twitter is another social media platform used for social protests. Because Twitter restricts user postings to 140 characters, this limitation created speed in sending messages, or tweets, with the subsequent advantage of these tweets sending news in real time (Westerman, Spence, and Van Der Heide, 2012). Unlike Facebook's connection model, these tweets are normally visible to every other viewer. The real-time nature of tweets and the ability to search by topic enables a large number of followers to discover information on a particular subject and to participate. An example of a Twitter protest movement occurred in Mexico in 2009 when the government tried to institute a tax on Internet usage. A single legislator posted a protesting tweet that within 10 days produced 100,000 supporting tweets. After a few weeks of protests, the Internet tax was repealed (Sandoval-Almazan and Gil-Garcia, 2013).

Social media allows protestors to organize their thoughts and to synchronize their actions. However, the exact impact of their effect cannot be measured. Social media-inspired protests seem to be most successful where the government is constrained by the public sphere. In more repressive regimes, social media may have inspired the people to consider alternative regimes but these protests were successful per se when the governments, due to economic and other factors, had become weakened (Shirky, 2011).

10.3 Business

Business traditionally has had a high degree of communication control over marketing. They used paid agents (such as advertising agencies, marketing research firms, and public

Social Media and Big Data

relations consultants) to coordinate their company-led product promotions in terms of their medium, frequency, advertising content, and timing. Any product information outside these bounds were through consumer word-of-mouth whose impact was restricted due to limited dissemination (Mangold and Faulds, 2009).

With the advent of social media, businesses' degree of communication control has dramatically been reduced. The locus of control has shifted to the experiences of individual consumers who share their experiences on various social media platforms, many of which are fully autonomous of businesses and their agents (Mangold and Faulds, 2009). Consumers have switched from business-controlled traditional media to social media sources to conduct their own searches upon which they base their purchasing decisions. Furthermore, information obtained from social media sources is considered more trustworthy than that obtained from corporate sources (Ahn, Oh, and Kim, 2013). This shift has given consumers unprecedented power in the marketplace and has overpoweringly impacted all facets of consumer behavior (Mangold and Faulds, 2009).

Besides marketing promotion, social media has found that a majority of social media users (78%) found that their online interactions with people have made them more open to the idea of sharing with strangers. This willingness to share indicates that social media has been instrumental in breaking down trust barriers. This sharing may be in many forms such as sharing one's expertise to develop a solution to a problem (programmer's forums, open source software) to sharing of physical goods (John, 2013).

In order to manage social media's influence on business, it is suggested that marketing managers embrace social media and redirect its influences. One suggestion is to use company-sponsored sites to mimic the virtual community of like-minded individuals that social media provides. For example, RoadRunner Records provides a forum section to gather fans of rock and metal music to promote their music genres' discussion and to promote their products. Another suggestion is to utilize blogs to permit consumers to provide feedback about products whether in the form of congratulations, criticisms, and helpful recommendations. This feedback, whatever the form, helps develop a community where transparent conversion is stimulated and customer commitment is increased. Toyota not only encourages feedback from its customers, via its blog, but also from journalists and even rival companies (Mangold and Faulds, 2009).

To determine the influence traditional companies have had on social media, a survey of the number of Facebook "likes" was taken of five of the world's top consumer corporations, as defined by Chen (2015). The results of the survey are shown in Table 10.1. Given that Facebook has reached over 1.5 billion monthly users by September 30, 2015, the number of "likes" or acknowledgements from this huge population base is relatively small. The company with the largest "adherents" was Samsung (Mobile), which suggests a popular

TABLE 10.1

Facebook Company Pages and "Likes"

Company	Number of "Likes"*
Volkswagen	24.04 million
Wells Fargo	853,756
Toyota (USA)	2.6 million
Apple	9.268 million
Samsung (Mobile)	42 million

* As of September 30, 2015.

product among a media and Internet savvy crowd, while the smallest following was Wells Fargo, a banking conglomerate, with a diverse base of customers.

10.4 Introduction to Big Data

10.4.1 Definition

The term Big Data is often defined through its characteristics of volume, velocity, and variety (Diebold, 2003). Volume refers to the huge amount of data that must be considered; velocity refers to the speed needed to process and analyze this data; and variety refers to the structure (or lack thereof) within this data (Warin and Sanger, 2014).

As the data sources change, the nature of data is evolving. In 2013, only 20% of the world's data is structured (typically processed by traditional systems) while the remaining is unstructured (Nemschoff, 2013). The prominence of unstructured data entails a number of challenges such as data variability and data complexity. Because each type of data has its own characteristics and handling requirements, structuring and integrating this data into a common schema for analysis is multifaceted and difficult but is a prerequisite for unified analysis (Composite Software, 2013; Peng et al., 2008; Swoyer, 2013). Data integration for relational databases stress unity of data, despite increased complexity and cost. This data unification comes at a price in terms of increased costs and huge amounts of time. On the other hand, Big Data integration, given the constraints of velocity, volume, and variety, is willing to give up some aspects of data unity in return for improved performance and increased simplicity (Composite Software, 2013; Swoyer, 2013).

In traditional Big Data structuring, concepts from nonlinear system identification (Billings, 2012) are applied to large sets of sparse data (Delort, 2012) to indicate associations, dependencies, and forecasts of outcomes and behaviors (Billings, 2012).

10.4.2 Traditional Structuring Techniques

The first step in the integration of heterogeneous data is to resolve the value, syntax, semantic, and structural differences among the data sources (Seligman et al., 2002). Data value and semantic consistencies often arise (Geng and Kong, 2008). An example of data value inconsistency may be the use of two different representations of an address for a person, such as "84 Asher Str" and "Eighty Four Asher Street," while an example of data semantic inconsistency might be having a person's address both as "ClientAddress" and "PersonAddress" entities (Boufares and Salem, 2012).

In order to handle data value and semantic inconsistencies, some researchers leave out conflicting data from a query ("No gossiping") or use a trusted third party for guidance ("Trust Your Friends"). More automated resolution practices include randomly choosing one out of the many conflicting alternatives ("Roll the Dice"), choose the most common value ("Cry with Wolves"), and choose the most recently updated value ("Keep up to Date") (Bleiholder and Naumann, 2006). The strategy chosen often depends on the domain expert guidance and the presence of metadata. If certain metadata is available, the "Trust Your Friends" and "Keep Up to Date" may be chosen (Bleiholder and Naumann, 2006). The expert user may choose the practice "Keep up to Date" for conflicting addresses yet choose

Social Media and Big Data

"Cry with Wolves" for multiple conflicting values with the assumption that uncommon values may be the result of data entry errors.

Domain experts may be used to determine semantic similarity between different attributes. The attributes *Purchaser* and *Client*, created by modelers with different viewpoints, have similar but slightly different semantics but may be grouped at the global level into the attribute *Consumer*. Often two attributes will require bridging information to merge into a conceptual attribute. An example might be *Account* and *Annuity* requiring the bridging information of pension to explain the concept global attribute of *Pension* (Geng and Kong, 2008). Similarly, two attributes with the same name, such as *Cost*, may have two entirely different meanings, such as *TotalCost* and *UnitCost*. Visa versa, two differently named attributes, such as *Sellers* and *Vendors*, may refer to the same entity (Reddy et al., 1994).

Other techniques include using Bayesian decision theory to find similarities among different concepts and then attributes. The Cupid approach first uses domain-specific dictionary and thesaurus lookups for terms, and then uses these terms with a similarity coefficient, based on linguistic similarities, to match schemas, with their relationships and attributes. It is assumed that the shorter the similarity distance between terms the more closely related the terms must be (Villányi and Martinek, 2012). These related attributes, with their calculated relationships, are amalgamated into an ontology (Duong et al., 2009).

These semantic discovery techniques, with their automated mappings, are not proficient at defining intricate contextual entities with an error rate of 50% as demonstrated in experiments (Reynaud, Sirot, and Vodislav, 2001). To address this problem of incorrectness, some researchers will mark these automated mappings as tentative to be resolved later through domain experts (Geng and Kong, 2008).

10.4.3 Social Media Analysis and Structuring Techniques

Traditional business analytics, based on more structured and predictable business data, are often impractical when dealing with social media, due to its constant evolving nature, large human element, and lack of clear structure. Consequently, social media analytics require new, in addition to traditional, techniques in order to derive insights from social media (Hussain and Vatrapu, 2014).

Some examples of traditional techniques used to structure data within social media include image-recognition algorithms to identify any relations between a multitude of images and audio deciphering techniques to identify audio content. Video, partially due to its complex nature and partially due to its immense volume, poses a challenge. Video is usually separated into audio and video constituents (Goplan, 2012). The video constituent is often split into one or more frames where the entities within the frame(s) are determined via feature identification algorithms (Zhu et al., 2015). Despite the use of these techniques, there is no standard set of methods that identifies action within video. Action is often thought to constitute the content and semantic meaning of the video (Goplan, 2012).

Existing attributes within social media such as URLs, hashtags, words, @usernames, and selected phrases, are often used to categorize groups and structure data (Lieberman, 2014). Batool et al. (2013) structures tweets using the existing structural attributes of Username, TweetDate, Status, TweetID, and Image. Keywords are identified and analyzed using Markov-based taggers and statistical methods to determine further semantic meaning and structure (Batool et al., 2013). Multidimensional analysis using sentiment (positive/negative), frequency, and correlation analysis was performed using a small set of keywords to determine attributes in tweets (Kim et al., 2012). Buono et al. (2005) extracted a small predetermined number of events from a given domain of tweets in order to establish pattern(s) of topics. A social media platform, Twitter, is often used for experimentation due to the huge size of its available data, accessibility, and ease of analysis (relative to other social media formats) (Tufecki, 2014). However, due to its 140-character limitation, only a short description can be given, which prevents use of traditional topic discovery methods (Yin et al., 2013).

Traditional statistical analyses, such as factor analyses, cannot always provide the needed structuring information. The use of time series techniques, such as Fourier, gives only a one-dimensional analysis view of data: its evolution through time. Warin and Sanger (2014) combine these time analysis and frequency dimensions to create the pace of evolution, which is based on financial modeling. This model is used to both analyze an evolving trend in social media, within the event context of the time tweeted, and to determine, from the frequency posted, its importance.

These categories may be grouped into five trends of social media analysis (Warin and Sanger 2014):

1. Constant rate of posts over social networking website
2. High return and low variance (high growth rate of posts with constant rates of growth indicating an interesting topic that is engaging more and more people)
3. High return and high variance (a small increase in posts with high volatility indicating a topic that is growing slowly in engagement with varying interest levels)
4. Low variance and low return (a steady decrease in posts indicating a topic that is progressively losing interest among participants)
5. Low return and high variance (small number of participants that post infrequently indicating that a topic is of small interest with little currency)

The use of metadata, cross-referencing, and patterns are critical parts to deriving meaning from otherwise undecipherable content. Human behavior has a highly predictive and repetitive component to it. An example might be encrypted cellphone communication, which is enigmatic to derive content from; however, when cross-referenced with different data items that we have a relationship with, such as using bus tickets and paying with credit cards, compared with the aggregate norm of other people, may indicate an outlier and help provide clearer meaning of their conversation (Corera, 2015).

10.4.4 Big Data Architectures

Although data has been traditionally handled by a relational database model due to the model's maturity, standardization, and solid mathematical basis (SyonCloud, 2013), relational databases are often ineffective in handling large data sets (Agrawal, Das, and El Abbadi, 2010) As a specialized solution, graph databases are utilized when the relationships between data items (nodes of information) are more important than the data items themselves with the disadvantage of added complexity. Key-value properties are used to look up both nodes and relationships. In order to utilize such a database, the nodes or entities first must be discovered and then the relationships between them identified (Burtica et al., 2012).

Using network theory, nodes (denoting data items or individual actors within this network) and relationships (denoting associations between entities including employees,

Social Media and Big Data

Facebook friends, e-mail correspondence, hyperlinks, and Twitter responses) are incorporated into the graph database. Social networks, represented by graph databases, have been used to represent and analyze the data contained within these databases such as determining and analyzing corporate structures, client relationships, and authorship (Lieberman, 2014).

An example of a social network used in a traditional business setting is the supermarket. Food items are represented as entities and groups of entities that are purchased together are represented by associations with transaction rates/value weightings. The association with the heaviest weighting is not necessarily of interest; for example, it is commonly known that burgers and buns are purchased together. The most valuable information is what is unknown, that is, what entity is common to all groups, which, in this case, might be milk. Using this knowledge, supermarkets can attract all types of shoppers by promoting and discounting milk (Lieberman, 2014).

10.4.5 Ontology

In conjunction with the nodes and relationships of a graph database, an ontology is needed to map data from various sources into a global schema that can be translated into a graph database structure.

Because Big Data is comprised of data from various sources, each with varying structure, nomenclature, and content, there is a need to have a common global schema with clear and single-set definitions of data attributes and relations (Reddy et al., 1994). In order to manage this heterogeneous data, an n-layer ontology level is used where the topmost layer provides a global uniform view of data that is useful for analysis; the middle layer provides a logical view of a standardized set of names; and the bottom layer contains the original data elements mapped to names in the middle layer (Composite Software, 2013). With traditional data, common buiness terms and definitions are used in the middle layer to provide a standardized set of terms to diverse terms used in the lower layer (Bertino, 1991). Because the data sources and content frequently change, there is a need to quickly update the data mappings within the ontology to the global schema (Geng and Yong, 2008).

Given the even more rapidly changing nature of content and relationships among data present in social media, we propose another layer to this ontology. On top of the topmost layer, which represents the global schema, we propose a time-based layer that holds mapping from the global schema to a particular point in time. As a topic's (which may be represented as a single item in the global schema) meaning and importance shifts with time, the time-topic tuple provides a unique identifier for that topic at a particular point in time. Furthermore, this added ontology layer provides the ability to analyze the changing nature of a single topic over time.

10.5 Case Studies

10.5.1 Airbnb

An example of Big Data structuring within social media is the website Airbnb. Airbnb started in 2007 when several roommates rented out air mattresses on their floor for conference attendees who had no other place to stay. It evolved into a booking service for hosts and guests worldwide; by 2012, it was worth $1.3 billion and had 10 million nights of bookings. The success of the company has been attributed to the "sharing" economy that was redeveloped using technology. The idea of a sharing economy has been better received by people in older age demographics, who were used to "barter and share" economies, than those in early age demographics (Salter, 2012). It could be argued that Airbnb is a return to the old social world of sharing among kindred spirits (an old-fashioned trip that meant staying with friends/relatives rather than hotels) that has reemerged through social media (John, 2013). Guttentag (2013), after studying factors motivating an Airbnb stay versus a hotel stay, confirmed that a "drive for community" or social interactions was one of the main reasons.

In order to both build a predictive model of future needs and stays and to structure its rentals, Airbnb extracts "words of interest" from site descriptions and reviews. Using the Stanford Part of Speech Tagger, with custom-built algorithms within it, 150 different attributes (such as beaches, hiking) are extracted from these descriptions and reviews, and conjoined with location to form structures on which predictive mining can occur (McMillan, 2014). The selection of a small number of attributes is justified by the work of other researchers who found that the top keywords, or selected attributes, occur in less than 10% of the word structures of a description or review yet form the key motivators for an Airbnb selection. In contrast to hotels, whose keyword clusters often focus on location, Airbnb word clusters focus on type of neighborhood (Tussyadiah and Zach, 2012).

This preference for types of neighborhoods had to be included in the location query for possible Airbnb hosts. Originally, an Airbnb location query returned the highest number of hosts, using a given distance from the user-specified location, using date, price, and other parameters as filters. This strict distance-based query showed preference to hosts in the city center while ignoring hosts in the suburbs where many users prefer to stopover. Furthermore, the distance-based query ignored the differing occupant densities of cities. To take these preferred suburb hosts into account, the distance-based query was replaced by a conditional probability query. A conditional probability query is centered on a given location with the probability of possible bookings based on bookings and distances for this location in the past. This conditional probability distance also had a skew—many past bookings depended on a nearby venue or event that the current booker might not be interested in. Consequently, Airbnb used normalized conditional booking per location to smooth out a spate of bookings based on a single event and give a broader range of bookings that a current booker might be interested in (Newman, 2015).

One of the features of Airbnb is for visitors to leave a review of their place with a short textual description and a rating out of 5 stars. The collective statistics on past individual ratings for a place is provided for future visitors. This rating system, which is used to identify good places to stay from worse ones, relies on one of social media's advantages in that potential visitors view other past visitor's ratings of an establishment as more trustworthy than business/host ratings of their institution (Ahn, Oh, and Kim, 2013).

In order to structure the facilities offered and the quality of accommodation offered, reliance should be placed on "keywords of interest" and preferred neighborhood locations, based on normalized past visit history per location, along with aggregate past visitor's ratings, which are more in line with social media's preferences rather than traditional lodging attributes of location, facilities, type of room, and so on.

Social Media and Big Data

189

10.5.2 #FeesMustFall

An example of Big Data analysis and subsequent structuring of a political movement, through tweets, is the #FeesMustFall campaign. An analysis of the #FeesMustFall movement is extremely complex. Using graph-based analysis and Lieberman (2014) categories, these tweets, using localized hashtags and location, were grouped into communities, centered around universities, with strong interconnections (denoted by retweets or @ mentions) among almost all users. Very few users were peripheral (Findlay, 2015). Lieberman (2014) would classify this as an in-group (dense interconnections within the group with few interconnections outside the group), yet this classification is faulty as there is evidence of interconnectivity of this movement with similar movements worldwide (Baloyi and Issacs, 2015; Chunylall, 2015). Even the in-group model is simplistic as the most numerous tweets had a hashtag of #douniates, which would denote a hub model. #douniates, based in New York and focused on #BlackLivesMatter (a movement that originated as a protest against police brutality and widened into government institutionalized causes; Cartegena, 2015), retweeted to an independent audience. Each community initially had a unique hashtag but after October 21, 2015, when student protesters were confronted by police at the Parliament Buildings in Cape Town, these hashtags consolidated into a single hashtag, #FeesMustFall (Findlay, 2015). The importance of this covalence is indicated by the government's short-lived attempts to ban this hashtag (Chunylall, 2015). The nature of the movement changed from a protest over student tuition fees to demanding the resignation of the education minister and finally demanding change to the South African government (Findlay, 2015).

In terms of Big Data structure, this analysis indicates the importance of time, domain, and frequency components within data and the quick-changing evolution of themes and hashtag postings within a movement in social media in contrast to the more stable structure of traditional data (Millham, 2016). Initial hashtags, which might be used to classify social media postings as data classification attributes, evolve over time and with this change comes the changing schema of a database (indicating the requirement of a time-specific ontology layer).

10.6 Conclusion

In this chapter, examples of the pervasiveness of social media on our lives were given. These examples include the use of social media to coordinate the rescue of a hijacked man, disaster relief, and the use of social media as a form of social control. With extensiveness of social media in so many people's lives comes the dimension of Big Data: the volume and velocity of a huge number of individual interactions and the variety of formats given the range of social media platforms.

Because this huge amount of data needs to be structured for future analysis, a few traditional structuring techniques were mentioned along with additional techniques used for social media. The part of ontologies were used to provide a link between native social media sources and a global uniform schema that can be more easily used for analysis. Because social media has a critical time component within its interactions, unlike most traditional data, the use of a time-based layer within the ontology was proposed to aid better structuring and understanding. Graph-based databases for Big Data were proposed as a way to mimic the relationship structure of social media and to utilize this structure to find insights into the data that it held.

The role of social media in political protests and business was mentioned as providing a voice to the formerly voiceless and in coordinating actions. Two case studies, one business based and the other political based, were used to illustrate not only the role that social media played within them but also to show how the information within these case studies could be structured for Big Data analysis.

References

Agrawal, D., Das, S., and El Abbadi, A. (2010). Big data and cloud computing: New wine or just new bottles? *Proceedings of the VLDB Endowment*, 3(1–2), 1647–1648.

Ahn, J., Oh, S., and Kim, H. (2013, July). Korean pop takes off! Social media strategy of Korean entertainment industry. In *2013 10th International Conference on Service Systems and Service Management (ICSSSM)* (pp. 774–777). IEEE.

Baloyi, B. and Issacs, G. (2015). South Africa's "fees must fall" protests are about more than tuition costs. *CNN*. Accessed November 10, 2015. http://edition.cnn.com/2015/10/27/africa/fees-must-fall-student-protest-south-africa-explainer/.

Batool, R., Khattak, A. S., Maqbool, J., and Lee, S. (2013). Precise tweet classification and sentiment analysis. In *2013 IEEE/ACIS 12th International Conference on Computer and Information Science (ICIS)* (pp. 461–466).

Bertino, E. (1991). Integration of heterogeneous data repositories by using object-oriented views. In *Proceedings First International Workshop on Interoperability in Multidatabase Systems* (pp. 22–29). IEEE.

Billings, K. (2012). Oracle takes you through the four phases of achieving Big Data insight. Intel IT Center.

Bleiholder, J. and Naumann, F. (2006). Conflict handling strategies in an integrated information system. Humboldt-Universität zu Berlin, Institut für Informatik.

Boufares, F. and Salem, A. B. (2012). Heterogeneous data-integration and data quality: Overview of conflicts. In *2012 6th International Conference on Sciences of Electronics, Technologies of Information and Telecommunications (SETIT)* (pp. 867–874). IEEE.

Buono, P., Aris, A., Plaisant, C., Khella, A., and Shneiderman, B. (2005). Interactive pattern search in time series. Electronic Imaging 2005. International Society for Optics and Photonics.

Burtica, R., Mocanu, E. M., Andreica, M. I., and Tapus, N. (2012). Practical application and evaluation of no-SQL databases in cloud computing. In *2012 IEEE International Systems Conference (SysCon)* (pp. 1–6). IEEE.

Cartegena, J. (2015). I am Puerto Rican and Black Lives Matter. *HuffPost Latino Voices*. Accessed November 10, 2015. http://www.huffingtonpost.com/juan-cartegena/i-am-puerto-rican-and-black-lives-matter_b_8493646.html.

Chen, L. 2015. The world's largest companies 2015. *Forbes*. Accessed December 16, 2016. http://www.forbes.com/sites/liyanchen/2015/05/06/the-worlds-largest-companies/.

Chunylall, R. (2015). #FeesMustFall: A movement of shares, likes, tweets and posts. *Thought Leader*. Accessed November 10, 2015. http://thoughtleader.co.za/rasvanthchunylall/2015/10/29/feesmustfall-a-movement-of-shares-likes-tweets-and-posts/.

Composite Software. (2013). Data abstraction best practices. Accessed December 22, 2015. http://purl.manticoretechnology.com/ImgHost/582/12917/2013/resources/datasheets/Composite_Data_Abstraction_Best_Practices_2013.pdf.

Corera, G. (2015). Will Big Data lead to Big Brother? *BBC*. November 10, 2015. http://www.bbc.com/news/magazine-34810066.

Delort, P. (2012). Big Data in biosciences. Big Data Conference, Paris. http://www.bigdataparis.com/documents/Pierre-Delort-INSERM.pdf#page=5.

Diebold, F. X. (2003, January). "Big Data" dynamic factor models for macroeconomic measurement and forecasting. In *Advances in Economics and Econometrics: Theory and Applications, Eighth World Congress of the Econometric Society*, edited by M. Dewatripont, L. P. Hansen, and S. Turnovsky, pp. 115–122.

Duong, T. H., Jo, G., Jung, J. J., and Nguyen, N. T. (2009). Complexity analysis of ontology integration methodologies: A comparative study. *Journal of Universal Computer Science*, 15(4), 877–897.

Ellison, N. (2007). Social network sites: Definition, history, and scholarship. *Journal of Computer-Mediated Communication*, 13(1), 210–230.

Findlay, K. (2015, October 30). The birth of a movement: #FeesMustFall on Twitter. *Daily Maverick*. Accessed November 10, 2015. http://www.dailymaverick.co.za/article/2015-10-30-the-birth-of-a-movement-feesmustfall-on-twitter/#.VkLwcqPovIU.

Fuchs, C. (2006). The self-organization of cyberprotest. In *The Internet Society II: Advances in Education, Commerce and Governance*, edited by K. Morgan, C. Brebbia, A. Carlos and J. Michael Spector, pp. 275–295. Southampton, Boston: WIT Press.

Geng, Y. and Kong, X. (2008). The key technologies of heterogeneous data integration system based on ontology. Second International Symposium on Intelligent Information Technology Application. IEEE.

Gopalan, R. S. (2012). Big Data integration. Accessed August 14, 2013. http://bigdataintegration.blogspot.com/.

Guttentag, D. (2013). Airbnb: Disruptive innovation and the rise of an informal tourism accommodation sector. *Current Issues in Tourism*, forthcoming.

Hussain, A. and Vatrapu, R. (2014). Social data analytics tool: Design, development, and demonstrative case studies. IEEE 18th International Enterprise Distributed Object Computing Conference Workshops and Demonstrations (EDOCW). IEEE.

Idugboe, D. (2015). Why you shouldn't abandon email marketing for social media. *SMedia*. Accessed December 16, 2015. http://www.smedio.com/why-social-media-is-yet-to-destroy-email-marketing/.

John, N. A. (2013). The social logics of sharing. *The Communication Review*, 16(3), 113–131.

Joseph, S. (2012). Social media, political change, and human rights. *Boston College International and Comparative Law Review*, 35, 145–188.

Kim, J. S., Yang, M. H., Hwang, Y. J., Jeon, S. H., Kim, K. Y., Jung, I. S., Choi, C. H., Cho, W. S., and Na, J. H. (2012). Customer preference analysis based on SNS data. Second International Conference on Cloud and Green Computing (CGC). IEEE.

Lieberman, M. (2014). Visualizing Big Data: Social network analysis. Digital Research Conference.

Mangold, W. G. and Faulds, D. J. (2009). Social media: The new hybrid element of the promotion mix. *Business Horizons*, 52(4), 357–365.

McMillan, R. (2014). Airbnb is quietly building the smartest travel agent of all time. *Wired*. Accessed November 10, 2015. http://www.wired.com/2014/07/airbnb_recommendations/.

Millham, R. (2016). Theme evolution and structure in Twitter: A case study of South Africa student protests of 2015. IEEE International Conference on Big Data Analytics, Hangzhou, China.

Nemschoff, M. (2013). Big Data: 5 major advantages of Hadoop. ITProPortal.com.

Neumayer, C. and Raffl, C. (2008, October). Facebook for global protest: The potential and limits of social software for grassroots activism. Prato CIRN 2008 Community Informatics Conference: ICTs for Social Inclusion: What Is the Reality?

Newman, R. (2015). At Airbnb, data science belongs everywhere: Insights from five years of hyper-growth. Airbnb. Accessed November 10, 2015. http://nerds.airbnb.com/scaling-data-science/.

Peary, B. D., Shaw, R., and Takeuchi, Y. (2012). Utilization of social media in the east Japan earthquake and tsunami and its effectiveness. *Journal of Natural Disaster Science*, 34(1), 3–18.

Peng, Y., Kou, G., Shi, Y., and Chen, Z. (2008). A descriptive framework for the field of data mining and knowledge discovery. *International Journal of Information Technology and Decision Making*, 7(4), 639–682.

Peters, L. (2012, April 7, 12:11 pm). Twitter post. https://twitter.com/onebadvillynn/status/188705676149792769.

Reddy, M., Prasad, B. E., Reddy, P. G., and Gupta, A. (1994). A methodology for integration of heterogeneous databases. *IEEE Transactions on Knowledge and Data Engineering*, 6(6), 920–933.

Reynaud, C., Sirot, J. P., and Vodislav, D. (2001). Semantic integration of XML heterogeneous data sources. In *International Symposium on Database Engineering and Applications* (pp. 199–208). IEEE.

Rheingold, H. (2002). *Smart Mobs: The Next Social Revolution*. Cambridge, MA: Perseus Books Group.

Ronson, J. (2015a, February 12). How one stupid tweet blew up Justine Sacco's life. *New York Times Magazine*. Accessed December 22, 2015. http://www.nytimes.com/2015/02/15/magazine/how-one-stupid-tweet-ruined-justine-saccos-life.html?_r=0.

Ronson, J. (2015b, December 20). How the online hate mob set its sights on me. *The Guardian*. http://www.theguardian.com/media/2015/dec/20/social-media-twitter-online-shame?CMP=share_btn_tw.

Salter, J. (2012, September 7). Airbnb: The story behind the $1.3bn room-letting website. *The Telegraph*. Accessed November 10, 2015. http://www.telegraph.co.uk/technology/news/9525267/Airbnb-The-story-behind-the-1.3bn-room-letting-website.html.

Sandoval-Almazan, R. and Gil-Garcia, J. R. (2013, January). Cyberactivism through social media: Twitter, YouTube, and the Mexican political movement. I'm Number 132. In *46th Hawaii International Conference on System Sciences (HICSS)* (pp. 1704–1713). IEEE.

Seligman, L. J., Rosenthal, A., Lehner, P. E., and Smith, A. (2002). Data integration: Where does the time go? *IEEE Data Engineering Bulletin*, 25(3), 3–10.

Shirky, C. (2011). The political power of social media. *Foreign Affairs*, 90(1), 28–41.

Smith, D. (2012). Twitter helps save South African carjacking victim. *The Guardian*. Accessed December 22, 2015. http://www.theguardian.com/world/2012/apr/11/twitter-south-african-carjacking-victim.

Strømmen-Bakhtiar, A. (2012, June). An essay on the emerging political economy and the future of the social media. In *6th IEEE International Conference on Digital Ecosystems Technologies (DEST)* (pp. 1–8). IEEE.

Swoyer, S. (2013). Big Data and Hadoop: The end of ETL? In *Big Data Integration*.

Syoncloud. (2013). Overview of Big Data and NoSQL Technologies as of January 2013. Accessed December 22, 2015. http://www.syoncloud.com/big_data_technology_overview.

Tufekci, Z. (2014). Big questions for social media big data: Representativeness, validity and other methodological pitfalls. In *Proceedings of the 8th International Conference on Weblogs and Social Media, ICWSM 2014* (pp. 505–514). AAAI Press. arXiv preprint arXiv:1403.7400.

Tussyadiah, I. and Zach, F. (2012, June 5). Hotels vs. peer-to-peer accommodation rentals: Text analytics of consumer reviews in Portland, Oregon. Tourism Travel and Research Association: Advancing Tourism Research Globally. Paper 2. http://scholarworks.umass.edu/ttra/ttra2015/Academic_Papers_Oral/2.

Villanyi, B. and Martinek, P. (2012, November). Towards a novel approach of structural schema matching. In *IEEE 13th International Symposium on Computational Intelligence and Informatics (CINTI)* (pp. 103–107).

Warin, T. and Sanger, W. (2014). Structuring Big Data: How financial models may help. *Journal of Computer Science and Technology*, 2(1), 1.

Waterflow, L. (2015, February 16). "I lost my job, my reputation and I'm not able to date anymore." *Daily Mail*. Accessed December 22, 2015. http://www.dailymail.co.uk/femail/article-2955322/Justine-Sacco-reveals-destroyed-life-racist-tweet-trip-Africa.html.

Westerman, D., Spence, P. R., and Van Der Heide, B. (2012). A social network as information: The effect of system generated reports of connectedness on credibility on Twitter. *Computers in Human Behavior*, 28(1), 199–206.

Yin, H., Cui, B., Hua, L., Huang, Y., and Yao, J. (2013). A unified model for stable and temporal topic detection from social media data. In *IEEE 29th International Conference on Data Engineering (ICDE)* (pp. 661–672).

Zhu, Y., Kiros, R., Zemel, R., Salakhutdinov, R., Urtasun, R., Torralba, A., and Fidler, S. (2015). Aligning books and movies: Towards story-like visual explanations by watching movies and reading books. In *Proceedings of the IEEE International Conference on Computer Vision* (pp. 19–27).

Authors

Richard Millham is currently a research professor at Durban University of Technology in Durban, South Africa. His research interests lie in software and data evolution, cloud computing, Big Data, and social media. Before serving as an academic in South Africa, Bahamas, South Sudan, Ghana, and the United Kingdom, he worked for over 13 years in the information technology sector in diverse fields such as oil/gas, finance, transportation, telecommunications, education, and property management. He completed his PhD at De Montfort University in Leicester, UK. He is a chartered engineer and senior member of IEEE.

Surendra Thakur has a DTech in information and communication technology from Durban University of Technology, South Africa. His thesis was a multidisciplinary effort combining computer science, engineering, biometrics as well as political science to propose and analyze an optimal mobile voting election solution. Thakur is the KZN e-Skills director. It is in this capacity that he evangelizes online etiquette as well as safe internet for parents through public lectures, radio, and a popular newspaper column, "DigiTalk." He is a past treasurer of the Computer Society of South Africa.

11

Big Data Integration, Privacy, and Security

Rafael Souza and Chandrakant Patil

CONTENTS

11.1 Introduction 196
11.2 Big Data Revolution 196
11.3 Explaining the Term Big Data 197
11.4 Great Benefits of Unforeseen Uses of Big Data 198
11.5 Big Data Information Violations and Identification Fraud 199
     11.5.1 Information Breaches 200
     11.5.2 Identification Fraud 202
11.6 Data Determinism: The Advantages of Algorithms 203
     11.6.1 Better Transparency Is a Doubtful Remedy 204
     11.6.2 Big Data and Wealth Discrimination 205
11.7 Big Data and Customer Choice: Do Customers Get the Things They Need? 206
11.8 Privacy and Security Challenges 207
     11.8.1 Best Security Practices for Nonrelational Data Hubs 207
     11.8.2 Reusable and Scalable Privacy-Preserving Analytics and Data Mining 207
     11.8.3 Information Provenance 208
     11.8.4 Secure Transactions and Data-Storage Logs 208
     11.8.5 Secure Implementations in Development Frameworks 208
     11.8.6 Cryptographically Applied Access Control and Communicating Securely ... 209
     11.8.7 Endpoint Input Filtering/Validation 209
     11.8.8 Modular Audits 210
     11.8.9 Real-Time Compliance and Security Testing 210
11.9 Conclusion 210
References 211
Authors 212

ABSTRACT   Big Data is transformative, ubiquitous technology that is not going to end and just keeps going rapidly. Companies are rapidly executing Big Data projects to deliberately change their business prototypes to speed up their strategic growth, build their main products, and expand their worldwide existence. However, as these technologies grow they confront an increasing number of global laws and measures. Therefore, companies must look for opportunities and difficulties as they develop their Big Data governance projects to enhance Big Data's features, while properly addressing issues of global privacy, security, and compliance.

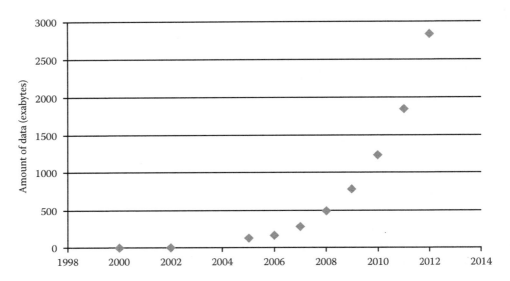

FIGURE 11.1
Digital data created worldwide.

11.1 Introduction

Big Data describes the huge levels of authorities and electronic information businesses gather about our environment as well as us. Daily, we create 2.5 quintillion bytes of information, so much that 92% of the information these days has been developed in the past couple of years alone (Figure 11.1). Privacy and security problems are amplified by the speed, quantity, and variety of data we have, including large-scale infrastructures, diversity of information sources and platforms, buffering nature of data acquisition, and high-volume intercloud transfer. Using scale infrastructures that are large and a diversity of application system distributed across large networks of computers raises the attack area of the whole system.

Conventional protection mechanisms that are customized to procuring small-scale, fixed (compared to buffering) information are insufficient. For instance, a lot of outliers would be generated by stats for anomaly diagnosis. Likewise, it is unclear the best way to retrofit provenance in infrastructures that are available these days. Buffering information requires extremely quick reaction times from privacy and protection options.

11.2 Big Data Revolution

The information technology (IT) revolution has created an information revolution, now usually called "Big Data," in which huge quantities of information can be cost-effectively gathered, stored, and examined. About one-third of the information gathered worldwide is believed to originate in the United States (Lenard and Rubin, 2015).

While it's possible to be suspicious of the hoopla surrounding Big Data, it certainly produces the prospect of major innovation in particular industries in addition to the general market. Reviews by McKinsey Global Institute and the World Economic Forum, among others, characterize the potential advantages for scam defense, government solutions, healthcare, retail, and manufacturing. McKinsey estimates that statistics and Big Data can give advantages for healthcare alone greater than $300 million per annum. Increases in the entire market can be as much as $610 million in price economies and yearly efficiency.

Concerns about invasion of privacy by governments have also been raised by the development of Big Data. A lot of the matter is related to an application and the collection of information by authorities for national security functions, a problem we don't tackle here. Major concerns are also indicated regarding surveillance uses of Big Data by businesses.

FTC Chairwoman Edith Ramirez (2013) addressed the privacy concerns of Big Data, including whether Big Data is connected with a concomitant rise in privacy damages and in the importance of government actions. She also proposes that we ought to appear to the "recognizable options," the Fair Information Privacy Practices (FIPPs) calling for notice and selection, using standards and limitations, and information minimization to resolve any privacy issues caused by Big Data.

This chapter targets the following queries that, although not new, are becoming more prominent regarding Big Data:

- How should we feel concerning the reuse of information, that is, using information for purposes not initially recognized or actually imagined?
- Likewise, how should we feel regarding the mixed utilization of information from resources that are different?
- What are the consequences of Big Data for information security, identification fraud, and information breaches?
- What are the consequences of Big Data for utilizing algorithms to profile people?
- What are the implications for functions including advertising, work, and credit choices?

We reason that there's no proof at this point that using Big Data for many functions as well as business low-surveillance has triggered privacy invasion. Also, the "recognizable options" connected with FIPPs are a potentially significant obstacle to a lot of the creation we expect to result from the Big Data revolution.

11.3 Explaining the Term Big Data

Even though the word is in widespread usage, there's no extensive definition of Big Data. McKinsey explains Big Data as discussing "datasets whose dimension is beyond the capability of typical database applications tools to capture, save, handle and assess." Mayer-Schönberger and Cukier (2014), in their current publication on Big Data, concentrate on the information that is generated: "big information describes matters you can do at a large-scale that cannot be completed in a smaller one, to take out new penetrations or create new types of worth, in methods that alter markets, organizations, the connection between people and authorities, and more." They concentrate on the power of large data sets to give correlations between variants that provide significant public and personal gains. Einav and Levin (2013) highlighted this point and discussed the possible groundbreaking ramifications of information on economic evaluation. Large data's potential comes from "the recognition of new designs in behavior or action, as well as the improvement of predictive designs, that might have already been difficult or impossible with smaller trials, fewer variants, or more aggregation." Information is actually accessible in real time, at a bigger scale, with less construction, as well as on various sorts of variants.

11.4 Great Benefits of Unforeseen Uses of Big Data

Among the "recognizable options" long encouraged by privacy advocates is the fact that information should only be gathered for an identified purpose. That is mirrored in the FIPPs dating back to the 1970s, the Organization for Economic and Co-Operation Development (OECD) privacy rules of 1980, present European Union rules, as well as the guidelines of the U.S. Federal Trade Commission's 2012 Privacy Report. According to FTC Chairwoman Ramirez (2013), the primary commandment of info cleanliness is "Thou will not accumulate and store individual info unneeded to an identified goal." Likewise, FTC Commissioner Julie Brill laments the reality that companies "without our understanding or permission, may generate huge amounts of private information on the topic of individuals to make use of for functions we do not anticipate or understand."

Ramirez's (2013) first commandment is especially ill-suited for Big Data and is inconsistent with the rest of her speech where she highlights valuable uses of Big Data, including enhancing standard healthcare while cutting costs, producing more accurate weather predictions, predicting maximum electricity usage, and providing better products and solutions to customers at lower prices. These beneficial functions include utilizing health-related information and energy bill records as well as other information for purposes other than those for which they were initially gathered.

Furthermore, the government itself regularly breaks the info cleanliness commandment. It failed to realize that information from its results might afterward be employed, for example, to find out their eligibility for health insurance subsidies when individuals paid their taxes. People could not have been notified of the possible use, which has been just lately discovered.

Big Data almost always entails uses of information that is not expected, because large data evaluation includes discovering patterns and correlations that may otherwise not be seen. Mayer-Schönberger and Cukier (2014) stress that "in a big data period, state-of-the-art extra uses have not been envisioned when the information is first accumulated. … [W]ith big data, the worth of information no more rests only in its primary objective. As we have argued, it's today in extra uses."

The poster child for Big Data is Yahoo Influenza. Analyzing 450 million models, investigators determined 45 key phrases that may forecast the spread of flu faster as opposed to the Centers for Disease Control, which utilizes doctors' reports. By monitoring how often people looked for phrases like "grippe" and "cough medicine" utilizing the search engine Yahoo, an outbreak of influenza may be seen a week or two ahead of CDC reports. Utilizing information from web searches to determine Yahoo Flu could not have been foreseen when these data were gathered.

The usage of information isn't, though, a trend new or limited to the electronic age. Mayer-Schönberger and Cukier (2014) offer the instance of Commander Mathew Maury, who, during the 1800s, utilized information from logbooks of previous ocean trips to

Big Data Integration, Privacy, and Security   199

formulate paths that are more effective and mapped out transport lanes that are still in use nowadays. His data were additionally utilized to set the first transatlantic telegraph cable. Maury "chose advice created for one function and transformed it into something else."

The types of usage of information varies. In healthcare, for example, the Danish Cancer Society compared Denmark's nationwide registry of cancer individuals with mobile telephone customer information to examine whether phone use raised the threat of cancer. The U.S. Food and Drug Administration employed Kaiser Permanente's database of 1.4 million individuals to demonstrate that the arthritis medication Vioxx raised the potential for heart attacks and strokes. The CDC joined flight records, disorder reviews, and market information to monitor health dangers.

Levin and Einav's study showed that economists are now utilizing large-scale, real-time information to predict economic action and better monitor utilizing actions that supplement established government figures.

In the private sector, Big Data is used to produce products that create great value for customers and businesses. ZestFinance, utilizing several more variants than conventional credit grading, helps lenders determine whether to provide modest, short-term loans to individuals who are otherwise bad credit risks. This provides an improved option to those who otherwise may depend on payday lenders and loan sharks.

Two successful startups, Farecast, bought by Microsoft, and Decide.com, recently bought by eBay, utilize Big Data to assist buyers to find the best prices. Farecast utilizes billions of trip cost records to forecast the movements of airfares; saving customers an average of $50 per ticket. Decide.com predicts price movements for numerous products with possible savings for customers of about $100 per item.

Information gathered on over 65 million consumers places and unites them with additional information to directly help provide location-specific services and marketing.

Big Data can also be accustomed to guarding against undesirable activities. As Mayer-Schönberger and Cukier (2014) note, "The recognition of credit card fraud functions by trying to find defects, as well as the most effective method to discover them would be to crunch all of the information as an alternative to a sample." Einav and Levin (2013) mention a "Palo Alto firm, Palantir, which is now a multibillion-dollar enterprise by building algorithms that may be used to identify terrorist threats utilizing communications as well as additional information, and also to discover deceptive conduct in healthcare and financial services." In addition, they mention work from an organization at Dartmouth utilizing large samples of Medicare promises to show considerable unexplained variance in Medicare spending per enrollee that may be due to issues or scams.

Recent research by the Direct Marketing Association found that person-level customer information was an essential part in making over $150 million in advertising solutions and that the capability was needed by more than 70% of the solutions to switch information between companies. These advertising solutions, therefore, are especially precious to newcomers and smaller companies, and decrease the expense of companies that are fitting with prospective buyers in a market (Libert, 2010).

11.5 Big Data Information Violations and Identification Fraud

Information Violations and Identification Fraud could increase or reduce with the help of Big Data. Market failure might be indicated by these safety problems due to the issue of imposing costs on the perpetrators, who might not be able to stay anonymous. Countervailing powers, nevertheless, provide powerful incentives for information holders (e.g., creditors) to protect their information, while the information itself may be helpful in avoiding fraud, as mentioned earlier.

In her address, Chairwoman Ramirez (2013) indicates that Big Data raises concerns related to identification fraud and information violations. It's beneficial, therefore, to analyze if the growth of information has led to a greater prevalence of identification fraud and information violations (Libert, 2015).

11.5.1 Information Breaches

There are two sources of information on data breaches: the Identity Theft Resource Center and the Privacy Rights Clearinghouse. These two resources aggregate info on data breaches in the press, community databases, and press releases from state governments; yet, the yearly totals change somewhat according to strategy as well as their individual meanings of a data violation. Figure 11.2 indicates the number of breaches is slightly upward since 2005.

Information Breaches are strictly an Internet Phenomenon, therefore, it is not inappropriate to flatten them by a way of measuring action that is online. The danger of a data breach continues to be relatively steady, as shown in Figure 11.3, when associated with the amount of e-commerce.

More significant compared to the variety of violations is the number of records undermined as well as the number of records endangered deflated by some measure of coverage, for example, bucks that are e-commerce. This is shown in Figures 11.4 and 11.5, respectively.

All in all, the tendency in records broken into since 2005 is relatively steady or decreasing slightly, as well as the trend in records broken deflated by a quantity that in e-commerce is not significantly more positive.

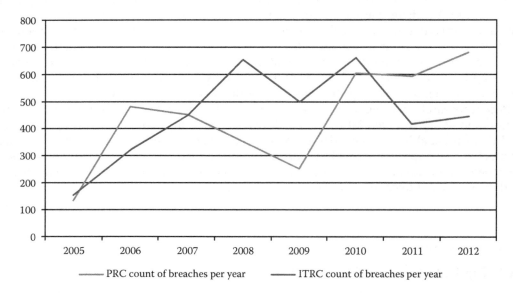

FIGURE 11.2
Data breaches per year in the United States.

Big Data Integration, Privacy, and Security

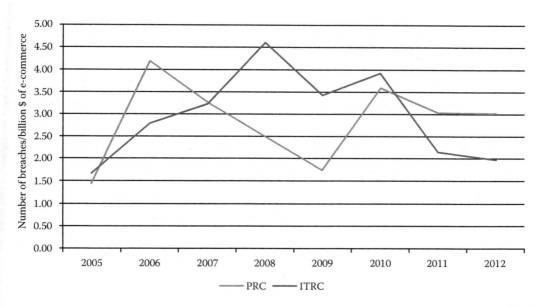

FIGURE 11.3
United States data breaches deflated per year by e-commerce.

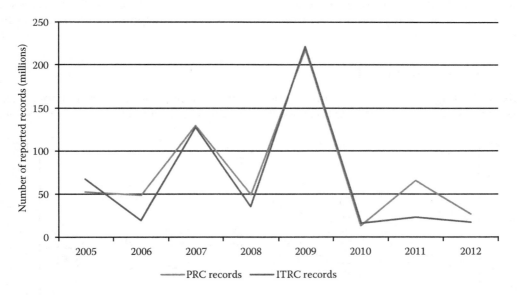

FIGURE 11.4
Number of records undermined by information breaches.

The information on violations and identification fraud do not include the entire system. However, there's absolutely no sign that they went up together with the growth of Big Data.

You might anticipate that identification fraud would be reduced by using Big Data, because creditors, who carry all the expenses, have powerful incentives to police abuse of the cards. One clear approach is tracking purchases and informing customers when purchases appear to be beyond their typical behavior, as ascertained by evaluation of

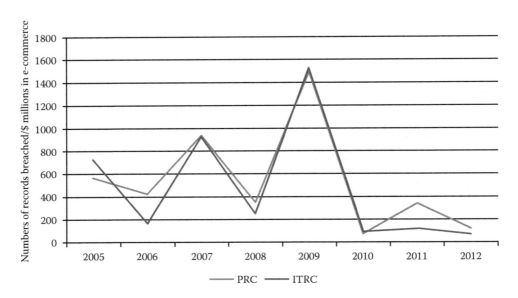

FIGURE 11.5
Number of records undermined by information breaches deflated by e-commerce.

Big Data even though these firms understandably tend not to promote their processes. Notice this monitoring calls for the use of information for purposes other than that for which they were initially gathered.

11.5.2 Identification Fraud

Javelin Strategy and Research compiles the statistically representative chain on identification fraud that we have not been aware of. These data are presented in Figure 11.6. Despite

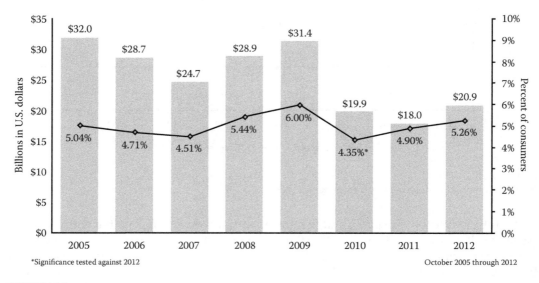

FIGURE 11.6
Overall identification fraud rate and whole fraud sum by year.

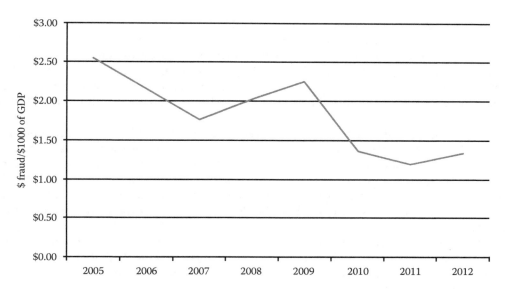

FIGURE 11.7
Yearly expense of identification fraud deflated by GDP.

concerns expressed by the FTC and others, the general prevalence of identification fraud has not been irregular since 2005. Throughout the same interval, the overall dollar sum of scams has dropped, from an average $29.1 million for 2005–2009 to $19.6 million for 2010–2012 (Zvarevashe et al., 2014).

To better understand what has occurred to the "threat" of identification scams, we must change the information on identification scams by some measure of exposure. Figure 11.7 displays that the cost of identification fraud per $1,000 GDP has fallen since 2005. If the identity fraud cost information were collapsed by e-commerce retail revenue the downward trend would come to the top, because e-commerce industry has developed much faster than GDP. Nevertheless, gross domestic product might be a more suitable deflator, since the majority of identification fraud is due to offline conduct.

11.6 Data Determinism: The Advantages of Algorithms

The efficient utilization of individuals' information has been practiced for years. The direct-marketing business, for instance, has for decades constructed e-mail lists of customers thinking about services and particular products. Likewise, essential variables that indicate danger to find out whether and at what prices to provide insurance contracts are used by the market.

A theme throughout Big Data research is the fact that using information to come up with models that are predictive, including variants that are apparently unrelated, is not harmless to customers. As FTC Chairwoman Ramirez (2013) stated, "there's an alternative danger which is a byproduct of big data stats, specifically, that big data is going to be utilized to produce decisions about people, not based on real details, but on implications or correlations which may be unwarranted." She additionally highlights, "an error rate of just one-in-ten, or one-in-a-hundred, might be bearable to the business. To the customer who is miscategorized, nevertheless, that classification may sense like arbitrariness-by-algorithm."

This point was also made by Commissioner Brill: They (information agents) fill all this information into complex calculations that spew away amazingly private predictions about our wellness, financial position, pursuits, sexual preference, religions, politics and habits. Increasingly our data fuel more than just what advertising we're served (Slashdot Media, 2014).

Naturally, such distinctions can be produced. Actually the academic screening business relies on such a correlation. For example, the government, such as the FTC, utilizes course positions that attorneys are selecting. Usage of test scores and qualifications is popular in America. The conclusions are based on "small data"—one test rating or one information level. If more data points are employed in making conclusions, then it's more unlikely that any single information point is likely to be determinative that the right conclusion will probably be achieved.

Business organizations that allocate resources to task complicated evaluation and collecting information do so as it is in their interest to make judgments that are more precise. Therefore, using Big Data should result in fewer customers being misclassified and arbitrariness in decision making.

It's uncertain what "inferences or correlations could be unwarranted." Insurers usually offer a reduction on car insurance, for example, to students with good scores. In addition, they identify clients based on sex and age. This is possible because the information describes that there's a correlation coefficient between variants and injury prices.

The employment of more options authorized by Big Data should result in more precise conclusions that also may be "more honest." For example, ZestFinance, as previously explained, utilizes its Big Data examination to give loans to people who otherwise might not qualify. Yet another illustration is the better use of information by conditional parole panels to help determine parole. Whether it is more reasonable is not clear, but advocates consider using Big Data this way to help decide which criminals ought to be reintroduced into society, and provide more precise forecasts on the chances of recidivism, possibly leading to a decrease in prison costs.

11.6.1 Better Transparency Is a Doubtful Remedy

The worry in regard to the effect of miscategorizing people generally results in the advice the algorithms need to be more transparent and there ought to be "processes to remediate choices that adversely affect people that have been incorrectly classified by a correlation coefficient," according to Commissioner Brill's "Reclaim Your Name" effort. One important data brokerage, Acxiom, has had a step on that path with its aboutthedata.com website, allowing people to see and possibly appropriate information in Acxiom's document. For example, it is unclear that an individual rejected for credit by a complex formula would primarily benefit by being shown the equation involved. An instance of a computation based on a complicated formula, the credit score, is practically not possible to show even to an educated buyer due to nonlinearities and interactions in the way in which the rating is entered into by components.

Also, digital info is commonly used in sophisticated ways that can be impossible or hard to describe. It might not be possible for websites to meaningfully share these details through a notice, and the hours customers would have to devote to comprehending it. Actually, according to the Wall Street Journal show, it seems that lots of professionals don't themselves understand the ways they are using information. In Lenard and Rubin

Big Data Integration, Privacy, and Security

(2015), there's a complicated schematic showing the uses of information by 2001. That schematic is hardly easy to check out and since that time, the program has not become simpler.

Offering customers the capacity to improve their lots could be harder than it might seem. Some of the difficulties are administrative. Customers do possess the right to improve information utilized in determining their credit ratings, but it's not easy to achieve this. People have a great deal more info about themselves than insurers, lenders, and companies. Uneven info is a characteristic of some marketplaces that possibly can cause marketplace dislocation.

Someone who believes she's been incorrectly classified has an interest in fixing incorrect information if the information has an adverse impact. But she may also be interested in "correcting" valid information, which could negatively alter her choice, or adding wrong information that could have a positive impact. Differentiating between these different "corrections" might be rather challenging.

Also, if people were allowed to easily gain access to their information, this might also make it easier for counterfeiters to gain access to the same information. If criminals have use of large quantities of information about a person, they can more readily defraud that person (possibly by producing purchases that might be in keeping with using the individual's behavior so that you can fool the bank card firm's tracking attempts). Therefore, simple observations are at best a two-edged blade.

11.6.2 Big Data and Wealth Discrimination

Some authors claim that the utilization of Big Data in promotion choices favors the wealthy over poor people. A few especially inflammatory quotations from experts include, "Ever-increasing data-collection and evaluation possess the capacity to worsen course differences" and "Big Data—elegance, profiling, monitoring, exclusion—endanger the self determination and personal independence of poor people more than another group." One author theorized that "to woo the quality consumers, they provide attractive discounts and promotional material—use your commitment card to get Beluga caviar; get a complimentary bottle of Wine. However apparently the retail merchants can not consider a reduction for their advertising endeavors. Who then pays the price tag on the affluent shoppers' high-end goods? You guessed it, the remainder of us—with cost increases on goods like bread and butter."

The debate that data collection favors the wealthy over the poor is generally offered without proof. Probably the issue expressed by these authors pertains to price discrimination, involving charging different prices to various customers for the same merchandise according to their readiness to afford it.

Nevertheless, price discrimination may be financially successful, if it raises total output in an industry. If airlines were unable to charge flight-changing costs, there might be fewer flights. Several digital items like applications and programs have high fixed (total cost) but low or even zero marginal costs, and price discrimination could be crucial to the creation of the products.

Cost discrimination includes billing costs according to a consumer's willingness to spend, which is absolutely associated to a consumer's ability to afford items. This means a cost-discriminating company will most likely charge lower costs to lower-income customers. Therefore, opposite to the aforementioned theories, using Big Data, to the degree it facilitates price discrimination, should operate to the benefit of lower-income customers.

11.7 Big Data and Customer Choice: Do Customers Get the Things They Need?

Two additional themes working through a few of the current privacy materials imply that the utilization of information and algorithms might create "damages" rather distinctive from what we usually believe of as privacy and protection injuries (i.e., damages that include the vulnerability of individuals' information to folks who should not view them). Some authors claim that Big Data may ease controlling customers to buy stuff they do not really need. Others are worried that customers may also get too much of what it is that they need; that they're going to reside in a "filter bubble" discovered by Big Data (Manyika et al., 2011).

The books on abuse of algorithms do not present any evidence that is not consistent with our theory that there's little obvious damage in the proper usage of information collected by businesses. For example, Calo's types of "objective solitude damages" come with utilization of blood check info for driving under the influence of alcohol; info utilized to get a no-travel listing; and cops use of advice from a therapist (Calo, 2011). Not one of these calls for information that is from a business. The single example that he uses is commercially from Google advertising in Gmail. In this example, the customer voluntarily utilizes the support in full understanding he may receive advertising that is focused. Also, the "damage" determined is high risk and rather indirect—consumers utilizing the support will not be aware of any loss.

More typically, it's tough to draw a line between what's called "exploitation" and the information that assists a customer making a purchase. By way of example, in another study, Calo (2011) covers chances that are money-making for companies to capitalize on behavior that is unreasonable. For instance, he indicates delivering a text from a store to an overweight customer who is attempting to stop snacking. A doughnut might be wanted by the customer, although Calo (2011) believes he should not have one.

As Calo (2011) admits, making the most of unreasonable behavior will be difficult (maybe impossible) as it will be exceedingly hard to find out what's reasonable to get a certain buyer. Also, he will not clarify why companies might wish to get this done. Utilizing Big Data sets, companies may decide when they can promote products and most of the time that would be to the customers who really need the product. Also, while some companies may make an effort to market goods the buyer doesn't actually need, the others would be attempting to sell goods the customer does need and these companies could be assumed to win out.

The essential issue with this particular point of an investigation is that the privacy advocates and authors of the topic do not seem to trust the customers for whom they claim to represent. Additionally, this is evident in authors who convey anxiety about customers residing in a filter bubble. Dwork and Mulligan (2013) are worried that filter bubbles may eliminate "the tumult of popular community forums—footpaths, community parks, and road corners—where a measure of randomness and volatility produces a mixture of findings and meetings that lead to a more educated society."

If customers need assortment, algorithms and Big Data, especially as they get more advanced, will be useful in supplying businesses with that. On the other hand, the belief that algorithms may offer customers too much of the things they need for the cost that is right for them is a more revolutionary thought with uncertain consequences. Does it suggest we have to restrict utilization and the collection of information to intentionally create calculations that are less precise? That does not appear to make sense.

Big Data Integration, Privacy, and Security

11.8 Privacy and Security Challenges

So on the basis of the research published about Big Data, here are the top nine privacy and security challenges:

1. Best security practices for nonrelational data hubs
2. Reusable and scalable privacy-preserving analytics and data mining
3. Information provenance
4. Secure transactions and data-storage logs
5. Secure implementations in development frameworks
6. Cryptographically applied access-control and communicating securely
7. Endpoint input filtering/validation
8. Modular audits
9. Real-time compliance and security testing

11.8.1 Best Security Practices for Nonrelational Data Hubs

Nonrelational data hubs popularized by NoSQL databases are still evolving to safety facilities. For example, strong alternatives to NoSQL treatment are not mature. NoSQL databases were assembled to handle distinct problems presented by the statistics world, thus safety was never a concern of the product at any given point of its own layout phase. Computer programmers utilizing databases that are NoSQL typically add security. No assistance is provided by NoSQL databases for applying it expressly in the database. Nevertheless, additional difficulties are posed by the clustering facet of NoSQL sources to the robustness of safety methods that are discussed (Mora et al., 2015).

Business organizations working with large, unorganized data sets may gain by moving from a conventional relational database into a NoSQL database when it comes to adapting/running enormous quantity of information. NoSQL databases security rely on external enforcing mechanisms. To prevent security events, security procedures must be reviewed by the organization for its middleware and firmware and at the same moment strengthen the NoSQL database without compromising on its functional characteristics to fit its counterpart relational databases.

11.8.2 Reusable and Scalable Privacy-Preserving Analytics and Data Mining

Possibly empowering invasions of privacy can be seen as an unpleasant reflection of Big Data, decreased civil liberties, invasive advertising, and increase state as well as condition control.

A recently available evaluation of how information analytics are being leveraged by firms for advertising functions found an instance in which a retail merchant could see that a teenager was pregnant before her dad knew. Likewise, anonymizing information for statistics just isn't sufficient to preserve consumer privacy. For example, AOL launched the search that anonymized logs for educational goals, but consumers were readily recognized by people who knew them. When consumers of the anonymized data set were identified by correlating their film ratings with IMDB ratings, the same issue was confronted by Netflix. Thus, it is critical to set up tips and guidelines for preventing accidental privacy reports.

Employees are always mining and examining consumer data gathered by corporations and authorities, and also possibly external company associates or contractors. A malicious insider could remove personal info from clients and or associates and may mistreat these data sets.

Likewise, intelligence organizations need huge quantities of information. The resources are numerous and could contain chat rooms, weblogs that are private, and community hubs. Most information that is accumulated is, nevertheless, harmless in character, does not need to be kept, and anonymity is maintained.

Scalable and strong privacy-maintaining mining calculations increases the likelihood of gathering info that is useful to boost consumer security.

11.8.3 Information Provenance

Provenance metadata may increase as a result of substantial provenance charts created from provenance in sophistication—empowered development surroundings in data programs that are big. Evaluation of such big provenance graphs to find metadata dependence for security/secrecy programs is computationally extensive.

A few safety programs that are essential need the annals of an electronic document, such as information regarding its development, for example, to ascertain the truth of the databases for study inspections or finding insider trading for commercial businesses. These safety evaluations need calculations that are quick to take care of the provenance metadata including those records that are time-sensitive in nature. Additionally, information origin matches review logs for conformity needs, like Sarbanes-Oxley or Payment Card Industry (PCI).

11.8.4 Secure Transactions and Data-Storage Logs

Transaction and information logs are saved in multiple-tiered storage press. Manually transferring data between grades provides the IT supervisor direct control over when and exactly what information is transferred. As the size and dimensions of data set continues to be growing rapidly, so the availability and scalability have pushed to have an auto-tiering for Big Data storage management. Auto-tiering options tend not to keep an eye on where the information is saved, which presents new problems to protected data storage. New systems are not holding the preserve for 24/7 availability and to combat unauthorized access (Inukollu et al., 2014).

A manufacturing company would like to incorporate information from different sections. Some of the information is seldom recovered, while the same information pools are always utilized by some departments. An automobile-grade storage program may conserve the manufacturing company cash by drawing the rarely applied information into a lower (and more affordable) grade. Nevertheless, this info might result in outcomes research and development is not aware of, but include essential information that is known. Because safety is reduced in lower-grade storage, the business should study tiering schemes.

11.8.5 Secure Implementations in Development Frameworks

Development frameworks that are distributed use parallelism in storage and computation to process enormous quantities of information. A favorite illustration is the MapReduce framework, which divides an input document into numerous chunks. In the initial stage

Big Data Integration, Privacy, and Security

of MapReduce, a mapper performs some calculation for every chunk says the information and results from inventory of key/value sets. In another words, the values belong to each distinct key are combined by a reducer and outputs the result. There are just two main assault prevention steps: procuring the information in the existence of a sure mapper and ensuring the mappers.

Sure mappers can yield erroneous results that may subsequently create aggregate outcomes that are incorrect. With data sets that are big, it's difficult to spot, causing mistakes that are major, particularly for fiscal and medical calculations.

Promotion services for the client or specific advertisements usually analyze buyer information. These jobs call for highly similar computations over large data sets and, therefore, are especially suited for MapReduce frameworks like Hadoop. On the other hand, accidental or deliberate leaks may be contained by the information mappers. For example, a value that is very exceptional may be emitted by a mapper by examining a document that is private, sabotaging users' privacy.

11.8.6 Cryptographically Applied Access Control and Communicating Securely

To make sure that the many delicate information that is private is end to end only accessible and protected to the entities that are approved, information must be protected depending on access-control procedures. Special research on this topic, including aspect-based encryption (ABE), has to be made more affluent, more successful, and scalable. To make positive equity, understanding, and validation on the list of things that are dispersed, a protected communication platform must be executed.

Delicate information is typically stored unencrypted in the cloud. The problem with securing information, particularly Big Data sets, is the all-or-nothing access coverage of encoded information, disallowing customers to readily perform little-grained activities like queries or discussing records. By using a public-key cryptosystem where aspects associated with the information encoded work to discover the tips, this issue is alleviated by ABE. However, there is unencrypted information that is less delicate at the same time, for example, information helpful for stats. Such information must be conveyed in a safe and agreed upon manner, utilizing a communication platform that is cryptographically protected.

11.8.7 Endpoint Input Filtering/Validation

Several Big Data use-cases in business configurations demand data collection from several resources, including endpoint apparatus. For example, a security info and event management (SIEM) system might accumulate event logs from numerous components devices and software within an enterprise community. A crucial problem in the data-collection procedure is input approval: How do we trust the info? How can we verify a supply of feedback information is nonmalicious and how may we filter harmful input signals from our selection? Input validation and selection is a challenging obstacle presented by certain input signal resources, particularly with the bring-your-own-device (BYOD) version.

Equally, information recovered from comments, ballots, and climate sensors delivered by a program revealed that the iPhone had an affirmation issue that was similar. A driven opponent could have the ability to produce "rogue" digital detectors, or spoof iPhone IDs to rig the outcomes. This is further complicated by the quantity of information gathered, which might surpass numerous readings/ballots. Algorithms must be produced to verify the input signal for Big Data sets to execute these tasks efficiently (Big Data and Privacy Making, 2013).

11.8.8 Modular Audits

With real-time safety monitoring, we strive to be informed at the instant an assault takes place. In fact, this is not going to necessarily be the case (e.g., fresh strikes, skipped actual benefits). So that you can get to the underside of a strike that is missed, review advice is needed. Auditing is not new, but the range and granularity may not be the same. We must manage an increase of information items, which likely are (although maybe not always) spread.

Conformity requirements (e.g., PCI, HIPAA, Sarbanes-Oxley) need financial companies to supply granular auditing records. Furthermore, the increasing loss of records containing info that was personal is estimated at $200/report. Legal law—with respect to the geographic area—may follow in the event of a data breach. Financial Organizations require access to large data sets that include Personal Information (PI) such as social security number. Accessibility is wanted by marketing companies, for example, for private social networking info to enhance their client-centric strategy regarding online advertising.

11.8.9 Real-Time Compliance and Security Testing

Real-time protection monitoring is really difficult, provided the amount of alarms generated by safety apparatus. These alarms (related or not) lead to a lot of false-positives, which are widely ignored or just "clicked away," as people cannot handle the sheer number. This issue may increase with Big Data, provided the speed and the amount of information channels. Nevertheless, Big Data systems also offer an opportunity: these technologies do enable statistics and rapid running of various kinds of information, which in its turn may be used to supply, as an example, real-time anomaly diagnosis according to safety stats that are scalable.

Many businesses and authorities (agencies) may reap the benefits of real-time protection stats although the use-cases vary. All these will not be new, but the distinction is the fact that we have more information at our disposal to produce more rapid and better choices (e.g., fewer false-positives) in that respect. Nevertheless, new use-cases could be described or we are able to change present use-cases instead of Big Data. For example, the wellness sector mainly profits from data systems that are big, possibly saving billions to the taxpayer, getting more precise using claims payment and diminishing the scams associated with statements. Yet, the records kept must be certified with Health Insurance Portability and Accountability Act (HIPAA) or local ordinances, which demand careful defense of health information. Finding in real-time the collection of information that is personal, accidental, or deliberate, enables the healthcare professional to avoid further abuse and to timely fix the harm produced.

11.9 Conclusion

The possibility of Big Data could be distinct from "small data" concerning their significant impacts on the market and particular industries. There isn't any proven reason for privacy concerns as a result of Big Data. But the concerns are not irrelevant:

- Will there be evidence and market failure of harm to customers? Current research on Big Data doesn't supply such evidence, at the very least as much as the proper usage of information for business purposes can be involved. Also, we've uncovered

Big Data Integration, Privacy, and Security

no signs of a rise in harm to customers from information violations or identification fraud.

- The general options recommended by regulators would probably not yield exclusive results.

Any effort to restrict "dangerous" uses of advice may limit beneficial purposes at the same time. The FTC is seen by authors including Calo as (2011) a white knight, and Chairwoman Ramirez (2013) additionally implies "substantive supervision" as a cure for the things they see as damages to customers. On the other hand, the FTC has frequently paid off consumer welfare by an extreme management of advice and has demonstrated itself to be an overprotective steward. Even though the primary job of a regulator like the FTC should be to execute a cost-benefit evaluation in making its current privacy tips, it has not done so. With this dearth of evaluation and info, especially in a modern marketplace including the digital utilization of advice, it is more likely that innovation will stop rather than providing net benefits. The "recognizable options"—the FIPPs that will restrict the reuse or sharing of information—would look to be especially dangerous since they do not apply to the new ways Big Data is used.

It's not possible to visualize programs without information being consumed by them, creating new types of information, and including data-driven calculations. Program surroundings become networked, as calculating surroundings become more affordable, and analytics and system environments become shared on encryption, protection, access control, and the cloud expose problems that need to be dealt with in a way that is systematic.

In this chapter, we emphasized the top security and privacy issues that must be resolved to make computing facilities and large data processing better. Some traditional components in this set of top problems that are particular to Big Data originate from using several facilities grades (both storage and computer science) for running Big Data, using new computing infrastructures including NoSQL databases (for rapid throughput required by Big Data amounts) that never have been completely checked for safety problems, the low scalability of encryption for large data sets, low-scalability of real-time tracking methods that may be useful for smaller amounts of information, the heterogeneity of devices that generate the information, and distress together with the abundance of varied legal and coverage constraints that result in random strategies for ensuring safety and privacy. And there are lot of other difficulties too which assaults the particular area of the complete information processing facilities that is being examined for all kind of risks.

References

Big Data and Privacy: Making Ends Meet. Future of Privacy Forum. Stanford Law School, The Center for Internet and Society. September 2013.

Calo, R. The Boundaries of Privacy Harm. Indiana Law Journal. November 2011.

Dwork, C.; Mulligan, D. K. It's Not Privacy and It's Not Fair. Stanford Law Review Online. June 2013.

Einav, L.; Levin, J. The Data Revolution and Economic Analysis. NBER Conference. April 2013.

Inukollu, V. N.; Arsi, S.; Ravuri, S. R. Security Issues Associated with Big Data in Cloud Computing. IJNSA, May 2014.

Lenard, T. M.; Rubin, P. H. The Big Data Revolution: Privacy Considerations. Technology Policy Institute. December 2015.
Libert, B. *The Big Data Revolution*. New Word City Inc. December 2015.
Libert, B. *Social Nation*. Wiley. September 2010.
Manyika, J.; Chui, M.; Brown, B.; Bughin, J.; Dobbs, R. Big Data: The Next Frontier for Innovation, Competition, and Productivity. McKinsey Global Institute. McKinsey and Company. 2011.
Mayer-Schönberger, V.; Cukier, K. Big Data: A Revolution That Will Transform How We Live, Work, and Think. Mariner Books. March 2014.
Mora, A. C.; Chen, Y; Fuchs, A.; Lane, A. Big Data Security and Privacy Challenges. November 2015.
Ramirez, E. The Privacy Challenges of Big Data: A View from the Lifeguard's Chair. Speech at Technology Policy Institute. August 2013.
Slashdot Media, SourceForge, Free(Code). 10 Ways to Build a Better Big Data Security Strategy. January 2014.
Zvarevashe, K.; Mutandavari, M.; Gotora, T. A Survey of the Security Use Cases in Big Data. *International Journal of Innovative Research in Computer and Communication Engineering*, 2(5), May 2014.

Authors

Rafael Souza is currently working as an information security consultant at CIPHER Intelligence Lab, Sao Paulo, Brazil. In addition, he is chief information security officer (CISO) at Hackersonlineclub.com. He has been listed in multiple halls of fame as a security researcher including Microsoft, Apple, and Forbes.

Chandrakant Patil is cofounder and chief technical officer (CTO) at Texec Private Limited, Pune, India. He is also the chief security officer (CSO) at Hackersonlineclub.com. He has delivered numerous trainings and workshops on information security across the globe and has been a consistent writer for widely known security and technology magazines.

12

Paradigm Shifts from E-Governance to S-Governance

Akshi Kumar and Abhilasha Sharma

CONTENTS

12.1 Introduction 214
12.2 Introduction to E-Governance 215
    12.2.1 What Is E-Governance? 216
    12.2.2 Impact of E-Governance 216
    12.2.3 SWOT Analysis of E-Governance 217
    12.2.4 PEST Analysis of E-Governance 221
12.3 Paradigm Shift to S-Governance 223
    12.3.1 What Is S-Governance? 223
    12.3.2 Social Model of Governance 224
    12.3.3 Big Data and Its Categories 224
    12.3.4 Impact of Big Data on Governance 226
    12.3.5 SWOT Analysis of Government Using Big Data 226
12.4 Sentiment Mining for S-Governance 229
    12.4.1 What Is Sentiment Mining? 230
    12.4.2 Approaches to Sentiment Mining 230
    12.4.3 Sentiment Intelligence: The "S" in S-Governance 230
    12.4.4 Sentiment Governance: Research and Practice 231
12.5 Conclusion 232
References 233
Authors 234

ABSTRACT "Democracy is the government of the people, by the people and for the people." The evolution of governance models should pertinently adhere to this and investigate the underlying potential, opportunities, power, and capabilities of novel, emerging Internet technologies. The emergence of the social web and the exponential data generated consequently can be analyzed to give the human touch to governance. In this chapter we discuss the paradigm shifts from e-governance to s-governance characterizing a social model of governance that is envisioned to be democratic, transparent, and accountable. As a step toward intelligent governance, we expound a new perspective of "sentiment" in s-governance to understand the human element of Big Data. The impact of Big Data on governance facilitated by application of sentiment mining is exemplified by demonstrating its use in research and practice.

213

12.1 Introduction

The notion of governance is innate to any society. *Governance* is defined as a tool to perceive and formulate decisions and their implementation that empower stakeholders, especially citizens. It is about administering and identifying the work culture of an organization and/or country that is appropriate, dynamic, and progressive. More formally, according to *Wikipedia*, governance refers to "all processes of governing, whether undertaken by a government, market or network, whether over a family, tribe, formal or informal organization or territory and whether through laws, norms, power or language." With great power comes great responsibility, as goes the age-old adage. If governance intends to control decisions and manage the resources of a country, then good governance is about making sure that the promised purpose of power helps to enhance the quality of life enjoyed by all citizens. With the evolving information and communication technologies (ICT), the affiliation between government and people has expounded a distinct dimension toward a resilient democratic aura for a country. Along with tapping the telecommunication mechanism, e-governance constantly strives to capture the diversification of intellectual attitude and working practices that can be incorporated in a government's course of action, operation, and approaches to serve the society in a better and reliable way. Thus, the transformation of the web into a ubiquitous tool for "e-activities," where its use has pervaded to the realms of day-to-day work, information retrieval, and business management (Bhatia and Kumar, 2008), has been associated with the governance for the sake of providing an accountable, transparent, fast, and economical channel to broadcast information for the execution of government administration activities, introducing the term *e-governance*. E-governance can bring forth new concepts of citizenship, both in terms of citizen needs and responsibilities. Its objective is to engage, enable, and empower the citizen (United Nations Educational Scientific and Cultural Organization [UNESCO], 2005).

According to the Internet Society's "Global Internet Report" (2015), there are more than 3 billion people online worldwide using the Internet for communicating, sharing, finding information, publishing, and commerce, among others. Statistics also reveal that more than 2 billion people worldwide have social accounts (Facebook, Twitter, etc.). The collaborative and participative facet of the social web (Weber, 2009) is used to facilitate interaction between people and can offer a substantial, unparalleled platform for extensive involvement of citizens in government. The shifts from passive to active to the current need of interactive governance can thus be conceptualized, giving insight to the social model of governance (Figure 12.1). The emergence of the social web and the exponential data generated consequently can be mobilized to define an *s-governance* model (where *s* stands for "social"), a model of government–citizen engagement/participation/communication/relationship that complements the web-based e-government services.

Big Data is full of chats, web forums, online discussions, blogs, comments, pictures, documents, commercial transactions, machine-generated data web logs, and so on. Besides public views, assessment, mind-set, and conception toward entities, personal, concerns, events, theme, and their attributes, opinion mining is the linchpin of societal web. Such a massive volume of opinionated text requires opinion mining, to transform the unstructured data into operational wisdom. The social web is undoubtedly the pulse of the nation and in order to make this emerging phenomenon healthy, progressive, and prolific, collective intelligence plays a vital role.

As a step toward intelligent governance, in this chapter we explicate a new perspective of "sentiment" in s-governance to comprehend the human element of Big Data. The idea

Paradigm Shifts from E-Governance to S-Governance 215

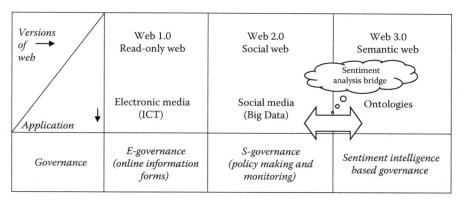

FIGURE 12.1
Evolution of web governance.

is to investigate the impact of Big Data on governance facilitated by application of sentiment mining to build a nation that's powerful, viable, and more stabilized via governance that is democratic, transparent, accountable, intelligent, and reliable. This transition from e-governance to s-governance should be essentially cohesive and coherent, and we investigate its development to examine its emerging initiatives, validity, and precision.

12.2 Introduction to E-Governance

Governance is about conducting, directing, and exercising power and lock in to ensure the reach of an organization is well-suited, vigorous, and effective. It is a mechanism of formation of decisions and their implementation, which constitutes usability, applicability, and steering the resources of a country.

At the same time, good governance has to establish consensus among the stakeholders of a country with the goal to improve the quality of life enjoyed by all citizens. In resolution 2000/64, the United Nations Commission on Human Rights identified the key attributes of good governance:

- Transparency
- Responsibility
- Accountability
- Participation
- Responsiveness (to the needs of people) (United Nations Human Rights, Office of the High Commissioner [OHCHR], n.d.)

Thus, to elevate the process of good governance and in accordance to the identified attributes, electronic media have been associated with the governance for the sake of providing an accountable, transparent, fast, and economical channel to broadcast information for the execution of government administration activities, introducing the term e-governance.

12.2.1 What Is E-Governance?

E-governance is the implementation of information and communication technology (ICT) for offering the government services in a convenient, efficient, and transparent manner. As the Internet is the most significant innovation of information technology (IT), making communication flexible and at low cost regardless of the geographical distance, governments are embracing the Internet to maximize automated service delivery and minimize bureaucrats' involvement in routine operations (Avny, 2007).

With the evolving ICT, the affiliation between government and people has provided and contributed a new dimension to a sturdy democratic climate for a country. Along with introducing a telecommunication mechanism, e-governance is continuously struggling for the diversification of intellectual attitude and working practices to incorporate government course of action, operation, and approaches in order to serve society better.

ICT is heavily used in private sectors like in e-commerce, but e-governance has yet to reach that level. E-governance is also a form of e-business in government as it provides the structure for communicating with business partners and also provides e-transactional services (Backus, 2001). E-governance provides an e-infrastructure for delivery of e-services such as interaction between government and citizens (G2C), government and business (G2B), government and government (G2G), and government and its employees (G2E) (McNulty, 2014). The aim of e-governance is to provide all the government services efficiently and effectively to the public in a locality while maintaining the transparency and reliability at an economical price (National e-Governance Plan [NeGP], n.d.).

12.2.2 Impact of E-Governance

E-governance initiatives have demonstrated marked impact on society. With the expansion in use of e-governance services by its stakeholders, their viewpoints toward government are changing. The key benefits that facilitate this idea of progressive governance are (Chandra and Malaya, 2011)

- Good governance—With the advent of e-governance, the policies of the government are visible to the public, exposing government performance to a wider audience. This encourages the government to build more suitable policies effectively and efficiently.

- Trust and accountability—Due to e-governance, citizens are able to use services 24/7. They can complete forms after business hours, check the content uploaded by the government anytime and give their feedback, or inquire through e-mail. Service delivery levels have improved remarkably.

- Citizen's awareness and empowerment—The content on e-governance websites provides information about working policies of the government creating awareness for citizens. As a result, citizens can question the actions of regulators and bring issues to the forefront, thus increasing the transparency and empowering them.

- Citizen's welfare—The integration of ICT and e-governance is providing the services and social support to all the citizens equally. It also helps in reducing poverty by giving the prices of every item on e-governance web portals, helping the citizens to find the required item at the least cost (Saith, Vijayabaskar, and Gayathri, 2008).

Paradigm Shifts from E-Governance to S-Governance

- Democracy—Because of e-governance, citizens are aware of the policies at issue and they can give their suggestions with the help of social networking websites of e-governance.
- Nation's economic growth—E-governance molds government activities such that they are transparent to the public, establish a corruption-free government, and also increase the business opportunities thus strengthening the nation's economic growth. Moreover, the streamlining of administrative processes has improved the workflow.
- 24/7 service model—Services such as bill and tax payments are available 24/7, so citizens can pay at any time. Also, e-governance is providing services for transportation like booking tickets in advance while sitting at home. These services are making the life of citizens easy (Pathak and Kaur, 2014) and also contribute to increased revenues.

12.2.3 SWOT Analysis of E-Governance

Figure 12.2 represents a strengths, weaknesses, opportunities, and threats (SWOT) analysis of e-governance.

Strengths

- Transparency—Government, business interactions, financial transactions, and the amount spent on any policy will be visible to citizens. It builds the trust of business and citizens in the government. Moreover, because of e-governance web portals, progress of any project is visible to the public.

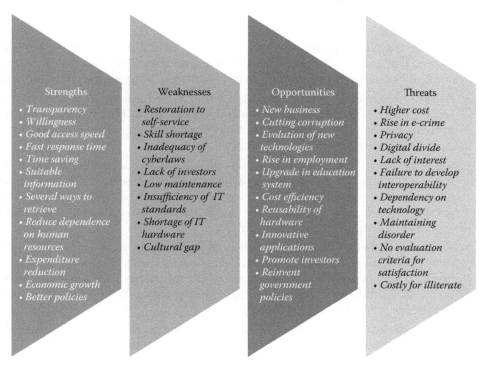

FIGURE 12.2
E-governance, a SWOT analysis.

- Willingness—Government is willing to adopt e-governance, and citizens are also eager to learn IT skills (Verma et al., 2012). As government is trying to provide more e-services to citizens, the new generation prefers to use it as a more convenient and cost-effective option.

- Good access speed—Information can be attainted quickly because of ICT and can be fetched at any time, as a 24/7 model is used. In traditional systems, services are available only during working hours (usually 9 A.M. to 5 P.M.) and for which one needs to be there at office premises, whereas an e-governance portal can be accessible anywhere anytime.

- Fast response time—Information can be attainted quickly because of ICT and response to queries sent through e-mail is swift (Damian, Segundo, and Merlo, 2014), which is dissimilar to the earlier, long-established manner of communication. With the use of e-services like e-mail, discussion forums, and social networking websites, anyone can get a response to their queries in a very short time.

- Time saving—Citizens do not have to physically go to various governmental agencies and wait in line to conduct government business; now they can do this by sitting anywhere with their smart devices, saving a lot of time.

- Suitable information—Various websites offer distinct services available in multiple languages to help citizens conveniently find the desired information. Even in a single country there are multiple languages being used, so the information is made available accordingly and the services are provided in such a way that there are different web portals for the variety of services, for example, one portal relates to information on agriculture whereas the other may relate to tax payment.

- Several ways to retrieve—Information is provided in polymorphic forms such as text and video (Damian, Segundo, and Merlo, 2014). Many citizens are illiterate or they might not understand the language in which information is provided, so they look toward the alternate mode of presentation like images, videos, and audio. It helps in maintaining the interest of citizens using e-governance services.

- Reduce dependence on human resources—ITC reduces dependence on civil servants, as much of the work is done automatically, although it also requires humans for maintaining those machines. Moreover, the efficiency of civil servants is improved by this automation.

- Expenditure reduction—Overall costs will be reduced, as many employees will be replaced by computers, and fully automated services cost less than manual services. Though the setup cost will be higher as compared to the salary expenditure of employees every month, the maintenance cost will be much less when incorporated in day-to-day life.

- Economic growth—Merging the ideas of public and private sector will help raise business and help rapidly develop infrastructure for e-governance. New business brings profit to government, too. The tax money paid because of these businesses is raising the economic condition of the country. Also, it will provide better control on expenditure.

- Better policies—Government will be able to focus more on making better policies rather than solving public and employee's disputes. Also, feedback and opinion of citizens about policies will be immediately visible to policy makers. Simultaneously, performance indicators can also be added.

Paradigm Shifts from E-Governance to S-Governance

Weaknesses

- Restoration to self-service—Stakeholders are hesitant to use electronic services (Agnihotri and Sharma, 2015), specifically the older generation, who may not be tech savvy, are habitual to the conventional ways of governance and it is hard to accustom them to use e-services.
- Skill shortage—Older employees in public offices may not be computer illiterate. Most of the people working in government agencies need to learn how to use the software providing e-governance services efficiently and effectively.
- Inadequacy of cyberlaws—Citizens are concerned for their privacy (Singh and Chander, 2012). Because of the lack of implementation of cyberlaws, more cybercrimes are happening these days, like denial-of-service (DoS) and spoofing attacks, breaching the privacy of citizens and making it difficult for government to provide them 24/7 service.
- Lack of investors—Funds are needed to implement e-governance, which requires training people, purchasing expensive hardware like servers, and high-speed Internet connection. Insufficient funds is a major weakness that hinders the implementation of the e-governance model.
- Low maintenance—Quality and usefulness of information and services is not well maintained. Many times content is not regularly updated on websites, and sometimes because of cyberattacks or other problems of the server, the website is not available to the public. Unresponsive links will erode the interest and trust of citizens in e-services (Verma et al., 2012).
- Insufficiency of IT standards—IT standards and software licenses are not properly implemented. IT standards help companies to develop quality software needed for e-governance projects, and these software should be certified by the suitable software license, but government doesn't have the proper standards and license for maintaining the quality of the software.
- Shortage of IT hardware—There is a deficiency of infrastructure needed for providing Internet services and database servers for maintaining the data of a nation. Database servers are the essential requisite for implementing the e-governance project and the shortage of them is affecting the development. A proper location is also needed to securely manage the database.
- Cultural gap—Some regions don't have access to ICT or have only restricted access, creating differences between the people, taking away the right of equality. And every state in a nation has a different culture so the websites should contain information according to their culture too, like different languages. Providing services to every location and in a user-friendly manner is very difficult.

Opportunities

- New business—With the evolution of e-governance, many startups have come up. It helps in extension of existing business models and creates the opportunity of new business forecast and proposals universally by outsourcing the projects, like spreading of local area networks (LANs), software for providing e-services like websites, and mobile applications.
- Cutting corruption—Corruption will be controlled as the work will be automated and transparency will be maintained. With the advent of e-governance, information about every business transaction will be updated on the web

portals, so anyone can question the usage of funds. Moreover, automated procedures will reduce discretionary powers of government officials substantially controlling corruption.

- Evolution of new technologies—Technologies like cloud computing and social networks can be used to strengthen the e-governance (FORSEE Partnership, 2013). Many new technologies are coming in practice whose potential can be exploited for e-governance services.
- Rise in employment—Skilled developers and information managers will be needed as the traditional government agencies will be updated with e-governance services.
- Upgrade in education system—Computer education will be given in schools, as it will become a necessity for enjoying e-services, resulting in more computer-literate citizens.
- Cost efficiency—Fully automated systems have an overall cost less than manual systems (Verma et al., 2012). Citizens are offered low-cost services, where just with the help of Internet connectivity most information is accessed and transactions are done.
- Reusability of hardware—As reusable secondhand hardware is available at a cheap rate, poor people can also have access to mobile phones (Singh and Chander, 2012).
- Innovative applications—Applications such as mobile alerts are being developed to help people make effective use of e-governance (FORSEE Partnership, 2013). These new applications benefit both businesses and citizens.
- Promote investors—Growing interest of investors for e-governance results in hike of public sector funding as digitization of governance speeds new business along with transparency.
- Reinvent government policies—Procedures of many services are being changed, making e-governance a more custom-oriented organization (Avny, 2007), making it more effective for every citizen to use its services.

Threats

- Higher cost—The cost of the Internet, like broadband subscription, is not affordable for most of the population of a nation. To use the e-services they need an Internet connection, so every citizen would not be able to benefit from e-governance.
- Rise in e-crime—Cyberterrorism and cybercrimes, like DoS attacks, lead to unavailability of a website. Inadequacy of cyberlaws will lead to a rise in cybercrimes, putting the privacy of citizens at risk.
- Privacy—Violation of security and copyright issues leads to misuse of information. Information about each citizen will be available on the database servers of the government, so access to such information by terrorists and hackers, or by higher government officials having access permission (possibility/probability of leaking confidential information, if any), leads to a constant danger to citizens' privacy.
- Digital divide—Some areas of the nation do not have access or have restricted access to the Internet (Avny, 2007), meaning some citizens have access to better services and others do not.

- Lack of interest—Some people hesitate in using e-governance web portals (Damain, Segundo, and Merlo, 2014). Many people fear their privacy or getting into a cyberfraud, so they don't try to use e-services.
- Failure to develop interoperability—There are problems in developing proper interface between internal and external government (Ha and Coghill, 2006). As state governments have different web portals, maintaining an interface between different states and national portals would be difficult, as the proper synchronization is needed between them.
- Dependency on technology—Even a minor error in software could stop the whole work or may lead to loss of data (Ha and Coghill, 2006).
- Maintaining disorder—Maintenance and upgrading is a problem, as unavailability of the latest information will lead to misunderstanding, and the trust of citizens in e-governance will be lost.
- No evaluation criteria for satisfaction—Barrier in evaluating e-governance performance, as it is difficult to quantify public services and it is strenuous to measure citizens' demand and their satisfaction from services (Avny, 2007).
- Costly for illiterate—Older and poor people who are computer ignorant will be at a loss, as the automated services will cost less than manual services (Avny, 2007).

12.2.4 PEST Analysis of E-Governance

PEST (political, economical, social, and technical) analysis is performed to understand how these four factors affect the performance and activities of e-governance (Figure 12.3) (Backus, 2001; Ha and Coghill, 2006; Verma et al., 2012).

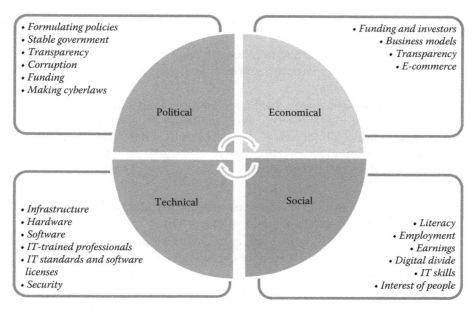

FIGURE 12.3
PEST analysis of e-governance.

Political

- Formulating policies—As the structure of making new policies is transparent, citizens should be flexible enough for embracing the changes.
- Stable government—E-governance is affected every time by the change in government, as new government officials bring change to policy making and decision making processes.
- Transparency—Transparency builds the trust of stakeholders and its gains could be achieved by various e-applications, for example, information dissemination to a large audience.
- Corruption—Administrative corruption is reduced by eliminating the need for intermediaries.
- Funding—It determines the budget for the resources required for e-governance like database servers.
- Making cyberlaws—Enforcing cyberlaws will prevent cybercrimes and maintain the privacy and security of citizens.

Economical

- Funding and investors—Careful management of available resources is a crucial requisite for governing bodies. Funding determines the budget required for the resources of e-governance (e.g., cost for database servers) and investors are desired to allocate capital for their prospective monetary returns. Hence, a congenial infrastructure for e-governance could be built only when the funds provided by the investors are sufficient.
- Business models—In the e-governance business model, administration is citizen oriented as public and private sectors deliver paperless services resulting in improved process efficiency and product efficacy. E-governance is expanding the sphere of new business prospects all over the world, as outsourcing is being done for the IT service industry.
- Transparency—Transparency builds the trust of stakeholders and its gains could be achieved by various e-applications, such as information dissemination to a large audience.
- E-commerce—E-commerce facilitates trading in products and services by using electronic media that changed the relative significance of time as the strength indicator of a country's economic state. It has become a part and parcel of transactions made in daily lifestyle and maintaining its security is indispensable to avoid fake transactions.

Social

- Literacy—The education level of citizens severely affects their ability to properly utilize the services provided by e-governance.
- Employment—There is an exponential rise in employment vacancies in the IT service industry with the advent of e-governance.
- Earnings—The income of citizens is an another crucial factor to determine whether they can afford Internet plans.
- Digital divide—Citizens who live within those geographical areas of a nation where ICT services are not accessible are not able to avail e-governance services.

Paradigm Shifts from E-Governance to S-Governance

- IT skills—IT skills of people affect their efficiency of utilization of e-governance services.
- Interest of people—The acceptance of e-services provided by e-governance depends heavily upon the acceptance and resistance of the citizens.

Technical

- Infrastructure—The infrastructure for e-governance should have proper database servers, LAN settings, and smart devices like a computer, as the inadequate place for storage affects the project. For example, wide area networks (WANs) have still not been spread over the nation.
- Hardware—Availability of hardware is a basic requisite through which they can access various e-governance web portals.
- Software—Software should be easy to learn, use, and reliable, having attractive GUI maintaining the interest of the public.
- IT-trained professionals—Employees should have IT skills so that they can properly work on the systems.
- IT standards and software licenses—IT standards should be followed for maintaining the websites, and developed or outsourced software should have proper licenses.
- Security—Public privacy should be maintained, else they lose trust in e-governance (e.g., certain websites ask for personal details of citizens).

12.3 Paradigm Shift to S-Governance

E-governance has generated a micro impact for achieving the goals of good governance. To improve the scope of implementation of good governance and to generate a macro impact, a paradigm shift is desired that entails harnessing active participation of stakeholders (citizens/businesses) using the social web. The extensive involvement of citizens in governance measures at all levels by various online discussion forums is increasing exponentially by the rapid usage of the Internet and web by the means of e-governance, which is a vital application area of Web 1.0. Various web applications can be effectively classified with the abstraction of web evolution.

The next version of the web, i.e., Web 2.0, is designed for a social effect, and its collaborative and participative aspect has been used to reinforce interaction among people with similar preferences and interest; also termed as *Social Web*, coined by Howard Rheingold in 1996 (Weber, 2009). The social web is a set of social relations that link people through the World Wide Web (Halpin and Tuffield, 2010).

12.3.1 What Is S-Governance?

The social web is a set/cluster of societal relations and affiliations that connect people across the globe to encompass various software, websites, application packages, and so on, in order to prop and boost social interaction. It is a mode of communication that uses existing innovative techniques for sharing information, thoughts, and opinion prolifically.

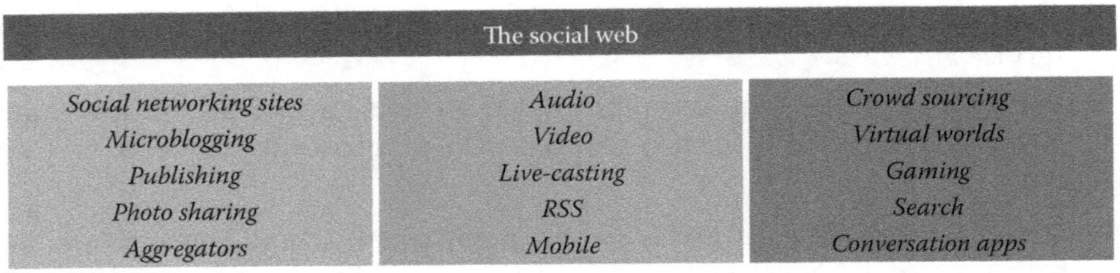

The social web		
Social networking sites	Audio	Crowd sourcing
Microblogging	Video	Virtual worlds
Publishing	Live-casting	Gaming
Photo sharing	RSS	Search
Aggregators	Mobile	Conversation apps

FIGURE 12.4
Components of the social web.

All government organizations should mobilize this social facet of the web with a view to reach out to more citizens in order to analyze the reaction of the public for the adoption of the social web in governance. The emergence of the social web in governance give rise to the term *social governance* (*s-governance*); an extension of e-governance which with the aid of social media can grasp the social buzz and retort to issues.

12.3.2 Social Model of Governance

The social model of governance provides various contributing components and parameters of the social web in the evolution of s-governance. All the elements might become powerful tools for recasting governance. Persuasive software packages, web applications, praxis, and processes need to be evolved for s-governance.

Social governance is a compilation of protocols, practices, plans, and informative sources that allow us to regulate the social web. A powerful social governance model empowers citizens by providing them a social platform to represent and choose the way they want to interact with government and keep lawmakers liable. It allows one to keep the social activities on track and line up with the government plan of action and targets. A huge amount of data is an outcome of all the applications of the social web (listed in Figure 12.4) that can be viewed as Big Data.

12.3.3 Big Data and Its Categories

Big Data is used to refer to the collection of data sets that are too large and complex to handle and process using traditional data processing applications (Figure 12.5). It usually includes data sets with sizes beyond the ability of commonly used software tools to capture, curate, manage, and process data within a tolerable elapsed time. Big Data is a trending set of techniques that demand new ways of consolidation of various methods to uncover hidden information from the massive and complex raw supply of data.

This is one of the reasons why even systematic and efficient databases tend to fail in handling such enormous amount of data and hence collapse. Following are the four types of Big Data that aid business (Ingram Micro Advisor, 2015):

- Prescriptive (How can we make it happen?)—In prescriptive analysis, there is extra focus paid on specific questions. It prescribes a variety of possible actions and the details of what and how the steps in the analysis will take place. For example, prescriptive analysis is done on various structured and unstructured data sets in

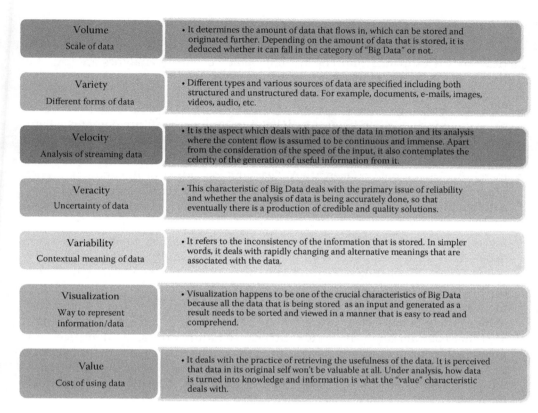

FIGURE 12.5
Seven V's of Big Data: Its characteristics. (From McNulty, E., 2014, Understanding Big Data: The seven V's, *Dataconomy*, http://dataconomy.com/seven-vs-big-data/; Optimus Information, 2015, Understanding the 7 V's of Big Data, http://www.optimusinfo.com/tag/big-data/.)

the oil industry to access and promote further performances in the optimization of fracking in the fields.
- Predictive (What will happen?)—Analysis of data sets is used to gain useful information and predict future outcomes and trends. It does not guarantee certainty but forecasts what might happen. For example, restaurants use predictive analysis on the projection of the menu, food, and staff needs, which eventually lead to enhancement in the business.
- Diagnostic (Why did it happen?)—It is the process of going deeper in the studying of data to understand why some things happened and why the steps taken were taken. It provides a better understanding of situations and answers particular questions related to it.
- Descriptive (What happened?)—It is the namesake for data mining, which indirectly uncovers patterns by studying the data sets of past and present events. It describes raw data and presents something that is interpretable to the user. For example, descriptive analysis is used in examining electricity usage to help plan power needs and optimal prices.

12.3.4 Impact of Big Data on Governance

An e-government model utilizing ICT and resulting in Big Data is anticipated to reduce costs (Kalbande, Deshpande, and Popat, 2015). Some benefits of analytics are (Agnihotri and Sharma, 2015)

- Predictive policing—Data when analyzed and processed for future cause of action helps in giving a view of the future. It helps in finding the future domains where problems can take place. By such policing we can make efforts to improve the future.
- Increasing operational efficiency—A clear understanding of the analysis report provides a specific area to work upon as per the specific requirement. Working on a defined field increases the operational efficiency and gives rise to an accurate result.
- Better consumer services—Analysis gives a clear insight to what the customer needs. Providing consumers with what they want is itself a quality service. By keeping track of consumers' behavior on different services and later analyzing it gives rise to better service.
- Identification of new market—Big Data analysis gives rise to new areas to work upon, as it has a clear insight of the behavior of the current market or the area that is under analysis. Factors that cause failure are easily identified and gives rise to finding a new market to work upon. Apart from these benefits there are other benefits too that are not discussed here, including compliance with regulations, informing strategic directions, and identifying new product services.

12.3.5 SWOT Analysis of Government Using Big Data

Figure 12.6 represents a strengths, weaknesses, opportunities, and threats (SWOT) analysis of government using Big Data.

Strengths
- Satisfies multiple basic functions—Quickly stores, converts, transfers, and analyzes the massive amounts of constantly updated, structured, and unstructured data. For implementing into e-governance successfully, there is the need to manage the records of all the citizens.
- Helps unveil new information—Provides collection of technologies and methodologies to create useful information and patterns out of unstructured data. It helps in analyzing citizens' data and reviewing of earlier policies for making new policies.
- User convenient—The process of Big Data provides services that make it economical, efficient, and easier for users to manipulate. E-governance minimizes the need of physical presence, as users can fill/update details and pay bills from home.
- Heterogeneous data sources—Various data sources bring in all kinds of information that may be useful to industries and organizations. E-governance web

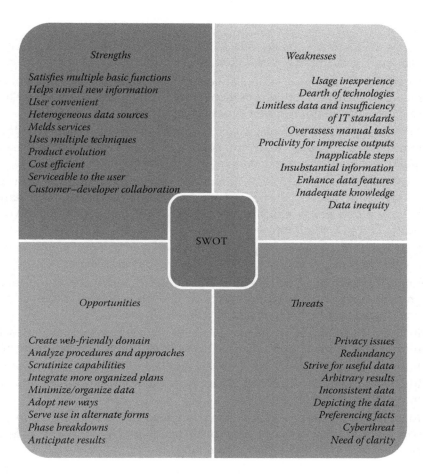

FIGURE 12.6
SWOT analysis of government using Big Data.

portals contain data in many languages and in many forms like text, video, and audio for better understanding by citizens.

- Melds services—Integrates software, hardware, and application services to build the industry capabilities.
- Uses multiple techniques—Generates unprecedented knowledge by using gathering and data mining techniques. This knowledge can further help in pattern recognition and decision making.
- Product evolution—Helps redevelop a product by evaluating its past and future scope like reforming government policies after getting public opinions.
- Cost efficient—Tends to reduce costs while at the same time produces improved output, as computers replace the human labor.
- Serviceable to the user—Develops and installs interactive and dynamic systems, allowing users to benefit from the data.
- Customer–developer collaboration—Increases customer–developer interaction (as the customer is also treated as a source of data).

Weaknesses

- Usage inexperience—There is lack of experience in using Big Data techniques. Old employees in the public sector are unable to use computers efficiently.

- Dearth of technologies—There are insufficient technologies to support all formats, since current implementations have complex logic. Also there are very few investors left for funding new technologies.

- Limitless data and insufficiency of IT standards—As the IT standards are not maintained properly in e-governance, it is difficult to store and process a large amount of data within conventional systems of organizations.

- Overassess manual tasks—Requires excessive human interpretation to process the patterns created from various sources. Due to shortage of IT hardware, there is a deficiency of infrastructure, like database servers in e-governance, needed for providing Internet services.

- Proclivity for imprecise outputs—Validation of output needs new approaches on how to measure accuracy. Data validation has to be done.

- Inapplicable steps—Some steps are irrelevant in analyzing Big Data sources and will not be replaced/undertaken by other processes. The same is the case with e-governance due to low IT standards.

- Insubstantial information—Some databases may include records for which there may only be limited information available. But all values of interest are missing.

- Enhance data features—The timeline, relevance, and accuracy of data needs to be enhanced. Even in e-governance the quality of information is not well maintained.

- Inadequate knowledge—Lack of comprehending the comparability of data sources. The knowledge for the four different models cannot be generalized; each model has to be handled differently.

- Data inequity—Data suffers discrimination on the basis of priority and how to sell it.

Opportunities

- Create web-friendly domain—A web-accessible environment for storage and analysis of large-scale data sets can be created and be used as a "sandbox" and act as a catalyst for evolving of a new business through e-governance.

- Analyze procedures and approaches—Explore/implement new methodologies that improve efficiency in existing business domains. It should seek to utilize the new data sources, technologies presented by Big Data to meet emerging needs like e-governance can be a reason for a rise in employment, as skilled labor is required for managing.

- Scrutinize capabilities—Consider all capability elements to ensure that the end result is well-integrated. Applications such as alert mobiles are being developed to help people connect with e-governance.

- Integrate more organized plans—Structured field tests for surveys are likely to be replaced by feasibility studies of new sources. This makes the surveys faster and more efficient, reducing the needed effort.

- Minimize/organize data—Reducing the bulk data by transforming the data into matrices or subsampling to make data small enough to manage.

Paradigm Shifts from E-Governance to S-Governance

- Adopt new ways—A meta-analysis approach (comparing results from a number of studies) should be considered. Some innovative applications are also made to connect with e-governance applications.
- Usage in alternate forms—Could be used as auxiliary information to improve all or part of the existing survey.
- Phase breakdowns—There may be a need to introduce an initial exploration phase as insights are investigated and potential of the Big Data source is evaluated.
- Anticipate results—Predictive analysis of Big Data may help assess risks. This analysis is also helpful in deciding which policies can be adopted for the nation's development.

Threats

- Privacy issues—Confidentiality may become an issue in the future. Violation of security and copyright issues leads to misuse of information.
- Redundancy—No distinct supply of data for output may lead to "mix-match" data and chaos, maintenance, and upgrade issues.
- Strive for useful data—Poses challenges in the production of quality statistical information. User may provide disguised and misleading data.
- Arbitrary results—It is unpredictable to produce confirmed output, as errors can occur at any stage, initial or final.
- Inconsistent data—All types of data sources can potentially suffer from partial nonresponse (values for specific variables are missing). Cybercrime also affects the availability and quality of data.
- Depicting the data—The representative way of data makes it difficult to see its value. Complex visualization presentations of data enhances the nonreadability of the data.
- Preferencing facts—The data needs to be prioritized, as private/confidential data may prove to be hazardous. Some of the information should be accessible only to higher-level civil authorities.
- Cyberthreat—Threat of security. If anyone gets access to the database of e-governance, the privacy of citizens will be at risk and at the same time the crucial information about government could be used by terrorists and criminals.
- Need of clarity—Lack of transparency may lead to losing people's trust in organizations that use Big Data. Trust of the public is very important for maintaining interest in using e-services provided by government.

12.4 Sentiment Mining for S-Governance

The social web contributes toward the interconnection of societal dynamics, and the next version of web, that is, Web 3.0, also called the semantic web, intends to assign meaning to the enormous amount of data piled up on social media. Sentiment mining (or analysis) acts as a bridge between the social and semantic web in order to extract or mine sentiment and opinion from the huge bulk of Big Data available on social web. Social web has brought about a paradigm shift from e-governance to s-governance, introducing sentiment by exploring/mining of Big Data with the usage of sentiment mining in research and practice.

12.4.1 What Is Sentiment Mining?

Sentiment mining (or opinion analysis) is a field of study that tends to use natural language processing techniques to extract, capture, or identify the attitude (otherwise sentiment) of a person with respect to a particular subject. It is the automated mining of attitudes, opinions, and emotions from text, speech, and database sources through natural language processing (NLP).

The primary task is to opinionate, that is, to sort and categorize one's perspective into positive, negative, or neutral views. Once this is done, it can be further subcategorized into two parts: one of them focusing on the information that is factual, more likely to be an objective description of a unit, while the other emphasizes on sentiments that are subjective in the expression of the feelings of the opinion holder. Both of them hold equal importance in deducing conclusions.

12.4.2 Approaches to Sentiment Mining

Analyzing the content of social media for sentiment mining is a tiresome task, as it requires a thorough and extensive knowledge of the rules associated with NLP, for example, syntactic and semantic, explicit and implicit, and regular and irregular language rules. Three main techniques used in the procedure of sentiment classification are as follows:

- The machine learning approach can be grouped into supervised and unsupervised learning methods. In the supervised method, learning done from training data is applied to new test data, whereas in the unsupervised method there is no prior learning (i.e., no training data), and the task is to find hidden structures in the unlabeled data.

- The Lexicon-based approach tends to be dependent on the sentiment vocabulary that provides a collection of known and precompiled sentiment terms. It is also further divided into two categories, namely, the dictionary-based approach and the corpus-based approach which uses statistical or semantic methods to find sentiment polarity and determines the emotional affinity of words, which is to learn their probabilistic affective scores from large corpora.

- The hybrid approach is the combination of both the above mentioned methods and plays an important role in decision making as the techniques of both the approaches are collaborated for a better result.

12.4.3 Sentiment Intelligence: The "S" in S-Governance

Sentimental intelligence is a conjunction of intelligence, empathy, and sentiments to enhance opinion and comprehend social interactive dynamics. It is the capability of voicing and monitoring public opinion enabling apt classification of sentiments, which guides and impacts thinking attitude and aptitude.

Convergence of sentiment intelligence in social governance tends to make a nation or organization more powerful, viable, and stable by amplifying collective intelligence through sharing knowledge, skilled methodologies, and strategies. Applying sentiment intelligence in s-governance (usage of the social web in governance) requires sentiment mining to transform the unstructured data into operational wisdom.

Social web applications turn out huge pools of data (viewed as Big Data), which requires new techniques and technologies to shape rational meaning out of it. By virtue of the social web adoption, society can take advantage of social platforms involving huge user participation. The pressing need is to recognize the significance of the human element in the form of sentiment intelligence for the development of a democratic nation by executing s-governance.

12.4.4 Sentiment Governance: Research and Practice

Sentiment governance is comprised of two factors in the domain of governance: social and sentimental. The social factor refers to societal interaction of person/entity for their collective coexistence, and sentimental describes an expression of strong influence/emotion of people/society. Both the parameters are vitally important for the execution of social and sentimental intelligence based governance. The goal of social and sentimental intelligence-based governance is to look toward the concerned audience and give credence to their views and thoughts for the purpose of airing information, looking for civic inputs in policy making and employment, and granting access to services, to edify and foster stakeholders.

The statistics in Table 12.1 figure out the popularity of social networks, rated by frequency of operational accounts. Figure 12.7 represents the number of active users over various social media channels.

TABLE 12.1

Statistics of Usage of Web Data

Application	Usage of Web Data[a]
Facebook	149 million visitors per month
Twitter	90 million visitors per month
YouTube	More than 4 billion videos viewed per day; 60 hours of videos uploaded every minute
Flickr	Hosts more than 6 billion photo images
Wikipedia	Hosts over 20 million articles attracting over 365 million readers

Source: Statista: The Statistics Portal, 2015, http://www.statista.com/statistics/272014/global-social-networks-ranked-by-number-of-users/.

[a] As of August 2015.

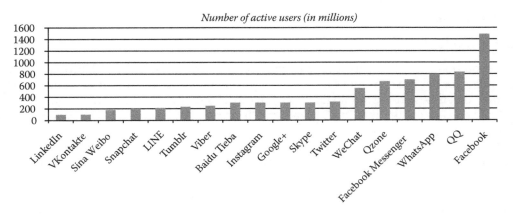

FIGURE 12.7

Count of active users over social web. (From Statista: The Statistics Portal, 2015, http://www.statista.com/statistics/272014/global-social-networks-ranked-by-number-of-users/.)

232   *The Human Element of Big Data*

TABLE 12.2

Embrace of Social Web Data in Indian Governance

Government Agency	Stats over Social Media Channels
Indian Public Diplomacy Division of Ministry of External Affairs	Twitter account with 138,004 followers and more than 4158 tweets posted till date
Planning Commission of India	Facebook page of Planning Commission having 57,360 likes and Twitter account with 164,227 followers
Delhi Traffic Police	Twitter account with 83,404 followers and 177,956 likes on Facebook
State Bank of India	Facebook page with 46,648 likes
Aam Aadmi Party Campaign	Maintains various Twitter and Facebook pages
Prime Minister Narendra Modi Social Media Account	Provides information of forthcoming policies through various social applications, including Facebook, Twitter, YouTube, Google+

Growing recognition and popularity of social media inspired governments to adopt it, and it is certainly becoming a great podium for various governing divisions and authorities at universal, federal, regional, and provincial levels. Table 12.2 shows the use of social media by varies Indian governing bodies (Agrawal, 2015).

The banes and boons of the social web go hand in hand especially in fidelity of governance where the integrity of a country is on high risk. In reference to society, the public can be broadly classified into three categories:

- Social (pertaining to human services and welfare; active and positive elements)
- Unsocial (not inclined to society; passive and neutral elements)
- Antisocial (ruinous to the interests of society; destructive and negative elements)

There is a need to identify and minimize the malicious activities done over the social web by applying sentiment intelligence in a very focalized and precise manner for careful analysis of the facet and viewpoint of people to work in a favorable and supporting direction in enrichment of the people, by the people, and for the people.

12.5 Conclusion

The evolution of web technology has pushed the government toward process reengineering, evoking the concept of a proactive, pro-people, and maximum governance. This chapter discusses the technologies that have bridged the divide between government and citizens effectually making a paradigm shift from pure politics-based governance to society-managed governance.

We tracked the electronic journey of governance by first expounding and reviewing the e-governance platform and then demonstrating s-governance as an empowering tool that embarks a transparent, accountable, and digitally advanced social governance model.

The amount of data generated due to the active participation on social media can be mined for extracting views of citizens toward government practices, policies, rules, and for their performance monitoring. As a promising effort in this direction, gauging the sentiment from citizen participation is geared toward a progressive governance.

References

Agnihotri, N. and Sharma, A. K. (2015). Big Data analysis and its need for effective e-governance. *IJIACS*, 4.

Agrawal, H. (2015, May 5). How Indian government is using social-media. *Shout Me Loud* (blog). http://www.shoutmeloud.com/indian-government-into-social-media.html.

Avny, A. (2007). SWOT analysis of e-Government. *Annals of University of Bucharest, Economic and Administrative Series*, (1), 43–54.

Backus, M. (2001). E-governance in developing countries. *IICD Research Brief*, 1(3).

Bhatia, M. P. S. and Kumar, A. (2008). Information retrieval and machine learning: Supporting technologies for web mining research and practice. *Webology*, 5(2).

Chandra, D. G. and Malaya, D. B. (2011, December). Problems and prospects of e-Governance in India. In *2011 World Congress on Information and Communication Technologies (WICT)* (pp. 42–47). IEEE.

Damian, I. P., Segundo, J. S., and Merlo, E. M. (2014). SWOT analysis of the services provided by e-government sites in Brazil. *Procedia Computer Science*, 33, 130–135.

FORSEE Partnership. (2012). eGovernment PESTLE and SWOT Analysis. https://www.google.co.in/url?sa=t&rct=j&q=&esrc=s&source=web&cd=1&cad=rja&uact=8&ved=0ahUKEwiG9ryS073KAhUJA3MKHfxSARsQFggbMAA&url=http%3A%2F%2Fwww.southeast-europe.net%2Fdocument.cmt%3Fid%3D529&usg=AFQjCNFds6sr5CNOOw92KgIsbcbxE3TD2w&bvm=bv.112454388,d.bGQ.

Ha, H. and Coghill, K. (2006). E-government in Singapore—A SWOT and PEST analysis. *Asia-Pacific Social Science Review*, 6(2), 103–130.

Halpin, H. and Tuffield, M. (2010). A standards-based, open and privacy-aware social web. W3C Social Web Incubator Group Report.

Ingram Micro Advisor. (2015, March 23). Four types of Big Data analytics and examples of their use. http://www.ingrammicroadvisor.com/data-center/four-types-of-big-data-analytics-and-examples-of-their-use.

Internet Society. (2015). Global Internet report 2015. http://www.internetsociety.org/globalinternetreport/assets/download/IS_web.pdf.

Kalbande, S., Deshpande, S., and Popat, M. (2015). Review paper on use of Big Data in e-governance of India. *International Journal for Research in Emerging Science and Technology*, 2(1), 395–403.

McNulty, E. (2014, May 22). Understanding Big Data: The seven V's. *Dataconomy*. http://dataconomy.com/seven-vs-big-data/.

National e-Governance Plan (NeGP). (n.d.). http://www.negp.gov.in.

Optimus Information. (2015, August 18). Understanding the 7 V's of Big Data [blog]. http://www.optimusinfo.com/tag/big-data/.

Pathak, M. and Kaur, G. (2014). Impact of e-governance on public sector services. *International Journal of Emerging Research in Management and Technology*, 3(4), 100–103.

Saith, A., Vijayabaskar, M., and Gayathri, V. (Eds.). (2008). *ICTs and Indian Social Change: Diffusion, Poverty, Governance*. SAGE Publications India.

Singh, V. and Chander, S. (2012). E-governance in Punjab—A SWOT analysis. *International Journal of Management, IT and Engineering*, 2(6), 99–110.

United Nations Educational, Scientific, and Cultural Organization (UNESCO). (2005). Defining E-governance. http://portal.unesco.org/ci/en/ev.php-URL_ID=4404&URL_DO=DO_TOPIC&URL_SECTION=201.html.

United Nations Human Rights, Office of the High Commissioner. (n.d.). Good governance and human rights. http://www.ohchr.org/EN/Issues/Development/GoodGovernance/Pages/GoodGovernanceIndex.aspxm.

Verma, S., Kumari, S., Arteimi, M., Deiri, A., and Kumar, R. (2012). Challenges in developing citizen-centric e-governance in Libya. *International Arab Journal of e-Technology*, 2(3), 152–160.

Weber, L. (2009). *Marketing to the Social Web: How Digital Customer Communities Build Your Business*. John Wiley & Sons.

Authors

Akshi Kumar earned a PhD in computer engineering at the University of Delhi. She earned an MTech (master of technology) and BE (bachelor of engineering) in computer engineering. She is an assistant professor in the Department of Computer Engineering at Delhi Technological University, Delhi, India. She is an editorial review board member for the *International Journal of Computational Intelligence and Information Security*; *International Journal of Computer Science and Information Security*; *Interdisciplinary Journal of Information, Knowledge and Management*; and *Webology*. She is a life member of the Indian Society for Technical Education (ISTE), International Association of Computer Science and Information Technology (IACSIT), International Association of Engineers (IAENG), IAENG Society of Computer Science, and the Internet Computing Community (ICC). She has many publications to her credit in various journals and international conferences. Her research interests include the areas of web search and mining, intelligent information retrieval, sentiment analysis, and web-enabled software engineering.

Abhilasha Sharma is an assistant professor in the Department of Computer Science and Engineering at Delhi Technological University, Delhi, India. She has 8 years of work experience in industry, research, and academics. She earned an MTech (master of technology) and BTech (bachelor of technology) in information technology. She is pursuing a PhD in information technology at the Delhi Technological University, Delhi, India. Her research area includes software engineering, software testing, web applications, web engineering, sentiment analysis, and web-based software engineering.

Section IV

Case Studies for the Human Element of Big Data: Analytics and Performance

13

Interactive Visual Analysis of Traffic Big Data

Zhihan Lv, Xiaoming Li, Weixi Wang, Jinxing Hu, and Ling Yin

CONTENTS

13.1 Introduction 238
13.2 Big Data Generation and Current Situation 240
    13.2.1 Basic Traffic Information Management Subsystem 241
    13.2.2 Dynamic Traffic Information Processing Subsystem 241
    13.2.3 Dynamic Traffic Network Analysis Subsystem 241
    13.2.4 Planning Decision Making Auxiliary Subsystem 241
    13.2.5 3D Traffic Geographic Information Subsystem 242
13.3 Impact of Big Data Technology on Geographical Information Systems (GIS) 242
    13.3.1 Impact on Government Agencies and for Geographic Information
        Industry 242
    13.3.2 Development of GIS in Large Data 242
        13.3.2.1 GIS Development Model in Large Data 242
        13.3.2.2 Application of Big Data Technology in the Field of GIS 243
        13.3.2.3 Challenge of GIS in Big Data 243
13.4 System Division 243
13.5 Key Technology of the Platform 251
    13.5.1 Fault-Tolerance Processing of Transportation 251
    13.5.2 Integration of Multivariate and Heterogeneous Transportation Data 251
    13.5.3 Storage and Calculation of Mass Transportation Information 252
    13.5.4 Analysis and Prediction of Real-Time Dynamic Transportation Flow 252
    13.5.5 Three-Dimensional Analysis of Real-Time Transportation Information 252
13.6 Advantages of Platform Solution 253
    13.6.1 High Usability and High Stability 253
    13.6.2 High Performance and Real-Time Performance 253
    13.6.3 High Compatibility and Easy Access to Information 253
13.7 Analysis of Bus Passenger Flow in the City 253
    13.7.1 Analysis of Bus Service Scope 253
    13.7.2 Relevant Bus Flow Analysis of the Junction 253
13.8 Passenger Flow Analysis of Public Transportation Transfer 254
13.9 Human Factors in Traffic Geographical Information Systems 257
    13.9.1 Traffic Information Fault-Tolerance Processing 257
    13.9.2 Multielement Isomeric Traffic Data Integration 257
    13.9.3 Mass Traffic Information Storage and Computing 258
13.10 Conclusion 258
13.11 Future Work 259
Glossary 260
References 260
Authors 262

ABSTRACT The creation of new technologies like cloud computing and the Internet of Things has indeed brought great chances for the evolution of wise transportation. Being an efficient integration of data processing technology, communication transmission technology, Internet technology, and intelligent sensor technology, wise transportation has been applied into the whole transportation system, which is quite comprehensive and systematic. This system is of great importance especially in terms of a comparative larger space–time scale. If a comparison is made with intelligent transportation, it might be found that the wise transportation system could not only be used to lay comparative greater emphasis over the exploitation and utilization of data but also be used to accumulate and deliver data. The system puts more focus on the decision-making reaction, knowledge discovery, and traffic analysis of the information. This new concept covers a number of tasks where traditions have been overtaken by intelligent technology, which requires manual resolution and discrimination to achieve the optimization. In addition, with the development of car networking, wise transportation pays greater attention to the interconnection between the transportation information system and other information systems to the maximum extent possible. Then, it is obvious that the deeper analysis of the transportation data and further efficient management are the key takeaways in the promotion of wise transportation. It takes mining, integrating, and collecting the transportation information in different fields and hence it could play a more crucial role in easing traffic jams, ensuring the transportation security, and guaranteeing the efficiency of the transportation.

Catering to the need of various parties involved in transportation, a cloud service platform for intelligent transportation serves as a timely comprehensive service platform, which enriches transportation information. The development of such a platform relies on the increasingly mature cloud computing technology and the Internet of Things, and contributes to addressing such defects as insufficient processing capacity of traditional information and platform information and the current channels for information interaction. Traffic data are large in quantity, diverse, predictable, and real-time, and hence are within the category of Big Data.

A cloud service platform is proposed in this chapter, which is aimed at wise transportation, facilitating unified management, and mining analysis of the huge number of the multivariate and heterogeneous dynamic transportation information, providing real-time transportation information, increasing the utilization efficiency of transportation, promoting transportation management and service level of travel information, and providing decision support of transportation management by virtual reality.

13.1 Introduction

Nowadays, there is an increasing interest in using virtual reality geographical information system (VRGIS), which can obtain the landscape geospatial data dynamically, and perform rich visual 3D analysis, calculations, and management based on geographical information system (GIS) data (Haklay, 2002; Huang et al., 2001). As a medium composed of interactive computer simulations that sense the participant's position and actions, and replaces or augments the feedback to one or more senses, virtual reality gives the feeling of being mentally immersed or present in the simulation (a virtual world). With several characteristics, such as large scale, diverse predictability, and timeliness, traffic data falls in the range of definition of Big Data (Briggs, 2012). In addition to the spatial data integration, new user interfaces for geodatabases are also expected (Breunig and Zlatanova, 2011). Therefore, the management and development of traffic Big Data with virtual reality technology is a promising and inspiring approach.

The urban comprehensive passenger transportation hub is a key node of the urban transportation network. With various forms of traffic flows (for example, rail, bus, taxi, and long-distance passenger transportation) connected with the hub and complicated forms of transfer among them, the passenger flow transportation efficiency will affect the whole transportation network. In full consideration of the height of the entire hub, the trend of information technology development and application and other aspects, it is necessary to research the real-time state information of the urban comprehensive passenger transportation hub. First, for the daily management of the transportation hub, on one hand, the real-time publication of accessibility of all types of passenger flows plays an important role in improving the hub's service quality and optimizing the whole transportation system; on the other hand, researching residents' long-term traveling needs and the spatial and temporal distribution of passenger flows can help us grasp the law of passenger flows and estimate the passenger flows, so as to take administrative measures ahead of time. Second, for the planning of the transportation hub in Shenzhen, China, evaluating the service scope and serviceability of the existing transportation hubs is the basis for future planning and construction of transportation hubs. Finally, for the technical level, the integration of diversified real-time dynamic transportation information is the inevitable trend. The storage, analysis, and 3D visualization of real-time dynamic transportation information for single nodes in the transportation network and GIS Transport and other technical trials help to provide technical references for using the diversified real-time dynamic transportation information during the integrated construction of municipal services. Some previous work has inspired our work (Zhong, Arisona et al., 2014; Zhong, Huang et al., 2014).

The creation of new technologies like cloud computing and Internet of Things has indeed brought great possibility for the evolution of wise transportation. Being an efficient integration of data processing technology, communication transmission technology, Internet technology, and intelligent sensor technology, wise transportation has been applied to the whole transportation system, which is quite comprehensive and systematic. This system is of great importance, especially in terms of a comparative larger space–time scale. If a comparison is made with intelligent transportation, it might be found that the wise transportation system could not only be used to lay comparative greater emphasis over the exploitation and utilization of data but also be used to accumulate and deliver data. The system put more focus on the decision-making reaction, knowledge discovery, and traffic analysis of the information. Some tasks' prerequisites have been replaced by the intelligent technology, which requires manual resolution and discrimination to realize the optimization. Because of the rapid development of car networking, wise transportation puts more focus on the interconnection of the transportation information system and some other transportation systems. Then we could predict what the future efficient management would be like. Wise transportation requires the integration and collection of transportation information from a number of fields and then the information will be excavated fully to play a role in easing traffic jams, ensuring transportation security, and guaranteeing the efficiency of transportation.

Confronting different traffic actors, cloud computing designed for wise transportation offers a real-time comprehensive service platform, enriching the information of transportation. The construction of the platform relies on the more mature Internet of Things and cloud computing. The incompetent processing ability of platform information and traditional information and the poor information interaction channel should be improved (Breunig and Zlatanova, 2011). There are a number of characteristics of traffic data, including real time, diverse predicable, and large scale, that fall into the range of Big Data definition (Briggs, 2012).

13.2 Big Data Generation and Current Situation

Current major software devices cannot organize, process, manage, and capture Big Data, or a huge amount of data, in a timely fashion to aid business decision-making purposes. Big Data has large data (volume), is fast (velocity), is varied (variety), and has other characteristics (Qingquan and Deren, 2014).

The first literature concerning Big Data presents an analysis over the open source project. At that time, Big Data was used to describe a large number of data sets, which need to be processed or analyzed for the updating of the web search index. With the release of the Google File System (GFS) and Google MapReduce, Big Data has more applications, describing a large number of statistics and covering the rate of processing data. The earliest proposed Big Data era has come, it is the world's leading consulting company McKinsey. McKinsey has pointed out in a research report that the data has penetrated into every industry. It has gradually become an important production factor, and the use of mass data will herald a new wave of productivity growth and consumer surplus (Shahrokni et al., 2014).

Big Data has been attached with the coming of the era of the cloud. Compared with traditional data, the proportion of Big Data is large. In a sense, Big Data is the frontier technology of data analysis. In short, it is the ability to quickly obtain valuable information from various types of data.

Today, Big Data has gradually infiltrated every aspect of our social life. With the rise of social networks, a large number of user-generated content (UGC), audio, text information, video, pictures, etc., the amount of data from other external things is even greater, plus the mobile Internet contributes more accurate and faster collection of user information, such as location, life information, and other data. But because the pace of data development is too fast and leads to higher requirements for hardware, there will be technical problems. Although the development of Big Data is still in its primary stage in China, the commercial value of Big Data has already appeared. First, the data on hands in gold, transaction data can produce good benefits; second, based on data mining, new business models were born using different angles or a new focus on data analysis. The benefits include, helping companies do internal data mining or focus on optimization, help companies find new customers more accurately, reduce marketing costs, improve corporate sales, and increase profits (Sui, 2014).

In the future, the data will become the largest trading commodity. But the data is too big which is limited by, big large amount of data, data types, and the value of non-standardized data characterize data. Therefore, the value of Big Data is obtained by data sharing and cross-multiplexing. The future of Big Data will also affect the infrastructure, data providers, managers, regulators, and data center, and so on. These will make Big Data into a huge potential industry. According to statistics, the value of market of large data is $51, while in 2017, this scale is expected to rise to $530 (Chen, Chen, and Gong, 2015).

13.2.1 Basic Traffic Information Management Subsystem

The basic traffic information management subsystem has been adopted for the central controlling of traffic-related urban space data. It has also been adopted for the establishment of multiresolution and multiscale space information, which includes a traffic facility database, 3D model database, satellite image database, and vector database (Briggs, 2012). With the technological support of 3D traffic geographic information, this inferior system offers various functions, including information upgrading, information inquiry, and map visualization of various kinds of traffic information.

13.2.2 Dynamic Traffic Information Processing Subsystem

The dynamic traffic information processing subsystem has been connected with the collection port of traffic information. This system could be applied to the data acquisition and also to the preprocessing of dynamic traffic statistics (for example, converting, updating, loading, and fault-tolerance processing) (Che, Khodayar, and Shahidehpour, 2014; Che and Shahidehpour, 2014). It has been used to offer various models for the integration of data, for example, regional network traffic flow, microcosmic traffic flow, time–space complementation, historical analysis, and weight fusion analysis model.

13.2.3 Dynamic Traffic Network Analysis Subsystem

The dynamic traffic network analysis subsystem has been used for the prediction of the entire network and the analysis of traffic flow based on the output of the dynamic information processing system of the transportation. It has many functions, including the analysis of congestion conditions of different road sections, the prediction of transportation modes of the entire network, the prediction of the severity of the traffic system, the transportation modes after several hours or even several minutes (including common public transportation, rail traffic, and road traffic), and the design of the accessibility of real-time network nodes.

13.2.4 Planning Decision Making Auxiliary Subsystem

The planning decision making auxiliary subsystem provides data analysis of long-term traffic events and traffic flow of specific network nodes (for example, daily passenger-car flow, passenger-car flow in different periods, and the condition of traffic events in specific road sections), hence making it more convenient for the supervision system to acknowledge the long-term conditions for some important nodes and the entire traffic system, taking this as the major factor when making a decision. Furthermore, the spatial and temporal analysis will track the data of every car with the assistance of the road network offered by the Internet of Cars, which has been utilized to form a comprehensive and continuous origin and destination (OD) database for motor vehicle traveling. This database has been used together with the card data of public transportation and hence offers a comprehensive OD database for traveling about the transportation modes (Jiang et al., 2014). This system offers the OD analysis function with different transportation modes, offering important support to the design of traffic systems. This system could also be used for the discussion about traveling behaviors of taxi route, taxi flow, taxi speed, and public transportation under extreme weather conditions (like heavy fog, typhoons, and rainstorms) and in specific periods of time (like holidays, festivals, and other important events), so as to offer the analysis and a predictive function of abnormal flow of the traffic system.

13.2.5 3D Traffic Geographic Information Subsystem

The 3D traffic geographic information subsystem has been applied to the 3D visualization of data analysis outcomes and spatial information. The fundamental functions of the 3D geographic information system include landform video, setting of eagle-eye map, setting of indoor negation mode, setting of 3D mode, setting of navigation mode, area measurement, vertical distance measurement, spatial distance measurement, horizontal distance measurement, coverage control, underground mode, setting of sun and time, and the selection of various operations and objects (H. Z. Li et al., 2013). This system also provides support for the 3D visualization query and expression of network flow congestion conditions of multiscale traffic, the query and expression of different traffic incidence, the visualization of a decision-making strategy, and the analysis mode of traffic with the support of the 3D space data model.

13.3 Impact of Big Data Technology on Geographical Information Systems (GIS)

13.3.1 Impact on Government Agencies and for Geographic Information Industry

The arrival of the era of Big Data, to some extent, is a new challenge to the mapping geographic information sector. Big Data applications are bound to bring the healthy development for the future of the department of surveying and mapping geographic information (Li, Lv, Zhang et al., 2015). But it is gratifying that the State Bureau of Surveying and Mapping Geographic Information has been fully aware of this and plans to carry out the monitoring of geographical conditions and is constantly promoting the application of geographic information data in China.

The arrival of Big Data for the geographic information enterprises is not only the driving force to promote business transformation, but also means increased business opportunities (H. Lin et al., 2013). Enterprises need to rethink existing models, and combine technology and operations management to seize upon the business opportunities brought about by Big Data.

13.3.2 Development of GIS in Large Data

13.3.2.1 GIS Development Model in Large Data

With the continuous advance of the application of large data, as well as the sustainable evolution of cloud computing, the Internet of Things, and the mobile Internet, generally speaking, geographic information systems have enjoyed a rapid development (K. P. Lin et al., 2013). In support of large data technology and mobile Internet, mobile GIS terminal applications can get full data support. At the same time, mobile GIS can get all kinds of GIS services through network and cloud services, such as tile services, analysis services, and through the development of terminal applications, to achieve the reuse of existing GIS services, the terminal application, and server applications to achieve organic integration. With the interaction of GIS services, the function of large computation and high load is processed by the back-end, and the implementation of the extended mobile GIS application is further implemented. The application service platform is the support system of GIS, which serves as an open resource sharing and application integration (Lv, 2013). It will be able to offer a number of back-end functions. At the same time, these data can be effectively integrated with the different application or industry data sources (Lv et al., 2012). Finally, it is the Big Data that provide meaningful understanding, that is, information sharing regarding geographic information technology will be able to provide more users with effective and unified data display means.

13.3.2.2 Application of Big Data Technology in the Field of GIS

At present, the problem of mass data storage and processing in the field of GIS is becoming more prominent, such as the application of remote sensing technology to capture geographic information, real three-dimensional GIS data volume surge, and so on. For large data storage, analysis, and processing and other issues, research is particularly critical (Zhou et al., 2010.) If the problem is solved, information regarding remote sensing data and the 3D geographic space will be more accurate.

13.3.2.3 Challenge of GIS in Big Data

The volume of geographic data is growing, and the spatial data are not structured, so the spatial data sets have the typical characteristics of large data (Lv, Esteve et al., 2015). So the problem of storage of massive spatial data has been a key research topic in GIS. How to share Big Data in GIS, how to manage and protect large data files, how to solve a large number of data, and other issues will become the new challenges faced by GIS.

Due to the large number and variety of GIS data information, the original data organization, analysis, and processing methods have become increasingly unable to adapt to this huge amount of data. So improving the real-time update rate of the data and the ability of mass computing to meet the needs of users are challenges in the era of Big Data (Lv, Feng et al., 2015).

13.4 System Division

Nowadays, there's quite a few visual display and integrated analyses concerning the multiple real-time dynamic information over the traffic system. However, the application examples and research for this topic is limited. This study takes the Comprehensive Transportation Junction in Shenzhen as the example. This study utilizes the dynamic traffic information that is continuously changing to manage controlling and analyzing the temporal and spatial distribution of the passenger flow or traffic flow, taking special periods and different periods as examples. Currently the adopting data includes the taxi statistics, the database also covers the card swiping statistics of public transport and the traffic information of long distance.

It has been proven that virtual environments could promote the public understanding of 3D planning statistics (Lv, Feng et al., 2015). To share every department's information resources and the geospatial information's dynamic tracking, an integrated information system has been constructed. The application of virtual reality has been taken as the visual means that could change the old city image (Lv, Feng et al., 2014).

Geographic statistical analysis has been used to help conduct data analysis and decision-making. 2D visualization has been overlapped with a white background over the 3D virtual reality environment, as it is a less demanding display mechanism, lessening the user's cognitive workload (Lv, Feng et al., 2015). The creation of this world covers 3D GIS analysis, dynamic comprehensive statistics mining of the transportation, comprehensive analysis of public transportation's service capacity, comprehensive analysis over the travel time, and dynamic traffic data in the long term.

Generally speaking, this system could be classified into seven modules, namely, the bus transfer module, statistical analysis module, passenger flow forecasting module, OD analysis module, dynamic traffic circle module, real-time traffic status module, and common tool module. The proposed system is based upon the Web VR engine and Web VRGIS (Lv, Li et al., 2015).

The fundamental functions of the program include changing the mouse to the dragging mode and identify the 3D earth dragging in any direction based on the moving directions of the mouse. Then, it needs a click for further recovery. Despite the map diminishing and magnification display operations, it has been possible to be aware of the flight of the systematic map over the displaying of the panorama location of Shenzhen with the assistance of the panoramic function. The operating approaches of rotating and sliding have also been provided. The compass function could imply the current direction. Once you click the compass button, the map will calibrate its direction automatically and then move to the north direction.

To demonstrate the property of the road, video, picture, or text could be added over the surface or right over the terrain. Apart from that, 3D models, 2D faces, 2D lines, and vector data could also be added right above the land surface.

The function of a real-time report of the road condition could help to load the information and display it with a panoramic perspective, just like what is shown from Figure 13.1 and Figure 13.2. The function of accessibility analysis could display and analyze the accessible scope covered by the Futian Transportation hub in a specific time period with a panoramic form (Figure 13.3).

The OD analysis of transportation could be used to analyze the number of metro trains and other vehicles coming from a hub to every regional center based on the statistics of the taxis going out and in the Transportation Hub of Futian. The system will demonstrate the taxis from the Futian hub to every regional center with trains to every metro station at every metro station's location with various cylinders, as shown in Figure 13.4.

The function of passenger flow forecasting is to display and analyze monthly and daily taxi passenger flows based upon the historical data via the passenger flow analysis method. Curve graphs and bar graphs have been used to display the monthly and daily passenger flow volume through the taxi from the Futian Hub, just like what is displayed in Figure 13.5.

The bus transfer function is based upon the route data of the bus in Shenzhen city combined with the algorithm of the bus transfer. The query of bus transfer and three-dimensional transfer functions has been provided. By getting into the terminal station and original station and clicking the "More" button, the transfer route will be shown in greater detail. If you click the transfer route button, then the system will start to display. Every transfer station and other station will be shown on the 3D map where the bus will appear and pass, as shown in Figure 13.6.

The cloud service platform that targets the wise transportation needs to be managed with a unified system or undertake a mining analysis of the large numbers of heterogeneous

Interactive Visual Analysis of Traffic Big Data

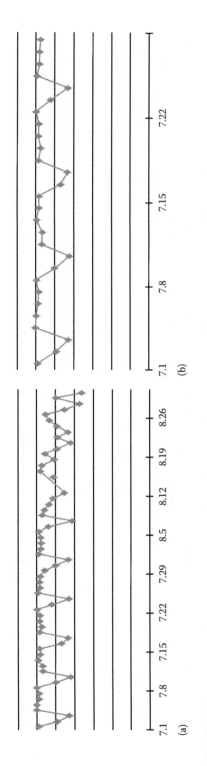

FIGURE 13.1
(a) The statistics of the daily amount for the swiping of bus card from July to August. (b) Daily amount for the swiping of bus card in four weeks (July).

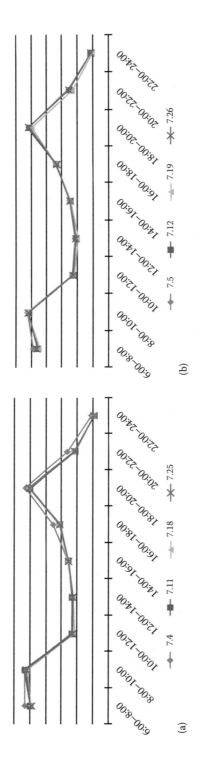

FIGURE 13.2
(a) The statistic figure for the amount of the swiping of bus card during various periods on Monday in July. (b) The statistic chart for the amount of the swiping of bus card during various periods on Tuesday in July.

Interactive Visual Analysis of Traffic Big Data

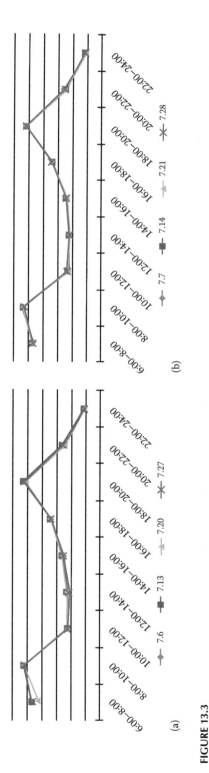

FIGURE 13.3
(a) The statistic chart for the amount of the swiping of bus card during various periods on Wednesday in July. (b) The statistic chart for the amount of the swiping of bus card during various periods on Thursday in July.

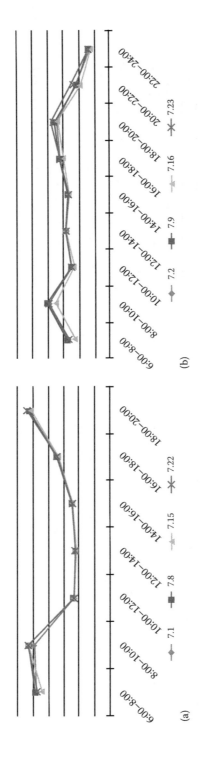

FIGURE 13.4
(a) The statistic chart for the amount of the swiping of bus card during various periods on Saturday in July. (b) The statistic chart for the amount of the swiping of bus card during various periods on Friday in July.

Interactive Visual Analysis of Traffic Big Data 249

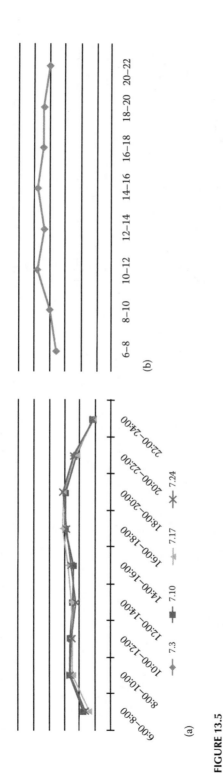

FIGURE 13.5
(a) The statistic chart for the amount of the swiping of bus card during various periods on Sunday in July. (b) Average time for transferring from subway to bus (minutes) during various periods.

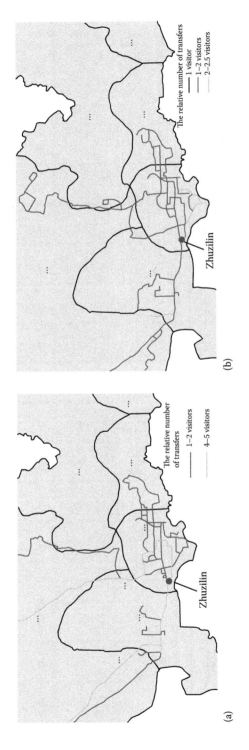

FIGURE 13.6
(a) The main transfer bus routes after getting off the Zhuzilin subway station and relative transfer volume of the routes. (b) The bus route taken before transferring to the subway in Zhuzilin and the relative transfer volume of various routes.

and multivariate dynamic transportation information, increasing the transportation efficiency and offering the real-time report about transportation, promoting the travel information's service level and then the transportation management through virtual reality. The goals of the concrete research are listed next.

Fully integrating the transportation includes carrying the management and processing over the heterogeneous and multivariate transportation statistics, and supporting the interconnection between other information systems and transportation data systems to develop the interactive cooperation between the industrial department and other functional departments, and promoting the maximum utilization and sharing of resources.

Carrying out analysis and deep data excavation over the multisource statistics makes the transportation participants and the traffic warden understand and master both the real-time transportation condition and variation trends through analyzing and comparing historical and real-time data. Long-term analysis could result in informative and correct data support for the leadership's decisions.

The 3D visualization of the city has been made to display different kinds of resource data and object data management in the community, named the virtual community (Lu et al., 2013) based upon the RIA. According to Zhang et al. (2009), the 2D visualization of statistical analysis could be overlapped with the virtual reality environment of 3D, as it is more intuitive. It is also a less cognitive demanding display mechanism, lessening the user's cognitive workload. The proposed platform has been based upon the Web VR engine and Web VRGIS (Lv et al., 2011), which has been extended to the virtual city and has been used to forecast and analyze city traffic (Li, Lv, Hu et al., 2015).

13.5 Key Technology of the Platform

13.5.1 Fault-Tolerance Processing of Transportation

Because of the mistake or the breakdown of the transmission equipment and traffic sensor, it is inevitable that losses and mistakes take place in transportation statistics. Thus, the original statistics should amend the incomplete statistics and get rid of the abnormal data and to ensure the correctness and integrity of the statistics. The major research of the processing of fault-tolerance includes the judging of the incomplete data, amending the missing data, and identifying the abnormal data. The judging of the missing data has been done to keep scanning the dynamic data in a specific time period based on the stated data collection format and time (Lv, Li et al., 2014). Confirming the abnormal data requires distinguishing if the fault data is the real abnormal traffic data that is generated because of the abnormal weather or traffic accident. Amending the incomplete data needs to utilize the mathematic model that has been used in the prediction and analysis, and hence supplements the incomplete data.

13.5.2 Integration of Multivariate and Heterogeneous Transportation Data

The collection approaches of transportation statistics include manual work, microwave sensor, camera, and probe vehicle (Lv et al., 2013). Since the source statistics collected possesses different timing, position, accuracy, and structure, the heterogeneous and multivariate transportation statistics should be integrated before the transportation analysis. Together with the development of the network communication technology and the development of the sensor technology, the transportation statistics' multivariate heterogeneity has been becoming more prominent and the related challenges concerning data integration are more difficult. The major work of data integration has taken the statistics' advantage through promoting the data accuracy and lifting the coverage range of the network (Lv, Su et al., 2014). Meanwhile, conducting the superposition calculation, cross-checking, and complementation over the temporal-spatial data via different statistical and data models, and conducting processing over the multisource statistics form a more comprehensive description of transportation. On the other hand, viewing the discrete vehicles as the fundamental description unit is a more accurate statistic integration than the collection section from a micro perspective and leads to more accurate information about transportation.

13.5.3 Storage and Calculation of Mass Transportation Information

Since the transportation data capacity is huge, the updating frequent, and the source rich and diverse, the managing and storing of the mass statistics in a satisfying and reliable application is an important element in wise transportation construction. For the storage of the mass data, a database for convenient and quick management and inquiry could be established. Besides, high-efficient transmission is supposed to be realized under the limited Internet band. Meanwhile, the application, analysis, integration, and acquisition of the mass transportation data take the support from a relative high-powered computer platform. It also needs to offer the same powerful network services and computing ability as a "super computer" via the construction of the cloud platform for the government service.

13.5.4 Analysis and Prediction of Real-Time Dynamic Transportation Flow

Real-time prediction and analysis of the transportation flow have always been the most difficult in the analysis of the transportation. As the changes in the transportation network has been complicated and fast, along with the growing of dynamic statistics of transportation, it has always been a high requirement to predict the traffic flow of different transportation methods and real-time analysis crossing the Internet. Most research covers the analysis of road congestion, judging the seriousness of traffic accidents, forecasting the impact of space and time over the scope of a traffic jam, and predicting the road speed of different transportation means, after only several hours or minutes based upon the data integration.

13.5.5 Three-Dimensional Analysis of Real-Time Transportation Information

Along with the evolution of the 3D geographical information system and people's requirements for a realistic 3D scene, it has become necessary to build up the 3D geographical system. The major research work covers a wide range of areas, including the inquiry of the transportation network layering, the inquiry of the different transportation accidents, 3D visual representation, analysis of the model research, and the inquiry over the different transportation accidents based upon the 3D statistics mode (Lv et al., 2011).

Interactive Visual Analysis of Traffic Big Data

13.6 Advantages of Platform Solution

13.6.1 High Usability and High Stability

Ensuring the stable and safe operations of the mechanism through cloud technology, distributed computation, and utilization of virtualization promotes the disaster toleration and safety of the system.

13.6.2 High Performance and Real-Time Performance

Breaking the bottleneck of the performance of old architecture based upon the cloud computing system architecture leads to easy processing of mass statistics, intelligent management over the transportation information, and real-time monitoring, which meets the requirement of high performance of the dynamic information's real-time processing.

13.6.3 High Compatibility and Easy Access to Information

The application load has rather easy expansion, extensive compatibility, and strong adaptability. The compatibility covers a wide range of channels for the information issuing, for example, 3G wireless, the Internet, and public switched telephone network (PSTN), which have been used to support devices like the tablet PC, PDA, and PC.

13.7 Analysis of Bus Passenger Flow in the City

13.7.1 Analysis of Bus Service Scope

Currently, there are 47 bus routines in Shenzhen City, passing the transportation junction of Fukuda. If the residents choose the bus route to travel, which is 500 meters from them in most cases, then they also need to take 500 meters to go to the buffer zone where bus 47 can go to both directions. This buffer area is over 400 square meters. There is a nonstop bus line heading for Zhuzilin, which could offer the residents traffic convenience for at least 400 square meters.

13.7.2 Relevant Bus Flow Analysis of the Junction

The data from Shenzhen Tong, which is the citizens' use of bus cards in Shenzhen, includes the type and the ID, namely, the type of vehicle the passengers are taking and their card numbers. For instance, 21 refers to swiping the card for entry of the subway, while 22 refers to swiping the card for the subway, and 31 refers to swiping the card to board the bus. There is also information about the bus line, time, and device ID. For example, the bus route taken by the passenger, the time when the passenger swipes the car and boards the bus, and the number of the swiping machine where the passengers swiped the card will be stored on this card. Since the card can only store the time when the passenger swipes the card and the bus line taken by the passenger, there's no information recorded about the passenger getting off and getting on the station. The time the passenger getting off the bus will not be recorded either. Thus, the data of the Shenzhen Tong bus card will not support the proper bus flow analysis, which is related with the junction. Therefore, the study could only provide the analysis of the 47 bus lines related with the junction of Fukuda and the information of the flow law in every station to forecast the bus flow of this junction. Figure 13.1 is the daily flow data about the bus route, which has been directly connected with the transportation junction of Fukuda. It can be easily seen that despite the large-scale activities and special holidays, the related bus flow changes regularly over the seven days. Figure 13.1 also shows the data of the passenger flow in different periods on the same day each week from July to August. It is easily can be seen that the periodicity has become rather obvious.

13.8 Passenger Flow Analysis of Public Transportation Transfer

The public transportation transfers cover various modes, like bus–water, subway–bus, and bus–bus transportation modes. Theoretically, the public transportation's exponential function involves 2 as the base number. However, for a particular transportation junction, there have been many different types. For the concrete study for the transportation junction in Zhuzilin, based upon the geographic location and designing structure of Zhuzilin and considering the features of the utilization of the nearby land and the time–space distribution of current passenger flow statistics, some passengers will transfer definitely (see Table 13.1).

The key modes for study are as follows:

- Transfer between the subway and bus at the station of Zhuzilin
- Transfer between the bus and subway at the station of Zhuzilin

Other transfer modes, like the transfer between buses to another vehicle, are not analyzed in the study since there are no statistics concerning coming from the Shenzhen Tong. The following text presents the analysis over the three modes with the aim to obtain the

TABLE 13.1

Proportion of the Main Transfer Bus Passenger Volume to Zhuzilin after Subway Transfer

Main Bus Route Taken First	Percentage
392	5%
43	2.5%
66	1.8%
B728	1.75%
338	1.5%
392 interval line	1.25%
113	1.25%
70	1.25%
M250	1.25%
3	1.21%

Interactive Visual Analysis of Traffic Big Data

transfer modes in the juncture of Zhuzilin, the mutual relations, and the inner structure of the mode.

The transfer between the subway and other vehicles is a quite important transfer mode. This study defines the swiping records of the bus card in half an hour when the passenger gets off at the Zhuzilin transfer station and then transfers to a bus. Figure 13.6 presents the location distribution of the bus lines that have been designed as transfer stations after passengers get off from the Zhuzilin station. In the figure, the color of the line indicates the quantity of the passengers flow. The transfer volume is the real number of transfer passengers in related vehicle lines in the Zhuzilin transfer station. There are different types of passenger flows predicting the models and the common models are the time series prediction model and regression prediction model.

Taking a subway to Zhulin and then taking the bus to the final destination is a key transfer mode. The statistics resources could be the Shenzhen Tong records where passengers need to swipe the cards when they get off the bus and later get into the subway station of Zhuzilin through card swiping again in one hour. Figure 13.6 is the bus lines geographic distribution. The different colors of the transportation routes indicate the total transfer volume.

The third transfer mode is based upon the second one in which the passengers will take a bus first and later transfer to the Loo line and then head for the transportation juncture of Zhuzilin. The Shenzhen Tong records are the data source where the passengers will swipe the cards when they get off the buses and later swipe the card again if they are going to board a Lobo line and then get off at the transfer station of Zhuzilin after getting off in an hour. After the analysis, we could obtain 10 major bus lines.

The geographic distribution of 10 major lines is presented next. The distribution of passengers is average. Judging from the surface, it seems the Luobo line runs parallel to the No. 338 bus for 30 km. However, they still serve as the secondary transfer mode where passengers could board the bus first and then change into the Luobao line and head for the transportation juncture of Zhuzilin. It still ranks as the top 5 route. After tracking the passengers who hold a one-card record, it can be found that the majority of the passengers will choose the Luobao line after getting off the bus. They mainly get off from three stations: Guwu, Hourui, and the East Airport. These three stations are located in the neighborhood of the Luobao line or the terminal of the Luobao line. Then, it could be understood that passengers will board the No. 338 bus and then head for Fuyongzhen or Shajin Town rather than the Zhuzilin juncture. Judging from the analysis of the one-card data, it will take 40 to 50 minutes to go to Zhuzilin from Guwu, Hourui, or the East Airport. However, passengers who choose to head for Zhuzilin directly will spend more than 90 minutes on the road, as the bus speed is less than 18 km per hour. With the aim to avoid peak hours and reach Zhuzilin on time, passengers would likely transfer to the Luobao line. Then, it can be seen that the transfer of the different transportation means could somehow utilize the blind spots of the transportation and promote transportation efficiency. The geographical distribution of Luobao line and No. 338 line is as follows:

According to the statistics, the average time passengers spend from the moment they get off from the subway and then change to the bus is 11 minutes. Figure 13.7 has presented the related statistics.

As shown in Figure 13.5, if passengers swipe their cards when they get off the subway and change to the bus, the average time period is during the morning peak hours, which means between 6 a.m. and 10 a.m. During the morning peak hours, the average transfer time is 9 to 19 minutes (Table 13.2).

The evening peak hours are from 4 p.m. to 8 p.m. The transferring time on average is 11 minutes. However, the average transfer time during nonpeak hours will be longer compared

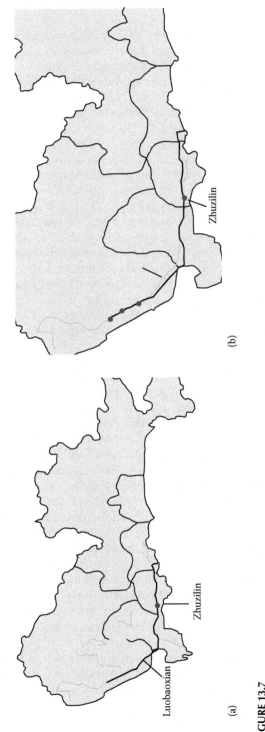

FIGURE 13.7
(a) The 10 main bus routes to Zhuzilin. (b) The geographic distribution diagram for No. 338 bus and Lobo route.

Interactive Visual Analysis of Traffic Big Data

TABLE 13.2

Average Time for Transferring and Standard Deviation

Period	Average Time for Transferring (Minutes)	Standard Deviation of Transfer Time
6 a.m.–8 a.m.	9	6.380525236
8 a.m.–10 a.m.	10	7.071766835
10 a.m.–12 a.m.	12	7.297721547
12 a.m.–2 p.m.	11	6.848422948
2 p.m.–4 p.m.	12	7.229369224
4 p.m.–6 p.m.	11	7.075560019
6 p.m.–8 p.m.	11	6.794950708
8 p.m.–10 p.m.	10	6.198755368

to peak hours. For instance, from 2 p.m. to 4 p.m. and 10 a.m. to 12 a.m., the average transferring time passengers spend will be 12 minutes. Then, it can be inferred that the passengers who need to transfer at the Zhuzilin station have not hit the predicted saturation capacity yet. That is to say, the transfer order is quite good and the efficiency of transfer is high.

The transfer time passengers spend during the off-peak hours is 1 to 2 minutes longer compared to peak hours. We could interpret it like this: First, the passengers who need the transfer are off or on duty in fixed lines during the peak hour and they have been quite familiar with the lines and they have exact clear goals. Under a situation like this, quickening the step could short the transferring time if the transfer line is not quite crowded. Second, there will be more buses for the same line during the peak hour, greatly reducing the waiting time passengers spent in the station.

13.9 Human Factors in Traffic Geographical Information Systems

13.9.1 Traffic Information Fault-Tolerance Processing

Because of the deviation, breakdown of the data recording, as well as other reasons, the traffic data and the transmission devices could inevitably have missing data, errors, and other problems. Thus, the platform has been used to detect the raw data, removing the abnormal statistics and amending the incomplete statistics, ensuring the correctness and integrity of the data. The processing of fault tolerance mainly covers amending the incomplete data, judging the obliterated data, and identifying the abnormal data. Obliterated data has been used mainly for the continuous scanning over the dynamic statistics in a specific period of time corresponding to the data collection format and time (Tan et al., 2011). In the process of the abnormal data identification, the abnormal statistics are the statistics involving equipment failure or valid traffic abnormal statistics generated by abnormal weather, traffic events, and so on. For the amending of the abnormal statistics, a mathematical model has been adopted for the prediction and analysis to amend the incomplete statistics.

13.9.2 Multielement Isomeric Traffic Data Integration

Traffic data collection has various modes, including manual labor, microwave, radar, camera, and floating car. Statistics collected from various sources are different in time, position, accuracy, and structure (Tan et al., 2014). Turns out, the multielement isomeric traffic statistics should be the subject of statistics integration before the analysis of the traffic data. With the rapid development of intelligent sensing advanced technology and the Internet of Cars, the multielement isomeric nature of the traffic statistics as well as the network communication technology, the isomeric nature of the traffic statistics are highlighted with the passing of time, leading to greater challenges for the data integration.

Different kinds of statistics have been used to promote the network coverage and data accuracy. Meanwhile, space data is inferior to superposition computing, mutual verification, and complementation via different statistical models and data models, in order to form more comprehensive descriptions of the traffic and to deal with the multisource statistics. The collected information about road segments is inferior to the accurate data integration if it is analyzed from a microcosmic perspective and hence it obtains more accurate information about the traffic.

13.9.3 Mass Traffic Information Storage and Computing

Traffic statistics needs frequent updating and has diversified sources. It is important for the establishment of wise transportation to effectively manage and store the mass statistics and try to make them satisfy the standards set by the application of a traffic system for high reliability and high availability. For the storage of such mass statistics, it has been necessary to build a database that features convenient and rapid management and query, and realizes the high-efficiency statistics transmission with limited network bandwidth. Meanwhile, it also needs the support from the computer platform for application, analysis, integration, and acquisition of mass traffic statistics to forecast and analyze the dynamic flow at the same time. The real-time forecasting and analysis over the traffic flow has always been a problem over the traffic analysis. Changes occurring in the traffic network have been rather complicated and rapid. With the promotion of the upgrading pace of the dynamic statistics of the traffic system, there are increasing standards of the real-time forecasting and analysis over the traffic capacity of different transportation modes. Judging from the perspective of data integration, this platform has been used to discuss the congestion level of the road, predict the space–time impact of the traffic incidence, judge the severity of traffic incidents, and also predict the sections of road in the entire system after several hours or minutes.

13.10 Conclusion

With the promotion of the 3D system and people's growing demands over the 3D scene, it is an inexorable trend to build a 3D information system. This platform actually supports the network flow with multiscales and visualization expression. Research about the spatial analysis model and the visualization of the decision-making process is based upon the 3D space statistics model. This platform has adopted cloud computing, distributed computation, and virtualization to ensure the stable and safe operation of the system, promoting the disaster tolerance and security of the statistics and the entire system to the maximum level (Wang et al., 2012). Judging from the system framework possessed by the cloud system, this platform has broken the old system's performance bottleneck, achieving the intelligent monitoring and realizing the real time processing. It has been characterized with strong load adaptability, easy expansion, and wide compatibility (Xu et al., 2014). This

Interactive Visual Analysis of Traffic Big Data 259

platform will be compatible with the distribution modes of multichannel information, which includes 3G wireless, the Internet, and PSTN, and provides support to the terminals of information distribution like the tablet PC, mobile phone, PDA, and PC.

In this study, the transportation junction of Futian was the research subject. The temporal and spatial distribution rules over the service and passenger flow of all transportation means were found by conducting data analysis over the daily time-phased passenger flow and daily long-term passenger flow in the transportation junction in Futian based on the statistics like long- and short-term prediction, transportation data of long-distance passengers, floating car and taxi data, and card data about the Shenzhen Tong. The different passenger flow does not hit the upper limit even during peak hours on holidays, with no obvious congestion or transfer. In the short term, different transportation means enjoying a rather stable passenger flow. In addition, the prediction model of the time-phased passenger has been reliable. The major junction service group has been distributed in the Futian District, Nanshan District, and the Luohu District, covering about 9 km around the transportation junction.

It can be seen that the traveling time has been taken as an index being used to conduct a set of studies and analyses over the accessibility of the public transportation system in the transportation junction of Futian. It has been found that the fluctuation in traveling time has also been viewed as an index to comprehend the reliability of the junction system. The general reliability was high and there's only poor reliability during peak hours in the Bao'an station and Huaqiang North station. The lively working region is not an exception. For the areas with strong entertainment facilities like Honey Lake, it also has poor reliability during peak traveling.

However, the 3D application in Shenzhen proves that the 3D analysis and visualization is a useful device for social services and agencies for directly analyzing and browsing Big Data concerning the city.

The traffic statistics of the city have a number of features like real-time, diverse, predictable, and large scale, falling into the range of Big Data's depiction. This chapter promoted a cloud service platform targeting wise transportation, which is to conduct mining analysis and unified management over the large numbers of heterogeneous and multivariate dynamic information about the traffic, offering real-time information of the traffic, promoting transportation utilization efficiency, and enhancing the service level and transportation management of travel information. This will result in the virtual reality offering decision support to transportation management.

13.11 Future Work

Through long-term analysis and monitoring, the prediction about the passenger flow was based upon the condition that combines urban planning with economic development. Future analysis will be determined by the travel behavior of human beings, as well as their influence over public buses, taxi routes, and traveling speed as well as the weather conditions (e.g., heavy fog, typhoons, and rainstorms). More in-depth analyses can forecast and monitor large-scale events and make decisions during emergency evacuations. Apart from the city, ocean statistics will be combined into the well-established platform (Su et al., 2014), where we will adopt the spatiotemporal visualization to be the representative method. A number of novel interaction approaches have been considered to be adopted in our future work (Lv, 2013), the grid system, and the data management algorithm (Che et al., 2014).

Glossary

Big Data: Big Data, involves the amount of data (volume), timeliness (velocity), diversity (variety), and accuracy (veracity). Big Data refers to the huge amount of data that cannot pass through current mainstream software tools. Once captured, managed, processed, and finished, Big Data could help make business decisions within a reasonable time.

Passenger flow forecasting: The passenger flow forecast refers to the index reflecting the demand characteristics of traffic passenger flow by forecasting the cross-sectional flow of urban transport lines within a certain period and interstation origin destination (OD). Upon planning the traffic network, the passenger flow analysis result of different traffic network schemes is the main content upon which the line network is selected. There are many kinds of traffic passenger flow forecast models, and the common models include regression forecast and time series prediction.

System: This research takes the Shenzhen Futian Comprehensive Transportation Junction as the case, and makes use of continuous, multiple real-time dynamic traffic information (currently using taxi data, the database also includes card swiping data of public transport, and long-distance passenger traffic information, etc.) to monitor and analyze the spatial and temporal distribution of passenger flow under different means of transportation and service capacity of junction from multidimensional space-time perspectives such as different periods and special periods.

Virtual geographical environment: Virtual environments have proven to significantly improve public understanding of 3D planning data. To share the information resources of all departments and the dynamic tracking for the geospatial information of population and companies, an integrated information system of social services is constructed. The use of virtual reality as visual means has changed the traditional image of the city.

VRGIS: The virtual reality geographical information system can obtain the landscape geospatial data dynamically, and perform rich visual 3D analysis, calculations, and managements based on geographical information system (GIS) data. VRGIS can be regarded as a special "traditional" GIS, which has the functions of storage, processing, query, and analysis of spatial data of traditional GIS system, but the VR technology is the main user interface and interactive method. An ideal VRGIS should have the following features: (1) the real performance of spatial data; (2) the user can observe from any angle, immersed in real-time interaction, and can be used in the choice of geographical range free migration; (3) basic GIS function; (4) the user interface is a natural and complete part.

References

Breunig, M. and S. Zlatanova. (2011). Review: 3D geo-database research: Retrospective and future directions. *Computers and Geosciences* 37(7): 791–803.

Briggs, F. (2012). Large data—Great opportunities. Presented at IDF2012, Beijing.

Che, L., M. Khodayar, and M. Shahidehpour. (2014). Adaptive protection system for microgrids: Protection practices of a functional microgrid system. *IEEE Electrification Magazine* 2(1): 66–80.

Che, L. and M. Shahidehpour. (2014). DC microgrids: Economic operation and enhancement of resilience by hierarchical control. *IEEE Transactions Smart Grid* 5(5): 2517–2526.

Chen, Z., N. Chen, and J. Gong. (2015). Design and implementation of the real-time GIS data model and sensor web service platform for environmental Big Data management with the Apache Storm. Fourth International Conference on Agro-Geoinformatics, IEEE.

Chow, E., A. Hammad, and P. Gauthier. (2011). Multi-touch screens for navigating 3D virtual environments in participatory urban planning. In *CHI '11 Extended Abstracts on Human Factors in Computing Systems*, pp. 2395–2400, New York, ACM.

Haklay, M. E. (2002). Virtual reality and GIS: Applications, trends and directions. In P. Fisher and D. Unwin, editors, *Virtual Reality in Geography*, pp. 47–57. New York, Taylor & Francis.

Huang, B., B. Jiang, and H. Li. (2001). An integration of GIS, virtual reality and the internet for visualization, analysis and exploration of spatial data. *International Journal of Geographical Information Science* 15(5): 439–456.

Jiang, D., Z. Xu, P. Zhang, and T. Zhu. (2014). A transform domain-based anomaly detection approach to network-wide traffic. *Journal of Network and Computer Applications* 40: 292–306.

Li, H.-Z., S. Guo, C.-J. Li, and J.-Q. Sun. (2013). A hybrid annual power load forecasting model based on generalized regression neural network with fruit fly optimization algorithm. *Knowledge-Based Systems* 37: 378–387.

Li, X., Z. Lv, B. Zhang, W. Wang, S. Feng, and J. Hu. (2015). WebVRGIS based city Big Data 3D visualization and analysis. IEEE Pacific Visualization Symposium (PacificVis).

Li, X., Z. Lv, J. Hu, B. Zhang, L. Yin, C. Zhong, W. Wang, and S. Feng. (2015). Traffic management and forecasting system based on 3D GIS. 15th IEEE/ACM International Symposium on Cluster, Cloud and Grid Computing (CCGrid).

Lin, H., M. Chen, G. Lu, Q. Zhu, J. Gong, X. You, Y. Wen, B. Xu, and M. Hu. (2013). Virtual geographic environments (VGEs): A new generation of geographic analysis tool. *Earth-Science Reviews* 126: 74–84.

Lohr, S. (2012). The Age of Big Data. *New York Times*, February 11.

Lu, Z., S. U. Rehman, and G. Chen. (2013). WebVRGIS: WebGIS based interactive online 3D virtual community. In *2013 International Conference Virtual Reality and Visualization (ICVRV)*, pp. 94–99. IEEE.

Lv, Z. (2013). Wearable smartphone: Wearable hybrid framework for hand and foot gesture interaction on smartphone. In *2013 IEEE International Conference on Computer Vision Workshops*, pp. 436–443. IEEE.

Lv, Z., G. Chen, C. Zhong, Y. Han, and Y. Y. Qi. (2012). A framework for multi-dimensional webGIS based interactive online virtual community. *Advanced Science Letters* 7(1): 215–219.

Lv, Z., C. Esteve, J. Chirivella, and P. Gagliardo. (2015). A game based assistive tool for rehabilitation of dysphonic patients. 2015 3rd Workshop on Virtual and Augmented Assistive Technology (VAAT). IEEE.

Lv, Z., L. Feng, H. Li, and S. Feng. (2014). Hand-free motion interaction on Google glass. SIGGRAPH Asia 2014 Mobile Graphics and Interactive Applications. ACM.

Lv, Z., L. Feng, S. Feng, and H. Li. (2015). Extending touch-less interaction on vision based wearable device. IEEE Virtual Reality Conference 2015, March 23–27, Arles, France.

Lv, Z., A. Halawani, S. Feng, H. Li, and S. U. (2014). Multimodal hand and foot gesture interaction for handheld devices. *ACM Transactions on Multimedia Computing, Communications, and Applications*, 11(1): 10:1–10:19.

Lv, Z., X. Li, J. Hu, L. Yin, B. Zhang, and S. Feng. (2015). Virtual geographic environment based coach passenger flow forecasting. IEEE Computational Intelligence and Virtual Environments for Measurement Systems and Applications (CIVEMSA).

Lv, Z., X. Li, B. Zhang, W. Wang, S. Feng, and J. Hu. (2015). Big city 3D visual analysis. 36th Annual Conference of the European Association for Computer Graphics (Eurographics2015).

Lv, Z., S. Rhman, and G. Chen. (2013). WebVRGIS: A p2p network engine for VR data and GIS analysis. In M. Lee, A. Hirose, Z.-G. Hou, and R. Kil, editors, *Neural Information Processing* (vol. 8226 of Lecture Notes in Computer Science), pp. 503–510. Springer, Berlin, Heidelberg.

Lv, Z. and T. Su. (2014). 3D seabed modeling and visualization on ubiquitous context. In *SIGGRAPH Asia 2014 Posters*, p. 33. ACM.

Lv, Z., T. Su, X. Li, and S. Feng. (2015). 3D visual analysis of seabed on smartphone. *2015 IEEE Pacific Visualization Symposium (PacificVis)*. IEEE.

Lv, Z., T. Yin, Y. Han, Y. Chen, and G. Chen. (2011). WebVR—Web virtual reality engine based on P2P network. *Journal of Networks* 6(7): 990–998.

Porathe, T. and J. Prison. (2011). Design of human-map system interaction. In *CHI '08 Extended Abstracts on Human Factors in Computing Systems*, pp. 2859–2864, New York, ACM.

Qingquan, L. I. and L. I. Deren. (2014). Big Data GIS. Geomatics and Information Science of Wuhan University.

Shahrokni, H., B. Van der Heijde, D. Lazarevic, and N. Brandt. (2014). Big Data GIS Analytics towards Efficient Waste Management in Stockholm. *Advances in Computer Science Research*, 140–147.

Su, T., Z. Lv, S. Gao, X. Li, and H. Lv. (2014). 3D seabed: 3D modeling and visualization platform for the seabed. In *2014 IEEE International Conference on Multimedia and Expo Workshops (ICMEW)*, pp. 1–6. IEEE.

Sui, D. (2014). Open GIS for Big Data: Opportunities and impediments. *Progress in Geography* 33(6): 723–737.

Tan, J., X. Fan, and F. Deng. (2011). Design and key technology of urban landscape 3D visualization system. *Procedia Environmental Sciences* 10: 1238–1243.

Tan, J., X. Fan, and Y. Ren. (2014). Methodology for geographical data evolution: Three-dimensional particle-based real-time snow simulation with remote-sensing data. *Journal of Applied Remote Sensing* 8(1): 084598–084598.

Wang, Y., W. Jiang, and G. Agrawal. (2012). SciMATE: A novel MapReduce-like framework for multiple scientific data formats. In *2012 12th IEEE/ACM International Symposium Cluster, Cloud and Grid Computing (CCGrid)*, pp. 443–450. IEEE.

Xu, J., D. Vazquez, A. M. Lopez, J. Marin, and D. Ponsa. (2014). Learning a part-based pedestrian detector in a virtual world. *IEEE Transactions on Intelligent Transportation Systems* 15(5), 2121–2131.

Zhang, M., Z. Lv, X. Zhang, G. Chen, and K. Zhang. (2009). Research and application of the 3D virtual community based on WEBVR and RIA. *Computer and Information Science* 2(1): P84.

Zhang, M., Y. Sun, S. Dang, and K. Petrou. (2014). Smart grid-oriented algorithm of data retrieval and processing based on cRIO. ISEEE.

Zhong, C., S. M. Arisona, X. Huang, M. Batty, and G. Schmitt. (2014). Detecting the dynamics of urban structure through spatial network analysis. *International Journal of Geographical Information Science* 28(11): 2178–2199.

Zhong, C., X. Huang, S. M. Arisona, G. Schmitt, and M. Batty. (2014). Inferring building functions from a probabilistic model using public transportation data. *Computers, Environment and Urban Systems* 48: 124–137.

Zhou, X., D. Di, X. Yang, and D. Wu. (2010). Location optimization of urban passenger transportation terminal. In *Proceedings of the 2010 International Conference on Optoelectronics and Image Processing*, pp. 668–671. IEEE Computer Society.

Authors

Zhihan Lv is a native Chinese. He is an engineer and researcher of virtual/augmented reality and multimedia. He has plenty of work experience in virtual reality and augmented reality projects, and application of computer visualization and computer vision. His research application fields widely range from everyday life to traditional research fields (i.e., geography, biology, medicine). He has recently successfully completed several projects on PCs, websites, smartphones, and smartglasses.

Xiaoming Li was born in Shandong, China, in 1984. He earned a PhD from Wuhan University of China with a major in photogrammetry and remote sensing in 2011. He is currently a researcher at Shenzhen Research Center of Digital City Engineering. Li is mainly engaged in the research of 3D GIS and VGE, and city Big Data management.

Weixi Wang was born in Henan, China, in 1978. He earned a PhD from Liaoning Project Technology University of China with a major in geodesy and survey engineering in 2007 and completed his post-doctoral fellowship at Wuhan University of China in 2013. He is currently a researcher at Shenzhen Research Center of Digital City Engineering. Wang is mainly engaged in the research of BIM and 3D GIS and VGE.

Jinxing Hu was born in Hennan, China, in 1974. He earned a PhD from Perking University of China with a major in GIS in 2003. He is currently a researcher and director assistant at High Performance Computing Research Center at Shenzhen Institutes of Advanced Technology (SIAT), Chinese Academy of Science, China. Hu is mainly engaged in the research of integration of 3S application, reference, and core application of digital city, analysis of disaster monitoring, and traffic data mining.

Ling Yin earned a PhD at the University of Tennessee with a major in geography in 2011. She is a researcher at High Performance Computing Research Center at Shenzhen Institutes of Advanced Technology (SIAT), Chinese Academy of Science, China. She is engaged in spatial-temporal GIS, T-GIS, spatio-temporal data mining, and time-geography research.

14

Prospect of Big Data Technologies in Healthcare

Raghavendra Kankanady and Marilyn Wells

CONTENTS

14.1 Introduction 266
14.2 Big Data in Healthcare 266
    14.2.1 What Is the Role of Big Data in Healthcare? 266
    14.2.2 How to Apply Big Data Technologies to Healthcare 268
14.3 Introduction to Electronic Medical Record (EMR) System 269
    14.3.1 What Is an EMR? 269
    14.3.2 Types of EMRs 269
    14.3.3 Desirable Characteristics of EMRs 269
    14.3.4 Challenges with EMRs 272
    14.3.5 EMRs for Healthcare Data Analytics 273
14.4 Integrating EMR through NoSQL Datastores 273
    14.4.1 Key-Value Datastore 273
           14.4.1.1 Key-Value Datastore Data Model 274
    14.4.2 Document Datastore 274
           14.4.2.1 Document Datastore Data Model 274
    14.4.3 Column Datastore 275
           14.4.3.1 Column Store Data Model 275
    14.4.4 Graph Datastore 276
           14.4.4.1 Graph Datastore Data Model 276
    14.4.5 NoSQL Datastore Usage Scenarios 277
    14.4.6 Benefits of NoSQL Datastore 278
14.5 Conclusion 278
References 279
Authors 279

ABSTRACT In the recent decade we have seen the digitization of healthcare records. This has opened a new era for information flow. Digitization has led to large amounts of data being generated by the healthcare industry. The vast amount of data collected is usually controlled by different hospitals, surgeries, clinics, allied health, and administrative departments in data silos. A consolidated and integrated approach to Big Data can help the healthcare industry with problems of escalating healthcare spending, variability related to quality of patient care, biomedical research, disease prevention, and also help patients reduce total treatment costs. Big Data analysis can also help physicians, pharmaceutical companies, patients, and other healthcare stakeholders identify value and opportunities in the large quantities of data collected for further exploration and analysis. The Big Data revolution in the healthcare industry is in its early days and most of the value created is still unclaimed to a large extent. Applications of Big Data technologies to healthcare and some of the ways of extracting value

265

from electronic medical records (EMRs) using Big Data analytics is explained in this chapter. This chapter also identifies some of the key issues and challenges within EMRs, which needs addressing prior to realizing the full potential of Big Data technologies.

14.1 Introduction

From banking to the retail industry, many sectors to some extent have adapted to Big Data analytics. The healthcare industry has lagged in adaptation of this technology. Part of the problem could be resistance to change, underinvestment in technology due to uncertain returns, and organizational structural issues with reference to consolidation and standardization of data. A series of converging trends, such as demand for better data, cost pressures in the form of reform, significant advances in technology, and changing government regulations for making data publicly available is bringing the healthcare industry to a tipping point where Big Data technologies can play a major role in transforming the healthcare industry. Big Data technologies can also foster healthcare system for data feedback loop.

14.2 Big Data in Healthcare

14.2.1 What Is the Role of Big Data in Healthcare?

A broad range of healthcare information is available about patients in different areas of healthcare. Physicians, nurses, and hospitals are using computer-based record systems for storing patient data. Hospitals and healthcare providers who are participating in health information exchange are getting connected electronically. With time, more hospitals and care providers are joining the healthcare information ecosystem. This is creating large quantities of data that is available for further analysis and economic value creation.

Large volumes of patient information are created by physicians during the course of patient lifecycle management in areas such as hospitals, clinics, laboratories, and medical offices. For example, when the patient visits the physician for the first time, a patient file is created that includes the patient's personal details, medical history, medications, diagnosis, current treatment, allergies, insurance details, and other significant medical information. This file can also include laboratory test results, x-rays, scanned images, and other treatments administered. If the patient is referred to another physician for consultation, then the referred physician's diagnosis, corresponding hospital's information, clinical information, and laboratory results are updated to the patient file. Laboratory results can be in various formats such as magnetic resonance images, electrocardiograph data, and blood test concentrations. Hospitals and clinics may also use a combination of paper-based records and electronic data for managing patient records. This creates a lot of structured and unstructured data during the entire patient management lifecycle.

Big Data technologies can assist in patient management. Patient management could be improved in both quality and efficiency by effective information management using Big Data technologies. Predictions can be made using data analytics with reference to readmissions, adverse events, optimized treatment plans, and early identifications of a worsening health state of a patient. Interoperable standards for information exchange are also being created by both public and private sector organizations. Integrating Big Data technologies into patient management systems will develop and deliver a healthcare system that is more coordinated and effective. Real-time access to patient information using Big Data technologies can help reduce patient readmissions by enabling care coordinators to book appointments with primary care physicians. It is known that the most powerful predictor of not having a readmission is that the patient has scheduled an appointment with their primary care physician with seven days of discharge.

Accountable care organizations (ACOs) are using Big Data technologies to improve the quality of healthcare and reduce healthcare costs. ACOs have established Big Data warehouses to optimize healthcare services (Conn 2015). A Big Data warehouse will let ACOs pull information from a variety of sources to help optimize care for individual patients and for the overall enrolled population. ACOs primarily are using data already pooled in their own and their partner providers' EMR (electronic medical record) systems. For the majority of ACOs accessing and analyzing smaller pods of data, sharing information and sharing of results are the formidable information challenges faced. Big Data technologies can assist ACOs with integrating data from various data sources and provide a comprehensive analysis of patient records for effective patient management.

Big Data technologies can also help personalize healthcare to patients. Data-driven and networks-driven thinking and methods can play a critical role in the emergence of personalized healthcare (Chawla and Davis 2013). Analytics can bring in an order of understanding to the personalized healthcare complexity. As EMR systems for healthcare become globally available, personal health information management will also emerge. For the next big steps in healthcare to happen, it requires Big Data technologies to discover deep insights about patient similarities and hereditary relationships, and to provide personal disease risk profiles for individual patients. This provides opportunities for proactive disease management, proactive medicine, and patient empowerment. This also leads to a reduction in patient readmissions.

Healthcare can move from a disease-centered model toward a patient-centered model. A physician's decision making is based on clinical expertise, diagnosis, and various tests in a disease-centered model. Patients can receive healthcare services that are based on individual needs with oversight and advice from healthcare providers in a patient-centered model. Patients can have a personalized care system in a patient-centered model. Advanced Big Data analytical solutions can contribute toward this shift, that is, from a disease-centered model that is based on population-based evidence for decision making to a patient-centered model that is the integration of an individual-and population-based evidence system. The patient-centered model and advanced analytics will enable patients to answer questions such as: What are the risks of me developing a particular disease? What is the best method to manage my disease? Who is the best available care provider for this particular disease or for my disease risk profile? What strategies and wellness programs should I use? Developing wellness strategies, identifying risk profiles, and predictive analysis can lead to better management of health and empower patients. This will also enable patients to have an informed dialogue with their physician that lead to patients' overall improved well-being.

Big Data technologies can also provide physicians a boundless experience to gauge the impact of a patient's disease toward developing other diseases in the future. It can assist in finding out if there are other patients with similar symptoms, not only with respect to major issues (common symptoms) but also with respect to rare issues. Disease interactions, symptoms, clinically reported traits, and a patient's biological information can help identify possible health risks, their causes, and comorbidities.

14.2.2 How to Apply Big Data Technologies to Healthcare

There are lots of articles and books that describe Big Data from a technology perspective. Apache Hadoop and NoSQL databases are the most prominent Big Data technologies presently used (Oracle 2013). NoSQL databases can be seen as an enabling technology behind Big Data analytical capabilities. The flexible nature of the NoSQL databases makes analytics possible for Big Data technologies.

Some of the challenges faced by health IT managers when implementing Big Data technologies are

- What value and insights can be possibly extracted using Big Data technologies?
- What will be the integration methodology with existing data warehousing solutions?
- Can the current data warehousing solution be extended or expanded for Big Data capabilities?
- What will be the cost of implementing new Big Data solutions as compared to augmenting it with existing solutions?
- What is the impact on existing governance structure and information management if Big Data solutions are implemented?
- Can the Big Data solutions be implemented in a phased approach?
- What skills are needed to build and run the Big Data solutions?
- Can the existing data stored in data warehouse solutions also be used to derive insights?
- Can the Big Data solution help to reduce the complexity of data integration from different data sources?

There are no guidelines that outline what insights can be achieved by Big Data solutions. Healthcare organizations also doubt if the value and insights that they seek can be addressed by using Big Data solutions. The actual scenarios need to be identified by the organization as they evolve over time. Having data scientist skills may also be key in determining important use cases and business scenarios, which if implemented can bring significant value to the organization. A data scientist will be able to understand the key performance metrics for healthcare and apply statistical analysis to the data for the key use cases identified in healthcare. It's also helpful to study the industry for what other players are doing before implementing Big Data technologies in the organization (Mysore and Jain 2013).

Data analysis has been focused on structured data in healthcare for many years. The focus needs to shift on unstructured data, like the data residing in images, unstructured physician notes, patient satisfaction surveys, information monitored by state and federal government groups, and data published by healthcare organizations (Davenport and Dyché 2013), as well as the structured data for successful extraction of value from Big Data technologies. The amount of healthcare data held in computers in the form of EMRs such as clinical records and medical images has grown exponentially. This provides an opportunity to collaborate and extract economic value from EMR information using Big Data analytics. Big Data technologies and EMR systems can be used to provide efficient patient management, personalized healthcare, and predictive analytics to patients.

Prospect of Big Data Technologies in Healthcare

14.3 Introduction to Electronic Medical Record (EMR) System

14.3.1 What Is an EMR?

An EMR system is a medical records system that is used to create and electronically maintain patient data (Pearson 2014). This system captures disease information, symptoms, diagnosis, lab records, prescribed medications, treatments, and medical procedure information about patients. Data can be input using various sources such as graphical user interfaces having touch screens in tablet computers or portable computers connected wirelessly or wired to the network. Authorized healthcare providers are able to access, analyze, update, and electronically annotate patient data. EMR systems are also referred to as electronic health record (EHR) systems in some instances. These systems can also consist of other data components such as medication administration, nursing notes, care plan, daily information charting, physician referrals, past medical history, discharge history, diaries, and immunizations. The system can also access other reference databases for practice guidelines and consultation regarding medications and allergies (Evans 1999).

EMR systems consist of structured data, and narrative text and scanned images, which are unstructured data. The data stored in EMR systems permits analysis of patient information to identify patterns and disease relationships. Decision-making tools can be integrated into the EMR system if the record is structured and if defined terminologies are used. The data that is stored in these EMR systems have to be accurate and complete. With data errors in information, EMRs can be worthless for statistical analysis, medical research, and health policy purposes. Good recordkeeping has to be implemented for EMR systems, which will keep the data free of errors. Good recordkeeping also saves time and improves the quality of patient documentation, minimizes administrative tasks, and minimizes patient-related risks. In the future it may be necessary to incorporate different kinds of more standardized instruments and semistructured electronic interviews in the EHR systems. It will be also important to implement standardized codes and systematic terminologies to the EMR systems so that the information contained can be used for better healthcare management, clinical research, and health services planning and analysis.

14.3.2 Types of EMRs

EMRs are classified into the record types shown in Table 14.1 according to the ISO standard (ISO/TR 20514:2005). Table 14.2 outlines the types of users of EHR systems (Häyrinen, Saranto, and Nykänen 2009).

14.3.3 Desirable Characteristics of EMRs

Mandl et al. (2001) have summarized the desirable characteristics of EMRs that are required to comply with public standards and patient control, as the following:

Comprehensiveness—EMR records must be comprehensive. Care is provided to patients by physicians at different hospitals, nurses, different pharmacists, and ancillary healthcare providers. In a patient's lifetime, he may visit different hospitals at different locations and different cities. EMRs should contain information about a patient's medical history at other hospitals and also outpatient history. Outpatient history should be comprehensive with a history of visits, disease

TABLE 14.1

Types of EMRs

EMR Type	Definition
Electronic medical record (EMR)	Generally focused on medical care
Departmental EMR	Contains information entered by a single hospital department
	Picture archiving and communication system (PACS)
	Anesthesia records
	Intensive care records
	Ambulatory records
	Emergency department system
	Pathology laboratory system
	Oncology records
	Cardiology records
	Operation theater records
	Gynecology records
	Internal medicine records
	Pharmacy systems
	Geriatric center records
	Diabetes clinic records
	Radiology reporting system
Interdepartmental EMR	Contains information from two or more hospital departments
	Obstetric records for inpatient and outpatient clinics
	Prescribing system
Hospital EMR	Contains all or most of a patient's clinical information from a particular hospital
Interhospital EMR	Contains a patient's medical information from two or more hospitals
Electronic patient record (EPR)	Contains all or most of a patient's clinical information from a particular hospital
Computerized patient record (CPR)	Contains all or most of a patient's clinical information from a particular hospital
Electronic healthcare record (EHCR)	Contains all patient health information
Personal health record	Controlled by the patient and contains information at least partly entered by the patient
Computerized medical record	Created by image scanning of a paper-based health record
Digital medical record	A web-based record maintained by a healthcare provider
Clinical data repository	An operational datastore that holds and manages clinical data collected from health service providers
Electronic client record	Scope is defined by healthcare professionals other than physicians, e.g., by physiotherapists or social workers
Virtual EHR	No authoritative definition
Population health record	Contains aggregated and usually deidentified data

history, diagnoses, and referrals. Hospital records should consist of nursing notes, medications, problem lists, procedures, patient–provider communications, discharge summaries, and patient directives. EMR information should also contain a patient's lifetime medical information for predictive and retrospective analysis.

Accessibility—Patient records will have to be always accessible. Access to patient records may be needed on a regular basis, for example, during scheduled visits to the doctor or on an ad-hoc basis in an emergency situation. The requirement

Prospect of Big Data Technologies in Healthcare

TABLE 14.2

EHR User Types

User	Component of EHR
Nurse	Daily charting, medication administration, physical assessment, admission nursing note, nursing care plan
Physician	Referral, present problems, past medical history, lifestyle, physical examination, diagnoses, tests, procedures, treatment, medication, discharge
Patient	History, diaries, tests
Parents	History
Secretarial staff	Procedures, problems, diagnoses, findings, immunization
Pharmacists	Medication
Healthcare providers	Referral, present problems, past medical history, lifestyle, physical examination, diagnoses, tests, procedures, treatment, medication, discharge, administration of medication, admission nursing note, daily charting

to access the information can be from anywhere, from the patient's usual place of care or far from home. The information should be available even when the patient is not in a position to provide consent for use, for example, in case of emergencies or when the patient is unconscious. Policy may be necessary to dictate its use in such situations. Patient records should be accessible universally, such as on the World Wide Web, with the patient's consent.

Interoperability—EMR information should be interoperable. Different EMR systems should be able to collect and share information, i.e., they should be able to accept radiological and laboratory results from multiple sources. Interoperability of data is the key. Without interoperability, electronic medical records will remain fragmented. Further semantic interoperability should also be achieved for international terminologies.

Confidentiality—Patients should be able to choose who will be allowed to access, examine, and alter their medical records. However, there is a risk of receiving uninformed and thus inferior care due to this scenario. Patients will have to determine the degree of confidentiality, which will fall between receiving informed care by physicians and medical practitioners, and privacy. Individuals may have preferences about who is allowed to see which type of data. Individuals should be able to grant access rights to healthcare providers based on their role type. For example, patients may not like all healthcare providers to access their psychiatric information, whereas they may be happy sharing immunization information with all providers. A confidentiality override policy may be required in case of an emergency for authenticated care providers. Use of a confidentiality override policy in this scenario should trigger an audit at a later date.

Accountability—Accountability should be built into the EMR system. Patients should be able to identify who has accessed their information, for what purpose, and under what circumstances. Policies and compliance requirements should be constructed to enforce accountability. Logs should be generated for all access and modification of patient records. These logs should be visible to patients for their individual records. Patients should also be able to challenge the information recorded in EMRs and annotate it if required. However, it will create data integrity issues if the patients are able to modify or delete the recorded information.

Deletion of records should not be permitted. Reliable authentication mechanisms and appropriate compliance requirements can enforce accountability in the EMR system.

Flexibility—Flexibility is important with information handling in EMR systems. Patients should be able to grant access to medical researchers or selected personnel who are researching to improve medical knowledge. This can be based on ethical policies or decisions about specific studies. For example, ethical policy may define that data can be used in a nonidentifiable and non-reidentifiable form. Patients should also be able to provide limited access to some segments for their records, for example, writing/updating lab results while not permitting everyone to read it.

14.3.4 Challenges with EMRs

Deployment and successful use of EMR systems poses many challenges.

- A patient's medical history may be stored in different hospitals, clinics, and laboratories, which may be located remotely.
- Patient information may vary from one healthcare provider to another.
- Patient information may not be available to a remote care provider.
- Patient information may not be available to one care provider while being edited at another care provider's location.
- Patient information may not be available during the time of record creation and record update.
- Special and specific treatments administered by physicians, abnormal lab results, and relationships among the patient data for special cases may not be apparent within the patient's EMR.
- Access to specific data when needed for analysis may be difficult.
- A variety of data formats makes it difficult for data integration, electronic data processing, use, and maintenance of patient information.
- Consolidation of care providers into health maintenance organizations (HMOs) and preferred provider organizations (PPOs) creates issues in transfer and maintenance of patient data in large organizations that have numerous remote locations. In this scenario patient records may be scattered across multiple sites and will be fragmented, which will be an obstacle of effective care, analysis, and research. Care providers may find it difficult to administer effective care.
- Security of patient privacy is also becoming a challenge as more information becomes public. Stakeholders need to ensure that safeguards are in place to prevent organizations from releasing patient's information without consent and ensuring privacy.

The World Wide Web can provide the technical infrastructure on which longitudinal medical records can be built and that can be integrated across sites. A good EMR system has to address the aforementioned challenges and has to be integrated, interoperable, and standardized for it to be successful and effective in healthcare.

Prospect of Big Data Technologies in Healthcare 273

14.3.5 EMRs for Healthcare Data Analytics

There are various EMR types. The large quantities of information collected by the EMR systems can be used for different types of data analysis in healthcare. Big Data technologies applied to healthcare can go a long way in transforming healthcare. Chen, Chiang, and Storey (2012) have identified the following use cases for healthcare data analytics using EMR information:

- Genomics and sequence analysis and visualization
- EMR association mining and clustering
- Health social media monitoring and analysis
- Health text analytics
- Health ontology
- Patient network analysis
- Adverse drug side-effect analysis
- Privacy-preserving data mining

14.4 Integrating EMR through NoSQL Datastores

EMRs are loosely structured; clinical notes contain rich diverse information that is usually unstructured. Unstructured data does not align with relational databases. Relational databases require structured data. Organizations may require lots of databases with different goals to tailor to the needs of the unstructured data. Having lots of databases has considerable overhead and communication between these databases is also difficult. For solving this issue with unstructured data, researchers have created NoSQL datastores. These datastores allow unstructured data to be stored in a form that is closely approximated to its original representation. NoSQL datastores have generated significant interest in the field of healthcare informatics. NoSQL datastores have no schema. NoSQL databases have four classes or properties. They are

- Key-value
- Document
- Column
- Graph

14.4.1 Key-Value Datastore

Key-value datastores have the following characteristics:

- Keys are used to access data blobs
- Values contain varied data types (videos, images)
- Pros: Scalable, simple API (put, get, delete)
- Cons: Queries cannot be generated based on content values

Examples include Redis and DynamoDB.

14.4.1.1 Key-Value Datastore Data Model

Relational databases have a defined schema, i.e., table names, column names, primary keys, foreign keys, and primary and foreign key relationships between different tables. All records have the same set of columns. Key-value datastores don't have a predefined schema. A table in a key-value datastore is a set of collection of items and each item is a collection of its attributes. A key-value datastore is defined by a primary key, and it does not require the user to predefine all attributes of the items. Items in key-value datastores can have any number of attributes. Currently, the upper limit on the size of an item is 400 KB for DynamoDB. Item size is calculated by the length of its attribute name and its value. Every attribute is a name-value pair. An attribute can be a set, single value, or an object. When the user creates a table, in addition to the table name, the user must specify the primary key of the table. For example, the storing of products in a key-value datastore is represented by a product table and product ID as the primary key. The primary key is used to uniquely identify products/items so that no two products have the same product ID. The user can store various kinds of products/items in the table. The user can store one book item and two computer items. The ID is the only required attribute.

There are two types of primary keys:

- Partition key—This is a simple primary key and is composed of one attribute. This key determines the partition where the item will be stored. Two items cannot have the same partition key.
- Partition and sort key—This key consists of two attributes. The first attribute is the partition and the second attribute is sort. The partition key determines where the items will be stored. The sort key determines how the items will be sorted. Items with the same partition key are stored together. Items can have the same partition key value, but must have a different sort key value.

14.4.2 Document Datastore

The document datastores have the following characteristics:

- Data is stored in nested hierarchies.
- Data is stored as documents.
- Logical data is stored together as a unit.
- Document items can be queried.
- Pros: No object-relational mapping layer, ideal for search.
- Cons: Complex to implement, incompatible with SQL.

Examples include MongoDB, CouchDB, and RavenDB.

14.4.2.1 Document Datastore Data Model

The data model of MongoDB, which is a document datastore, is explained as follows. Document datastores store data as documents. These documents are in a form of binary representation call Binary JSON (BSON). BSON is an extension of JavaScript Object Notation (JSON) representation and includes additional data types such as int, long, and floating point. JSON is a lightweight, text-based, language-independent data interchange

Prospect of Big Data Technologies in Healthcare   275

format (Crockford 2006). JSON defines a small set of formatting rules for the portable representation of structured data. JSON can represent four primitive data types (i.e., strings, numbers, Boolean, and null) and two structured types (i.e., objects and arrays). Object is a collection of name/value pairs. Name is string and value can be string, Boolean, number, null, array, or object and array (an ordered sequence of values).

BSON documents are organized as collections. Collections are similar to tables in relational databases and documents are similar to rows and fields are similar to columns. Document consists of one or more fields. Every file will contain a value (int, long, objects, arrays, and subdocuments). For example, in a blogging application the relational database would use the data model comprised of multiple tables. In document datastore, the data would be modeled as two collections, one for the user and the other for articles. In each blog, the document may contain multiple comments, multiple tags, and multiple categories. Documents have all the data for a given record in a single document, whereas in a relational database the information for a given record is spread across many tables. A document store database reduces the need to join separate tables, as the data is more localized. This improves the performance of the database and a single read request can retrieve all fields from the document. The documents are also closely aligned to the structure of object-oriented programming languages. This makes development efforts faster and developers can easily map application data to the data stored in the document datastore.

14.4.3 Column Datastore

Column datastores have the following characteristics:

- Key includes a row, column family, and column name.
- Stores versioned blobs in one large table.
- Queries can be run using column names, column families, and rows.
- Pros: Good scale out, versioning.
- Cons: Column designs are important and queries cannot be performed on blob content.

Examples include Bigtable, Cassandra, and HBase.

14.4.3.1 Column Store Data Model

In a column datastore, data is stored in rows and columns. This is not similar to the relational database schema of rows and columns. The model is multidimensional in a column store database. The data model consists of the following:

- Table—A table is made up of multiple rows.
- Row—The row consists of a row key and columns with values. Row keys are used to sort the rows alphabetically. The aim of the row key is to sort the rows in a way that the related rows are near each other. This makes the design aspect of the row keys important. For example, for the website domains org.apache and org.apache.mail, it will be good to store the domains in the reverse order, so that these website domains are near each other rather than being spread out based on the value of the subdomains.

- Column—A column consists of two parts: a column family and column qualifier. These parts are delimited by a colon separator. Every row in the table has the same column family. Column families have a set of storage properties that define data compression, memory cache, and encoding properties for its values. Column families are used to physically collocate sets of columns and their values for performance reasons. A column qualifier provides an index to the data. For example, if the content in the column family is .pdf, then the qualifier will be :pdf; and if the content is an image, the column family will be :gif. Column qualifiers are editable and may vary between rows, whereas a column family is fixed at the time of table creation.
- Cell—The cell consists of data value. A cell is a combination of a row, column family, and column qualifier. The cell contains a value and timestamp, which is written beside every value. The timestamp represents the server time when the data was written or when the data was last updated.

14.4.4 Graph Datastore

Graph datastores have the following characteristics:

- Data is stored in nodes defined by relationships and properties.
- Queries are really graph traversals.
- Ideal when relationships between data is key (e.g., social networks).
- Pros: Enable fast search of the networks and public linked data sets.
- Cons: Large graphs do not fit into the RAM and can cause scalability issues. It also requires the use of specialized query languages such as SPARQL for querying the database.

Examples include Stardog and Neo4j.

14.4.4.1 Graph Datastore Data Model

In a graph-based model, every node is a labeled user. This indicates the user's role within the network. The node is connected with other nodes using relationships. A graph is made up of nodes, relationships, properties, and labels. A labeled property graph has the following characteristics (Robinson, Webber, and Eifrem 2015):

- It contains nodes and relationships.
- Nodes contain properties. The nodes store properties in the form of key-value pairs. The keys are strings and values can store primitive data types, strings, objects, and arrays. Nodes can be tagged with labels. Labels group the node and indicate the role that they play within the data set.
- The relationships connect the nodes and provides structure to the graph. They have a start point and an end node, direction, and a name. The relationships add semantic clarity to the structure. Similar to nodes, the relationships have properties. The properties provide additional metadata and are particularly useful for graph algorithms, adding additional information to relationships and for constraining queries during data analysis.

14.4.5 NoSQL Datastore Usage Scenarios

Each type of datastore can be used for different scenarios such as

- If the requirement is to store and retrieve nontransparent data items using a key, a key-value datastore can be used (e.g., DynamoDB).
- If the requirement is to store records with many attributes, but with few fields and analytical functions, a column-oriented database can be used (e.g., HBase).
- If the requirement is to search for a value associated with the key and update it on the basis of individual attributes within the value, a document database can be used (e.g., MongoDB).
- If the requirement is to store friend-of-a-friend data types that demand complex joinings of multiple tables, then a graph database can be used (e.g., Neo4j).

These scenarios show the possible flexibility of NoSQL datastores, though the scenarios are not hard and fast rules of mapping SQL datastore types to EMR system requirements. There are only a few EMR systems that are being designed to work with multiple types of datastores or to query from different datastores. The polyglot persistence concept is also emerging. The lack of progress in the use of multiple datastores in EMR systems is due to the need of a unique query language or application programming interface (API) for communication between multiple NoSQL datastores as well as between relational databases and NoSQL datastores. A combination of a variety of datastore types such as relational databases for structured data (e.g., financial data), NoSQL datastores such as document datastore for semistructured data such as laboratory images, and graph-based databases for maintaining data containing relationships such as patient–doctor interactions and patient symptoms and diagnosis can help drive up the economic value of information in EMR systems and Big Data technologies.

Figure 14.1 depicts a polyglot datastore for an EMR system. Here a combination of relational and NoSQL data stores are used for storing data from different data models

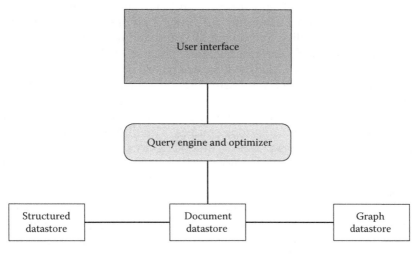

FIGURE 14.1
EMR system.

(Kaur and Rani 2015). The query engine optimizer is used to query the different data models, where the query will be routed to the appropriate datastore based on the data type. The user interface (UI) is an EMR UI where the user interacts with the EMR system.

14.4.6 Benefits of NoSQL Datastore

NoSQL databases provide superior performance and are more scalable. The data model in NoSQL addresses several issues that cannot be addressed by the relational databases, such as

- Storing large volumes of structured, semistructured, and unstructured data
- Implementation of object-oriented framework
- Enabling developers to develop codes in quick iteration
- Scale-out architecture, which is efficient and cost effective

14.5 Conclusion

Healthcare is slowing progressing towards a patient-centered model from a disease-centered model. Physicians' decision making is focused on their clinical expertise, symptoms, diagnosis, data from various tests, and medical evidence. Patients actively participate and receive care based on their individual needs and preferences in a patient-centered model. Patients will be provided oversight and advice from their care providers. Big Data technologies can be used to add economic value to healthcare. Data analytics can be used to extract value from new healthcare models such as patient-centered models and integrated EMR systems. While the prospect of use of Big Data in healthcare seems undisputed, there is considerable work to be done in addressing the key challenges and issues to improve EMR's analytical capability and efficiency in the healthcare industry. The key challenges that need addressing are systems architecture, security and privacy of patient information, flexibility, interoperability, and defining standards for EMRs, prior to realizing benefits from Big Data technologies. The use of EMR systems improves the task efficiency and improves the quality of patient record documentation. Big Data analytics incorporated in EMR systems can improve the disease predictability and prevention. Continued meaningful use of EMR systems and reinforcing their use as an instrument in patient care can improve patient management. Data integration strategies will have to be developed to integrate data from various sources. The different sources should include smart devices, embedded medical devices, mobile devices, and alternate patient engagement channels such as hospital kiosks and affinity websites. Technical barriers have to be simplified to share information with other organizations to ensure comprehensiveness of patient information. Clinical messaging protocols have to be standardized. Healthcare providers will have to participate in health information exchange and pursue data sharing opportunities through partnerships with other private institutions. With the key challenges addressed, the prospect of Big Data technologies promises to bring innovation and transformational change to the healthcare sector.

References

Amazon Web Services. 2012. "Amazon DynamoDB."

Apache Software Foundation. 2015. "Apache HBase reference guide."

Chawla, N., and Davis, D. 2013. "Bringing Big Data to personalized healthcare: A patient-centered framework," *JGIM: Journal of General Internal Medicine* 28: 660–665.

Chen, H., Chiang, R., and Storey, V. C. 2012. "Business intelligence and analytics: From Big Data to big impact," *MIS Quarterly* 36(4): 1165–1188.

Conn, J. 2015. "Big Data learning curve," *Modern Healthcare* 45(3): 22, 24–25.

Crockford, D. 2006. "The application/JSON media type for Javascript Object Notation (JSON)," RFC 4627. The Internet Society.

Davenport, T. H., and Dyché, J. 2013. "Big Data in big companies," International Institute for Analytics.

Evans, J. 1999. "Electronic medical records system," US Patent 5,924,074, filed September 27, 1996, issued July 13, 1999.

Häyrinen, K., Saranto, K., and Nykänen, P. 2009. "Definition, structure, content, use and impacts of electronic health records: A review of the research literature," *International Journal of Medical Informatics* 77(5): 291–304.

ISO/TR 20514:2005. 2005. "Health informatics—Electronic health record—Definition, scope, and context."

Kaur, K., and Rani, R. 2015. "Managing data in healthcare information systems: Many models, one solution," *Computer* 48(3): 52–59.

Mandl, K., Markwell, D., MacDonald, R., and Szolovits, P. 2001. "Public Standards and patients' control: How to keep electronic medical records accessible but private," *BMJ* 322: 283.

MongoDB. 2015. "MongoDB architecture guide."

Mysore, D., Khupat, S., and Jain, S. 2013. "Big Data architecture and patterns, part 2: How to know if a Big Data solution is right for your organization," IBM developerWorks.

Oracle. 2013. "Information management and Big Data: A reference architecture."

Pearson, M. 2014. "Aintree University Hospital NHS Foundation Trust rolls out new electronic medical records system to improve the quality of patient care," *International Journal of Integrated Care (IJIC)* 14: 148–152.

Robinson, I., Webber, J., and Eifrem, E. 2015. *Graph Databases*, O'Reilly Media, Sebastopol, CA.

Authors

Raghavendra Kankanady is currently working as a senior architect in the IT industry. He has completed his masters of engineering in information technology and an executive MBA from Royal Melbourne Institute of Technology (RMIT). His specialties include technology planning and data science. He is currently pursuing his PhD in health informatics from Central Queensland University (CQU). He has published many papers and book chapters on healthcare informatics.

 **Marilyn Wells** joined Central Queensland University in February 2006. Prior to joining the university, she was with the University of Western Sydney (UWS) and taught in the areas of information systems and knowledge management. Prior to joining UWS, Wells held various senior management positions in insurance and environmental industry, and worked in the information systems, finance, and administration areas. Wells research interests involve the issues surrounding organizational change, particularly as it applies to changing information systems, resistance to change, and the power redistribution that generally follows such change. Wells is specifically interested in how behavioral issues facilitate knowledge transfer during collaborative tasks in a changing environment.

15

Big Data Suite for Market Prediction and Reducing Complexity Using Bloom Filter

Mayank Bhushan, Apoorva Gupta, and Sumit Kumar Yadav

CONTENTS

15.1 Advances in Big Data 282
    15.1.1 Big Data Applications..283
    15.1.2 Tools and Technologies for Big Data.....................................283
    15.1.3 Application in Market Trend Analysis 287
15.2 Introduction to Algorithms 288
    15.2.1 Differential Evolution (DE)..289
    15.2.2 Genetic Algorithm (GA)..290
    15.2.3 Objective Function Used in DE and GA for Sentiment Analysis 290
    15.2.4 Case Study: Sentiment Analysis Using DE and GA 291
        15.2.4.1 Comparison Database 291
15.3 Reduce Time and Space Complexity with Big Data...........................291
    15.3.1 Bloom Filter..294
    15.3.2 Implementation of Bloom Filter with Big Data....................295
15.4 Applications of Bloom Filter Using MapReduce 297
15.5 Human Contributions in Big Data and Recent Advancements 298
    15.5.1 Human Contribution in Big Data 298
        15.5.1.1 Healthcare 298
        15.5.1.2 Understanding and Targeting Customers........298
        15.5.1.3 Optimizing Business Processes 298
        15.5.1.4 Performance Optimization 298
    15.5.2 Big Data Benefits 298
    15.5.3 Future Perspective 299
15.6 Conclusion 300
References...300
Authors..301

ABSTRACT A Bloom filter is helpful for achieving fast results and optimization in Big Data applications. Further, the probabilistic approach can be extended for market predictions. A varied number of algorithms can be used for attaining optimized results. Two such algorithms providing suitable results are differential evolution and genetic algorithms. Customer reviews are optimized using differential evolution (DE) and the genetic algorithm (GA) are also discussed in this chapter.

15.1 Advances in Big Data

Today is the era of social media: establishing new connections, social networking, online shopping, web postings, online lectures, blogging, and much more. "Daily data" as comments on Facebook, likes, video and picture posts, tweets, and millions of videos on YouTube are just common examples of the sources of millions and trillions of data that is being stored and uploaded/downloaded every day over the Internet. The exponential growth of data is challenging for Facebook, Yahoo, Google, Amazon, and Microsoft. The term "Big Data" is used to refer to the collection of data sets that are too large and complex to handle and process using traditional data processing applications.

Business intelligence and market predictions are major technology trends, as per the IBM tech trends report. Figure 15.1 shows properties of Big Data. The two interrelated terms—business intelligence and market predictions—form a crucial part of today's business culture that primarily targets improved customer satisfaction leading to enhanced company profits and a better company reputation among their customers and the service providers. There has been tremendous growth in these fields during the past decades with a handful of related academic and industry publications. It is believed by many market researchers that there exists a "conversation" between business providers and customers, providing a unique opportunity for the business, instead of the conventional long-accepted business–customer marketing. This supports a two-way conversation between the customer and the business providers wherein the customer's reviews regarding any service, product, platform, etc., provided by the business are of prime importance. The improvement in any product/service, the likelihood of a product/service, the future sustainability of a product in the market majorly depends on the customer reviews that further influence and also attract other customers, increasing company profits.

These reviews form the silent marketing strategy that formulates not only customer satisfaction but at the same time advertises the product/services for other customers. Hence, there has been a tremendous need for devising a mechanism such that these reviews can provide maximum benefit to the company.

Business intelligence for predictive marketing and enhanced business profits are the primary concerns. The project aims at performing intelligent business through analyzing the product reviews such that the reviews categorized as positive and negative form the

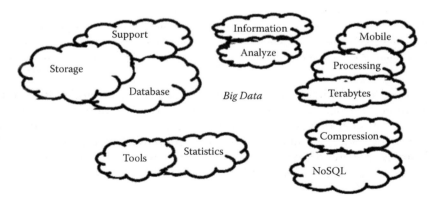

FIGURE 15.1
Big Data characteristics.

Big Data Suite for Market Prediction and Reducing Complexity Using Bloom Filter 283

basis for recommending a product or not, and also whether to consider the reviews for the product by different customers as useful in analyzing the customer satisfaction for the product (Chen, Chiang, and Storey, 2012).

15.1.1 Big Data Applications

Studying the current market statistics in order to predict future market trends not only fetches benefits to the company but at the same time it is important for a good customer–business relationship in order to maintain customer trust and enhance profits with greater market sustainability. Keeping in mind such an objective market prediction have become one of the prime areas of research for market analysts. There are predictive models giving a link between the dependent and the explanatory variables (e.g., next likely customer based on their preference, fraud detection), descriptive models giving collaborative data elements having similar characteristics (e.g., product preference, profitability, customer segmentation as per their social responses), and decision models that provide an optimal solution to make a desired decision (e.g., resource optimization, scheduling) (Oracle, 2010). This is very well elaborated in Table 15.1.

15.1.2 Tools and Technologies for Big Data

There are many tools and technologies required for Big Data solutions for getting optimized solutions in accessing and utilizing the millions and trillions megabyte zettabyte chunks of data (McAuley and Leskovec, 2013).

Traditionally it may be feasible to analyze limited data storage over the server which was stored over the file systems. The data-intensive companies (Google, Yahoo, Amazon, and Microsoft) had to figure out the on-demand books, websites, and popular people, and thus decide what kind of ads actually appealed to the audience. The existing tools and SQL-based query analysis tools were not sufficient enough for meeting the growing data analysis demands failing at tackling multiplatform, storage of data requiring multiplatform codes.

Hadoop is a distributive open source framework for writing and running distributed applications that process large amounts of data. The key features offered by Hadoop are

- Accessibility—Hadoop runs on large clusters of commodity machines and provides easy access to all the systems overcoming the barriers of distance.
- Robust—Hadoop can easily overcome the frequent machine malfunctions since it runs on commodity hardware.
- Scalable—Hadoop scales linearly to handle larger data by adding more nodes to the cluster.
- Simple—The simplicity of Hadoop lies in writing quick efficient parallel programs giving the programmer the advantage of using programs in any language (Java, Python).
- Cost effective—Hadoop proves to be cost effective in using commodity hardware and not expensive servers.

The working environment in Hadoop is given by its Hadoop ecosystem (Figure 15.2). Hadoop provides various analysis tools, data warehousing, data querying, and data mining tools inclusive of machine learning algorithms, such that Hadoop may be used for the analysis of Big Data.

TABLE 15.1

Business Intelligent Applications with Functionality Overview

	Data	Analytics	Impact	Functionality	Application
E-commerce and market intelligence	1. Logs 2. Transaction records 3. Social comments 4. Reviews 5. Content generated by customer 6. Responses 7. Feedback forms 8. Informal opinions	1. Sentiment analysis 2. Opinion mining 3. Association rule 4. Data segmentation 5. Text analysis 6. Web analysis 7. Social network analysis 8. Anomaly detection and analysis	1. Marketing 2. Recommender engines 3. Customer satisfaction 4. Increased sales 5. Enhanced profits 6. Advertising	1. Classification 2. Regression 3. Anomaly detection 4. Association rules 5. Clustering 6. Feature extraction	1. Recommender systems 2. Social media modeling 3. Virtual games 4. Market basket analysis 5. Fraud detection 6. Employee retention 7. Network intrusion
Science and technology	1. Sensor and network content 2. System generated data 3. Large scale records 4. Multiple modality	1. Analytical and mathematical models	1. Technological advances 2. Space observations 3. Interplanetary conclusions 4. Archeological advances 5. Natural calamities prediction	1. Association rules 2. Feature extraction 3. Attribute importance	1. Knowledge discovery 2. Hypothesis testing 3. Link analysis
Health	1. Health records 2. Genomics and sequential data 3. Patient social media	1. Clustering 2. Genomics and sequence analysis 3. Ontology 4. Data mining 5. Patient social analysis 6. Drug analysis	1. Improved healthcare 2. Enhanced life expectancy 3. Quality services 4. Customer satisfaction	1. Classification 2. Clustering 3. Attribute importance	1. Human plant genomics 2. Healthcare decision support 3. Patient social analysis 4. Predicting future diseases 5. Protein analysis 6. Surgery preparation 7. Customer profitability modeling

(Continued)

TABLE 15.1 (CONTINUED)

Business Intelligent Applications with Functionality Overview

	Data	Analytics	Impact	Functionality	Application
Security and safety	1. Criminal records 2. Terrorism databases 3. Viruses, cyberattacks, botnets 4. Crime maps	1. Cyberattacks 2. Criminal network analysis 3. Multilingual text analysis 4. Sentiment analysis 5. Criminal association rule and clustering	1. Improved public safety 2. Enhanced security	1. Feature extraction 2. Anomaly detection 3. Classification 4. Association rules	1. Text analysis 2. Fraud detection 3. Credit default modeling 4. Link analysis
Government and politics	1. Citizen feedback and comments 2. Legacy systems 3. Citizen conversation	1. Content analytics 2. Sentiment analysis 3. Information collaboration	1. Better decision making 2. Empowering citizens 3. Equality 4. Participation 5. Enhanced transparency	1. Classification 2. Attribute importance 3. Association rules	1. E-polling 2. Citizen participation 3. Response modeling 4. Text analysis and search

Source: C. Aggarwal, C. Procopiuc, P. S. Yu, 2002, *IEEE Transactions on Knowledge and Data Engineering* 14(1): 52–62; V. Ravi, H. Kurniawan, P. NweeKok Thai, P. Ravi Kumar, 2007, *Applied Soft Computing* 8(1): 305–315; N. Raj Kiran, V. Ravi, 2007, *Journal of Systems and Software* 81(4): 576–583; A. Pratap, C. S. Kanimozhiselvi, R. Vijaykumar, K.V. Pramod, 2014, *International Journal of Soft Computing and Engineering (IJSCE)*, 4(3); G. Acampora, G. Cosma, 2014, A Hybrid Computational Intelligence Approach for Efficiently Evaluating Customer Sentiments in E-Commerce Reviews, *2014 IEEE Symposium on Intelligent Agents*, 73–80.

286 · The Human Element of Big Data

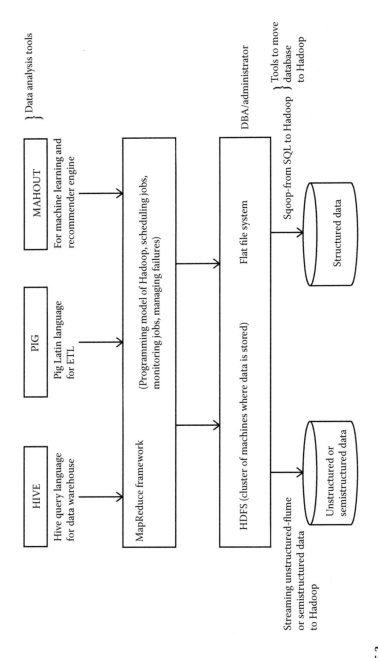

FIGURE 15.2
Hadoop ecosystem.

Big Data Suite for Market Prediction and Reducing Complexity Using Bloom Filter   287

Above all the layers of the Hadoop ecosystem lays the Apache Oozie for workflow management. Hadoop is written in Java. All the tools are open source and enable successful management of data having a distributed file system.

The initial release of the Hadoop 1.0 architecture had the following disadvantages:

- No horizontal scalability of NameNodes, that is, only one NameNode for a Hadoop cluster, and if one NameNode fails the entire system goes down.
- It does not provide NameNode high availability, i.e., single point of failure.
- May have an overburdened JobTracker.
- Does not support multitenancy, i.e., only one type of job can run or one batch may be executed at a time.

Despite the disadvantages, Hadoop 1.0 is still preferred and widely used as compared to YARN (Hadoop 2.0 architecture), due to the large 1.0 architecture acceptance in various industries and organizations such that they may get accustomed at first and then may shift to the updated versions of Hadoop.

15.1.3 Application in Market Trend Analysis

There have been many areas of emerging research such as

- Big Data analytics—Web mining, cloud computing, Hadoop, data mining, cloud security, parallel DBMS, MapReduce, spatial mining, temporal mining, machine learning
- Text analytics—Statistical NLP, sentiment analysis, multilingual analysis, speech analysis, relevance feedback, search engine optimizations, query processing, Hadoop, MapReduce
- Web analytics—Web crawling, mushups, cloud services, social marketing, web-based auctions, Internet security
- Network analytics—Link mining, fraud detection, community detection, trust/reputation, criminal networks
- Mobile analytics—Web services, smartphone platform, games, mobile social networking

There are a number of advantages for bringing the data extraction and mining tools to data, including

- Cost efficient and increased speed—The need to extract and transform data is eliminated as the data is moved to another environment.
- The process becomes iterative, increasing the overall quality of the output. It facilitates the optimization of the output process since when many scenarios are run simultaneously, it gives an opportunity to decide the best output.
- Predictive analytics impacts the business directly and has now become a part of the standard business process.
- Moreover, creativity is added to the entire process of analysis using predictive analytics and data tools together. Without reassessing the source data, multiple analyses and experimenting on them can be easily carried out.

There are chances that analysts can easily model wrong real-world problems leading to a completely worse scenario. Reality is expected to "fit the model." This significant change in data interpretation is called "outliers." However, it is human tendency to forcefully fit the model in the designed predictive framework. Now comes into play the experimentation, which is vital for the model acceptance and model wide consistent absorption in the industry. The outcome of the predictive analytics is compared with the real outcomes mostly carried out in the operational environment.

A higher number of assumptions leads to a higher number of chances of failures. For creating a robust theory, it is expected to remove all the unnecessary elements as possible. This process is termed "Razor." For example, profit and customer satisfaction are the least reliable indicators of business success (Baiza-Yates and Ribeiro-Neto, 1999; Porter, 1980).

These unreliable sources of information are targeted in this project such that the reviews are also optimized using soft computing techniques (differential evolution and genetic algorithm) and the reviews with fake, unreliable customers are automatically not recommended making the predictions about the product acceptance more reliable.

Moreover, traditionally the reliable indicators for a better predictive model are cash flow and the time of delivery. They are closer to the direct measurement and observation.

All these are directly reflected through the reviews by different customers. So, in research these reviews are the primary source of predictive modeling and the business intelligence for incorporating a better architecture for customer satisfaction and enhanced business development including better future planning and increased profits.

15.2 Introduction to Algorithms

Many computational intelligent algorithms are applied for data analysis and obtaining optimized solutions. Genetic algorithm (GA) and differential evolution (DE) are rapidly growing and widely accepted fields in artificial intelligence. These are the most useful optimization techniques used in artificial intelligence.

Figure 15.3 gives the process of optimization of producing the output based on the fitness function by taking a set of input variables. The fitness function is used for the process of optimization and deducing results using differential evolution and genetic algorithms.

A novel computational intelligent framework is proposed for customer sentiment analysis using the textual reviews. The positive and negative sentiments are extracted from the selected reviews such that these are assigned a positive and negative numerical value in reference to the positive and negative sentiments present in the review (Suresh et al., 2008).

These reviews are further optimized using the soft computing approach, wherein the fitness function for analysis is propounded and the results are compared for the differential evolution and the genetic algorithm approaches used. The learning phase is comprised of NLP, sent words, and the database module. The learning phase gives the number of reviews and the sent words are present in the selected product reviews.

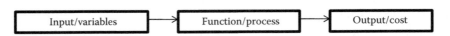

FIGURE 15.3
Process of optimization.

The evaluation phase deals with the soft computing module such that the fitness function propounded gives an optimized review analysis. The overall analysis predicts the popularity of the products in comparison to the review of the products of the same database. Also, the significance of any review is computed in terms of the lesser difference between the positive and the negative reviews about the product such that in case there is a huge difference between the two, the product review is regarded as less significant since there may be certain customers who give an extremely positive exceptional response about the product but there isn't any consistency in the positive feedback for the product. In other words, there is only one review that is extremely positive and the rest are coined positive reviews with very little positive values.

Therefore, in accordance to the reviews by different customers for a product, the product is recommended and further determines customer satisfaction and positivity for the product. This enables enhanced customer–business relationships and increased profits predicting the customer behavior in terms of their future purchasing habits and likelihood of purchasing the product (Abbass and Sarker, 2002).

15.2.1 Differential Evolution (DE)

The approach to an optimization problem (as mentioned in Figure 15.4) means first designing an objective function that can model problem objectives and, second, designing optimization methods that use an objective function.

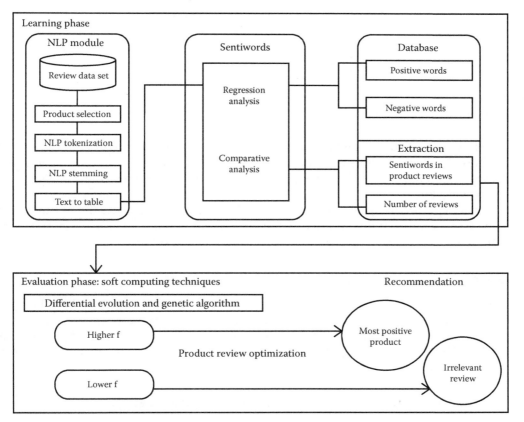

FIGURE 15.4
The methodology adapted for sentiment analysis.

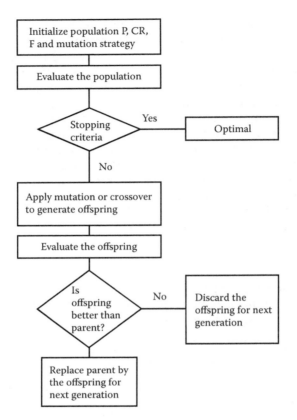

FIGURE 15.5
Flow diagram of DE algorithm.

DE serves as the most advantageous self-organizing scheme through the difference of two randomly chosen vectors that surpasses the already existing vector (Storn and Price, 1998). For computationally demanding optimizations, DE is the most suitable algorithm (Daoudi et al., 2014).

Evolutionary computing is developed from the interaction between the optimization and the biological evolution and hence, the DE algorithm emerges (Figure 15.5). Figure 15.5 gives the flow diagram of the differential evolution algorithm.

15.2.2 Genetic Algorithm (GA)

The genetic algorithm (GA) is the most widely accepted soft computing algorithm for optimized data analysis as per the required application. It is inspired from the natural life processes and the results give the fittest output in comparison to a number of populations generated. The methods incorporated are crossover, mutation, and then selection (Storn and Price, 1997).

15.2.3 Objective Function Used in DE and GA for Sentiment Analysis

The fitness is an important function that is responsible for the quality of the chromosomes. The chromosomes represent the sentiment words that are extracted from the review that

Big Data Suite for Market Prediction and Reducing Complexity Using Bloom Filter   291

are clustered between [1,k], where k is the number of clusters produced. In this chapter the function is two criterion functions combined to balance both positive sentiments (intracluster similarity) and negative sentiments (intercluster dissimilarity) (Abuobieda et al., 2013).

$$\text{Intracluster similarity function: } f1 = \sum l = 1k \; |c1| \sum s_i s_j sim_x(s_i s_j)$$
$$= \sum s_i \in c1 sim_x(s_i, s_j) \rightarrow max \tag{15.1}$$

where c is the cluster (c1 is the positive cluster representing the total number of positive words that act as reference), l is the cluster number, k is the total number of clusters required, sim is similarity, and x is the current selected similarity measure.

$$\text{Intercluster dissimilarity function: } f2 = \sum l = 1k - 1 \; 1/|c1| \; \sum m = 1 + 1k \; 1/|c2| \; \sum s_i \in c1$$
$$\sum s_j \in c2 sim_x(s_i, s_j) \tag{15.2}$$

where c2 is the negative cluster representing the total number of negative words that act as reference.

The objective fitness function is computed from Equations 15.1 and 15.2 as

$$f = f1/f2 \rightarrow max \tag{15.3}$$

Evolutionary algorithms are genetic, optimization algorithms that are biologically inspired mechanisms. Genetic algorithms are probalistic algorithms categorized under evolutionary algorithms. Nature is the inspirational source and enables efficient and effective problem solving. There exists an analogy in functioning of genetic algorithms with the natural processes/evolution.

15.2.4 Case Study: Sentiment Analysis Using DE and GA

15.2.4.1 Comparison Database

There is a list of positive and negative words at http://www.unc.edu/~ncaren/haphazard/. The database on which the sentiment analysis is performed was obtained from http://snap .stanford.edu/data/web-Amazon.html. From this database, three databases of size 20M were chosen for the product review analysis by the customers. The database extracted is Product_and_Accessories. Table 15.2 and Figure 15.6 provide the results of the analysis using differential evolution and genetic algorithms.

15.3 Reduce Time and Space Complexity with Big Data

As data structure is used to arrange data in a mannered way, a Bloom filter is an added preprocessing step with all queries involved in it. A Bloom filter is a space efficient way to store large data. It reduces complexity as well (Tarkoma, Rothenberg, and Lagerspetz, 2012), so that at the time of retrieval of data it can easily produce the result.

TABLE 15.2

Comparison Database for the Fitness Function Calculation Using DE and GA

Product ID	Number of Reviews	DE (f)	DE (NFE)	DE Elapsed Time (sec)	GA (f)	GA (NFE)	GA Elapsed Time	Recommendation
B000JVERTW	5	6.473058 e+010	1000	13.069793	6.473058 e+010	1	7.380601	Highly recommended
B000924R51	9	3.136944 e+010	1000	10.009981	3.136944 e+010	1	7.214541	Not recommended
B000F1UQJY	5	8.738629 e+010	1000	11.462348	8.738629 e+010	1	6.740137	Highly recommended
B00004WIN0	218	2.912876 e+010	1000	8.295068	2.912876 e+010	1	8.741099	Not recommended
B00004WINT	9	2.912876 e+010	1000	8.412276	2.912876 e+010	1	12.858335	Not recommended
B0006J27C4	92	3.883835 e+010	1000	5.560718	3.883835 e+010	1	6.654296	Not recommended
B000M9N5GA	23	3.107068 e+010	1000	11.811993	3.107068 e+010	1	9.621744	Not recommended
B000JUV21W	11	1.262246 e+010	1000	10.620127	1.262246 e+010	1	7.619004	Reviews are not reliable
B000F1UQWQ	69	4.766525 e+010	1000	8.272758	4.766525 e+010	1	6.319275	Recommended
B000FV8S58	56	3.883835 e+010	1000	12.098943	3.883835 e+010	1	6.141944	Not recommended
B000NJGDUY	18	3.883835 e+010	1000	7.460046	3.883835 e+010	1	6.29608	Not recommended
B000FPGZTA	40	3.155616 e+010	1000	7.973906	3.155616 e+010	1	13.331299	Not recommended
B0002VQ3SU	19	3.530759 e+010	1000	7.816322	3.530759 e+010	1	11.962311	Not recommended
B000P6CEYE	13	5.825752 e+010	1000	6.474509	5.825752 e+010	1	7.76768	Highly recommended
B0002DFW2Q	58	1.941917 e+010	1000	12.165299	1.941917 e+010	1	10.609424	Reviews are not reliable

Big Data Suite for Market Prediction and Reducing Complexity Using Bloom Filter 293

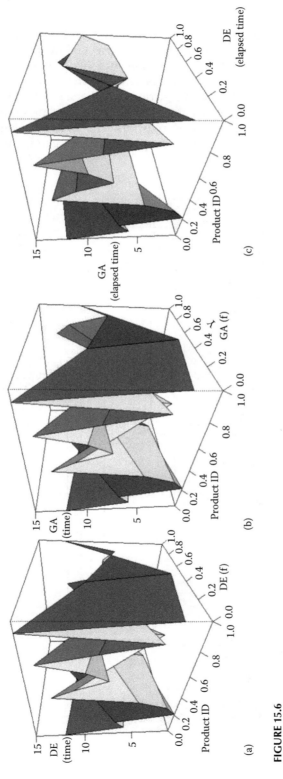

FIGURE 15.6
The relation between (a) fitness and time taken in DE, (b) GA, and (c) time-elapsed in DE and GA.

15.3.1 Bloom Filter

A Bloom filter is a probabilistic data structure that is space efficient with little error allowable when there is a test performed. There are two functions mainly in use in a Bloom filter: first is storing true values that return from the function and second is testing for values that were stored earlier. The first function accepts values to store it in bloom array according to its size that should be well calculated. The second justifies whether a function is present there. It provides a Boolean value for the result. If it gives all true values that are stored that means a value is present in the database, if any values return to false that means the value is not found there.

Figure 15.7 shows a string "Roonie is in the park" that is stored in an array using a Bloom filter.

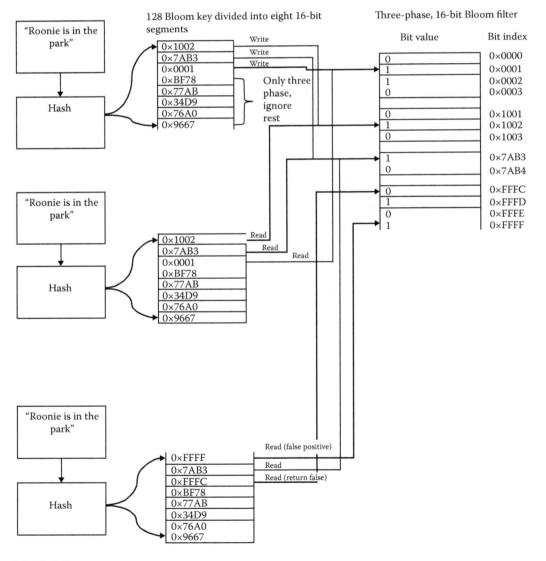

FIGURE 15.7
Working of a Bloom filter.

As a property of MD5, if there is change in even a single bit of a string, then the hash value will dramatically change. There may be a case when data is not present in an array that still results in showing of its presence (Chu et al., 1998).

An array may represent 1 or 0; if it represents 1 that means a string is present and this is the chance of false positive. Figure 15.7 shows a case of a false positive, as the first line is giving a false result in the array while the third string produces a false result. There may be case when all checking string in array represent 1 although element is not present in it. To avoid this situation, there is need to calculate an error probability.

A bloom filter can create an array to give information about whether to store the element. Following is the algorithm for creation of a Bloom filter.

15.3.2 Implementation of Bloom Filter with Big Data

Big Data refers to large amounts of data used for processing. Suppose there is a need to develop antivirus software; antivirus only functions well when there is use of a bulk database. A large database can easily and efficiently filter a virus. Thus any antivirus product should quickly and efficiently search for viruses.

A Bloom filter can approach this with an array system for further processing. This processing can use functions like join, search, etc. in an efficient manner. Using Bloom filter data can be optimized because it uses an array to store data so that fewer bits are used to check for data presence (Bhushan, Banerjee, and Yadav, 2014).

Figure 15.8 shows the structure of Hadoop using a Bloom filter, which optimizes the data storage on Hadoop. The working structure is as follows:

- First, the job is initialized and submitted to NameNode where JobTracker runs. NameNode consists of all information that needs to be executed in Hadoop. It is queued into the job queue to initialize the job. JobTracker reads job files from the distributed file system. Now JobTracker can create the MapReduce function.

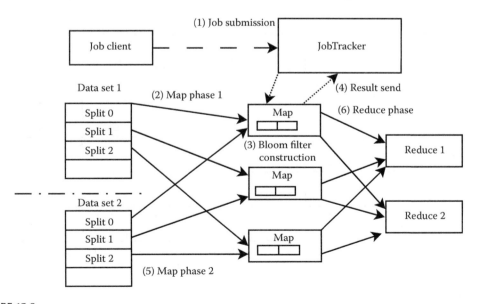

FIGURE 15.8
Data optimization with a Bloom filter.

- The Map phase for the first record map phase depends on splits. The number of splits is the same as the number of map functions. JobTracker assigns tasks for TaskTrackers. These TaskTrackers keep sending signals to prove its aliveness.
- Each mapper has its own result of <key, value> pair with a Bloom filter. These intermediate results need to be collected in JobTracker where all results are combined.
- Result combination. After completion of all tasks, TaskTrackers need to send results to the JobTracker. This time TaskTrackers will not submit the whole result; they will send only filtered records.
- The Map phase for the second record also does the same function as the first record and creates data with a Bloom filter. Now all data of second record with bloom filter submit to jobtracker where first record already there. Perform join operations with these filtered data.
- The last phase is the Reduce phase, which collects intermediate records and runs the Reduce function to provide results in an output path.

Construction of a Bloom filter provides facilities to utilize the bandwidth rate. Each mapper creates a Bloom filter array, which stores large amounts of data in small size. This will be transfered to the JobTracker where operations may be implemented. JobTracker constructs a global filter to execute operations (Bhushan, Banerjea, and Yadav, 2014).

Figure 15.9 is the result of error probability with respect to array size when 253,717 records were processed using Amazon EC2 in Table 15.3. As array size representing data storage so if array size is less then it show few space to store all data so that bring possibility of all 1 that is 'ffff' in array. It is necessary to make some calculation before defining array size so that data can be stored in the optimal way.

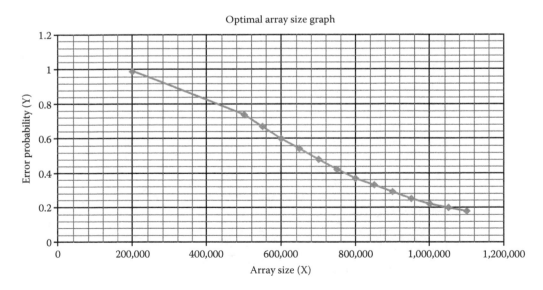

FIGURE 15.9
Result between array size and error probability in EC2 (Table 15.3).

TABLE 15.3

Error Probability Result with EC2

Array Size	Error Probability
500,000	0.74
550,000	0.67
600,000	0.6
650,000	0.54
700,000	0.48
750,000	0.42
800,000	0.37
850,000	0.33
900,000	0.29
950,000	0.25
1,000,000	0.22
1,050,000	0.2
1,100,000	0.177

15.4 Applications of Bloom Filter Using MapReduce

A Bloom filter provides functionality to reduce data that is redirected to reduce complexity for processing. This filter easily integrates with MapReduce and is an advantage over traditional systems in reading data. Locality sensitive filters can produce buckets for processing. These buckets can be formed to analyze specific behavior of data.

Hardware capacity thus becomes a performance bottleneck. Hardware capacity always limited, so that for large dataset it very tough to manage the task. The Hadoop function will reduce this problem and provide a storage solution up to a certain limit (Manber and Wu, 1994).

As the Bloom filter is space and time efficient , it is used in many areas of computer technology. There are lots of usages in network and data storage fields. In peer-to-peer (P2P) it brings a lot of changes to file sharing. The natural outcome of this was a system that could reproduce data as tables and partitions and could also give an SQL-like language for query and analysis.

Hive that is tool which use in Hadoop for data analytics can be useful for following purpose:

- Data organization—Data is organized consistently across all data sets and is stored compressed, partitioned, and sorted.
- Compression—Almost all data sets are stored as sequence files using the gzip codec. This is well worth the savings in terms of disk space.
- Partitioning—Most data sets are partitioned by date.
- Sorting—Each partition within a table is often sorted (and hash-partitioned) by a unique ID. This has a few key advantages:
  - It is easy to run sampled queries on such data sets.
  - Indexes on sorted data can be built (Reynolds and Vahdat, 2003).

15.5 Human Contributions in Big Data and Recent Advancements

15.5.1 Human Contribution in Big Data

Every field is somehow touched by Big Data and the research community is raising new questions.

15.5.1.1 Healthcare

Big Data can be applied in healthcare fields like medical image processing, medical signal processing, and genomics.

15.5.1.2 Understanding and Targeting Customers

Big Data is helpful in performing analysis of the existing profile of a customer, and one can better understand and target customers.

15.5.1.3 Optimizing Business Processes

Business processes use Big Data analytics for supply chain or delivery route optimization.

15.5.1.4 Performance Optimization

Big Data is not only useful for companies and governments, individuals can also improve and optimize their performance. Data can be generated from wearable devices such as smart watches or smart bracelets and later used for analysis purposes.

15.5.2 Big Data Benefits

Big Data is the real-time streaming of data. Big Data processing and collection is about understanding its properties. Big Data is defined by three V's: volume, velocity, and variety. Big Data offers a new horizon to the decision making and data mining for business companies. Mining Big Data uncovers the great opportunity to understand the market, its flow, customer demand, the utilization of resources, and so on.

Traditional databases that were collected could be arranged and processed in a regular fashion, but real-time data has several different properties, such as it is difficult to modify real-time continuous data and only traditional query tools can work this high volume of data. So to understand and control Big Data, new tools and schematic schemes were designed.

Big Data benefits include the following:

- Big Data is real-timed and hence is collected and stored in continuous streams of information and knowledge. This provides for day-by-day analysis, making it more thorough and provides a very detailed path for analysis.
- Big Data has several different faces that depend on its abstraction, that is, Big Data looks the way the user wants it to. Hence it is accessible to all types of executives.
- Big Data collection is a collection of a huge amount of data; this voluminous amount provides for a holistic view of fields.
- Big Data, due to its variety and velocity, is trustworthy. The quality of Big Data is very fine and hence responsible for better business decisions.

- Due to Big Data analysis, there is significant ease in risk analysis, as the success of a company depends on predicting the future risks about the economic and social factors. This predictive analysis using Big Data in the background speeds up the environmental changes with real-time speed.
- Big Data helps in profiling the increased rate of changes in the customer world as new possibilities emerge daily.
- Big Data helps in redeveloping products or services, as it provides the way to perceive the service or product in terms of customer adaption. Analysis of the opinions of many customers is only possible with Big Data analysis.
- Big Data is secure, and Big Data tools help you map the ins and outs of the data giving the opportunity for analyzing internal threats.
- Big Data helps in overall cost-reduction advantages. Technologies like Hadoop and other cloud-based analysis techniques allow for this substantial cost reduction.
- Big Data provides for better, detailed, and finer decision-making powers as the data is real-time and in huge volume.
- The most interesting use of Big Data analysis is its power to create new products and services to benefit customers.
- Big Data provides for individual customization capabilities to the product and services. This not only increases the experience of the customer but also provides for ownership for the customer.
- As companies create and store most of its transactional data in digital form, they collect more detailed and accurate information about performance on everything from product catalogs and product inventories, which therefore exposes variability and helps in boosting performance. In fact, some leading organizations are using this ability of Big Data to collect and analyze controlled experiments to make better management decisions.

15.5.3 Future Perspective

Every business problem today needs the involvement and use of data for its solution. Hence, the importance of maintenance of data automatically increases. Data collection and analysis is the only path of surviving this ever-changing technology, and data has become the virtual lifeline of business. Data collection results in Big Data due to expansion in the customer and market realms. Big Data analysis has always provided for the point-in-time recordings of business or other operational events making the decisions more accurate.

Almost 5 years ago, most of the available business data was at a very raw or coarse level, which represented precise and discrete transactions such as orders, purchases, line items, trade, and travel segments. With the help of Big Data, we now have the much-needed ability of capturing and analyzing such transactions and other processes on data, making it happen at a very finer and more granular level. Hence we moved from transactional to behavioral understanding due to an increase in verity and volume of data. A good example of this is the expanding world of e-commerce, and the contrast between tracking and analyzing purchases on the one hand, and the measurement and analysis of live visible data and its ability to understand customer behavior, on the other.

The new emerging application and the expanding market are generating this vast amount of data in unstructured and structured form. Big Data has the ability to process and store this huge voluminous data.

Due to vast expansion of the Internet and its applications, everyday people are generating information while driving cars or booking hotels, browsing the Internet or attending online classes; every move of today's generation and upcoming generation is based on the internet and connectivity, which in turn produces a huge volume of data manageable only via analysis. Although the true advantage of data largely depends on the actual opinions of the data scientists, the data does pose ultimate potentials.

15.6 Conclusion

The differential evolutionary algorithm and genetic algorithm are observed to be efficient algorithms in review optimizations and sentiment analysis on products, thus recommending the likely product benefitting market intelligence.

The approach can be used for sentiment analysis and imparting business intelligence on huge chunks of data sets using a Hadoop MapReduce framework. Also, the sentiment analysis is not restricted to the review data set used in this chapter; it can be applied to other opinion sites like Twitter and Facebook, e-commerce sites like Flipkart, and many others such that the objective can be modified as per the required analysis agenda.

Hadoop comes in the picture when bulk data needs to be processed. Use of a distributed join, reduced side join, and Bloom filter provide ways to optimize data usage. Simple MapReduce on join operation uses 127 bytes with use of traditional way, whereas on the same data set distributed cache writes only 94 bytes. Distributed caches do not use the reduce function, so the map output direct writes into HDFS (Hadoop Distributed File System). Reduce side join is also useful in optimization, as it does not use map side. It joins the data set on the reduce side and write outputs to HDFS.

Bloom filter is used for collecting data in array and any operation data of that array is used to reduce network traffic. By that, network traffic of data will decrease. There is analysis about requirements of this technology in big companies like Facebook and Yahoo. So with increasing popularity of this, there is leading techniques in the market for data analysis.

References

Abbass H. A., R. Sarker. (2002). The Pareto Differential Evolution Algorithm. *International Journal on Artificial Intelligence Tools* 11(4): 531–552.

Abuobieda, A., N. Salim, M. S. Binwahlan, A. H. Osman. (2013). Differential Evolution Cluster-Based Text Summarization Methods. International Conference on Computing, Electrical and Electronic Engineering (ICCEEE), IEEE.

Acampora, G., G. Cosma. (2014). A Hybrid Computational Intelligence Approach for Efficiently Evaluating Customer Sentiments in E-Commerce Reviews. *2014 IEEE Symposium on Intelligent Agents* 73–80.

Aggarwal, C., C. Procopiuc, P. S. Yu. (January/February 2002). Finding Localized Associations in Market Basket Data. *IEEE Transactions on Knowledge and Data Engineering* 14(1): 52–62.

Baiza-Yates, R., B. Ribeiro-Neto. (1999). *Modern Information Retrieval*. ACM Press/Addison-Wesley.

Bhushan M., S. Banerjea, S. K. Yadav. (September 2014). Bloom Filter Based Optimization on HBase with MapReduce. 2014 International Conference on Data Mining and Intelligent Computing (ICDMIC).

Chen, H., R. Chiang, V. Storey. (December 2012). Business Intelligence and Analytics: From Big Data to Big Impact. *MIS Quarterly*, 36(4): 1165–1188.

Chu, Y.-H., P. DesAutels, B. LaMacchia, P. Lipp. (1998). PICS Signed Labels (DSig) 1.0 Specification. Accessed February 5, 2014. http://www.w3.org/TR/1998/REC-DSig-label/MD5-10.

Daoudi, M., S. Hamena, Z. Benmounah, M. Batouche. (2014). Parallel Differential Evolution Clustering Algorithm Based on MapReduce. International Conference on Soft Computing and Pattern Recognition, IEEE.

Karwa, S., N. Chatterjee. (2014). Discrete Differential Evolution for Text Summarization. International Conference on Information Technology, IEEE.

Manber, U., S. Wu. (1994). An Algorithm for Approximate Membership Checking with Application to Password Security. *Information Processing Letters* 50(4): 191–197.

McAuley, J., J. Leskovec. (2013). Hidden Factors and Hidden Topics: Understanding Rating Dimensions with the Review Text. *Proceedings of the 7th ACM Conference on Recommender Systems, serRecSys '13*, pp. 165–172. http://doi.acm.org/10.1145/2507157.2507163.

Oracle. (September 2010). Predictive Analytics: Bringing the Tools to the Data.

Porter, M. (1980). An Algorithm for Suffix Stripping. *Program: Electronic Library and Information Systems* 14(3): 130–137.

Pratap, A., C. S. Kanimozhiselvi, R. Vijaykumar, K.V. Pramod. (July 2014). Soft Computing Models for the Predictive Grading of Childhood Autism: A Comparative Study. *International Journal of Soft Computing and Engineering (IJSCE)*, 4(3).

Raj Kiran, N., V. Ravi. (2007). Software Reliability Prediction by Soft Computing Techniques. *Journal of Systems and Software* 81(4): 576–583.

Ravi, V., H. Kurniawan, P. NweeKok Thai, P. Ravi Kumar. (2007). Soft Computing System for Bank Performance Prediction. *Applied Soft Computing* 8(1): 305–315.

Reynolds, P., A. Vahdat. (2003). Efficient Peer-to-Peer Keyword Searching. In *Middleware 03: ACM/IFIP/USENIX 2003 International Middleware Conference*, pp. 21–40. Springer-Verlag, New York.

Storn, R., K. Price. (1997). Differential Evolution—A Simple and Efficient Heuristic for Global Optimization over Continuous Spaces. *Journal for Global Optimization* 11(4): 341–359.

Suresh, K., S. Ghosh, D. Kundu, S. Das. (2008). Clustering with Multi-Objective Differential Evolution—A Comparative Study. The International Conference on Advanced Computing Technologies (ICACT 2008), Hyderabad, India.

Tarkoma, S., C. E. Rothenberg, E. Lagerspetz. (2012). Theory and Practice of Bloom Filters for Distributed Systems. *IEEE Communications Surveys and Tutorials* 14(1): 131–155.

Authors

Mayank Bhushan completed his MTech at Motilal Nehru National Institute of Technology Allahabad. He has 5 years of experience in academics. He specializes in Big Data, distributed systems, and database systems. He has seven international research papers published in reputed publications. He is the author of two books that are running in UPTU syllabus. He worked on retrieving of Big Data through Hadoop with use of a Bloom filter that provide faster access of data with removal of redundancy. He has certification in network management on Linux platforms from IIT-Kharagpur. He is also a guest lecturer in various organizations on Big Data topics. He is a member of CiRG India (Scientific Research Organization Reg. Under Society Registration Act XXI of 1860 Govt. of India).

Apoorva Gupta has completed her MTech in computer science and engineering from Amity University, Noida, India. Her active areas of research include Big Data, predictive analytics, business intelligence, and Big Data security and optimization algorithms. She has international research publications in the field of robotics, Kerberos, biometric templates, sentiment analysis, and business intelligence. She is NIIT certified in C++, data structures, Java programming using Java SE 6, and Oracle database 10g SQL. She also successfully completed three projects under the Defense Research and Development Organization (DRDO), India, titled "3D Laser Imaging System," "Security Audit Management System," and "Online Complaint Registration System." Her master's thesis was titled "Predictive Analytics Using Differential Evolution and Genetic Algorithm." She has research interest in Big Data analytics and has delivered a number of expert lectures on Big Data in the Delhi NCR colleges. She is a member of CiRGIndia (Scientific Research Organization Reg. Under Society Registration Act XXI of 1860 Govt. of India).

Sumit Kumar Yadav is working as an assistant professor, Computer Science Department, Indira Gandhi Delhi Technological University for Women, Government of Delhi. He has completed his MS at Indian Institute of Information Technology Allahabad and has a PhD in computer science from GGSIP University Dwarka, New Delhi. He has more than 5 years of experience in academics. He has specialization in Big Data analytics, intelligence system, information security, DBMS, text mining, and data warehouse. He has more than 15 international research publications. He has certification in IBM Academic Initiative Project Group. He has delivered Big Data lectures to various organizations including some research associations. He is a Member of CiRG India (Scientific Research Organization Reg. Under Society Registration Act XXI of 1860 Govt. of India).

16

Big Data Architecture for Climate Change and Disease Dynamics

Daphne Lopez and Gunasekaran Manogaran

CONTENTS

16.1 Introduction 304
16.2 Background 305
    16.2.1 Big Data 305
    16.2.2 Big Data Characteristics 305
    16.2.3 Big Data Challenges and Potential Solutions 307
    16.2.4 Big Data Applications 308
    16.2.5 Climate Big Data and Climate Change 309
    16.2.6 Role of Big Data in Climate Change 310
    16.2.7 Big Data in Healthcare 311
    16.2.8 Big Data in Climate Change and Healthcare 311
16.3 Lambda Architecture 312
    16.3.1 Batch Layer 313
    16.3.2 Speed Layer 313
    16.3.3 Serving Layer 313
16.4 Components of Lambda Architecture 314
    16.4.1 Data Sources 314
    16.4.2 Components of Data Ingestion Block 314
    16.4.3 Components of Batch Layer 316
    16.4.4 Components of Speed Layer 319
    16.4.5 Components of Serving Layer 319
16.5 Big Data Architecture for Climate Change and Disease Dynamics 319
    16.5.1 Data Ingestion Block 321
    16.5.2 Batch Layer Implementation 322
        16.5.2.1 Apache Hive 322
        16.5.2.2 Apache Hadoop MapReduce 322
        16.5.2.3 Pearson Correlation Coefficient 325
    16.5.3 Serving Layer Implementation 325
        16.5.3.1 Apache HBase 325
        16.5.3.2 Apache Hive–Apache HBase Integration 325
    16.5.4 Speed Layer Implementation 325
        16.5.4.1 Streaming Hive 325
    16.5.5 Visualizing Layer Implementation 326
        16.5.5.1 Geoprocessing Tools for Hadoop 326
        16.5.5.2 Apache Hive–ArcGIS Integration 327

303

16.6 Findings..327
16.7 Conclusion 329
Acknowledgment...329
References...329
Authors...332

ABSTRACT Big Data is playing a major role in many areas like social networks, health, and climate. The modern climate information framework produces several exabytes of data and so it is often called Climate Big Data. Climate Big Data can be used to monitor and predict climate change; in addition to that, it can also be used to predict the possible diseases and climate change scenario. Till recently, GIS technology has been used to store the climate data with the spatial reference, but day-by-day the volume, velocity, and variety of climate data is increasing toward the exabyte. This requires efficient techniques to store and display such huge amounts of spatial climate Big Data to the end users. The intention of this chapter is to propose a Big Data architecture that analyzes the characteristics of spatial climate Big Data and to study the impact of climate changes on the outbreak of dengue.

The proposed architecture was developed based on the existing lambda architecture. In addition to the features offered by lambda architecture, the proposed architecture consists of two new layers, namely, data ingestion block and visualizing layer. As like lambda architecture, the proposed architecture consists of a batch, speed, and serving layer. Proposed Big Data architecture mainly focuses on computing the monthly average maximum temperature, minimum temperature, precipitation, wind, relative humidity, and solar, and calculating the Pearson correlation coefficient between monthly average climate parameters and monthly dengue cases. Apache Hadoop MapReduce and Apache Hive are used to implement the batch layer. Implementation of the speed layer is done using Apache Hive streaming, Apache HBase is used to implement the serving layer, and ArcGIS 10.2 is used in this study for visualizing the results. The results show that our proposed architecture performs well in accurately predicting the correlation between the huge size of climate parameters and number of dengue cases.

16.1 Introduction

The promise of Big Data is real and currently a gap exists between its potential and realization. Much of the data acquired today is not in the structured format; hence heterogeneity, scale, timeliness, complexity, and privacy with Big Data pose challenges in every stage of processing (Thilagavathi et al., 2014; N. Victor et al., 2016). Big Data architecture enables users to access structured, semistructured, and unstructured data to discover patterns and useful information (Boja et al., 2012; Fan and Bifet, 2013; Ranjan, 2014). Many Big Data architectures have been developed recently for business development, remote sensing, and health science and climate simulation. The climate change simulation requires the integration of millions of observations collected daily and reanalyzing the past observations. Climate and epidemiology research continues to stretch computing capabilities and the proposed architecture provides Big Data a solution that is the need of the hour. Traditional early warning systems detect the outbreak mainly from virology and clinical data collected through health departments, randomized telephone polls, sensor networks, and so on. These systems suffer with the limitation of slow reporting time and missing out rapidly emerging diseases. The immediate need is to develop models for accurate and responsive predictions based on proprietary data.

Large repositories of geospatial and health data provide vital statistics on surveillance and epidemiological metrics, and valuable insight into the spatiotemporal determinants of disease and health. It has been recently recognized that a rise in emerging infectious diseases can be triggered by increased variability in climatic conditions and detrimental effects of extreme weather events, such as heat waves and cold spells (Chandy et al., 2013). Compilation of health and climate data, supported by geographical information systems (GIS) and satellite imagery, together with fine-tuned computational tools can facilitate the design and development of early warning systems for tracking health outcomes. This chapter aims to provide data-driven decision making on Big Data systems. While the potential benefits of Big Data are real and significant, and some initial successes have already been achieved, there remain many technical challenges that must be addressed to realize its full potential. The sheer size of the data, of course, is a major challenge, and is the challenge that is most easily recognized.

The proposed architecture is for continuous monitoring of information related to climatic change and public health as they unfold. These systems are, in most instances, timely surveillance systems that collect information on epidemic-prone diseases in order to trigger prompt public health interventions. Developing countries like India need an effective surveillance system and equity in health delivery programs for taking corrective actions to improve health conditions of vulnerable populations.

16.2 Background

16.2.1 Big Data

In general, Big Data is termed as a collection of huge data sets with a variety of types so that it becomes complex to process by using traditional data processing techniques or state-of-the-art data processing platforms. More commonly, a data set can be named Big Data if it is difficult to store, process, and visualize using current technologies. Recently the number of data provisions has increased, such as high throughput instruments, telescopes, sensor networks, and streaming machines, and these environments produce huge amounts of data (Lynch, 2008). Big Data has been playing a vital role in many environments. Many researchers suggest that Big Data is one of the best research frontiers at present and in the future (Khan et al., 2015). Big Data is listed among the "Top 10 Critical Tech Trends for the Next Five Years" and "Top 10 Strategic Technology Trends for 2013" (Savitz, 2012a,b). It has been applied in many fields, including public administration, scientific research, and business.

16.2.2 Big Data Characteristics

Big Data is defined by a number of V's (Figure 16.1); there are a variety of explanations from 3 V's to 10 V's as follows.

- Volume—The term volume describes the size of the data set. We currently see exponential growth in the size of the data, because the formats of data are myriad. For example, data can be found in the format of text, audio, videos, and large

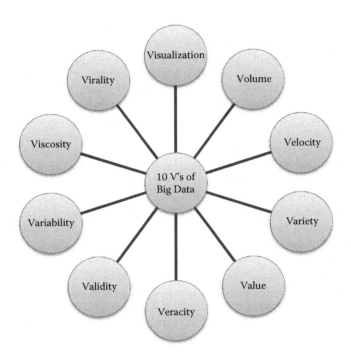

FIGURE 16.1
10 V's of Big Data.

images on our social networking sites. In general, it is normal to have terabytes and petabytes of the storage system for enterprises. In order to store such huge sizes of data, our traditional database system and architecture has to be improved. The big volume indeed represents Big Data.

- Velocity—The term velocity represents the speed of the data in and out. We currently see that the data explosion of the social media has changed. Up until the last decade it was believed that data of yesterday is recent. Nowadays, messages a few seconds old (a tweet, status updates, etc.) are not something of interest to users. They often discard old messages and pay attention to the most recent updates. The speed of the incoming data has reduced to fractions of seconds. This high velocity data represent Big Data.
- Variety—The term variety describes the range of data types and sources. In general, most organizations use the following type of data formats such as database, excel, and CSV, which can be stored in a simple text file. However, sometimes the data may not be in the prescribed format as we assume; it may be in the form of audio, video, SMS, pdf, or something we might have not thought about it. This can be overcome by developing data storage system that can store varieties of data.
- Value—The term value describes the worth of the data being extracted. Having endless amounts of data is one thing, but unless it can be turned into value it is useless. While there is a strong connection between data and insights, this does not always mean there is value in Big Data. The most important point to be considered is to understand the costs and benefits of collecting and analyzing the huge data. This value of data represents Big Data.

- **Veracity**—Veracity doesn't mean data quality; it's about data understandability. In other words, it assumes that data is being stored and mined properly to make it pertinent to the problem being analyzed. In order to use effective information from Big Data, the organization should perform data clean and process it to prevent "dirty data" from accumulating in the systems.
- **Validity**—Validity is similar to veracity. It checks whether the data is correct and accurate for the intended use. Clearly, valid data is the key to making the right decisions in the future.
- **Variability**—The term variability answers the following questions: Is the data consistent in terms of availability or interval of reporting? Does it accurately portray the event reported? When data contains many extreme values it presents a statistical problem to determine what to do with these "outlier" values, and whether they contain a new and important signal or are just noisy data.
- **Viscosity**—It describes the latency or lag time in the data transfer relative to the event being described. This is just as easily understood as an element of velocity.
- **Virality**—This defines the rate at which the data spreads and how often the data is picked up and repeated by other users or events.
- **Visualization**—The term visualization is used to help Big Data get a complete view of data and discover data values. Visualization will be a key to making Big Data an integral part of decision making and accessible to a large audience, and thus will be of great use.

16.2.3 Big Data Challenges and Potential Solutions

The rapid growth of data—both structured and unstructured—will present challenges as well as opportunities for organizations. The challenges (and solutions) discussed here are speed, data understanding, meaningful results, and outliers (Figure 16.2).

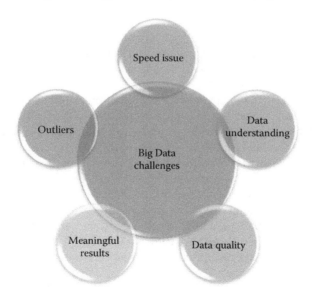

FIGURE 16.2
Big Data challenges.

Nowadays, the interest of organizations is not only to find and investigate the relevant data they need, but to find it very quickly. The visualization technique is used for analyzing and decision making, though it has its own limitations when analyzing huge volumes of data. Hardware is one possible solution to overcome this issue. Some organizations are using high-end memory and parallel processing platforms to crunch large volumes of data. In addition to that, loading data in-memory also solves many Big Data issues. Both approaches allow vendors to gain insights from the Big Data.

Even though more visualization tools are available, without understanding of data it is not possible to get useful information. One proper solution to this issue is to have the appropriate domain expertise in place to make people know where the data comes from, what kind of listeners will be consuming the data, and how well they understand the information.

Doing business insights and the decision-making process are not possible if the data is not accurate or timely. This is the most general challenge with any data analysis, and when considering Big Data, it becomes even more pronounced. To solve this issue, organizations need to have an information management or a data governance process in place to ensure that data is clean.

Getting meaningful results is not easy when processing extremely huge amounts of data or a variety of data. Consider 5 billion rows of data to be visualized in a graph; that would not be easy. This can be overcome by clustering data into a higher-level view where smaller groups of data become visible.

Visualization techniques represent outliers much faster than tables containing numbers and text. Users can simply identify the issues by glancing at a chart. In general, outliers present about 1% to 5% of overall data, but when working with huge amounts of data, viewing 1% to 5% of data is itself more complicated. One possible solution is to remove the outliers from the data or to generate an appropriate chart for the outliers. Though outliers are not representative of the data, they may also expose previously hidden and valuable business insights.

16.2.4 Big Data Applications

In this section we will explore how the applications of Big Data are likely to grow in the future and how they will essentially shape our real-time environment (Figure 16.3). The push toward collecting and analyzing large amounts of data in diverse application domains has motivated us to use a variety of applications such as health and human welfare, nature and natural processes, government and the public sector, commerce, business and economic systems, social networking and the Internet, and computational and experimental processes (Kambatla et al., 2014).

Clinical data are classified as imaging data, electronic medical records (EMRs), pharmaceutical data, data on personal practices and preferences (including exercise patterns, dietary habits, environmental factors), and financial/activity records. Successfully combining all these data provides a major enhancement in interventions, delivery, and well-being (Vayena et al., 2015). McKinsey Global Institute conducted a study in which it states that healthcare analytics could produce more than $300 billion in value every year (Manyika et al., 2011). Data is collected at point-of-care and is stored in extensively distributed repositories with huge access. For example, imaging data (MRI, fMRI) is frequently accessed overseas by skilled radiologists to deliver expert view and diagnoses (Kayyali et al., 2013).

The public sector and government also use Big Data analytics to maintain the General Services Administration (Wired, n.d.). Business services have been created, such as AWS

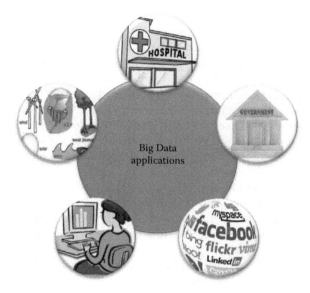

FIGURE 16.3
Major Big Data applications.

GovCloud, which exclusively aim to move exhaustive workloads to the cloud (Amazon Web Services, 2016). Thus, Big Data projects have significantly reduced execution time (both upload and download) and operational costs (Chandrasekaran and Kapoor, 2011; Kim et al., 2014).

Social networking and the Internet find extensive use worldwide. The latest news from Facebook states that 2 billion people are actively using social media each month (Kemp, 2014). Monitoring people's emotions and sentiment analysis have been applied in many areas to solve big issues (Shah et al., 2015; W. Wang et al., 2012).

Computing platforms too use Big Data to get high value insight. For example, quantum-mechanical modeling (Pandey and Ramesh, 2015), astrophysical simulations, and geo-spatial modeling (Mhlanga et al., 2015) use computational simulations and scientific instruments to model the real-time Big Data sets to bring in qualitative and quantitative changes in the near future (Reed and Dongarra, 2015).

Big Data also helps to save nature and natural processes as copious data being collected linking to our environmental footprint and its noticeable impact. This type of data is normally collected from satellite imagery, sensors, and radars to monitor the extreme weather events, deforestation, and urban encroachment. Thus, Big Data analytics has a major impact on sustainable development (Gijzen et al., 2013), land and water resources management (X. Wang and Sun, 2013), environmental impact assessment (Howe et al., 2008), natural resource management (Hampton et al., 2013), and global warming and climate change (Jang et al., 2015).

16.2.5 Climate Big Data and Climate Change

Climate data is observational data that is preferred to represent typical conditions. Data collected from the meteorological center and various research products give valuable information to the world. Meteorological and related data is most often used for weather forecasting. Moreover, subsequent analyses of the climate data for various purposes lead to a significant development in numerous applications. However, the main concern in the use of collected climatological data is not to only describe the data but to formulate inferences from the data that are more helpful to consumers of climatological information.

Statistical techniques are used to make inferences from raw climatological data. They serve as a bridge to fill the gap between raw data and useful information, and are used for examining data and climate models that are primarily used for climate prediction. As an example, statistical measures are used to find trends in climatological data such as the number of precipitation days. The World Climate Data and Monitoring Programme (WCDMP) is a program of the World Meteorological Organization's World Climate Programme (WCP) that facilitates the valuable collection and management of climate data and the observing of the global climate system. Climatologists use the term climate "normals" to compare current climatological trends to that of the past or what is considered "normal." A normal climate is described as the average of a climate parameter (e.g., precipitation) over a period. In general, the current climate normal period is calculated from January 1, 1961, to December 31, 1990.

World Weather Records (WWR), established in 1923, generates a huge volume of monthly temperature, wind speed, rainfall, precipitation, and pressure data from thousands of weather stations around the world. Some weather stations have been producing weather data since the early 1800s. The World Metrological Organization (WMO) is maintaining climate records by digital publication collected from thousands of stations worldwide. The first issue of publication included data from the earliest records available at that time up to 1920. Data have been collected for the periods 1921–1930 (2nd Series), 1931–1940 (3rd Series), 1941–1950 (4th Series), 1951–1960 (5th Series), 1961–1970 (6th Series), 1971–1980 (7th Series), 1981–1990 (8th Series), and 1991–2000 (9th Series).

In addition, the WMO Commission for Climatology (CCl) keeps a huge database to maintain data on world weather and climate extremes. The reports are verified and made available to worldwide users. The objective of this climate database is to record and validate extreme climate events, such as the highest/lowest recorded temperature, strongest wind speed, and greatest precipitation on Earth (over different time periods). It also maintains the world's most destructive storms, hurricanes, and tornadoes. The database was originally established by Arizona State University in the United States. The WMO measures the world surface temperature based on the air temperature at 1.25 to 2 meters over the surface level on the land. Sea surface temperature is measured by different observation stages such as ships and buoys. In order to measure the global precipitation data, rain gauge observations, and precipitation, estimates from satellites are used. The Global Precipitation Climatology Project (GPCP) is one of the World Climate Research Programme's core projects that give a complete source of information on worldwide precipitation. The following organizations maintain the global precipitation data sets: Global Precipitation Climatology Centre, hosted by Deutscher Wetterdienst of Germany; and the Climate Prediction Center and National Climatic Data Center, based in the United States.

16.2.6 Role of Big Data in Climate Change

Global climate change that plays a vital role in human life has become one of our era's biggest challenges in the 21st century. Many recent works are going on in geospatial (climate) Big Data (Lee and Kang, 2015; Nativi et al., 2015). Data science emphasizes more understanding of our global climate change data. Thus, compared to other fields where Big Data has been a great success story (Faghmous and Kumar, 2014), realizing global

Big Data Architecture for Climate Change and Disease Dynamics   311

climate change has forced researchers from various fields of science to stick together to attempt complicated research. Climate change researchers now deal with huge amounts of data about possible future climate change scenarios. They also require the climate data be readily accessible so that it can be used by researchers from different fields. Thus, the United States Environmental Protection Agency (2015) has developed new geospatial software, EnviroAtlas, for distributing and communicating the climate scenario information. This exclusive application allows people to use and search climate change information in an understandable format. EnviroAtlas also provides information on the impact of climate change on healthcare, society, and ecosystems (Pickard et al., 2015). Moreover, many researchers are focusing on processing climate Big Data. Recently researchers from NASA have identified Climate Analytics-as-a-Service (CAaaS), which is an extension of IaaS, PaaS, and SaaS enabled by cloud computing to fulfill the following features such as high performance, data proximal analytics, scalable data management (Big Data), software appliance virtualization, adaptive analytics, and a domain-harmonized API (Schnase et al., 2014). Similarly, the EUBrazilCC project has used the cloud computing Platform as a Service (PaaS) framework for Big Data analytics named PDAS for analysis of climate change and biodiversity data (Fiore et al., 2015).

16.2.7 Big Data in Healthcare

Apart from being used in the study of climate change, Big Data has had more impact in healthcare. Nowadays healthcare systems are quickly adopting clinical data, which will rapidly increase the size of health records that are available electronically. Simultaneously, rapid progress has been made in clinical analytics. For example, new methodologies for processing huge sizes of data and gleaning new insights from that analysis are part of what is known as Big Data. As a result, there are a number of options to use Big Data to reduce the costs of healthcare. A recent study expounds six use cases of Big Data to reduce the cost of patients, readmissions, triage, decompensation (when a patient's condition worsens), adverse events, and treatment optimization for diseases affecting multiple organ systems (Bates et al., 2014). In yet another study, Big Data use cases in healthcare have been classified into four broad categories such as administration and delivery, clinical decision support (with a subcategory of clinical information), consumer behavior, and support services (Hermon and Williams, 2014). Jee and Kim (2013) conducted a study that describes how to reshape the healthcare system based on Big Data analytics to select an appropriate treatment path, improvement of healthcare systems, and so on. These healthcare related use cases have used Big Data as (1) patient centered framework to estimate the cost incurred on healthcare, patient impact (outcomes), and reduce the readmission rates (Chawla and Davis, 2013; Groves et al., 2013; Koumpouros, 2014); and (2) virtual physiological human framework to produce robust and effective solutions in silico medicine (Viceconti et al., 2015).

16.2.8 Big Data in Climate Change and Healthcare

Big Data has a huge impact on climate change and healthcare, which had not been explored until recently. How well merging of climate and health data impacts Big Data analytics is explained next. Researchers from IBM, the University of California, and Johns Hopkins University have developed smart Big Data analytical tools for public health to monitor the outbreak of dengue fever and malaria. They have come out with the latest distributed computing technology and mathematical skills on an open source framework (IBM, 2013).

IBM scientists have also used existing vector borne disease models and the Spatiotemporal Epidemiological Modeler (STEM) tool with Big Data to develop new dengue fever and malaria models (Edlund et al., 2010; Stefan Edlund, 2016). Likewise, veterinary epidemiology researchers have used Big Data to model the spatial and temporal epidemiological analysis of animal and human health risks (Pfeiffer and Stevens, 2015). Our previous work describes the opportunities of using climate Big Data to predict H1N1 dynamics in Vellore, India (Lopez and Gunasekaran, 2015; Lopez et al., 2014).

16.3 Lambda Architecture

Lambda architecture (Figure 16.4), originally developed by Nathan Marz, is widely used in implementing Big Data systems. This architecture proposes three layers: batch, speed, and serving.

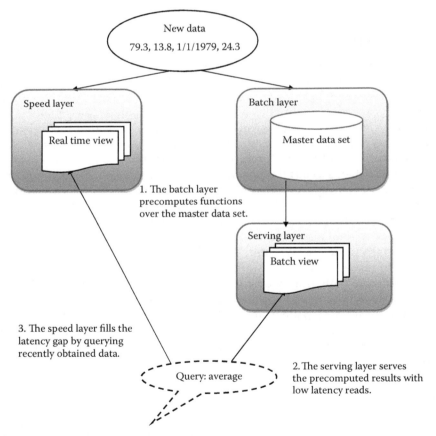

FIGURE 16.4
Lambda architecture.

Big Data Architecture for Climate Change and Disease Dynamics   313

16.3.1 Batch Layer

The batch layer of lambda architecture performs two main functions: (1) master data set management and (2) batch views precomputation. Master data management is the storage of very large lists of system records. In precomputation, the batch layer precomputes the master data set into batch views so that queries can be resolved with low latency. This requires a balance between what will be precomputed and what will be computed at execution time to complete the query. Doing a little bit of computation on the fly to complete queries avoids meaningless precomputation of large batch views. The key is to precompute essential information, hence a query can be completed quickly (Marz and Warren, 2015).

16.3.2 Speed Layer

Generating batch view involves scanning a huge size of raw data set that takes nearly a few hours to complete. During the scanning period, the batch view will be stale, but the user operates as usual and transaction information will be generated continuously. To answer the most recent up-to-date user's query, the most recent transaction needs to be stored and mixed into the real-time view. The real-time layer is intended to find the query results for the most recent incoming stream of data. Once query results are obtained, they should be stored in such a way that they will be queried by applications. It can be implemented using the Storm project that was originally created by Nathan Marz. The real-time layer also can store the query results (Marz and Warren, 2015).

16.3.3 Serving Layer

The serving layer is the last component of the batch section of the lambda architecture. It is tightly tied with the batch layer, because the batch layer is responsible for continually updating the serving layer views. These views will always be out of date due to the high-latency nature of batch computation. But this is not a concern, because the speed layer will be responsible for any data that is not yet available in the serving layer. As the batch layer does not display batch views, the batch views should be loaded elsewhere so that they will be efficiently queried to get necessary information out of the view. This is being done by the serving layer, a distributed database that stores batch views, and makes the batch views more efficiently queryable, and makes changes in updated versions of a batch view as they are provided by the batch layer.

The batch layer always takes a few hours to complete a single batch view update, whereas the serving layer updates its views within an hour. A serving layer database contains only updates of the most recent batch views and random reads. It does not allow random writes, because it may increase complexity in databases. Hence the serving layer is very easy to configure and operate (Kreps, 2016; Mapr.com, 2016; Marz and Warren, 2015).

Table 16.1 defines the number of tools that are available to implement the batch layer, speed layer, and serving layer of lambda architecture (Hausenblas and Bijnens, 2016). Figure 16.5 depicts the Cloudera Hadoop distribution with lambda architecture.

TABLE 16.1
Lambda Architecture Components

Batch Layer		Speed Layer		Serving Layer	
Technology	Language	Technology	Language	Technology	Language
Hadoop MapReduce	Java	Apache Strom	Clojure	ElephantDB	Clojure
Apache Spark	Scala, Java, Phyton	Apache Spark Streaming	Scala, Java, Phyton	SploutSQL	Java
Apache Hive	HiveQL, Java	Apache Samza	Scala, Java	Voldemort	Java
Apache Spark SQL	SQL, Scala, Java, Phyton	Apache S4	Java	HBase	Java
Apache Pig	Pig Latin, Java	Spring XD	Java	Druid	Java
Apache Spark	Pig Latin, Java	AWS Kinesis	Java		
Cascading/ Scalding	Java, Scala	Google Cloud Dataflow	Java		
Cascalog	Clojure	Hive Streaming	HiveQL, Java		
Crunch/ Scrunch	Java, Scala				
Pangool	Java				

16.4 Components of Lambda Architecture

16.4.1 Data Sources

The available Big Data sources include streaming data, rotating log files, batch files, and database data. Streaming data is mostly unstructured since data is injected continuously and so the data processing system must have the capabilities to handle high-speed data. Streaming data is processed by the "time windows" in memory. Rotating log files are normally generated by the machine for a period of time. In many cases, log files are structured or semistructured. Batch files are the large sets of data that are periodically (typically once in a day) injected into the local file system. Traditional examples of batch files are JSON or XML files injected from internal or external sources of the system. Traditional databases store the data in the structured form, for example, transaction data, employee profiles, and patient data are normally stored in a relational database management system (RDBMS). These are in a well-structured form.

16.4.2 Components of Data Ingestion Block

Apache Sqoop is a tool used for efficiently transferring huge data between Apache Hadoop and structured data stores such as relational databases. Sqoop can extract data from the Hadoop file system and export it into external structured data stores such as Teradata, Netezza, Oracle, MySQL, Postgres, and HSQLD. Apache Sqoop has the following functions to integrate bulk data movement between Hadoop and structured data stores:

- Sqoop performs huge data transformation between the mainframe and Hadoop Distributed File System (HDFS).
- It contains lightweight indexing and improved compression for efficient query performance.

Big Data Architecture for Climate Change and Disease Dynamics 315

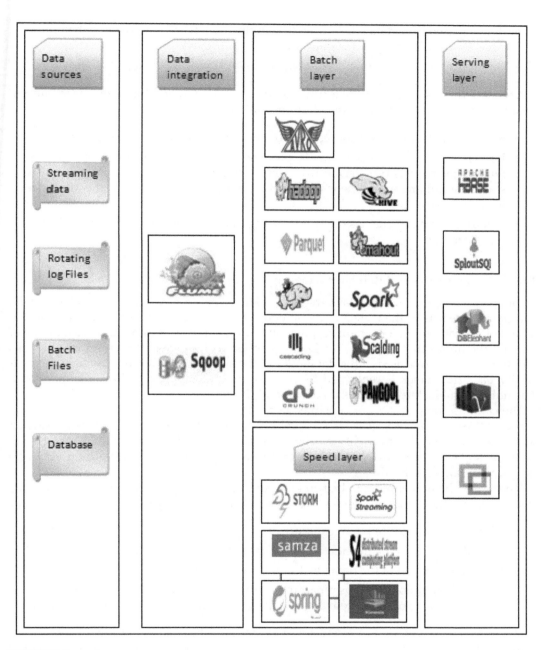

FIGURE 16.5
Cloudera distribution of lambda architecture.

- Transferring data from external storage and Enterprice Data Warehouse (EDW) into the Hadoop file system to optimize cost-effectiveness of combined data storage and processing.
- Better resource utilization and faster performance.
- Fast data transferring from external storage into the Hadoop system.

316   *The Human Element of Big Data*

- A schema-on-read data lake is used to combine structured data with unstructured data, so that efficiency of the data analysis is improved.
- Controlling and maintaining processing loads and excessive storage to other systems.

Apache Flume is used for transferring log files, batch files, and high-volume streaming data into HDFS for storage. Specifically, Flume allows users to

- Stream data from several sources into the Hadoop system for storage and analysis.
- Use channel-based transactions to promise reliable data delivery. For example, when a message is transferred from one system to another, two transactions are started simultaneously: one is represented on the receiver side and the other one is on the sender side.
- Horizontal scaling enables the system to ingest most recent data streams and additional storage.

16.4.3 Components of Batch Layer

Hadoop implements a master–slave architecture that consists of a namenode and datanode. The namenode acts as the master and datanodes act as slaves. The namenode controls the access of all datanodes. The main responsibility of datanodes is to manage the storage of data on the nodes that are running. Hadoop splits the huge file into a number of blocks and these blocks are stored in the datanodes of the system. In order to provide high availability, each data block is replicated to three different datanodes of the Hadoop system. The number of block replications is configurable by the user.

The Hadoop components are explained as follows.

Hadoop Distributed File System. HDFS is depicted in Figure 16.6. It was originally designed to run on a cluster of commodity hardware. The distributed data is stored in the HDFS. HDFS is suitable for many applications that have large data sets and is designed to be deployed on low-cost hardware.

Namenode. The namenode can be run on a commodity cluster hardware. In general, the system having the namenode serves as the master server and it does the following tasks:

- Manages the file system namespace.
- Periodically stores the metadata information of the data blocks.
- Stores the location of the data blocks on the datanode.
- Performs operations such as renaming, closing, and opening files and directories. If the namenode of the system crashes, then the entire Hadoop system goes down.

Datanode. The datanode is present in every node of the Hadoop cluster. These nodes concentrate on managing the data storage of their system and are responsible for the following tasks:

- Based on the client's request, they perform read and write operations on the Hadoop file systems.
- Performs operations such as block creation, deletion, and replication according to the instructions of the namenode.
- Stores blocks of data and later retrieves them. The datanodes periodically report about the block information to the namenode.

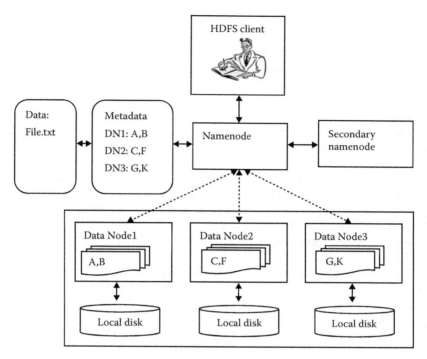

FIGURE 16.6
HDFS architecture.

Secondary namenode. The main function of the secondary namenode is to periodically copy and combine the namespace image and edit log. Once the name node crashes, then the namespace image stored in the secondary namenode can be used to restart the namenode.

JobTracker. JobTracker performs the scheduling client jobs that includes the creation of map and reduce tasks on the data nodes. In addition, JobTracker periodically checks the failed tasks and reschedules the failed tasks on another datanode. Generally, JobTracker runs on the namenode or on a separate node.

TaskTracker. TaskTracker runs on the datanodes of the Hadoop cluster. The main function of the task trackers is to run the map or reduce tasks assigned by the namenode and to periodically report about the status of the tasks to the namenode.

HDFS architecture does the following tasks:

- The distributed file system makes getting new data as simple as adding a new file to the folder, which contains the master data set.
- The huge size of data is distributed across a cluster of machines. As more machines are added, the storage space and I/O throughput increase.
- The distributed file system allows parallel processing across multiple machines using the MapReduce framework.
- The distributed file system allows disabling the ability to modify or delete files in the master data set folder. This feature protects the master data against bugs or human mistakes.

Hadoop MapReduce. Hadoop MapReduce is a programming model for processing the huge size of data sets across a Hadoop cluster. Data analysis follows the map and reduce process, and the Hadoop framework provides the scheduling, distribution, and parallelization services. In the MapReduce process, the top-level unit of work is a job. A job usually has a map and a reduce phase. Consider a MapReduce job that counts the number of word occurrences across a set of documents. In this problem the map phase counts the number of words in each document, then the reduce phase aggregates the per-document data into word counts spanning the entire collection. The map phase takes care of dividing the input data into a number of input splits across the Hadoop cluster. During the reduce phase, results from the map tasks are given as input to a set of parallel reduce tasks. The responsibility of the reduce tasks is to combine and consolidate the map output into final results. MapReduce operates based on the key-value pairs. Every MapReduce job takes a set of input key-value pairs and produces a set of output key-value pairs by passing the data through the map and reduce functions.

Hadoop MapReduce programming model does the following tasks:

- Programming languages can be chosen by developers. Languages such as C++, Java, or Python are best suited to run MapReduce jobs.
- MapReduce programming model can process petabytes of data, stored in the Hadoop cluster.
- Parallel processing of MapReduce can process the huge size of data in hours or minutes.
- MapReduce handles node failure on its own. If any one machine fails, another machine in the cluster has a copy of the same key-value pair, which can be used to solve the issue. The JobTracker is used to keep track of all the tasks.
- MapReduce moves the data only around the HDFS, not the other way. All processing tasks can be done on the physical node where the data resides. The MapReduce model extensively reduces the network I/O patterns and increases the processing speed.

Apache Pig. Apache Pig supports the generation of batch views. This query approach has several operations together in a single pipeline; so it reduces the number of data scanning. General data operations like filters, joins, and ordering, and nested data types like tuples, bags, and maps on structured, semistructured, or unstructured data can be performed. It is often used while joining new incremental data with the previous data results.

Apache Hive. Apache Hive also supports batch views generation in data warehousing. HiveQL is the query language for Hive, which converts normal SQL-like queries into MapReduce jobs executed on HDFS.

Cloudera Impala. Cloudera Impala can generate batch views using low-latency and high-performance SQL queries on data stored in HDFS. It supports fast responses to user queries, instead of long batch jobs historically related to SQL-on-Hadoop technologies. Impala can integrate with the Apache Hive metastore database so that users can share the tables and databases between both components. This high-level integration with Hive allows us to use either Hive or Impala to create queries and load data into the tables.

Apache Mahout. Apache Mahout is a scalable machine-learning technique that runs over the Hadoop MapReduce; it can generate more precise results for user queries. Machine learning is an artificial intelligence that enables systems to learn based on data alone; it offers an improved performance as more data is processed. It is the basis for several

Big Data Architecture for Climate Change and Disease Dynamics

technologies that are part of our day-to-day lives and includes filtering, clustering, classification, dimensionality reduction, and pattern mining.

Apache Hadoop YARN. Apache Hadoop YARN is used for master data management, which supports distributing Big Data analytics jobs by the MapReduce programming model and HDFS. YARN provides the following features for Enterprise Hadoop such as resource management, security, and data governance tools across the Hadoop system.

As its architectural center, YARN enhances a Hadoop compute cluster in the following ways:

- YARN allows open source or proprietary tools to use the Hadoop system for batch and real-time processing.
- YARN follows dynamic allocation of system resources that improves resource utilization compared to static MapReduce model rules used in early versions of Hadoop.
- Rapid expansion in the processing power of the data center allows YARN to manage petabytes of data across thousands of nodes in the cluster.
- Existing MapReduce applications are processed by YARN without any disruption.

Apache Parquest. Apache Parquest also supports master data management when a user needs columnar storage. Here, it doesn't load the entire data into the memory; instead it stores those data that are really required, thus reducing the required space in the memory as well as increasing the speed.

16.4.4 Components of Speed Layer

Apache Spark Streaming works based on a cluster computing framework. Unlike Hadoop's MapReduce paradigm, it follows in-memory primitives so that it can produce one hundred times faster output for user queries on stream of data. Spark streaming has been introduced as a part of Spark, which finds its application in real-time, for example, to control and monitor the access of users on a website and fraud detection in real time.

16.4.5 Components of Serving Layer

Apache HBase is a scalable and distributed database that stores the data on top of the HDFS. It was developed after Google's BigTable was identified and can store millions of rows and columns. In view of the fact that HBase follows the master–slave architecture, it is highly available to all nodes in the cluster.

16.5 Big Data Architecture for Climate Change and Disease Dynamics

Lambda architecture is both scalable and reliable for real-time applications and it focuses on handling huge workloads and use cases, but the lack of implementation with reference to this architecture is not familiar in real-time applications. Though the data source and data ingestion block are not well explained in Lambda architecture, this chapter gives a better understanding of them. The Hadoop local file system is used in this study to implement the data ingestion block. Three layers are associated with lambda architecture, namely, batch layer, speed layer, and serving layer. Apache Hadoop MapReduce and Apache Hive are used to implement the batch layer. Batch layer tools are implemented based on a scalable incremental method that stores incoming data in a cluster of commodity hardware and highly available storage engine. The batch layer also provides replay mechanisms in case of breakdown in any node of the cluster. Implementation of the speed layer is based on Apache Hive streaming. Unlike the batch layer, if any of the nodes fail in the cluster, the speed layer does not provide any recovery mechanism; so it drops the previous data and works with the most recent data available. The serving layer merges the results from the batch and speed layers and responds to the user query. Apache HBase is used to implement the serving layer and ArcGIS 10.2 is used in this study for visualizing the results. Proposed Big Data architecture mainly focuses on computing monthly average maximum temperature, minimum temperature, precipitation, wind, relative humidity, solar, and calculating the Pearson correlation coefficient between climate parameters and number of dengue infections.

The architecture in Figure 16.7 was developed based on the existing lambda architecture with two additional layers: the data ingestion block and visualizing layer. A number of data sources are elaborated in the data ingestion block. Normally data ingestion blocks are classified into four different types, namely, batch files, database data, rotating log files, and data streams. The data ingestion block is used for storing and handling climate and health data. Districtwise monthly dengue fever data is collected from multiple hospitals, district health officers, and the Ministry of Health and Family Welfare between January 1998 and December 2006 for Tamil Nadu, India (Chandy et al., 2013; Gunasekaran et al., 2011; Victor et al., 2007), which was chosen as our study area. Districtwise monthly dengue cases are stored in the Hadoop cluster nodes using Hive. Daily climate parameters

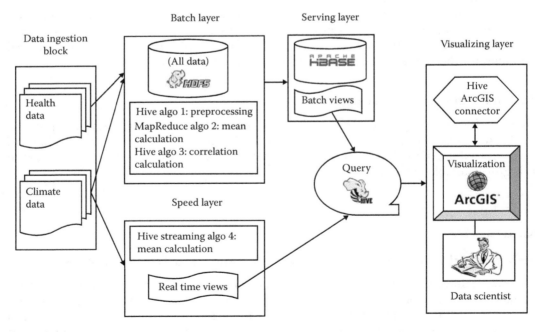

FIGURE 16.7
Proposed Big Data architecture.

```
Date,Longitude,Latitude,Elevation,MaxTemperature,MinTemperature,Precipitation,Wind,Relative
Humidity,Solar
1/1/1979,79.0625,13.8942003250122,409,24.001,17.365,0.3278742264,1.566199145656,0.8886190936,12.30403348,
1/2/1979,79.0625,13.8942003250122,409,25.817,14.111,0.0102996792,1.835927473671,0.873943504333,19.493721,
1/3/1979,79.0625,13.8942003250122,409,25.231,12.991,0.1.90932099044504,0.850141727895694,20.09739132,
1/4/1979,79.0625,13.8942003250122,409,25.162,12.907,0.1.86838639889342,0.835131190267102,20.104311348,
1/5/1979,79.0625,13.8942003250122,409,25.908,11.847,0.0781059168,1.6394340241707,0.802525084434,20.14002,
1/6/1979,79.0625,13.8942003250122,409,25.51,13.303,0.1441958544,1.87781918316264,0.834196067495133,18.93,
1/7/1979,79.0625,13.8942003250122,409,26.117,12.981,0,1.6757060896263,0.795431155405995,20.292809688,
1/8/1979,79.0625,13.8942003250122,409,26.701,14.226,0,1.49576174732698,0.766072592823415,20.412171432,
1/9/1979,79.0625,13.8942003250122,409,27.036,15.321,0,1.86507940597598,0.740040020348654,20.148522372,
1/10/1979,79.0625,13.8942003250122,409,25.813,13.84,0,2.09980346349538,0.80843842463949,20.31598458,
1/11/1979,79.0625,13.8942003250122,409,25.215,12.002,0,1.99474999541674,0.794919321398066,20.483435052,
1/12/1979,79.0625,13.8942003250122,409,25.506,10.974,0,1.594475807156,0.790534103060224,20.69099928,
1/13/1979,79.0625,13.8942003250122,409,26.329,14.381,0,1.71615448541087,0.76192037123461,20.681832168,
1/14/1979,79.0625,13.8942003250122,409,26.614,12.775,0,1.99117412616105,0.767678930018668,20.69740926,
1/15/1979,79.0625,13.8942003250122,409,26.903,13.428,0,2.10653682505959,0.723011561155546,20.887990308,
1/16/1979,79.0625,13.8942003250122,409,27.077,13.008,0,1.6733786779527,0.767045136865706,20.72435904,
1/17/1979,79.0625,13.8942003250122,409,27.086,13.333,0,1.82442404034068,0.808374437532221,20.569895568,
```

FIGURE 16.8
Raw weather station data.

like date, latitude, longitude, elevation, maximum temperature, minimum temperature, precipitation, wind, relative humidity, and solar are collected from multiple weather stations and stored in the Hadoop cluster nodes. The weather station normally generates unstructured data. As shown in Figure 16.8, a comma separates each piece of data. Hive is used to preprocess the comma-delimited values and it stores the huge size of rows into the Hadoop cluster nodes. Hive stores both climate and health data in a table format and MapReduce programming is applied.

In the batch layer, monthly mean maximum temperature, minimum temperature, precipitation, wind, relative humidity, and solar are calculated using the MapReduce algorithm and the result will be stored in the Hive table. The monthly average climate parameter table and monthly dengue case table are merged into a single table using Hive. Finally, the Pearson correlation coefficient is calculated using the built-in function corr() of Hive. The serving layer uses HBase to store Hive results as a column-oriented table. Batch views will be generated every hour to update the current climate and disease status.

To process the real-time climate data coming from multiple weather stations, the speed layer uses Hive Streaming. Using the Hive Streaming algorithm the average climate parameter value for most recent data is calculated. Finally, batch views and real-time views are combined to answer the user up-to-date queries. The visualizing layer has been developed based on the ArcGIS 10.2 Hive connecter. Hive results are in the form of a table that consists of the Pearson correlation coefficient between the dengue cases and climate parameter, latitude, and longitude for the specific location. Using latitude and longitude for each location, the correlation coefficient between the climate parameter and dengue cases are displayed in ArcGIS 10.2 for better and quick understanding. Implementation of the proposed architecture for climate change and dengue is elaborated in the following sections.

16.5.1 Data Ingestion Block

In the data ingestion block, daily climate parameters like date, latitude, longitude, elevation, maximum temperature, minimum temperature, precipitation, wind, relative humidity, and solar are collected from multiple weather stations where each piece of data is separated by a comma. As shown in Figure 16.18, climate data are collected from multiple weather stations from January 1, 1979, to December 31, 2014. It contains daywise climate data of about 432 years for the entire world. The proposed architecture uses the climate

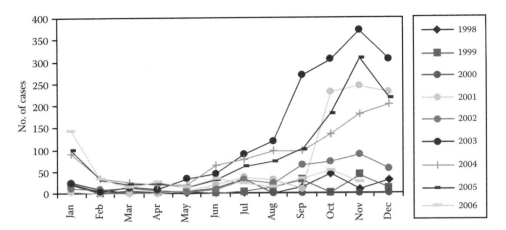

FIGURE 16.9
Monthly dengue cases.

data set of only 32 districts in the Tamil Nadu state, India. Each district contains 12,960 rows and 11 columns and so there are 4,14,720 rows and 352 columns in total for all districts in the Tamil Nadu state. Districtwise, monthly dengue fever data are collected from multiple hospitals, district health officers, and the Ministry of Health and Family Welfare between January 2000 and December 2014 for the study area (Figure 16.9).

16.5.2 Batch Layer Implementation

Implementation of the batch layer using Apache Hive and Apache MapReduce is illustrated in the following sections.

16.5.2.1 Apache Hive

Apache Hive provides an SQL interface and a relational model for analyzing, querying, and summarizing huge data sets stored in HDFS. HiveQL is a query language for Hive, which converts normal SQL-like queries into MapReduce jobs to be executed on HDFS. Unlike traditional SQL, HiveQL performs bulk loading of data into HDFS. The proposed architecture uses Hive to store 414,720 rows and 352 columns into HDFS. As shown in Figure 16.8, weather station data are separated by comma, so that it can be cleaned and loaded using Hive command, as shown in Figure 16.10.

16.5.2.2 Apache Hadoop MapReduce

In the new world of Big Data, open source projects like Hadoop have become the de facto processing platform for Big Data. Hadoop MapReduce is a subproject of the Apache Hadoop project. It is an open source software framework for distributed data processing of huge data sets on compute clusters of commodity hardware (Dean and Ghemawat, 2008). The framework takes care of node failure, task monitoring, and load balancing, and scheduling them.

The main objective of map–reduce is to split the input data set into independent chunks that can be processed in parallel. The primary objective of the Hadoop MapReduce framework is to sort the output of the maps, which are then input to the reduce tasks. Typically,

Big Data Architecture for Climate Change and Disease Dynamics

```
hive > CREATE TABLE IF NOT EXISTS climate (
     >     Date TEXT,
     >     Longitude DOUBLE,
     >     Latitude DOUBLE,
     >     Elevation DOUBLE,
     >     MaxTemperature DOUBLE,
     >     MinTemperature DOUBLE,
     >     Precipitation DOUBLE,
     >     Wind DOUBLE,
     >     RelativeHumidity DOUBLE,
     >     Solar DOUBLE)
     > ROW FORMAT DELIMITED FIELDS TERMINATED BY ',';

hive > LOAD DATA LOCAL INPATH '${env:HOME}/climatedata.txt'
     > INTO TABLE climate;
```

FIGURE 16.10
Apache Hive queries for data cleaning.

both the input and the output of the job are stored in a Hadoop file system. Proposed architecture uses Hadoop MapReduce framework to calculate the monthly mean of maximum temperature, minimum temperature, precipitation, wind, relative humidity, and solar. Figure 16.11 shows the key-value pair and Figure 16.12 shows the MapReduce mean algorithm. Calculated monthly mean climate parameters and monthly dengue cases are merged and stored into a single Hive table. As shown in Figure 16.13, the Pearson correlation between the two columns (monthly mean climate parameters and monthly dengue cases) can be calculated using the Hive aggregate built-in function corr(). The calculated Pearson correlation, latitude, and longitude for each location are stored in the HBase.

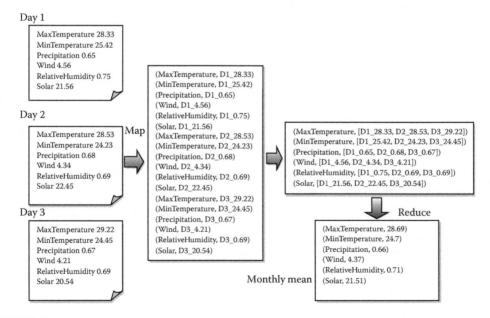

FIGURE 16.11
Key-value pair for the MapReduce mean algorithm.

```
Data:
day wise climate parametrs cpv collected from multiple weather station
Input:
ncp = name of the climate parameter
cpv = climate parameter value(daywise)
Output:
Monthly mean climate parameters cpv
Algorithm: Map
class MAPPER
   method INITIALIZE
     Sum = new ASSOCIATIVE ARRAY
     Count = new ASSOCIATIVE ARRAY
   method MAP(String ncp, double cpv);
     Sum{ncp} = Sum{ncp} + cpv
     Count{ncp} = Sum{ncp} + 1
   method CLOSE
     for all term ncp ∈ Sum do
     EmitIntermediate(string ncp, pair(Sum{ncp}, Count{ncp}))
Algorithm: Reduce
class REDUCER
   method REDUCE(String ncp, pairs[(sum₁, count₁)(sum₂, count₂) … ])
     double final_sum = 0.0;
     int final_count = 0;
     for all pair (Sum, Count) ∈ pairs[(sum₁, count₁)(sum₂, count₂) … ]do
     final_sum+= sum;
     final_count+= count;
double monthlymean_cpv = sum/count;
WriteToHBase(String ncp, double monthlymean_cpv);
```

FIGURE 16.12
MapReduce algorithm for monthly mean of climate parameters.

```
hive > CREATE TABLE IF NOT EXISTS monthly_mean (
     >     Date TEXT,
     >     Longitude DOUBLE,
     >     Latitude DOUBLE,
     >     Elevation DOUBLE,
     >     Mean_MaxTemperature DOUBLE,
     >     Mean_MinTemperature DOUBLE,
     >     Mean_Precipitation DOUBLE,
     >     Mean_Wind DOUBLE,
     >     Mean_RelativeHumidity DOUBLE,
     >     Mean_Solar DOUBLE)
     > ROW FORMAT DELIMITED FIELDS TERMINATED BY ',';

hive > LOAD DATA LOCAL INPATH '${env:HOME}/monthly_mean.txt'
     > INTO TABLE monthly_mean;

hive > ALTER TABLE monthly_mean ADD COLUMNS (monthly_infection INT);

hive > LOAD DATA LOCAL INPATH '${env:HOME}/monthly_infection.txt'
     > INTO TABLE monthly_mean monthly_infection;

hive > SELECT count(*), corr(mean_max_temp, monthly_infection) FROM
       monthly_mean;
```

FIGURE 16.13
Apache Hive queries for the Pearson correlation coefficient.

TABLE 16.2

Correlation Coefficient

Degree of Correlation	Coefficient r	Description
Perfect	Near ±1	Perfect correlation
High degree	±0.50 to ±1	Strong correlation
Moderate degree	±0.30 to ±0.49	Medium correlation
Low degree	Below ±0.29	Small correlation
No correlation	Zero	No correlation

16.5.2.3 Pearson Correlation Coefficient

The Pearson correlation coefficient is used to find the strength of a linear association between two variables, where the value $r = 1$ means a perfect positive correlation and the value $r = -1$ means a perfect negative correlation (Table 16.2). The proposed architecture uses the Pearson correlation coefficient to find the correlation between climate change and dengue. The Pearson correlation coefficient, r, is defined by

$$
r = \frac{\sum_i (x_i - \bar{x})(y_i - \bar{y})}{\sqrt{\sum_i (x_i - \bar{x})^2} \sqrt{\sum_i (y_i - \bar{y})^2}}
$$

16.5.3 Serving Layer Implementation

16.5.3.1 Apache HBase

HBase is a scalable and distributed database that stores the data on top of HDFS. It was developed after Google's BigTable was identified and it can store millions of rows and columns. HBase follows master–slave architecture; it is highly available to all nodes in the cluster. HBase is a columnar database, which means that instead of being organized by rows and columns, it is organized by column families, which are sets of related columns.

16.5.3.2 Apache Hive–Apache HBase Integration

Hive-HBase integration (Figure 16.14) gives us the ability to query HBase tables using the Hive Query Language (HQL). Mapping of existing HBase tables to Hive tables as well as creation of new HBase tables using HQL is also supported by Hive–HBase integration. Both reading data from HBase tables and inserting data into HBase tables are supported through HQL, including performing joins between Hive-mapped HBase tables and traditional Hive tables. Hive–HBase integration is used in this proposed architecture to store the Hive correlation result into HBase. Figure 16.14 shows the Hive queries for the Hive–HBase integration.

16.5.4 Speed Layer Implementation

16.5.4.1 Streaming Hive

Streaming processes can return zero or more rows of output for every given input, so it is possible to do aggregate operations like Hive's built-in sum() function. The proposed

```
hive > CREATE TABLE IF NOT EXISTS hbase_corr (
    >    Longitude DOUBLE,
    >    Latitude DOUBLE,
    >    Corr_Mean_MaxTemperature DOUBLE,
    >    Corr_MinTemperature DOUBLE,
    >    Corr_Precipitation DOUBLE,
    >    Corr_Wind DOUBLE,
    >    Corr_RelativeHumidity DOUBLE,
    >    Corr_Solar DOUBLE)
    > STORED BY 'org.apache.hadoop.hive.hbase.HBaseStorageHandler'
      WITH SERDEPROPERTIES ('hbase.columns.mapping' =         ':
      Longitude, f: Latitude, f: Corr_Mean_MaxTemperature, f:
      Corr_MinTemperature, f: Corr_Precipitation, f: Corr_Wind, f:
      Corr_RelativeHumidity, f: Corr_Solar')
      TBLPROPERTIES ('hbase.table.name' = 'corr');

hive > INSERT INTO TABLE hbase_corr SELECT * from monthly_mean;
```

FIGURE 16.14
Hive queries to store Hive correlation result into HBase.

```
#avg_cpv.pl
#cpv=climate parameter value
#sum_cpv=total climate parameter value
#avg_cpv=average climate parameter value
my $sum_cpv=0;
my $count_cpv=0;
while (<STDIN>) {
   my $climate_stream_data = $_;
   chomp($climate_stream_data);
   $sum_cpv=${sum_cpv}+${climate_stream_data};
   $count_cpv=$count_cpv+1;
}
$avg_cpv=$sum_cpv/$count_cpv;
print $avg_cpv;
```

FIGURE 16.15
Pseudocode for calculating average with streaming.

architecture consists of an accumulator before the loop that reads from the input stream (climate data) and outputs the sum after the completion of the input and divides the sum by the number of input data streams (Capriolo et al., 2012). Climate stream processing pseudocode is shown in Figure 16.15. In the speed layer, the pseudocode in Figure 16.15 is added to the distributed cache and is merged with the Transform query for processing the stream (Figure 16.16). The process returns a single row; it denotes the average of the climate parameter.

16.5.5 Visualizing Layer Implementation

16.5.5.1 Geoprocessing Tools for Hadoop

Geoprocessing Tools for Hadoop help us to integrate ArcGIS 10.2 with Hadoop. It provides tools to copy data files from ArcGIS to Hadoop, and copy files from Hadoop to ArcGIS (GitHub, 2016).

Big Data Architecture for Climate Change and Disease Dynamics

```
hive> CREATE TABLE average_cpv(avg_cpv INT);

hive> LOAD DATA LOCAL INPATH '${env:HOME}/data_to_avg_cpv.txt' INTO TABLE
average_cpv;
hive> ADD FILE ${env:HOME}/avg_cpv.pl;

hive> SELECT TRANSFORM (avg_cpv)
    > USING 'perl avg_cpv.pl' AS average FROM average_cpv;
```

FIGURE 16.16
Hive Transform query for streaming data.

```
hive > CREATE TABLE pearson_corr (
     >    Longitude DOUBLE,
     >    Latitude DOUBLE,
     >    Corr_Mean_MaxTemperature DOUBLE,
     >    Corr_MinTemperature DOUBLE,
     >    Corr_Precipitation DOUBLE,
     >    Corr_Wind DOUBLE,
     >    Corr_RelativeHumidity DOUBLE,
     >    ROW FORMAT SERDE 'com.esri.hadoop.hive.serde.JsonSerde'
     >    STORED AS INPUTFORMAT
     >    'com.esri.json.hadoop.EnclosedJsonInputFormat'
     > OUTPUTFORMAT
     >    'org.apache.hadoop.hive.ql.io.HiveIgnoreKeyTextOutputFormat';

hive > FROM (SELECT ST_Bin(0.5, ST_Point (longitude, latitude)) bin_id, *
     > FROM hbase_corr) bins
     > INSERT OVERWRITE TABLE pearson_corr
     > SELECT ST_BinEnvelope(0.5, bin_id) shape,
     > count(*)Corr_Mean_MaxTemperature GROUP BY bin_id;
```

FIGURE 16.17
Hive ArcGIS connecter.

16.5.5.2 Apache Hive–ArcGIS Integration

Correlation results from the Hive query can be geographically visualized using the Hive ArcGIS connecter. As shown in Figure 16.17, ArcGIS 10.2 is connected with the Hive query to visualize the output. Finally, the model can run and add the new feature class (Pearson correlation for each climate parameter) to the Tamil Nadu, India, map (Figure 16.20).

16.6 Findings

Figure 16.18 shows the daily climate data for January 1979 to December 2014. MapReduce-based monthly mean climate parameters are calculated and the result is shown in the graph in Figure 16.19. The Pearson correlation method is used to find the impact of the climate parameters and the infected cases. A sample study is done with the maximum temperature as one of the climate parameters and dengue infection cases for Tamil Nadu, India. The results are demonstrated in Figure 16.20.

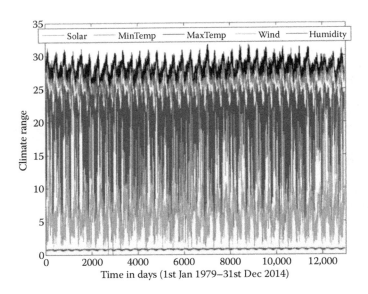

FIGURE 16.18
Daily climate range.

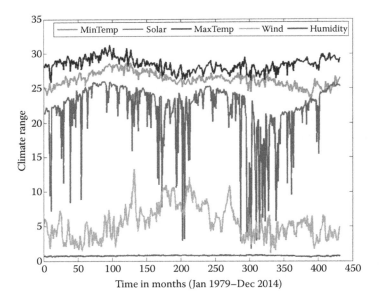

FIGURE 16.19
Monthly mean climate ranges.

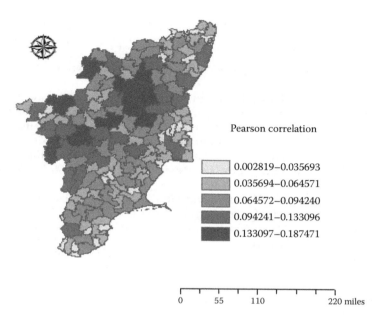

FIGURE 16.20
Sample ArcGIS correlation result between maximum temperature and dengue.

16.7 Conclusion

In summary, we have implemented a Big Data system to illustrate the impact of climate change in progression of disease, especially dengue. This chapter describes the advantages and application prospects from the GIS data distributed storage, user dynamic extraction, and fast processing of Big Data models and other aspects of the system. It mainly focuses on computing monthly average maximum temperature, minimum temperature, precipitation, wind, relative humidity, and solar, and calculating the Pearson correlation coefficient between climate parameters and number of dengue infections. The future extension of this work could be into more complex situations considering all the climate change parameters.

Acknowledgment

This work is funded by the Indian Council of Medical Research, Government of India, under Award Number 32/1/2010-ECD-I.

References

Amazon Web Services. (2016). AWS GovCloud (US) region overview—Government cloud computing. Retrieved January 8, 2016. https://aws.amazon.com/govcloud-us.

Bates, D. W., Saria, S., Ohno-Machado, L., Shah, A., and Escobar, G. (2014). Big Data in health care: Using analytics to identify and manage high-risk and high-cost patients. *Health Affairs, 33*(7), 1123–1131.

Boja, C., Pocovnicu, A., and Batagan, L. (2012). Distributed parallel architecture for Big Data. *Informatica Economica, 16*(2), 116–127.

Capriolo, E., Wampler, D., and Rutherglen, J. (2012). *Programming Hive*. O'Reilly Media.

Chandrasekaran, A. and Kapoor, M. (2011). State of cloud computing in the public sector—A strategic analysis of the business case and overview of initiatives across Asia Pacific. Frost & Sullivan. Retrieved January 8, 2016. http://www.frost.com/prod/servlet/cio/232651119.

Chandy, S., Ramanathan, K., Manoharan, A., Mathai, D., and Baruah, K. (2013). Assessing effect of climate on the incidence of dengue in Tamil Nadu. *Indian Journal of Medical Microbiology, 31*(3), 283.

Chawla, N. V. and Davis, D. A. (2013). Bringing Big Data to personalized healthcare: A patient-centered framework. *Journal of General Internal Medicine, 28*(3), 660–665.

Dean, J. and Ghemawat, S. (2008). MapReduce: Simplified data processing on large clusters. *Communications of the ACM, 51*(1), 107–113.

Edlund, S. B., Davis, M. A., and Kaufman, J. H. (2010, November). The spatiotemporal epidemiological modeler. In *Proceedings of the 1st ACM International Health Informatics Symposium* (pp. 817–820). ACM.

Faghmous, J. H. and Kumar, V. (2014). A Big Data guide to understanding climate change: The case for theory-guided data science. *Big Data, 2*(3), 155–163.

Fan, W. and Bifet, A. (2013). Mining Big Data: Current status, and forecast to the future. *ACM SIGKDD Explorations Newsletter, 14*(2), 1–5.

Fiore, S., Mancini, M., Elia, D., Nassisi, P., Brasileiro, F. V., and Blanquer, I. (2015, May). Big Data analytics for climate change and biodiversity in the EUBrazilCC federated cloud infrastructure. In *Proceedings of the 12th ACM International Conference on Computing Frontiers* (p. 52). ACM.

Gijzen, H. (2013). Development: Big Data for a sustainable future. *Nature, 502*(7469), 38.

GitHub. (2016). Esri/geoprocessing-tools-for-hadoop. Retrieved January 8, 2016. https://github.com/Esri/geoprocessing-tools-for-hadoop.

Groves, P., Kayyali, B., Knott, D., and Van Kuiken, S. (2013). The 'Big Data' revolution in healthcare. *McKinsey Quarterly* (32 pp.).

Gunasekaran, P., Kaveri, K., Mohana, S., Arunagiri, K., Babu, B. S., Priya, P. P., Kiruba, R., Kumar, V. S., and Sheriff, A. K. (2011). Dengue disease status in Chennai (2006–2008): A retrospective analysis. *Indian Journal of Medical Research, 133*(3), 322.

Hampton, S. E., Strasser, C. A., Tewksbury, J. J., Gram, W. K., Budden, A. E., Batcheller, A. L., Duke, C. S., and Porter, J. H. (2013). Big Data and the future of ecology. *Frontiers in Ecology and the Environment, 11*(3), 156–162.

Hausenblas, M. and Bijnens, N. (2016). Components. λ lambda-architecture.net. Retrieved January 8, 2016. http://lambda-architecture.net/components.

Hermon, R. and Williams, P. A. (2014). Big Data in healthcare: What is it used for? In *Proceedings of Australian eHealth Informatics and Security Conference*.

Howe, D., Costanzo, M., Fey, P., Gojobori, T., Hannick, L., Hide, W., Hill, D. P. et al. (2008). Big Data: The future of biocuration. *Nature, 455*(7209), 47–50.

IBM. (2013). Made in IBM Labs: Scientists Turn Data into Disease Detective to Predict Dengue Fever and Malaria Outbreaks. Retrieved January 8, 2016. https://www-03.ibm.com/press/uk/en/pressrelease/42103.wss.

Jang, S. M. and Hart, P. S. (2015). Polarized frames on "climate change" and "global warming" across countries and states: Evidence from Twitter big data. *Global Environmental Change, 32*, 11–17.

Jee, K. and Kim, G. H. (2013). Potentiality of Big Data in the medical sector: Focus on how to reshape the healthcare system. *Healthcare Informatics Research, 19*(2), 79–85.

Kambatla, K., Kollias, G., Kumar, V., and Grama, A. (2014). Trends in Big Data analytics. *Journal of Parallel and Distributed Computing*, 74(7), 2561–2573.

Kayyali, B., Knott, D., and Van Kuiken, S. (2013). The Big-Data revolution in US health care: Accelerating value and innovation. McKinsey & Company.

Kemp, S. (2014). Global social media users pass 2 billion. *We Are Social UK*. Retrieved January 8, 2016. http://wearesocial.net/blog/2014/08/global-social-media-users-pass-2-billion.

Khan, Z., Anjum, A., Soomro, K., and Tahir, M. A. (2015). Towards cloud based Big Data analytics for smart future cities. *Journal of Cloud Computing*, 4(1), 1–11.

Kim, G. H., Trimi, S., and Chung, J. H. (2014). Big-data applications in the government sector. *Communications of the ACM*, 57(3), 78–85.

Koumpouros, Y. (2014). Big Data in healthcare. In *Healthcare Administration: Concepts, Methodologies, Tools, and Applications: Concepts, Methodologies, Tools, and Applications*, edited by Information Resources Management Association (p. 23). IGI Global.

Kreps, J. (2016). Questioning the lambda architecture. *O'Reilly Radar*. Retrieved January 8, 2016. http://radar.oreilly.com/2014/07/questioning-the-lambda-architecture.html.

Lee, J. G. and Kang, M. (2015). Geospatial Big Data: Challenges and opportunities. *Big Data Research*, 2(2), 74–81.

Lopez, D. and Gunasekaran, M. (2015). Assessment of Vaccination Strategies Using Fuzzy Multi-criteria Decision Making. In *Proceedings of the Fifth International Conference on Fuzzy and Neuro Computing* (FANCCO-2015) (pp. 195–208). Springer International.

Lopez, D., Gunasekaran, M., Murugan, B. S., Kaur, H., and Abbas, K. M. (2014, October). Spatial Big Data analytics of influenza epidemic in Vellore, India. In *2014 IEEE International Conference on Big Data* (pp. 19–24). IEEE.

Lynch, C. (2008). Big Data: How do your data grow? *Nature*, 455(7209), 28–29.

Manyika, J., Chui, M., Brown, B., Bughin, J., Dobbs, R., Roxburgh, C., and Byers, A. H. (2011). Big Data: The next frontier for innovation, competition, and productivity. McKinsey Global Institute. Retrieved January 8, 2016. http://www.mckinsey.com/insights/business_technology/big _data_the_next_frontier_for_innovation.

Mapr.com. (2016). Lambda architecture. Retrieved January 8, 2016. https://www.mapr.com/developer central/lambda-architecture.

Marz, N. and Warren, J. (2015). *Big Data: Principles and Best Practices of Scalable Realtime Data Systems*. Manning Publications.

Mhlanga, F. S., Perry, E. L., and Kirchner, R. (2014). On adapting a war-gaming discrete event simulator with big data and geospatial modeling toward a predictive model ecosystem for interpersonal violence. In *2014 Proceedings of the Conference for Information Systems Applied Research*, Baltimore, MD, pp. 1–14. Available at http://proc.conisar.org/2014 /pdf/3305.pdf.

Nativi, S., Mazzetti, P., Santoro, M., Papeschi, F., Craglia, M., and Ochiai, O. (2015). Big Data challenges in building the Global Earth Observation System of Systems. *Environmental Modelling and Software*, 68, 1–26.

NIST Big Data Reference Architecture. (April 6, 2015). Draft Version 1, NIST Big Data Public Working Group Reference Architecture Subgroup (NBD-WG).

Pandey, A. and Ramesh, V. (2015). Quantum computing for Big Data analysis. *History*, 14(43), 98–104.

Pfeiffer, D. U. and Stevens, K. B. (2015). Spatial and temporal epidemiological analysis in the Big Data era. *Preventive Veterinary Medicine*, 122(1), 213–220.

Pickard, B. R., Baynes, J., Mehaffey, M., and Neale, A. C. (2015). Translating Big Data into big climate ideas. *Solutions*, 6(1), 64–73.

Ranjan, R. (2014). Streaming Big Data processing in datacenter clouds. *Cloud Computing, IEEE*, 1(1), 78–83.

Reed, D. A. and Dongarra, J. (2015). Exascale computing and Big Data. *Communications of the ACM*, 58(7), 56–68.

Savitz, E. (2012a). Gartner: 10 critical tech trends for the next five years. *Forbes*. Retrieved January 8, 2016. http://www.forbes.com/sites/ericsavitz/2012/10/22/gartner-10-critical-tech-trends-for-the-next-five-years.

Savitz, E. (2012b). Gartner: Top 10 strategic technology trends for 2013. *Forbes*. Retrieved January 8, 2016. http://www.forbes.com/sites/ericsavitz/2012/10/23/gartner-top-10-strategic-technology-trends-for-2013.

Schnase, J. L., Duffy, D. Q., Tamkin, G. S., Nadeau, D., Thompson, J. H., Grieg, C. M., McInerney, M. A., and Webster, W. P. (2014). MERRA analytic services: Meeting the Big Data challenges of climate science through cloud-enabled climate analytics-as-a-service. *Computers, Environment and Urban Systems*.

Shah, D. V., Cappella, J. N., and Neuman, W. R. (2015). Big Data, digital media, and computational social science possibilities and perils. *The ANNALS of the American Academy of Political and Social Science*, 659(1), 6–13.

Stefan Edlund, Y. (2016). The Spatiotemporal Epidemiological Modeler (STEM) Project. *Eclipse.org*. Retrieved January 8, 2016. http://www.eclipse.org/stem.

Thilagavathi, M., Lopez, D., and Murugan, B. S. (2014). Middleware for preserving privacy in Big Data. In *Handbook of Research on Cloud Infrastructures for Big Data Analytics* (p. 419).

US Environmental Protection Agency. (2015). EnviroAtlas. Retrieved January 8, 2016. http://enviroatlas.epa.gov/enviroatlas.

Vayena, E., Salathé, M., Madoff, L. C., and Brownstein, J. S. (2015). Ethical challenges of Big Data in public health. *PLoS Computational Biology*, 11(2), e1003904.

Viceconti, M., Hunter, P., and Hose, D. (2015). Big Data, big knowledge: Big Data for personalised healthcare. *IEEE Journal of Biomedical and Health Informatics*, 19(4), 1209–1215.

Victor, N., Lopez, D., and Abawajy, J. H. (2016). Privacy models for Big Data: A survey. *International Journal of Big Data Intelligence*, 3(1), 61–75.

Victor, T. J., Malathi, M., Asokan, R., and Padmanaban, P. (2007). Laboratory-based dengue fever surveillance in Tamil Nadu, India. *Indian Journal of Medical Research*, 126(2), 112.

Wang, W., Chen, L., Thirunarayan, K., and Sheth, A. P. (2012, September). Harnessing Twitter "Big Data" for automatic emotion identification. In *2012 International Conference on Privacy, Security, Risk and Trust (PASSAT), and 2012 International Conference on Social Computing (SocialCom)* (pp. 587–592). IEEE.

Wang, X. and Sun, Z. (2013). The design of water resources and hydropower cloud GIS platform based on Big Data. In *Geo-Informatics in Resource Management and Sustainable Ecosystem* (pp. 313–322). Springer Berlin Heidelberg.

Wired. (n.d.). 5 coolest government cloud projects. *Wired*. Retrieved January 8, 2016. http://www.wired.com/insights/2012/08/5-coolest-gov-cloud-projects.

Authors

Daphne Lopez is a professor in the School of Information Technology and Engineering, Vellore Institute of Technology University. Her research spans the fields of grid and cloud computing, spatial and temporal data mining, and Big Data. She has vast experience in teaching and industry. She is the author/coauthor of papers in conferences, book chapters, and journals. She serves as a reviewer in journals and conference proceedings. Prior to this, she worked in the software industry as a consultant in data warehouse and business intelligence. She is a member of the International Society for Infectious Diseases.

Gunasekaran Manogaran is currently pursuing a PhD in the School of Information Technology and Engineering, Vellore Institute of Technology University. He received his BE and MTech from Anna University and Vellore Institute of Technology University, respectively. He has worked as a research assistant for a project on spatial data mining funded by the Indian Council of Medical Research, Government of India. His current research interests include data mining, Big Data analytics, and soft computing. He is a member of the International Society for Infectious Diseases.

Index

Page numbers with f and t refer to figures and tables, respectively.

A

AaaS (Analysis as a Service), 71
Aam Aadmi Party Campaign, 232t
ABE (Aspect-based encryption), 209
Absorptive capacity, 90–91
ACAI (Access control and accounting infrastructure), 130
Access control, cryptographically applied, 209
Access control and accounting infrastructure (ACAI), 130
Accessibility, 270–271, 283
Accountability, 215, 216, 271–272
Accountable care organizations (ACO), 267
ACID, *see* Atomicity, consistency, isolated, and durable (ACID)
ACO (Accountable care organizations), 267
Advertising, 85t, 199, 284t
Agha-Soltan, Neda, 182
Agriculture, information quality, 85t
Airbnb, 187–188
Akka, 28
Algorithmic capabilities
    algorithms and organizational learning, 88–91
    data governance, 94–96, 94f
    organizational impacts and trade-offs, 91–94
    organizational learning
        absorptive capacity, 90–91
        algorithms and, 88–91
        definition, 88–89
        exploration and exploitation, 86, 90
        key constructs of, 86–88
        local versus global, 90
        simplification, 87, 89
        specialization, 87, 89
    reasons for failure, 97–101
    sectoral adoption of Big Data analytics, 82–86, 85t
Algorithms
    analysis of capabilities, *see* Algorithmic capabilities
    edge, 32

data determinism, 203–205
definition, 82
optimization, 288–289, 288f
organizational learning and, 88–91
organizational units and, 82–83
significance, 86
Amazon, 45, 72
Amazon AWS, 173
Amazon Echo, 169
Amazon Elastic Compute Cloud (EC2), 72, 73, 296f, 297t
Amazon Simple Storage Service (S3), 27, 29, 29f, 30, 72, 131
Amazon Web Services (AWS), 72, 73, 173, 314t
AMPLab (California), 19, 27, 39
Analysis as a Service (AaaS), 71
Analyze Data () function, 55
Andrade, Guilherme, 159
ANSI C++, 169
Antisocial public, 232
Apache Flink, 30–31, 32f, 33, 34, 36, 37, 39
Apache Flume, 20f, 27, 28, 29f, 30, 32f, 133, 316
Apache Hadoop
    architecture 1.0, 287
    CFile, 72
    data warehouse, 114
    ecosystem, *see* Apache Hadoop ecosystem
    geoprocessing tools, 326
    Hadoop-Based Intelligent Care System (HICS), 50, 55
    HDFS, *see* Hadoop Distributed File System (HDFS)
    JobTracker, 138
    key features, 283
    libraries, 54
    MapReduce, *see* Apache Hadoop MapReduce
    overview, 114, 131–132, 268
    Pcap Input, 54, 56
    -pcap-lib, 54, 56
    -pcap-serde, 54, 56
    services, 132–133
    significance, 283
    utilization in Big Data, 73–75, 74f
        overview, 73–74

335

336 *Index*

performance issues, 75
procedure to manage, 74, 74f
Apache Hadoop Distributed File System
(HDFS)
Apache Flink, 30, 31, 32f
Apache Spark, 27, 29, 29f
Apache YARN, 34
architecture, 133–134, 134f
batch layer and, 316
Fast Data Analytics Stack, 20f
functionalities, 132
Hadoop processing unit (HPU), 55
overview, 19, 114, 131, 132
significance, 72, 146
SQL Clients, 37
Sqoop and, 314
Apache Hadoop Ecosystem
Apache Hadoop, 145–146
Apache Mahout, 147
Apache Spark, 147
Apache YARN, 34
Big Data and, 145–147, 283, 286f, 287
Cascading, 37
Hadoop Distributed File System (HDFS), 146;
see also Apache Hadoop Distributed
File System (HDFS)
healthcare IoT and, 53f
MapReduce framework, 146–147, 146f, 147f
overview, 18, 19
Apache Hadoop MapReduce
algorithm, 138
analytics, 135, 135f
batch layer, 314t, 318, 322–323, 323f, 324f
Bloom filter, 297
clustering, 148f, 156–159
framework, 146–147, 146f, 147f
overview, 132
significance, 57, 134f, 135
clustering based on
DBCURE-MR, 148f, 158–159
Optimized Big Data K-means, 148f,
157–158, 157f
PKMeans, 148f, 156–157
Apache Hadoop YARN (Yet Another Resource
Negotiator), 34, 35f, 319
Apache HBase
definition, 131
NoSQL databases and, 27, 29, 30, 31
serving layer, 314t, 319, 320, 325, 326f
significance, 132, 133, 134f
Apache Hive
batch layer implementation, 322, 323f
as batching layer component, 314t, 318

definition, 132
serving layer implementation, 325
Apache HBase integration, 325, 326f
ArcGIS integration, 327, 327f
Pearson correlation coefficient, 324f
as serving layer component, 314t, 319
on Spark, 37
Apache Hive Streaming, 314t, 320f, 321, 325–326,
326f
Apache Ignite, 33
Apache Mahout, 39, 147, 318–319
Apache Mesos, 33, 34f
Apache MRQL, 36–37
Apache Nifi, 38
Apache Oozie, 133, 287
Apache Parquest, 319
Apache Pig, 38, 314t, 318
Apache S4, 39, 314t
Apache SAMOA, 39
Apache Samza, 39, 314t
Apache Software Foundation (ASF), 114
Apache Spark, 27–29, 29f, 34, 36, 147, 314t
Apache Spark ML Lib, 29, 29f, 38
Apache Spark ML Pipeline, 29, 29f
Apache SparkR, 28, 29, 29f
Apache Spark RDD, 33
Apache Spark SQL, 28, 29f, 314t
Apache Spark Streaming, 27, 28, 314t, 319
Apache Sqoop, 132, 314, 316
Apache Storm, 39, 314t
Apache SystemML, 38
Apache Tez, 34
Apache ZooKeeper, 35
Apple, 169, 170, 173, 183t
Application and user location diagram, 113
Application architecture
definition, 110, 115
impacts from Big Data, 115–118, 117f
objectives, 112
scope, 112–113
Application communication diagram, 113
Application components
data conversion components, 20f, 25–26,
36–38
data exploration components, 20f, 26, 40
integration components, 20f, 26, 40
machine learning components, 20f, 26, 38–39
technology choices, 36–40
Application/data matrix, 113
Application/function matrix, 112
Application Manager, 34, 35f
Application migration diagram, 113
Application portfolio catalog, 112

Index

Application/technology matrix, 113
Application use-case diagram, 113
Architectural requirements, 110
Architecture specials, 127
ASF (Apache Software Foundation), 114
Ashton, Kevin, 166
Aspect-based encryption (ABE), 209
Aster Data, 114
Asymmetric information quality, 84, 85t
Athos, 170
Atomicity, consistency, isolated, and durable
    (ACID), 114
AT&T, 65, 173
Audio, 240
Avro, 132
Awareness, of citizens, 216
AWS, *see* Amazon Web Services (AWS)
AWS Kinesis, 314t

B

Bahmani, Bahman, 159
Baidu Tieba, 231f
Balanced Iterative Reducing and Clustering
    using Hierarchies (BIRCH), 148f, 151, 152,
    152f
Batch layer
    in Cloudera distribution, 315f
    components, 316–319
    definition, 312f, 313, 314t
    implementation, 320, 320f, 322–325
Batool, Rabia, 185
Bayesian decision theory, 185
BDaaS (Big Data as a Service), 71
BDAS (Berkeley Data Analytics Stack), 20, 33
BFR Algorithm, 148–150, 148f
BI, *see* Business intelligence (BI)
Big Data
    analytics, *see* Big Data analytics
    applications, 283, 284t, 285t, 309f
    architecture, *see* Big Data architecture
    balanced approach, 13f
    benefits, 298–299
    challenges and potential solutions, 307–308
    characteristics, 225f, 282f, 305–307, 306f
        validity, 306f, 307f
        value, 144, 225f, 306, 306f
        variability, 144, 225f, 306f, 307
        variety, 127–128, 144, 184, 225f, 306, 306f
        velocity, 128–129, 144, 184, 225f, 306, 306f
        veracity, 144, 225f, 306f, 307
        virality, 306f, 307
        viscosity, 306f, 307

visualization, 144, 225f, 306f, 307
volume, 127, 128, 144, 184, 225f, 305–306,
    306f
climate change
    applications, 311–312
    batch layer implementation, 320, 320f,
        322–325
    data ingestion block, 314–316, 320, 320f,
        321–322, 322f
    findings, 327, 328f, 329f
    overview, 309–310, 319–321, 320f
    role, 310–311
    serving layer implementation, 320f, 325
    speed layer implementation, 320, 320f,
        325–326
    visualizing layer implementation, 326–327
cloud-computing ready platform, 115
clustering, *see* Big Data clustering
cost discrimination, 205
customer choice and, 206
data determinism, 203–205
definition, 50, 64, 68, 108, 126, 144, 184,
    197–198, 224, 260, 282, 305
Enterprise Architecture (EA)
    background and driving forces, 107–109
    entire information landscape (EIL), 111,
        112f, 115
    impacts on, 115–119, 119f, 120f, 121
    role in solutions, 109–111
essential classes of information, 67
examination, 65
functional issues, 67–68
future perspective, 299–300
geographic information systems (GIS)
    applications, 243
    challenge, 243
    development, 242–243
Hadoop utilization, 73–75, 74f
    overview, 73–74
    performance issues, 75
    procedure to manage, 74, 74f
handling, analysis issues, 68
healthcare, 266–268, 311–312
human elements, 13f
identification fraud, 202–203, 202f, 203f
impacts on governance, 226
implementation with Bloom filter, 295–296,
    295f, 296f, 297t
information breaches, 200–202, 200f, 201f, 202f
infrastructure
    ideal change, 129–130
    scientific data infrastructure (SDI)
        requirements, 130–131

major sources, 65, 66, 66f
market trend analysis and, 287–288
model, 127–129, 128f; *see also* Big Data,
  characteristics
ontology, 187
organization of storage for, 68
organization structure, 71–73
  Big Data package models, 71
  conveyed record framework, 71–72
  information stockpiling, 72
  information virtualization, 73
package models, 71
parallel programming models, 145–147
phenomenon, 108
privacy and security challenges, 207–210
properties, 282f
requirements in industries, 68–73
  data storage techniques used, 69, 70,
    70f
  existing types of data, 68, 69, 69f
  organization structure, 71–73
roles, in healthcare, 266–268
significance, 64–65, 126, 198–199
structuring techniques
  social media analysis, 185–186
  traditional, 184–185
study and estimation, 68
traffic, *see* Traffic Big Data
trends, 196, 196f
types, 224–225
usage and cost factors, 75–76
value of market, 240
V's
  validity, 306f, 307f
  value, 144, 225f, 306, 306f
  variability, 144, 225f, 306f, 307
  variety, 127–128, 144, 184, 225f, 306,
    306f
  velocity, 128–129, 144, 184, 225f, 306,
    306f
  veracity, 144, 225f, 306f, 307
  virality, 306f, 307
  viscosity, 306f, 307
  visualization, 144, 225f, 306f, 307
  volume, 127, 128, 144, 184, 225f, 305–306,
    306f
Big Data analytics
  actionable knowledge-as-a-service and, 12
  data mining toolbox, 6–8
    interactive generation and refinement
      of knowledge, 6
    knowledge artifacts interpretation, 7–8
    users' profile building, 7

decision making, 12–14
  challenges and opportunities, 12
  power of decision induction in data
    mining, 13, 13f
  prescriptive knowledge discovery, 13–14
definition, 18
Fast Data Analytics Stack and, 40–44
  mapping key requirements, 42, 44
  steps involved, 41–42
knowledge discovery, 4–6
  potentials and pitfalls, 5–6
  process of, 5, 5f
  relational dependencies and, 4–5
  state of the art and challenges of data
    mining, 4
lessons of machine learning, 8–11
  classify human expressions, 9–10, 10f
  expertise of human forecasting, 10–11, 11f
  human–machine interaction, 8–9, 9f
sectoral adoption, 82–86, 85t
solutions, role of Enterprise Architecture (EA),
    109–111
  technologies, 111, 112f, 113–115
  visual analytics complementarity and, 11–12
Big Data Appliance, 114
Big Data architecture
  capacity and scability considerations,
    139–140
  climate change and disease dynamics,
    319–327
    batch layer implementation, 322–325
    data ingestion block, 321–322
    overview, 319–321, 320f
    serving layer implementation, 325
    speed layer implementation, 325–326
    visualizing layer implementation,
      326–327
  performance parametric considerations,
    137–139
  social media and, 186–187
Big Data as a Service (BDaaS), 71
Big Data clustering
  challenges, 144
  definition, 144
  multiple machines technique, 154, 154f, 159
    MapReduce based, 148f, 156–159
    parallel, 148f, 155–156
  overview, 147, 148, 148f
  single machine technique, 148–154, 148f
    randomization techniques, 148f, 153–154
    sample-based, 148–153, 148f
  sizing, 137
BigTable, 72, 132, 319

Index 339

Binary JSON (BSON), 274, 275
BIRCH, *see* Balanced Iterative Reducing and Clustering using Hierarchies (BIRCH)
#BlackLivesMatter, 189
BlinkDB, 37, 43
Bloom filter
    implementation with Big Data, 295–296, 295f, 296f, 297t
    MapReduce, 297
    overview, 294–295, 294f
Bluemix, 173
Bluetooth, 51, 52, 168
Bluetooth LE, 169
Boutsidis, Christos, 154
Bradley, Paul S., 148
Brill, Julie, 198, 204
Brodley, Carla E., 154
BSON, *see* Binary JSON (BSON)
Business architecture
    definition, 110, 121
    impacts from Big Data, 121, 121t
    scope, 111–112
Business intelligence (BI), 109
Business service/function catalog, 111–112
Bus transfer analysis, 244, 250f

C

Caching, 31
Cai, Xiao, 159
Calo, M. Ryan, 206
Canary, 168
Cascading, 37–38
Cascalog, 314t
Case studies, 187–189
    #FeesMustFall, 189
    Airbnb, 187–188
Cassandra, 27, 29, 114, 133
CCl (Commission for Climatology), 310
CDC (Centers for Disease Control), 198, 199
Cells, column datastore, 276
Centers for Disease Control (CDC), 198, 199
CF (Clustering features), 152, 152f
CFile, 72
Charles, Jesse St., 159
Chen, C. L. Phillip, 5
Chen, Hsinchun, 109
Chen, Liyan, 183
Chevron Corporation, 126
Chiang, Roger H. L., 109
Chukwa, 133
Cisco, 173
CLARA (Clustering Large Applications), 151

CLARANS (Clustering Large Applications based on Randomized Sampling), 148f, 150–151
Clear Connect, 168
Climate, normal, 310
Climate change
    applications, 311–312
    batch layer implementation, 320, 320f, 322–325
    data ingestion block, 314–316, 320, 320f, 321–322, 322f
    findings, 327, 328f, 329f
    overview, 309–310, 319–321, 320f
    role, 310–311
    serving layer implementation, 320f, 325
    speed layer implementation, 320, 320f, 325–326
    visualizing layer implementation, 326–327
Climate Prediction Center and National Climatic Data Center, 310
Clinical data, 308
Clinical data repository, 270t
Clojure, 314t
Cloud computing, 115, 166
Cloudera Impala, 318
Cloud Stack, 73
Cloud storage systems, 29, 31
Clustering, 144
Clustering features (CF), 152, 152f
Clustering Large Applications (CLARA), 151
Clustering Large Applications based on Randomized Sampling (CLARANS), 148f, 150–151
Clustering size, 137
Clustering Using REpresentative (CURE), 148f, 153
Cluster level service, 24
Clusters, 133, 144
Clustrix, 114
CMD, 154
Colibri, 154
Collection unit, 54, 55, 56
Column datastores, 275–276
Column families, 276
Column qualifiers, 276
Columns, column datastore, 276
Commission for Climatology (CCl), 310
Competency traps, 87
Composite multimedia, 67
Comprehensiveness, 269–270
Comprehesive Transportation Junction (China), 243–251
    accessibility analysis, 244, 247f
    bus transfer analysis, 244, 250f

OD analysis, 244, 248f
  passenger flow forecasting, 244, 249f
  real-time status, 244, 245f, 246f
Compress set, 149
Computerized medical record, 270t
Computerized patient record (CPR), 270t
Computing Community Consortium, 108
Conceptual data diagram, 113
Concurrent activity, 138
Confidentiality, 175, 271
Confidentiality override policy, 271
Connectivity, as challenge, 175
Consul, 35
Consumer segmentation algorithms, 84
CONVAT-MR, 159
Coordinator node, 52
Core capabilities, 98
Cost discrimination, 205
Cost effective, 283
Cost of performance requirement, 42, 44
CouchDB, 114, 274
Counterintrusion techniques, 84
CPR (Computerized patient record), 270t
CPU, 139
CRISP-DM, *see* Cross Industry Standard
  Process for Data Mining (CRISP-DM)
Cross Industry Standard Process for Data
  Mining (CRISP-DM), 94, 94f
Crunch, 314t
Cui, Xiaohui, 159
Cukier, Kenneth, 107, 197, 198, 199
Cupid approach first, 185
CURE (Clustering Using REpresentative), 148f,
  153
Current Situation, 240
Customer demands, 83
Customer service, 121t
CX/CUR, 154

D

D1 layer (network infrastructure), 136, 136f
D2 layer (datacenter and computer facility), 136,
  136f
D3 layer (infrastructure virtualization), 136, 136f
D4 layer (scientific platform and instruments),
  136, 136f
D5 layer (federation), 136f, 137
D6 layer (scientific applications), 136f, 137
DaaS (Database as a Service), 71
DAG (Directed acyclic graph), 34, 145
Daily data, 282
Dallas Area Rapid Transit (DART), 173

Danish Cancer Society, 199
DART (Dallas Area Rapid Transit), 173
Dartmouth, 199
Dasgupta, Sanjoy, 154
Data analysis, human–machine interaction and,
  8–9, 9f
Data analysts, 8
Data architecture
  definition, 110
  impacts from Big Data, 118–119, 119f, 120f, 121
  scope, 113
Database as a Service (DaaS), 71
Database management system (DBMS), 66f, 71,
  111
Data breaches, *see* Information breaches
Datacenter and computer facility layer (D2),
  136, 136f
Data component catalog, 113
Data consumption capability, 20f, 23
Data conversion components, 20f, 25–26
  Apache MRQL, 36–37
  Apache Nifi, 38
  BlinkDB, 37
  Cascading, 37–38
  Hive on Spark, 37
  Sample Clean, 37
  SQL Clients, 37
  technologies for, 36–38
Data determinism, 203–205
Data dissemination diagram, 113
Data entity/business function matrix, 113
Data exploration components, 20f, 26, 40
Dataframe, 28, 29f
Data fusion techniques, 84
Data governance, findings, 94, 94f, 96
Data ingestion block, 314–316, 320, 320f, 321–322,
  322f
Data ingestion capability, 20f, 21–22
Data-intensive scientific discovery (DISD), 5
Data islands, *see* Semistructured data
Data items, 186
Data landscape, 111, 112f
Data locality, 114, 138
Data migration diagram, 113
Data mining
  power of decision induction in, 13, 13f
  privacy-preserving analytics, 207–208
  state of the art and challenges of, 4
Data mining toolbox, 6–8
  interactive generation and refinement
    of knowledge, 6
  knowledge artifacts interpretation, 7–8
  users' profile building, 7

Index

Data nodes, 138, 186, 276, 316
Data products, 18, 41, 44–45
Data relationships, 186, 276
Data scientists, 4, 8, 126, 268, 320f
Data security diagram, 113
DataSet API, 28, 29f
Data sources, 314
Data-storage logs, 208
Data warehousing appliances, 18, 19
Davenport, Thomas H., 8, 13
DBCURE-MR, 148f, 158–159
DBDC, *see* Distributed Density Based
    Clustering (DBDC)
DBMS, *see* Data base management system (DBMS)
DBSCAN, 159
DE, *see* Differential evolution (DE)
Decide.com, 199
Decision servers, 55
Deep data, 6, 7
Defense data, 66
Delhi Traffic Police, 232t
Delta Iterator, 30
Democracy, 217
Departmental EMR, 270t
Deutscher Wetterdienst, 310
Development frameworks, secure
    implementations, 208–209
Differential evolution (DE)
    overview, 289–290, 289f
    sentiment analysis and, 290–291, 292t, 293f
Digital India, 175
Digital medical record, 270t
Directed acyclic graph (DAG), 34, 145
Direct Marketing Association, 199
Discard set, 149
Discretized stream (DStream), 28, 29f
DISD (Data-intensive scientific discovery), 5
Disk, 140
Distributed caching feature, 24, 31–33
Distributed Density Based Clustering (DBDC),
    148f, 155, 155f
Distributed file system, 33
Distributed processing technology, 111
Distributed Relational Database Architecture, 116
Distributed Software Multi-threaded
    Transactional memory (DSMTX), 134
Distributed streaming ML algorithms, 39
Document datastore, 274–275
Documents, 120f, 121
Domain libraries, high level, 20f
#douniates, 189
Drineas, Petros, 154
Druid, 314t

Dryad, 145
DSMTX (Distributed Software Multi-threaded
    Transactional memory), 134
Duffy Marsan, Carolyn, 108
Dumbill, Edd, 108
Dwork, Cynthia, 206
Dynamic traffic network analysis subsystem,
    241
DynamoDB, 72, 273, 274, 277
DZone, 118

E

EBay, 199
EC2, *see* Amazon Elastic Compute Cloud (EC2)
ECL (Enterprise Control Language), 133
E-commerce, 121t, 201f, 202f, 284t
Economic growth, 217
Edge algorithm, 32
Education, 108
E-governance
    aim, 216
    definition, 216
    evolution, 215f
    impacts of, 216–217
    overview, 214
    PEST analysis, 221, 221f, 223
    significance, 216
Egyptian revolution (2011), 182
EHCR, *see* Electronic healthcare record
    (EHCR)
Einav, Liran, 197, 199
EIROforum Federated Identity Management
    Workshop, 130
Elastic Search, Logstash, Kibana (ELK), 35
Electronic client record, 270t
Electronic healthcare record (EHCR), 270t
Electronic medical record (EMR)
    challenges, 272
    characterisitics, 269–272
    definition, 269
    healthcare data analytics, 273
    integration through NoSQL datastores,
        273–278
        benefits, 278
        column datastores, 275–276
        document datastore, 274–275
        graph datastore, 276
        key-value datastores, 273–274
        usage scenarios, 277, 277f
    as record type, 270t
    record types, 270t
    user types, 271t

ElephantDB, 314t
ELK (Elastic Search, Logstash, Kibana), 35
Ellison, Nicole B., 180
EMC, 114
Emergency () functions, 55
Empowerment, of citizens, 216
EMR, *see* Electronic medical record (EMR)
Endpoint input filtering, 209
Energy sector, 83, 85t, 108
Enforcement procedures, 83
Enterprise Architecture (EA)
  Big Data
    background and driving forces, 107–109
    impacts on, 115–119, 119f, 120f, 121
    role in solutions, 109–111
  definition, 109–110
  entire information landscape (EIL), 111, 112f,
    115
  scope, 110
Enterprise Architecture Professional
  Organizations, 108
Enterprise Control Language (ECL), 133
Enterprise manageability diagram, 113
Entire information landscape (EIL), overview,
  111, 112f, 115
Enviroatlas, 311
EPA, *see* United States Environmental
  Protection Agency (EPA)
Epistemic uncertainty, 83
ERA, *see* European Research Area (ERA)
ES2, 72
Estrada, Joseph "Erap" Ejercito, 182
ETL, *see* Extraction, transformation, and load
  (ETL)
ETP EPoSS Project, 167
EUBrazilCC project, 311
Eucalyptus, 73
European Grid Infrastructure (EGI), 130
European Research Area (ERA), 130
European Technology Platform on Smart
  Systems Integration, 167
Exadata, 70
Exalogic, 70
Exalytics, 70
Experimentation, 10, 11
Exploitation, 206
Extraction, transformation, and load (ETL), 115,
  127, 135, 192, 286

F

Facebook, 65, 72, 75, 76, 108, 181, 183, 231f, 231t, 309
Facebook Messenger, 231f

FADI (Federated Access and Delivery
  Infrastructure), 137
Fair Information Privacy Practices (FIPP), 197
FARC, *see* Fuerzas Armadas Revolucionarias de
  Colombia—Ejército del Pueblo (FARC)
Farecast, 199
Fast data analytics core capabilities
  technology choices
    Apache Flink, 30–31, 32f
    Apache Spark, 27–29, 29f
Fast Data Analytics Stack
  Big Data analytics and, 40–44
    mapping key requirements, 42, 44
    steps involved, 41–42
  characteristics, 19
  deployment options, 44–45
  introduction, 18–19
  logical architecture, 20–26
    application components layer, 20f, 25–26
    fast data analytics core capabilities layer,
      20f, 21–23
    infrastructure services layer, 20f, 23–25
    overview, 20–21, 20f
  technology choices, 26–40
    application components, 36–40
    fast data analytics core capabilities,
      26–31
    infrastructure services, 31–36
Fast Data Analytics Technologies, 19, 20
Fayyad, Usama, 148
FDA, *see* U.S. Food and Drug Administration
  (FDA)
Federated Access and Delivery Infrastructure
  (FADI), 137
Federation layer (D5), 136f, 137
#FeesMustFall, 189
Fern, Xiaoli Zhang, 154
File servers, 19
Filter bubbles, 206
Finance data, 66
FINDCORE-MR, 159
Findings, 327
FIPP (Fair Information Privacy Practices),
  197
Fitbit, 173
Fitbit HR, 169
Flexibility, 272
Flickr, 231t
Flume TCP sockets, 30
Fork() system call, 145
Forrester Research, 167
Fourier technique, 186
Framework, 119f

Index   343

FSF (Free Software Foundation), 114
FTC, *see* U.S. Federal Trade Commission (FTC)
*Fuerzas Armadas Revolucionarias de Colombia—
    Ejército del Pueblo* (FARC), 182

G

GA, *see* Genetic algorithm (GA)
Ganglia, 35
Gartner Group, 109, 110, 126, 144
G-dbscan, 159
GDID, *see* Globally unique device identifier
    (GDID)
General Services Administration, 308
Genetic algorithm (GA), 290–291, 292t, 293f
Geographical information systems (GIS), 238
    development, 242–243
    government agencies and geographic
        information industry, 242
    human factors, 257–258
Geographic information subsystem, 3D traffic,
    242
GE's Industrial IoT cloud, 174
GFS, *see* Google File System (GFS)
GIS, *see* Geographical information systems (GIS)
Global Internet Report (2015), 214
Globally unique device identifier (GDID), 52, 54,
    55, 56
Global Precipitation Climatology Centre, 310
Global projection, 148f, 154
Global Resource Manager, 34, 35f
Globe information, 67
Google, 72, 76, 108
Google+, 231f
Google Cloud Dataflow, 314t
Google Docs, 182
Google File System (GFS), 71–72, 131, 132, 240
Google MapReduce, 240
Governance, 82, 214–215, 215f
Government, 121t, 285t
Graph datastore, 276
GraphX, 29, 29f
Greenplum, 114, 133
Group, Meta, 144
Gruman, G., 115
Guttentag, Daniel, 188

H

Hadoop, *see* Apache Hadoop
Hadoop 1.0 architecture, 287
Hadoop-Based Intelligent Care System (HICS),
    50, 55

Hadoop Distributed File System (HDFS), *see*
    Apache Hadoop Distributed File System
    (HDFS)
Hadoop Hive data warehouse, 114
Hadoop JobTracker, 138
Hadoop libraries, 54
Hadoop MapReduce, *see* Apache Hadoop
    MapReduce
Hadoop Pcap Input, 54, 56
Hadoop-pcap-lib, 54, 56
Hadoop-pcap-serde, 54, 56
Hadoop processing unit (HPU), 51, 55
Han, Jiawei, 152
HBase, *see* Apache HBase
HDFS, *see* Apache Hadoop Distributed File
    System (HDFS)
He, Yaobin, 159
Healthcare; *see also* Internet of Things (IoT)
    Big Data and, 121t, 266–268, 284t, 311
    data, 66
    data analytics, 273
    information quality, 85t
    Smart Everything and, 169–170
Healthcare providers, 271t
HEP (High Energy Physics), 130
HICS (Hadoop-Based Intelligent Care System),
    50, 55
High availability feature, 20f, 24, 35
High Energy Physics (HEP), 130
High-level domain libraries capability, 20f,
    22–23
High-performance computing (HPC), 133
High Performance Computing Cluster (HPCC),
    133
Hoffer, Jeffrey A., 119
Home Assistant, 169
Home automation (smart homes), 168–169
Home security, 168
HomeSeer, 169
Hospital EMR, 270t
HPC (High-performance computing), 133
HPCC (High Performance Computing Cluster),
    133
HPU (Hadoop processing unit), 51, 55
HSQLD (Hyper SQL Database), 314
Huang, Heng, 159
Hyper SQL Database (HSQLD), 314

I

IaaS, *see* Infrastructure as a service (IaaS)
IBM, *see* International Business Machines (IBM)
    Corporation

IBM Distributed Data Management
    Architecture, 116
IBM Research Lab, 38
IBM Systems Application Architecture, 116
IBM tech trends report, 282
Identification fraud, 202–203, 202f, 203f
Identity Theft Resource Center (ITRC), 200,
    200f, 201, 202f
IEEE 802.15.4, 54
IgniteRDD, 33
Images, 120f, 121
IMEX Research, 68, 69
Impact, definition, 110
Imperfect information quality, 85, 85t
Incomplete information quality, 84, 85t
IndexedRDD, 27
Indian Public Diplomacy Division of Ministry
    of External Affairs, 232t
Individual level failure, 97–98
Industrial Internet Consortium, 176
Information
    asymmetric information quality, 84, 85t
    breaches, 200–202, 200f, 201f, 202f
    economic definition, 83
    imperfect information quality, 85, 85t
    imperfection information quality, 85t
    incomplete information quality, 84, 85t
    uncertainty information quality, 83–84, 85t
Information breaches, 200–202, 200f, 201f, 202f
Information provenance, 208
Information stockpiling, 72
Information virtualization, 73
InfoSphere BigInsight, 114
Infrastructure as a service (IaaS), 73
Infrastructure services layer
    distributed caching feature, 24, 31–33
    high availability feature, 20f, 24, 35
    monitoring feature, 20f, 25, 35–36
    resource management feature, 20f, 24, 33–34,
        35f
    security feature, 20f, 25, 35
    technology choices, 31–36
Infrastructure virtualization (D3), 136, 136f
In-memory Databases, 18, 19
Innovation, architectural, 99
Instagram, 231f
Insteon, 169
Integration components, 20f, 26, 40
Integration with existing environment
    requirement, 42, 43–44
Intellectual rights, as challenge, 175
Intelligent building, 54
Interactive shells, 40

Interactive web interface, 40
Interdepartmental EMR, 270t
Interhospital EMR, 270t
Internal enterprise data, 120, 120f
International Business Machines (IBM)
    Corporation, 114, 173, 311
Internet data, 65
Internet of Cars, 241
Internet of Things (IoT)
    analytical architecture, 53–54, 53f
    background and driving forces, 49–51, 51f
    definition, 166, 167
    implementation and evaluation, 56–57, 57f,
        58, 58f
    intelligent building, 54–55
    proposed algorithm, 55–56
    sensor deployment scenario, 52–53, 52f
Internet of Things Consortium, 176
Internet Protocol Version 6 (IPv6), 49–50
Internet Society, 214
Interoperability, 175, 271
Intrinsic variability, 83
IPv6 (Internet Protocol Version 6), 49–50
Isolated data sets, *see* Structured data
Iterative development support requirement, 42, 44
Iterator, 30
ITRC, *see* Identity Theft Resource Center (ITRC)

J

Jacobs, Adam, 126
Java, 28, 29, 29f, 31, 32f, 45, 145, 147, 169, 314t
JavaScript Object Notation (JSON), 23, 37, 274,
    275, 314
Java Virtual Machine (JVM), 31
Javelin Strategy and Research, 202
Jawbone Up, 169
Jee, Kyoungyoung, 311
Jelly, 32f
Jha, Sanjay, 109
Ji, Changqing, 71
JobTracker, 317
Johannesburg carjacking (2012), 180–181
Johns Hopkins University, 311
Johnson, William B., 153
JSON, *see* JavaScript Object Notation (JSON)
Jupyter, 40
JVM (Java Virtual Machine), 31

K

Kafka, 27, 28, 29, 30
Kaiser Permanente, 199

Index 345

Kerberos, 36
KeystoneML, 39, 43
Key-value datastores, 273–274
KFS (Kosmos Distributed File System), 72
Kim, Gang-Hoon, 311
Kim, Younghoon, 158
Kinesis, 27, 28
Kitchin, Rob, 9, 10
Knowledge discovery, 4–6
   potentials and pitfalls, 5–6
   prescriptive, 13–14
   process of, 5, 5f
   relational dependencies and, 4–5
   state of the art and challenges of data
      mining, 4
Kosmos Distributed File System (KFS), 72

L

Lambda architecture
   batch layer
      in Cloudera distribution, 315f
      components, 316–319
      definition, 312f, 313, 314t
      implementation, 320, 320f, 322–325
   Cloudera distribution, 315f
   components, 314t
   data ingestion block
      components, 314–316
      implementation, 321–322, 322f
   data sources, 314
   illustration, 312f
   serving layer
      in Cloudera distribution, 315f
      components, 319
      definition, 312f, 313, 314t
      implementation, 320f, 325
   serving layer, in Cloudera distribution, 315f
   speed layer
      in Cloudera distribution, 315f
      components, 319
      definition, 312f, 313, 314t
      implementation, 320, 320f, 325–326
Laney, Doug, 108, 144
Lapkin, Anne, 108, 109
LDAP (Lightweight Directory Access Protocol),
   25, 36
Lenard, Thomas M., 204
Levin, Jonathan, 197, 199
Lieberman, Michael, 189
Liebowitz, Jay, 108
Lightweight Directory Access Protocol (LDAP),
   25, 36

Lindenstrauss, Joram, 153
LINE, 231f
LinkedIn, 108, 231f
Linux, 118
Little data, 120, 120f
Livny, Miron, 152
Llama, 72
Load balancer, 54
Locality preserving projection, 148f, 153–154
Logistics, 83
Low-Power Wireless Personal Area Network
   (6LoWPAN), 50
Lutron, 168

M

Machine learning (ML)
   algorithms, 29, 38, 39, 86
   classifiers, 55
   components, 20f, 26, 38–39
McKinsey Global Institute, 197, 240, 308
Mahalanabis distance, 150
Mainframe, 118
Mandl, Kenneth, 269
Manovich, Lev, 11
Manufacturing, 84, 85t, 171–172
Manyika, James, 108, 126
MapReduce, *see* Apache Hadoop MapReduce;
   Google MapReduce
MapReduce clustering
   DBCURE-MR, 148f, 158–159
   Optimized Big Data K-means, 148f, 157–158,
      157f
   PKMeans, 148f, 156–157
MapReduce framework, 146–147, 146f, 147f
Marketing, 85t, 284t
Market prediction, 282
Market Trend Analysis, 287
Markl, Volker, 30
Marz, Nathan, 312
Massively parallel processing (MPP), 114,
   133, 134
Master–slave approach, 24
Maury, Mathew, 198
Mayer-Schönberger, Victor, 107, 197, 198, 199
Medicare, 199
Membase, 114
Memory, 139
MERGE-CLS-MR, 159
Message Passing Interface (MPI), 145
Message queues, 19, 30
Metadata and lifecycle management layer,
   136f, 137

Meta Group, *see* Gartner Group
MFS (Moose File System), 72
Microsoft, 72, 118, 199
Microsoft Azure, 30, 114, 173
Microsoft's Big Data Solutions, 114
A Million Voices Against FARC group, 182
Mixed information, 67
Mobile analytics, 287
Mobile device data, 66
Modular audits, 210
Mohin, Sophie, 108
MongoDB, 30, 31, 274, 277
Monitoring
    definition, 83
    feature, 20f, 25, 35–36
Moore, Gordon, 126
Moore's law, 126
Moose File System (MFS), 72
MPI, *see* Message Passing Interface (MPI)
MPLS, *see* Multiprotocol Label Switching (MPLS)
MPP, *see* Massively parallel processing (MPP)
MQTT, 176
Mulligan, Deirdre K., 206
Multiple machines clustering, 154, 154f, 159
    MapReduce based, 148f, 156–159
        DBCURE-MR, 148f, 158–159
        Optimized Big Data K-means, 148f, 157–158, 157f
        PKMeans, 148f, 156–157
    parallel, 148f, 155–156
        Distributed Density Based Clustering (DBDC), 148f, 155, 155f, 161
        Parallel power iteration clustering (p-PIC), 148f, 155–156
Multiple programming paradigms capability, 20f, 23
Multiprotocol Label Switching (MPLS), 67
My data, 120, 120f
MyFitnessPal app, 169
MySQL, 314

N

Nagios, 35
NEIGHBOR-MR, 159
Neo4j, 276, 277
Nest, 169, 173
Netezza, 314
Netflix, 74, 166, 208
Network, 140
Network analytic approaches, 84
Network analytics, 287
Network infrastructure layer (D1), 136, 136f

Ng, Raymond T., 152
Nie, Feiping, 159
Node Manager, 34, 35f
Nodes, 186, 276
Nonrelational data hubs, best security practices, 207
NoSQL (Not Only SQL)
    databases
        Apache Flink, 30, 31
        Apache Spark, 27, 29
        Big Data, 131, 132f
        Fast Data Analytics, 18, 19, 21
        Healthcare IoT, 53f
        nonrelational data hubs, 207
        overview, 268
    datastores
        benefits, 278
        column datastores, 275–276
        document datastore, 274–275
        graph datastore, 276
        key-value datastores, 273–274
        usage scenarios, 277, 277f
NuoDB memsql, 114
Nurses, 271t

O

Objective catalog, 112
Objects, definition, 275
OD, *see* Origin and destination (OD)
OECD (Organization for Economic and Co-Operation Development), 198
Office of Digital Humanities, 7
OLAP (Online analytical processing), 70f, 135
OldSQL, 114
OLTP, *see* Online transaction processing (OLTP)
OMG Business Architecture Special Interest Group, 121
Online analytical processing (OLAP), 70f, 135
Online transaction processing (OLTP), 68, 70, 77, 111, 114, 118, 135
Ontology, 187
Open data, 120, 120f
The Open Group Architecture Framework (TOGAF), 115, 123
OpenHAB, 169
Open Interconnect Consortium, 176
OpenNebula, 73
Open Replica, 35
OpenStack, 73
Operation support and management service (OSMS), 136f, 137
Opinion analysis, *see* Sentiment mining

Index

Optimization algorithms, 83
Optimized Big Data K-means, 148f, 157–158, 157f
Oracle, 69, 111, 114, 314
Organizational impacts
    algorithms and organizational learning, 88–91
    data governance, 94–96, 94f
    organizational learning, *see* Organizational learning
    reasons for failure, 97–101
    sectoral adoption of Big Data analytics, 82–86, 85t
    trade-offs and, 91–94
Organizational learning
    absorptive capacity, 90–91
    algorithms and, 88–91
    definition, 88–89
    exploration and exploitation, 86, 90
    key constructs of, 86–88
    local versus global, 90
    simplification, 87, 89
    specialization, 87, 89
Organizational level failure, 98–101
    architectural innovation, 99–101
    inertia and core rigidities, 98–99
Organizational Talent, 176
Organization catalog, 111
Organization for Economic and Co-Operation Development (OECD), 198
Origin and destination (OD), 241, 244, 248f
OSGi, 169
OSMS (Operation support and management service), 136f, 137
Outliers, 11, 150, 152, 186, 196, 288, 308

P

PaaS (Platform as a Service), 71, 311
Palantir, 199
Palo Alto, 199
PAM (Partitioning Around Medoids), 150–151
Panahy, Payam Hassany Shariat, 118
Pangool, 314t
ParAccel, 114
Parallel clustering, 148f, 155–156
    Distributed Density Based Clustering (DBDC), 148f, 155, 155f
    parallel power iteration clustering (p-PIC), 148f, 155–156
Parallel K-Means (PKMeans) clustering, 148f, 156, 157
Parallel power iteration clustering (p-PIC), 148f, 155–156
Parents, 271t

Partition and sort key, 274
Partitioning Around Medoids (PAM), 150–151
Partition key, 274
Passenger flow analysis, bus, 253–254
Passenger flow forecasting, 244, 249f, 260
Patient management, 266–267
Patients, 271t
Payment Card Industry (PCI), 208
PDF (Portable Document Format), 120f, 121
Pearson correlation coefficient, 324f, 325, 325t
Personal health record, 270t
PEST analysis, *see* Political, economical, social, technical (PEST) analysis
Philips Hue lighting, 169
Physicians, 271t
Pictures, 240
Pig Latin, 314t
PKMeans, *see* Parallel K-Means (PKMeans) clustering
Planning Commission of India, 232t
Planning decision making auxiliary subsystem, 241–242
Platform, 251
Platform as a Service (PaaS), 71, 311
Pluggable Scheduler, 34, 35f
PMD, *see* Primary medical device (PMD)
PNUTS, 72
Political, economical, social, technical (PEST) analysis, 221, 221f, 223
Politics, 121t, 285t
Population health record, 270t
Portable cloud information analytics, 67
Portable Document Format (PDF), 120f, 121
Porter, Michael E., 111
POSIX threads, 145, 156
Postgres, 314
Potok, Thomas E., 159
p-PIC, *see* Parallel power iteration clustering (p-PIC)
PRC, *see* Privacy Rights Clearinghouse (PRC)
Prescott, Mary B., 119
PricewaterhouseCoopers (PwC) Consulting, 120
Pricing algorithms, 84
Primary keys, 274
Primary medical device (PMD), 51
Prime Minister Narendra Modi Social Media Account, 232t
Principles catalog, 111
Privacy, as challenge, 175
Privacy-preserving analytics, 207–208
Privacy Rights Clearinghouse (PRC), 200, 200f, 201f, 202f
Process/application realization diagram, 113

Project Tungsten, 28
Promotion algorithms, 84
Proprietary hardware technology, 111
Provenance metadata, 208
Pseudocode, 326f
Public policy, 176
PwC, *see* PricewaterhouseCoopers (PwC)
    Consulting
Python, 28, 29, 29f, 31, 32f, 39, 40, 147, 314t, 318
Python 3, 169

Q

QQ, 231f
Qzone, 231f

R

R (programming language), 28, 29f, 40
Rabbit MQ, 30
Ramakrishnan, Raghu, 152
Ramirez, Edith, 197, 198, 200, 203
Randomization clustering, 148f, 153–154
    global projection, 148f, 154
    locality preserving projection, 148f, 153–154
Raspberry-pi, 54
Rational Unified Process, 110
RavenDB, 274
Razor process, 288
RDBMS, *see* Relational database management
    system (RDBMS)
RDD, *see* Resilient Distributed Dataset (RDD)
Real time analytic processing (RTAP), 70f
Real-time compliance, 210
Redis, 30, 114, 273
Reduced code set, 111
Reina, Cory, 148
Relational database management system
    (RDBMS), 20, 29, 68, 69, 133, 314
Relational databases, 19, 30, 186, 274, 277, 278
REPTree, 55
Requirements, definition, 110
ResearchKit, 170
Resilient Distributed Dataset (RDD), 27, 29f
Resource management feature, 20f, 24, 33–35,
    34f, 35f
Resource managers, 35f
Retail industry, 75, 84, 85t, 121t, 171
Retained set, 149
RFID data, 66
Rheingold, Howard, 223
Riak, 114
RoadRunner Records, 183

Robertson, David C., 118
Robust feature, 283
Role catalog, 112
Ronson, Jon, 181
Rosenbush, Steven, 126
Ross, Jeanne W., 118
Rows, 275
Roxie, 133
RTAP, *see* Real time analytic processing (RTAP)
Rubin, Paul H., 204
Russom, Philip, 119

S

6LoWPAN, *see* Low-Power Wireless Personal
    Area Network (6LoWPAN)
S3, *see* Amazon Simple Storage Service (S3)
Sacco, Justine, 181
Salesforce, 174
Salim, S. E., 110
Sample-based clustering, 148–153, 148f
    BFR Algorithm, 148–150, 148f
    BIRCH, 148f, 151, 152, 152f
    CLARANS, 148f, 150–151
    CURE, 148f, 153
Sample Clean, 37, 43
Samsung, 183t
Samsung SmartThings, 169
Sanger, William, 186
SAVE DB () function, 55
Scala, 28, 29, 29f, 31, 32f, 39, 40, 314t
Scalable K-Means++, 159
Scalable processing capability, 20f, 22
Scalablility, 283
Scalding, 314t
Science and technology, 121t, 284t
Science data, 65
Scientific applications layer (D6), 136f, 137
Scientific data infrastructure (SDI)
    architectural model, 136–137, 136f
    requirements, 130–131
Scope, 110
Scrunch, 314t
Sears Holding Corporation, 126
Secondary namenode, 317f
Secretarial staff, 271t
Secure Sockets Layer (SSL), 25, 36
Security
    best practices for nonrelational data hubs,
        207
    Big Data applications, 285t
    as challenge, 175
    testing and real-time compliance, 210

Index 349

Security feature, 20f, 25, 36
Security info and event management (SIEM), 209
Security layer, 136f, 137
Semistructured data, 66, 66f, 135
Sensor data, 66
Sensor deployment scenario, 52
Sensors data, 66
Sentiment analysis, 6, 290–291
Sentiment governance, 231–232, 231f, 231t, 232t
Sentiment intelligence, 230–231
Sentiment mining, 229–232
   approaches, 230
   definition, 230
   overview, 229–230
   sentiment governance, 231–232, 231f, 231t, 232t
   sentiment intelligence, 230–231
Serving layer
   in Cloudera distribution, 315f
   components, 319
   definition, 312f, 313, 314t
   implementation, 320f, 325
S-governance
   definition, 214, 223–224
   evolution, 215f
   sentiment in, 214
   sentiment mining, 229–232
   significance, 224
Shared Secret, 36
Shipment data, 66
SIEM (Security info and event management), 209
SIENA Project, 130
Simplicity, 283
Sina Weibo, 231f
Single machine clustering, 148–154, 148f
   randomization, 148f, 153–154
      global projection, 148f, 154
      locality preserving projection, 148f, 153–154
   sample-based, 148–153, 148f
      BFR Algorithm, 148–150, 148f
      BIRCH, 148f, 151, 152, 152f
      CLARANS, 148f, 150–151
      CURE, 148f, 153
Singular value decomposition (SVD), 154
Skype, 231f
Smart Everything
   applications, 167–174
      customer-oriented, 168–171
      manufacturing, 171–172
      transportation, 172, 174, 174f

   challenges, 174–176
      connectivity, 175
      interoperability, 175–176
      organizational talent, 176
      privacy, confidentiality, and intellectual rights, 175
      public policy, 176
      security, 175
      technologies, 174–175
   definition, 167
   introduction, 165–167
Smart homes (home automation), 168–169
Snapchat, 231f
Social media
   Apache Flink, 30
   Apache Spark, 27
   Big Data structuring, 120f, 121, 185–186
   in business, 182, 183, 183t
   data from, 108, 134
   in events, 180–181
   governance, 181–182
   introduction to, 180–182
Social media analysis, 185
Social networks, definition, 180
Social public, 232
Social web, 223, 224f, 232t
Software distribution diagram, 113
Software engineering diagram, 113
Spark Kernel, 40
Sparkling Water, 39
SPEC (Standard Performance Corporation), 127
Specialization, 87, 89
Speed layer
   in Cloudera distribution, 315f
   components, 319
   definition, 312f, 313, 314t
   implementation, 320, 320f, 325–326
Splash, 38, 43
SploutSQL, 314t
Spring XD, 314t
SQL (Structured Query Language), 70, 314t
SQL Clients, 37
SSL (Secure Sockets Layer), 25, 36
Standard Performance Corporation (SPEC), 127
Stanford Part of Speech Tagger, 188
Stardog, 276
State Bank of India, 232t
STEM
Stochastic monitoring, 83
Stock market data, 66
Storey, Veda C., 109
Stratosphere, 30
Streaming data, 66

Streaming Technologies, 18, 19
Strengths, weaknesses, opportunities, and threats (SWOT) analysis
  Big Data on government, 226–229, 227f
  E-governance, 217–221
Structured data, 66
Structuring techniques
  social media analysis, 185–186
  traditional, 184–185
Supply chain management systems, 83
Surface data, 6
SVD, *see* Singular value decomposition (SVD)
SWOT analysis, *see* Strengths, weaknesses, opportunities, and threats (SWOT) analysis
System division, 243–244, 245f–249f
SystemML, 38, 43
Systems, definition, 260
Systems Network Architecture Distribution Services, 116

T

3D traffic geographic information subsystem, 242
24/7 service model, 217
Table
  column datastore, 275
  key value datastore, 274
Tachyon, 32
TaskTrackers, 317
Technische Universität (Berlin), 19, 30
Technologies, 111, 112f, 174–175
Technology architecture, 110, 113, 118
Technology portfolio catalog, 113
Technology standards catalog, 113
Telecommunications, 75, 84, 85t
Teradata, 314
Text analytics, 287
Thomas, Gwen, 118
Thor, 133
Time to market requirement, 41, 42–43
TOGAF (The Open Group Architecture Framework), 115, 123
Tōhoku earthquake and tsunami (2011), 181
Topi, Heikki, 119
Toyota, 183t
TPC (Transaction Processing Performance Council), 127
Traffic Big Data
  cloud-service platform
    advantages, 253
    key technology, 251–252

current situation, 240–242
  3D traffic geographic information subsystem, 242
  basic traffic information management subsystem, 241
  dynamic traffic information processing subsystem, 241
  dynamic traffic network analysis subsystem, 241
  overview, 240
  planning decision making auxiliary subsystem, 241–242
geographical information systems (GIS)
  development, 242–243
  government agencies and geographic information industry, 242
  human factors, 257–258
introduction, 238–240
passenger flow analysis
  bus, 253–254
  public transportation transfer, 254–257, 254t, 257t
system division, 243–244, 245f–249f, 250
Traffic information management subsystem, basic, 241
Traffic information processing subsystem, dynamic, 241
Transaction Processing Performance Council (TPC), 127
Transportation, 83, 85t, 108, 172, 174, 174f
Transportation hub, urban comprehensive passenger, 239
TrendWeight app, 169
Trust, 216
Tumblr, 231f
Twitter, 27, 29f, 30, 108, 181, 182, 186, 231f

U

UAP (Unified Analytics Platform), 114
UBUNTU, 51
UCI diabetes data set, 56
UCI ICU data set, 56–57
UCI repository, 56
UGC (User-generated content), 240
UK Future Internet Strategy Group Report, 130
Uncertainty information quality, 83–84, 85t
UNCHR (United Nations Commission on Human Rights), 215
Unified Analytics Platform (UAP), 114
United Nations Commission on Human Rights (UNCHR), 215
United Parcel Service (UPS), 65

Index

351

United States Environmental Protection Agency (EPA), 311
University of California, 311
Unsocial public, 232
Unstructured data, 66, 66f, 69f, 135
UPS (United Parcel Service), 65
User-generated content (UGC), 240
Users, 111, 112f, 271t
U.S. Federal Trade Commission (FTC), 198
U.S. Food and Drug Administration (FDA), 199

V

Validity, 306f, 307f
Value, 144, 225f, 306, 306f
Variability, 144, 225f, 306f, 307
Variety, 127–128, 144, 184, 225f, 306, 306f
Vasudeva, Anil, 68
Velocity, 128–129, 144, 184, 225f, 306, 306f
Velox, 39
Veracity, 144, 225f, 306f, 307
Vertica, 114
Viber, 231f
Videos, 120f, 121, 240
Vioxx, 199
Virality, 306f, 307
Virtual EHR, 270t
Virtual geographical environment, definition, 260
Virtual reality geographical information system (VRGIS), 238, 260
Viscosity, 306f, 307
Visualization, 144, 225f, 306f, 307
Visualization techniques, 4, 308
Visualizing Layer Implementation, 326
VKontakte, 231f
Voldemort, 314t
Volkswagen, 183t
VoltDB, 114
Volume, 127, 128, 144, 184, 225f, 305–306, 306f
VRGIS, see Virtual reality geographical information system (VRGIS)

W

Wal-Mart, 126
Walt Disney, 115
Wamba, Samuel Fosso, 10
Warin, Thierry, 186
WBAN (Wireless body area network), 49
WCP (World Climate Programme), 310
Web analytics, 287
Web logs, 120f, 121

WeChat, 231f
Weill, Peter, 118
Welfare, of citizens, 216
Wells Fargo, 183t
WeMo, 169
WhatsApp, 231f
White House, 65
Wi-Fi, 168, 169
Wikipedia, 231t
Wink Hub, 168
Wireless body area network (WBAN), 49
Wireless sensor networks (WSN), 49
WISDM lab data set, 57
WLCG, see Worldwide LHC Computing Grid (WLCG)
WMO, see World Metrological Organization (WMO)
Workplaces, 170–171
World Climate Data and Monitoring Programme (WCDMP), 310
World Climate Programme (WCP), 310
World Economic Forum, 197
World Metrological Organization (WMO), 310
World Weather Records (WWR), 310
Worldwide LHC Computing Grid (WLCG), 130
Wosh, 169
WSN (Wireless sensor networks), 49
WWR (World Weather Records), 310

X

Xeround, 114
XMPP, 176

Y

Yahoo, 72, 74, 76
Yahoo Influenza, 198
Young, Colleen, 108
YouTube, 166, 231t

Z

Zeppelin, 40
ZeroMQ, 27
ZestFinance, 199, 204
Zhang, Chun-Yang, 5
Zhang, Tian, 152
ZigBee, 51, 52, 54, 168, 176
Zimmerman, Alfred, 118
ZooKeeper, 35, 133
Zouzias, Anastasios, 154
Z-Wave, 168